Frommer's

3rd Edition

Virginia

by Bill Goodwin, Rena Bulkin, Gloria McDarrah, and Fred McDarrah

D0981420

Macmillan • USA

ABOUT THE AUTHORS

Born and raised in North Carolina, **Bill Goodwin** was an award-winning newspaper reporter before becoming a legal counsel and speech writer for two U.S. Senators, Sam Nunn of Georgia and the late Sam J. Ervin, Jr. of North Carolina. Now a full-time travel writer based in northern Virginia, Goodwin is the author of *Frommer's South Pacific* and co-author of *Frommer's Florida.* He also served as regional editor for the first edition of *Frommer's America on Wheels Mid-Atlantic.*

Rena Bulkin began her travel-writing career when she set out for Europe in search of adventure. She found it writing about hotels and restaurants for the *New York Times* International Edition. She has since authored 15 travel guides to far-flung destinations.

Gloria S. McDarrah is coauthor of *Museums of New York* and *The Artist's World* (a Photo-documetary of the abstract expressionist artists of New York City in the 50s and 60s), and is a book columnist for *Manhattan Spirit* and the book editor for *The Picture Professional.*

Fred W. McDarrah is the author of *The Beat Scene* and *Kerouak & Friends,* and coauthor of *Museums of New York, The Greenwich Village Guide,* and *The Artist's World.* He has been picture editor of *The Village Voice* since 1959, and won a Guggenheim Fellowship for photography.

MACMILLAN TRAVEL

A Simon & Schuster Macmillan Company
1633 Broadway
New York, NY 10019

Find us online at **http://www.mcp.com/mgr/travel** or
on America Online at **Keyword: SuperLibrary.**

ISBN 0-02-860704-X
ISSN 1058-4943

Editor: Alice K. Thompson
Production Editor: Pete Fornatale
Design by Michele Laseau
Digital Cartography by Ortelius Design and Devorah Wilkenfeld
Maps copyright © by Simon & Schuster, Inc.

SPECIAL SALES

Bulk purchases (10+ copies) of Frommer's travel guides are available to corporations at special discounts. The Special Sales Department can produce custom editions to be used as premiums and/or for sales promotion to suit individual needs. Existing editions can be produced with custom cover imprints such as corporate logos. For more information write to: Special Sales, Simon & Schuster, 1633 Broadway, New York, NY 10019.

Manufactured in the United States of America

Contents

List of Maps

AN INVITATION TO THE READER

In researching this book, we discovered many wonderful places—hotels, restaurants, shops, and more. We're sure you'll find others. Please tell us about them, so we can share the information with your fellow travelers in upcoming editions. If you were disappointed with a recommendation, we'd love to know that, too. Please write to:

Bill Goodwin
Frommer's Virginia, 3rd Edition
Macmillan Travel
1633 Broadway
New York, NY 10019

AN ADDITIONAL NOTE

Please be advised that travel information is subject to change at any time—and this is especially true of prices. We therefore suggest that you write or call ahead for confirmation when making your travel plans. The authors, editors, and publisher cannot be held responsible for the experiences of readers while traveling. Your safety is important to us, however, so we encourage you to stay alert and be aware of your surroundings. Keep a close eye on cameras, purses, and wallets, all favorite targets of thieves and pickpockets.

WHAT THE SYMBOLS MEAN

✪ **Frommer's Favorites**

Hotels, restaurants, attractions, and entertainment you should not miss.

✿ **Super-Special Values**

Hotels and restaurants that offer great value for your money.

The following abbreviations are used for credit cards:

AE	American Express	EU	Eurocard
CB	Carte Blanche	JCB	Japan Credit Bank
DC	Diners Club	MC	MasterCard
DISC	Discover	V	Visa
ER	enRoute		

The Best of Virginia

America's first permanent English-speaking colonists had a rough start at Jamestown in 1607, but within a few years the beautiful and bountiful land they called Virginia had greatly rewarded them for their courageous efforts. Almost 400 years later, the history-loving Commonwealth of Virginia rewards today's traveler with glimpses back to the colonial era, to the stirrings of revolution and the great victory that sealed independence for the United States, and to the bloody battles of the Civil War. The state abounds with historic homes and plantations, museums that recall the nation's storied past, and small towns that seem little changed since colonial times.

Fortunately, preservation hasn't been limited to historical landmarks. Conservation efforts have kept much of Virginia's wilderness looking much as it did in 1607, making the state a top destination for lovers of the great outdoors. Whether you like to hike, bike, birdwatch, fish, canoe, or boat—or just lie on a sandy beach—Virginia has a place to indulge your passion.

This chapter provides descriptions of what we consider some of the best experiences Virginia has to offer in a range of categories. Bear in mind that this is just an overview, and you'll surely come up with your own "bests" as you travel through the state.

Be sure to see the destination chapters later in this book for full details on the places mentioned in this chapter.

1 The Best of Colonial Virginia

- **Williamsburg, Jamestown & Yorktown:** Known as the Historic Triangle, these three towns are the finest examples of colonial America to be found anywhere. Thanks to an infusion of cash from the Rockefeller family, Colonial Williamsburg has been restored and rebuilt exactly as it appeared when it was the capital of Virginia from 1699 to 1780. The site of the original Jamestown settlement is now a national historical park, as is Yorktown, where George Washington bottled up Lord Cornwallis and won the American Revolution. See Chapter 11.
- **James River Plantations:** America's first great wealth was created by colonists who fanned out from Jamestown and hacked huge tobacco plantations out of Virginia's virgin forests. Today you can visit some of the great manses they built along the James River

between Williamsburg and Richmond. Descendants of the colonial planters still occupy some of these mansions. See Chapter 11.

- **Fredericksburg & the Northern Neck:** Not only did the Fredericksburg area play a role in the birth of a nation, it was the birthplace of George Washington, the father of that new nation. Also born here was James Monroe, who as president kept European powers out of the Americas by promulgating the Monroe Doctrine. A generation later, the great Confederate leader Robert E. Lee also was born here. Fredericksburg still retains much of the charm it had in those early days, and the birthplaces of Washington and Lee stand not far away from town on the Northern Neck. See Chapter 6.

- **Mount Vernon:** When he wasn't off surveying, fighting in the French and Indian Wars, leading the American Revolution, or serving as first president, George Washington made his home at a northern Virginia plantation 8 miles south of Alexandria. Restored as it was in Washington's day, Mount Vernon is America's second most visited historic home. See the Mount Vernon section in Chapter 5.

- **Charlottesville:** While Washington was the father of the United States, Thomas Jefferson was its intellectual genius. This scholar, lawyer, writer, and architect built two great monuments to himself—his lovely hilltop home Monticello, and the University of Virginia. Both still recall this great thinker and patriot. See Chapter 7.

- **Old Town Alexandria:** Although Alexandria is today very much part of metropolitan Washington, D.C., the historic district known as Old Town evokes the time when the nation's early leaders strolled its streets and partook of grog at Gadsby's Tavern. See Chapter 5.

- **Richmond:** Although Richmond is best known as the capital of the Confederacy, it played a major role in events leading up to the American Revolution. It was in Richmond's Christ Church that Patrick Henry shouted "Give me liberty, or give me death," thus inciting Virginia to join the rebellion. See Chapter 10.

2 The Best of Civil War Virginia

Some historians think the Civil War actually began in 1859 with John Brown's aborted antislavery raid on Harper's Ferry, then in Virginia. When the real fighting broke out in 1861 and the Confederacy moved its capital to Richmond, Virginia became the prime target of the Union armies. Consequently, Virginia saw more battles than any other state, as Robert E. Lee's Army of northern Virginia turned back one assault after another aimed at Richmond. Today's peaceful visitor can visit the sites of many key battles, all of them national historical parks.

- **Harper's Ferry:** Now just over the West Virginia line, Harper's Ferry National Historical Park is dedicated to John Brown's raid. The forces that captured and hung him were led by Robert E. Lee, then a Union officer. The old stone town has been preserved, and the historical park has lovely hiking trails overlooking the gorge where the Potomac and Shenandoah Rivers join and cut their way through the Blue Ridge. See Chapter 5.

- **Manassas:** The first battle of the war occurred along Bull Run near Manassas in northern Virginia, and it was a shock to the Union as Robert E. Lee, now commander of Confederate forces, engineered a surprising victory over a disorganized Union force. He won again here at the Second Battle of Manassas. See Chapter 5.

Virginia

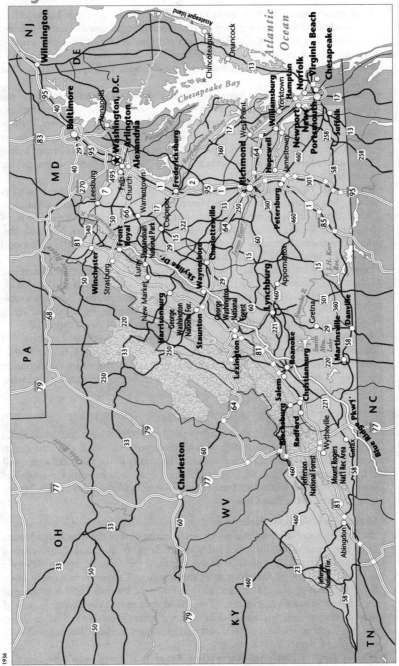

1936

- **Fredericksburg:** No other town in Virginia has as many significant battlefields as does Fredericksburg. Lee used the Rappahannock River as a natural line of defense, and he fought several major battles against Union armies trying to cross it near Fredericksburg and advance on Richmond. Today you can visit the battlefields in town and at Chancellorsville and the Wilderness all in an afternoon. See Chapter 6.
- **New Market:** While Lee was fending off the Union near Fredericksburg, the war was ebbing and flowing up and down the Shenandoah Valley, the Confederacy's breadbasket. The town of Winchester actually changed hands 72 times. Perhaps the war's most poignant battlefield is at New Market, where the corps of cadets from Virginia Military Institute marched up from Lexington and helped stop a larger union force. Ten of the teenagers were killed, and 47 were wounded. See Chapter 8.
- **Richmond:** The capital of the Confederacy, Richmond is loaded with reminders of the great conflict, including the Museum of the Confederacy and its adjacent White House of the Confederacy, home of President Jefferson Davis. The city's Monument Avenue is lined with statues of the great rebel leaders. Now suburbs, the city's eastern outskirts are ringed with battle sites, part of the Richmond National Battlefield Park. See Chapter 10.
- **Petersburg:** After nearly four years of frustration in trying to capture Richmond, Union Gen. Ulysses S. Grant finally bypassed Richmond in 1864 and headed for the important railroad junction of Petersburg, the lifeline of the Confederate capital. Even there he was forced into a siege situation, but finally in April of 1865, Grant broke through and forced Lee into retreat westward. See Chapter 10.
- **Appomattox Court House:** Lee fled for little more than a week until realizing that continuation of the war was fruitless. On April 9, 1865, he met Grant at Wilbur McLean's farmhouse and surrendered his sword. America's bloodiest conflict was over. Today the farmhouse is preserved as part of Appomattox Court House National Historical Park. See the Lynchburg section in Chapter 7.

3 The Best of the Great Outdoors

Virginia has hundreds of thousands of acres preserved in national and state parks, national forests, and national recreation areas. Especially in the mountains, you will find more than 1,000 miles of trails for hiking, biking, and horseback riding. The Chesapeake Bay offers fabulous boating and fishing, and the Atlantic beaches are among the best on the East Coast.

- **Shenandoah National Park:** More than two million visitors a year venture into the Shenandoah National Park, which straddles the crest of the Blue Ridge Mountains for more than 100 miles from Front Royal to Rockfish Gap between Charlottesville and Waynesville. Many visitors merely ride along the 105-mile Skyline Drive, one of America's most scenic routes. Others come to walk more than 500 miles of hiking trails, including 95 miles of Virginia's 450-mile share of the Maine-to-Georgia Appalachian Trail. Most trails start at the Skyline Drive and drop down into valleys, many of them with waterfalls. Even on the Skyline Drive, you are likely to encounter deer, and you may even see bear, bobcat, and wild turkey. See Chapter 8.
- **Mount Rogers National Recreation Area:** While you won't be alone in Shenandoah National Park, you could have a hiking, mountain biking, horseback

riding, or cross-country skiing trail all to yourself in Mount Rogers National Recreation Area. This wild wonderland in the Southwest Highlands occupies some 117,000 forested acres, including its namesake, Virginia's highest peak. Two of Virginia's finest "rails-to-trails" hiking, biking, and riding paths serve as bookends to the 60-mile-long recreation area: the New River Trail near Wytheville, and the Virginia Creeper Trail, from Mount Rogers to Abingdon. See Chapter 9.

- **Assateague Island:** Of all natural areas in Virginia, none surpasses Assateague Island, which keeps the Atlantic Ocean from the back bays of Chincoteague. Here you will find the famous wild ponies grazing in Chincoteague National Wildlife Refuge, and relatively tame humans strolling some 37 miles of pristine beach. Assateague Island is also one of the nation's prime bird-watching locales, for it is directly on the Atlantic Flyway. See the Eastern Shore section in Chapter 12.

- **Back Bay National Wildlife Refuge/False Cape State Park:** A mere 15 miles south of the heavily developed resort area of Virginia Beach, the beach of Back Bay National Wildlife Refuge does not allow sunbathing or swimming. But you can hike through the dunes or take a canoe into the marshes, another Atlantic Flyway landing zone for migrating birds. You *can* sunbathe and swim at the adjoining False Cape State Park, but it's so out-of-the-way that you'll have to bring your own drinking water. See the Virginia Beach section in Chapter 12.

- **The W&OD Trail:** Even in Virginia's metropolitan areas, it's possible to get away from it all. One fine example is the Washington & Old Dominion (W&OD) Trail, which begins in Arlington and ends 45 miles later in Purcellville at the edge of the Blue Ridge Mountains. Another rails-to-trails park, it follows an old railroad bed through the Washington, D.C., suburbs into the gorgeous Hunt Country. See the Arlington section in Chapter 5.

- **Front Royal:** Although the Shenandoah Valley town of Front Royal is best known as the northern entry to Shenandoah National Park, it's also Virginia's most popular spot for river rafting, canoeing, and kayaking—or just floating down the South Fork of the Shenandoah River in an inner tube. See Chapter 8.

4 The Best Scenic Drives

The best way—some of us think the *only* way—to see Virginia is by car, and with very good reason: The Old Dominion has some of America's most scenic drives.

- **Skyline Drive:** Few roads anywhere can top the Skyline Drive, which twists and turns 105 miles along the Blue Ridge crest in Shenandoah National Park. The views down over the rolling Piedmont to the east and the Shenandoah Valley to the west are nothing short of spectacular, especially during spring when the wildflowers are in bloom and in the fall when the leaves change color from green to brilliant hues of rust, orange, and yellow. See the Shenandoah National Park section in Chapter 8.

- **Blue Ridge Parkway:** Actually a continuation of the Skyline Drive, this road continues along the Blue Ridge crest all the way south to the Great Smoky Mountains National Park in North Carolina. Of the 218 miles in Virginia, the most scenic are north of Roanoke. Here you'll find it difficult to keep your eyes on the road, as the parkway often runs right along the ridgeline, with views down both sides of the mountain. See Chapter 9.

- **Colonial Parkway:** It's not very long, but the Colonial Parkway between Jamestown, Williamsburg, and Yorktown has its scenic merits, especially views of the James River near Jamestown and of the York River near Yorktown. The parkway goes through a tunnel under the heart of Colonial Williamsburg. See Chapter 11.

- **George Washington Memorial Parkway:** Stay away from this route during rush hour, when it becomes a major commuter artery into and out of Washington, D.C. But at any other time the "G.W. Parkway" is a great scenic drive along the Potomac River from I-495 at the Maryland line all the way to Mount Vernon. The river views of Washington are unparalleled. See Chapter 5.

- **Chesapeake Bay Bridge-Tunnel:** One of the manmade wonders of the world, the Chesapeake Bay Bridge-Tunnel runs for 17 miles over—and under—the mouth of the Chesapeake Bay between Norfolk and the Eastern Shore. You can barely see dry land when you're out in the middle. See Chapter 12.

- **Interstate 81:** Few interstate highways are as beautiful as I-81, which runs the entire length of Virginia from the Shenandoah Valley all the way through the Southwest Highlands to Tennessee. Alongside, the old Valley Pike (now U.S. 11) is a scenic excursion back to the 1950s, complete with old-fashioned gas stations, small motels, country stores, clapboard houses, and small-town restaurants. See Chapters 8 and 9.

- **Lexington to Hot Springs:** While I-81 runs down the floor of Virginia's great valleys, other roads offer a very different scenic treat by cutting across the mountains. One of these is Va. 39, which runs from Lexington to Hot Springs via the Goshen Pass, a picturesque gorge cut by the Maury River. You can make a loop by continuing north from Hot Springs via U.S. 220 to the beautiful village of Monterey in "Virginia's Switzerland." From Monterey, you can cross the mountains via U.S. 250 to Staunton and I-81. See "A Side Trip to Virginia's Switzerland," in the Staunton section of Chapter 8.

5   The Best of Small-Town Virginia

Another good reason to see Virginia by car is its many lovely small towns, the best of them capturing and keeping alive the state's storied history. This is especially true in the Shenandoah Valley, where first the Valley Pike, then U.S. 11 and now I-81, string together Winchester, Strasberg, Staunton, and Lexington, all possessed of 18th- and 19th-century brick and stone buildings.

- **Lexington:** Not only one of Virginia's but also one of America's best small towns, Lexington presents a lively college atmosphere in addition to a host of historical sights. It's home to Virginia Military Institute, where Gen. Thomas J. "Stonewall" Jackson taught and whose student body went off to the Civil War at New Market. After the war, Robert E. Lee came here as president of Washington College, now known as Washington and Lee University. And VMI was the alma mater of Gen. George C. Marshall, winner of the Nobel Peace Prize for the post–World War II Marshall Plan to rebuild Europe. Jackson and Lee are buried here, and the town has three fine museums dedicated to these great leaders. On top of all that, Lexington's downtown looks so much like it did when Jackson and Lee were here that only dirt had to be added to Main Street's pavement to film the movie *Sommersby*. See Chapter 8.

- **Abingdon:** Daniel Boone opened Virginia's Southwest Highlands to settlement in the 1770s, and it wasn't long before a thriving town grew up at Abingdon. Homes and buildings dating back to 1779 still line shady Main Street, making Abingdon a wonderful place for a stroll. The town's beauty has attracted a community of artists, craftspeople, and actors. The latter perform at the famous Barter Theatre, where you can still barter for a ticket. See Chapter 9.

- **Middleburg:** The self-proclaimed capital of Virginia's horse-loving Hunt Country, Middleburg takes up barely 6 blocks along U.S. 50, making it small enough to be digested in an afternoon. Some of the world's wealthiest individuals keep their horses near Middleburg, and the town has a host of upscale shops in buildings dating back to the 1700s. See the Hunt Country section in Chapter 5.

- **Waterford Village:** Founded by Quakers in the late 1700s, the little hamlet of Waterford went into a time capsule in 1870 when the railroad bypassed it in favor of nearby Leesburg. Today it looks very much as it did then, its houses carefully preserved by private owners. See the Hunt Country section in Chapter 5.

- **Monterey:** Over Shenandoah and Bull Pasture mountains from Staunton, the little village of Monterey appears more like New England than Virginia, with its white churches and clapboard homes nestled in a picturesque valley. Thousands of visitors make the trek over the mountains during the annual Highland Maple Festival in March. See "A Side Trip to Virginia's Switzerland," in the Staunton section of Chapter 8.

- **Onancock:** Relatively isolated on the Eastern Shore, little Onancock was incorporated in 1690 and was for more than two centuries an important Chesapeake Bay shipping port. The great ferries don't run anymore between Norfolk and Baltimore, and U.S. 13 passes a mile east of town, leaving Onancock as a lovely reminder of the old days of planters and merchants. See the Eastern Shore section in Chapter 12.

6 The Best Beaches

If you want to find a great beach in Virginia, just head east. The Atlantic Ocean surf beats all along the state's shoreline, from North Carolina to Maryland. Fortunately for conservationists, however, not all of this coastline is easily accessible to travelers.

- **Assateague Island:** One area you can reach is Assateague Island, mentioned above among the best of Virginia's great outdoors. This 37-mile-long barrier island is completely within the Assateague Island National Seashore, which has prevented all development along this stretch of golden sand. The National Park Service has been kind enough to build bathhouses and restrooms on one end of the beach; otherwise, it belongs to the seagulls and to hearty souls who don't mind a hike. The Virginia end of the island also is home to Chincoteague National Wildlife Refuge, where the famous Chincoteague wild horses roam. See the Eastern Shore section of Chapter 12.

- **Back Bay National Wildlife Refuge/False Cape State Park:** Also among the best of the great outdoors, these two preserves are just 15 miles south of—but a developed world removed—from Virginia Beach. You can't swim or sunbathe at the refuge's deserted beach, but you can hike or bike south to False Cape State Park. Carry your own drinking water—it's that isolated and undeveloped. See the Virginia Beach section in Chapter 12.

- **Virginia Beach:** Okay, it's developed, but this resort still has an expansive, fine-sand beach and excellent surf. The resort itself is one of Virginia's best family destinations, with much more to do than sun and swim. See the Virginia Beach section in Chapter 12.

- **Parramore and Cedar Islands:** Parramore is partially owned and preserved by the Nature Conservancy, and while Cedar has cottages on it, there is no way to reach either barrier island and their long, straight beaches except by boat. Those you can rent in the little town of Wachapreague on the mainland. See the Eastern Shore section in Chapter 12.

7 The Best Family Vacations

A vast majority of Virginia's visitors arrive by car, and most of them are families. Accordingly, the state's major attractions and resorts are well equipped to entertain and care for children. It's a great place for the kids to learn about American history, while at the same time having a good time at the beach or at one of the state's three major amusement parks.

- **Colonial Williamsburg:** The historic area of Colonial Williamsburg is the best place of all for children to get a quick lesson in American history. Here on the streets they might run into Thomas Jefferson (actually an actor) and have a conversation about the Declaration of Independence; practice marching and drilling with the 18th-century militia; or go to a special children's version of high tea at the Williamsburg Inn. As soon as they get bored, head for Busch Gardens Williamsburg or Water Country USA, two nearby theme parks. See Williamsburg in Chapter 11.
- **Virginia Beach:** First there's the beach, all 4 miles or so with lifeguards during summer. But that's not all Virginia Beach has to offer. Rainy days can be spent at the local Virginia Marine Science Museum—the state's most popular museum. And Norfolk's NAUTICUS, Hampton's Virginia Air and Space Center, and Colonial Williamsburg are all short drives away. See the Virginia Beach section in Chapter 12.
- **Northern Virginia:** Another good place for a history lesson is in northern Virginia, especially at Mount Vernon, Old Town Alexandria, and Arlington National Cemetery. Of course, Arlington is just across the Potomac River from Washington, D.C., where the kids can roam the National Air & Space Museum and other key attractions. See Chapter 5.
- **Shenandoah National Park:** Two lodges in the most popular part of Shenandoah National Park make this scenic wonderland a great place for family vacations. The kids can participate in ranger programs, hike to waterfalls, or go for a pony ride in the mountain forests. See the Shenandoah National Park in Chapter 8.
- **Chincoteague:** The little fishing village was the setting for Marguerite Henry's classic children's book *Misty of Chincoteague,* and there are plenty of wild horses (called ponies here) in Chincoteague National Wildlife Refuge on Assateague Island, which also has a lifeguarded beach for swimming during the summer. Best time to see the horses is during the annual pony swim the last week in July. See the Eastern Shore section in Chapter 12.
- **Richmond:** The state capital has several attractions of interest to children, including the hands-on Science Museum of Virginia. The big draws, however, are the wild rides and movie and TV characters at the huge Paramount's King's Dominion amusement park north of the city. See Chapter 10.

8 The Most Unusual Travel Experiences

A stuffed horse, a stalactite organ, an 18th-century version of today's Jacuzzi, and a cruise to Elizabethan times all make for unusual travel in Virginia.

- **Little Sorrel:** After he died of wounds accidentally inflicted by his own men at the Battle of Chancellorsville, Gen. Stonewall Jackson was brought home and buried in Lexington, where he had taught at Virginia Military Institute prior to the conflagration. One of the key exhibits at VMI's museum is the bullet-pierced raincoat Jackson was wearing that disastrous night. And thanks to taxidermy, there stands his favorite war horse, Little Sorrel. Nearby, Robert E. Lee's horse Traveller is buried just outside Lee Chapel, his master's resting place. See the Lexington section in Chapter 8.

- **Chimes Down Under:** There are several caverns under the Shenandoah Valley, but one of the most fascinating is at Luray. Through subterranean rooms more than 140 feet high comes beautiful organ music—but not from a man-made instrument. Well, almost not man-made. Thanks to modern technology, hammers striking million-year-old stalactites make this wonderful music. See the Luray section in Chapter 8.

- **Ancient Hot Tubs:** Eighteenth-century travelers couldn't climb into the hotel Jacuzzi after a rough day on the road—unless, that is, they pulled into Warm Springs. Since 1761, travelers have slipped their weary bodies into these natural rock pools whose circulating waters range from 94°F to 104°F. You can, too. See the Warm Springs & Hot Springs section in Chapter 8.

- **Hygh Tyde Tonyght:** Out in the Chesapeake Bay sits remote Tangier Island, whose residents have been so isolated over the centuries that they still speak with the Elizabethan brogue of their forebears. Out here, "high tide tonight" is pronounced *hygh tyde tonyght*—and narrow 17th-century lanes accommodate no modern automobiles. Cruises leave from Onancock on the Eastern Shore and from Reedville on the Northern Neck. See Chapters 6 and 12.

9 The Best Country Inns

With all of its old homes and gorgeous countryside, it's no wonder that Virginia is a hotbed of country inns and bed-and-breakfast establishments. Some have been in business since colonial times, and a few are among the best America has to offer. The following picks barely scratch the surface of the state's wonderful offerings:

- **Inn at Little Washington:** For the best, you need look no farther than the tiny Blue Ridge foothill village of Washington, which everyone in Virginia calls Little Washington. The rooms here were designed by an English decorator, but it's the romantic restaurant that draws the most raves, as co-owner and chef Patrick O'Connell relies on regional products to produce wonderful French cuisine. See the Front Royal section in Chapter 8.

- **Keswick Hall:** The creation of Sir Bernard Ashley, this Italinate villa in the town of Keswick outside Charlottesville has all the trappings of an English baronial estate, plus a golf course redesigned by Arnold Palmer. The entire establishment is graced with Sir Bernard's antiques and wallpaper, upholstery, and curtains designed by his late wife, Laura Ashley. See the Charlottesville section in Chapter 7.

- **Tides Inn:** Located in the town of Irvington, the Tides Inn is a sprawling resort complex beside a broad creek in Virginia's Tidewater area. The Stephens family has maintained a tradition of gracious service here since 1946. Guests can go boating on the Chesapeake Bay or play golf on a creekside course. See the Northern Neck section in Chapter 6.

- **Camberley's Martha Washington Inn:** Gracing Abingdon's historic district is this Greek Revival inn, whose center portion was built as a private home in 1832. You can sit in white-wicker rocking chairs on the front porch and watch the traffic on Main Street—or imagine Daniel Boone's dogs being attacked by wolves nearby. See the Abingdon section in Chapter 9.

- **Wayside Inn:** Located in the tiny Shenandoah Valley village of Middletown, the Wayside Inn has been serving travelers since stagecoaches started running on the Valley Pike (now U.S. 11) in 1797. Restored by an antiques collector in the 1960s, today's rooms are decorated with an assortment of 18th- and 19th-century pieces. The Wayside Theater is virtually next door, lending entertainment to a stop here. Just down the pike is another antique-laden historic relic, the Hotel Strasberg. See the Middletown & Strasberg section in Chapter 8.

- **Fort Lewis Lodge:** One of Virginia's most unusual country inns, the Fort Lewis Lodge in Millboro occupies an old mill and a rebuilt barn beside the Cowpasture River, just over the mountain from Warm Springs. A spiral staircase winds its way to three rooms inside the old silo beside the barn, and there are two log cabins with their own fireplaces. It's a great place to show urban kids a bit of farm life in beautiful surroundings. See the Warm Springs & Hot Springs section in Chapter 8.

- **L'Auberge Provençal** (White Post): Master chef Alain Borel and wife Celeste have created the look, feel, and cuisine of southern France in this 1750s farmhouse a few miles southeast of Winchester. Alain grows many of his own ingredients, and others he buys fresh from local farmers. See the Winchester section in Chapter 8.

10 The Best Luxury Lodgings

With deep enough pockets, you can enjoy some of the Mid-Atlantic's best luxury accommodations in Virginia. Here are some of the finest the Old Dominion has to offer.

- **The Homestead** (Hot Springs): Outstanding service, fine cuisine, and a myriad of recreational activities characterize this grand old establishment, in business since Thomas Jefferson's day. In fact, Jefferson was the first of seven presidents to stay here. The Homestead offers accommodations ranging from standard rooms to plush suites. And PGA pro Lanny Wadkins presides over its golf course, one of Virginia's finest. See the Warm Springs & Hot Springs section in Chapter 8.

- **Williamsburg Inn:** The Williamsburg Inn was built as part of the Colonial Williamsburg restoration but looks like it might have been here in 1750. If staying in the main inn with its superb service and cuisine won't do, you can opt for one of several restored colonial houses and taverns that have been converted into accommodations. As an added bonus, the Williamsburg offers not one but three fine golf courses. See the Williamsburg section in Chapter 11.

- **Jefferson Hotel:** A stunning beaux-arts Richmond landmark with Renaissance-style balconies and an Italian clock tower, the Jefferson was opened in 1895 by a wealthy resident who wanted his city to have one of America's finest hotels. A complete 1980s restoration restored it to its original splendor. See "Accommodations" in Chapter 10.

- **Hotel Roanoke & Conference Center:** The grand Tudor-style Hotel Roanoke stood in a wheat field when the Norfolk & Western Railroad built it in 1882 as the centerpiece of its new town called Roanoke. It was closed in 1989, but a $42 million renovation has completely restored its grand public areas to their original appearance and rebuilt all its rooms to modern standards. See the Roanoke section in Chapter 9.

- **Ritz-Carlton Pentagon City:** Although this Ritz-Carlton in Arlington was built in 1990 as part of a modern shopping mall, massive China cabinets, graceful wing chairs, plush sofas, Oriental rugs, crystal sconces, and a $2.5 million collection of 18th- and 19th-century paintings and antiques make it seem from another era. So does the superb service. See the Arlington section in Chapter 5.
- **Cavalier Hotel** (Virginia Beach): On a hill overlooking the Atlantic, the Cavalier has been a grand beach resort since 1927, and its older section still looks like it did back then—or when then–vice president Richard Nixon brought his family here for a beach vacation in the 1950s. There's a new wing beside the beach, but stay in the old section for charm. See the Virginia Beach section in Chapter 12.

11 The Best Moderately Priced Lodgings

Virginia has far too many wonderful, affordably priced lodgings to mention them all here. Here are some we like best:

- **Linden Row Inn:** One of the best-run hotels we've ever experienced, the Linden Row in Richmond consists of seven mid-19th-century row houses, all of them restored and furnished with late-Empire and early-Victorian pieces, beautiful wallpapers, damask draperies, flower-patterned carpets, and marble-top dressers. And it's convenient to downtown Richmond's historic sights. See "Accommodations" in Chapter 10.
- **Belle Grae Inn:** Owner Michael Organ gave up teaching at Mary Baldwin College in the 1980s to convert an 1873 hilltop Victorian house in Staunton into an inn. Today his establishment includes houses ringing an entire city block, and all of them are beautifully restored and furnished with period pieces. The cuisine here is the best in town. See the Staunton section in Chapter 8.
- **Kenmore Inn:** George Washington's brother-in-law, Fielding Lewis, once owned the property upon which sits this 1700s mansion right in Fredericksburg's Old Town historic district. A sweeping staircase leads to guest rooms furnished with four-poster beds and a mix of antiques. Four rooms have working fireplaces. See the Fredericksburg section in Chapter 6.
- **The Breakers Resort Inn:** Among the many cookie-cutter, high-rise buildings lining Virginia Beach's oceanfront, The Breakers stands out as a family-operated hotel that is friendly to families. Efficiencies here have fully equipped, money-saving kitchens. See the Virginia Beach section in Chapter 12.
- **Hart's Harbor House:** Unlike many small-town bed-and-breakfast owners who are expatriates from big cities, hosts Tom and Pat Hart of Hart's Harbor House are born-and-bred Wachapreaguers. Accordingly, their knowledge of the Eastern Shore is unsurpassed, and they are experts at arranging boat trips out to Parramore and Cedar islands along the Atlantic. Accommodations are in two Victorian houses they have restored (one's called Burton House Bed-and-Breakfast), both with charming screened porches. See the Eastern Shore section in Chapter 12.

12 The Best Inexpensive Lodgings

Virginia has any number of clean, comfortable motels of the Econo Lodge, Super 8, and Motel 6 variety. But for something with a little more uniqueness, we particularly like the following inexpensive accommodations:

- **Laurel Brigade Inn:** You need to reserve at least a month in advance for a room at the Leesburg Laurel Brigade Inn, a charmer going back to 1766 when an "ordinary" (tavern) stood here. Some of the rooms have fireplaces, just like in the old days. See the Hunt Country section in Chapter 5.

- **Fredericksburg Colonial Inn:** Don't be surprised to see Blues and Grays toting Civil War rifles in the lobby of the Fredericksburg Colonial Inn, so popular is this establishment with reenactment buffs. An avid collector, the owner has laden the rooms with antiques. See the Fredericksburg section in Chapter 6.
- **Americana Hotel:** When our parents brought one of us to Washington, D.C., in 1955, we stayed at an old-fashioned motel, one of many that lined U.S. 1 in Arlington. Only one of those motels remains among the high-rise buildings of what's now known as Crystal City: the Americana Hotel. In fact, the roadside sign here still says AMERICANA MOTEL. It's run by the same family, and it's as clean and comfortable as ever. See the Arlington section in Chapter 5.
- **Alpine Motel:** A holdover from the early 1960s, the immaculate, family-run Alpine Motel in Abingdon has extraordinarily large rooms—common in those days when cost-per-square-foot wasn't as high as today. Most of the rooms have mountain views. See the Abingdon section in Chapter 9.
- **Roseloe Motel:** You don't have to pay a fortune staying at The Homestead in Hot Springs to experience the area's famous thermal springs. Just drive 3 miles north to the Roseloe Motel, a clean, family operation across U.S. 220 from the lovely sounds of the Garth Newel Chamber Music Center. The hot pools at Warm Springs are a short drive away, and you can pay a lot less than the cost of a room to use The Homestead's superb recreational facilities. See the Warm Springs & Hot Springs section in Chapter 8.

13 The Best Culinary Experiences

Author William Styron, a native of southeastern Virginia, once said that the French consider smoke-cured Virginia hams to be America's only worthwhile contribution to the world's cuisine. That may be the opinion in Paris, but Virginians are also crazy about rockfish and crabs from the Chesapeake Bay and shad and trout from their rivers. Their farms produce a plethora of vegetables during the summer, and their orchards are famous for autumn apples. And let's not forget the peanut, one of Virginia's major crops. Following are some of the best places to sample Virginia's unique and very historic cuisine:

- **Inn at Little Washington** (Washington, Va.): Chef Patrick O'Connell constantly changes his basically French menu to take advantage of trout, Chesapeake Bay seafood, Virginia hams, and other delicacies at the romantic dining room of the Inn at Little Washington. The service here is extraordinarily attentive and unobtrusive. See the Front Royal section in Chapter 8.
- **Trellis Café, Restaurant & Grill** (Williamsburg): Chef Marcel Desaulniers has been nationally recognized for his outstanding regional cuisine, all of it emphasizing fresh local produce. Desaulniers has written three cookbooks, including *Death by Chocolate*. They don't raise cocoa in Virginia, but you can definitely die by it here. See the Williamsburg section in Chapter 11.
- **The Frog and the Redneck** (Richmond): The "Frog" stands for the French style of cooking learned and practiced by noted chef Jimmy Sneed. The "Redneck" comes from the local ingredients he uses in his gourmet alterations of traditional French dishes. You'll get Virginia ham and cantaloupe here, not Bayonne and melon. See "Dining" in Chapter 10.

- **Old Chickahominy House** (Williamsburg): Named for a nearby river, this reconstructed, antique-filled, 18th-century house is one of the best places to sample traditional Virginia fare such as Brunswick stew and Virginia ham on hot biscuits. See the Williamsburg section in Chapter 11.
- **Gadsby's Tavern** (Alexandria): George Washington said good-bye to his troops from the door of Gadsby's Tavern in Alexandria's Old Town historic district, and the old tavern looks much as it did then. In addition, a wait staff in colonial garb still serves chicken roasted on an open fire, buttermilk cake, and other dishes from that period. See the Alexandria section in Chapter 5.
- **The Green Tree** (Leesburg): Most of the dishes at The Green Tree are from faithfully reproduced 18th-century recipes garnered from the Library of Congress. A smoked sausage pie, a green-herb soup, and an oyster-flavored cabbage pie are featured offerings. See the Hunt Country section in Chapter 5.
- **The Log House 1776 Restaurant** (Wytheville): The name of The Log House 1776 Restaurant is appropriate because part of this establishment is contained in a log house built in 1776. Here you can order Thomas Jefferson's favorite, chicken marengo, or a very sweet Confederate beef-and-apple stew like the one Robert E. Lee fed his troops. See the Wytheville section in Chapter 9.
- **King's Barbeque** (Petersburg): Virginians love their smoked pork barbecue, and it doesn't get any better than at the two branches of King's Barbeque. Pork, beef, ribs, and chicken roast over an open pit right in the dining rooms, and the sauce is served on the side, not soaking the succulent meat and overpowering its smoked flavor. See "An Easy Excursion to Petersburg" in Chapter 10.

2 Getting to Know Virginia

No state in the nation can equal the Commonwealth of Virginia in its role as the cradle of the American republic. America originated at Jamestown and grew along the banks of the Rappahannock, the Potomac, and the James rivers. Spurred on by Virginia leaders like Patrick Henry, whose ringing denunciation of the Stamp Act inspired all 13 colonies, the desire for American independence grew strong. Tidewater planter George Mason wrote a Bill of Rights, and Virginia aristocrat Thomas Jefferson gave voice to this revolutionary philosophy in the ringing phrases of the Declaration of Independence. The mantle of responsibility for leading the new nation in its struggle for freedom and its first years as a republic fell on the most famous of all Virginians, George Washington.

With monuments and sites marking more than three centuries of American history, Virginia today is a pioneer in the field of historic preservation. Its landmarks and historic places, including its battlefields, are carefully restored and maintained, and its gem of an 18th-century restoration, Williamsburg, enjoys international renown.

While Virginia's place in U.S. history may be what first brings you to the Old Dominion, the commonwealth's natural beauty will lure you back again and again. From the pristine beaches of the Eastern Shore to the forests and highlands of western Virginia, visitors will find boundless opportunities for hiking, freshwater and ocean fishing, swimming, boating, sailing, and skiing. Overlooking the Shenandoah Valley and southwestern highlands, two of Virginia's many fabulously scenic routes—the Skyline Drive and Blue Ridge Parkway—carry motorists along the very spine of the Blue Ridge Mountains.

To this appealing mix of living history and outdoor fun, add a vibrant cultural scene that includes the nation's oldest repertory theater company, major art and science museums, a growing wine industry, and a culinary spectrum that ranges from Virginia ham to Chincoteague oysters. And that's not to mention the theme parks, the steeplechase race meets in Hunt Country, and the opportunities to sample farm life or test the waters at The Homestead, the nation's oldest spa hotel.

1 The Regions in Brief

Virginia is shaped like a triangle, with the base resting on the North Carolina and Tennessee borders. To the west are Kentucky and West Virginia; Maryland is to the north. The Potomac River, Chesapeake Bay, and Atlantic Ocean form the watery eastern boundary.

Along the eastern coast, the **Tidewater** (or coastal plain) is dominated by four rivers—the Potomac, Rappahannock, York, and James—that empty into the Chesapeake, one of the world's largest estuaries. These rivers divide the Tidewater into three peninsulas, or necks in local parlance. To the south, the Chesapeake meets the Atlantic Ocean at the great natural harbor of Hampton Roads.

The rolling hills of the **Piedmont** run through central Virginia, from Richmond, Charlottesville, and Lynchburg to the Hunt Country and suburban sprawl of northern Virginia. This farm country gently rises to meet the foothills of the **Blue Ridge Mountains.** Between the Blue Ridge and the Allegheny Mountains to the west, a series of gorgeous valleys—including the fabled Shenandoah—extends the length of the state, from the Potomac in the north to the Southwest Highlands near the borders of Tennessee and Kentucky.

Northern Virginia The fastest growing, most densely populated, and wealthiest part of the state, Northern Virginia today is much more than a suburban bedroom for government workers in Washington, D.C., for areas such as Tysons Corner have become unincorporated cities in their own right, with employment in high-tech service industries outstripping that of the federal government. Long known for its famous cemetery just across the Potomac from the nation's capital, Arlington today is a melting pot of immigrants from around the world—with a marvelous mix of ethnic cuisine to show for it. Centered around its historic Old Town, Alexandria offers fascinating daytime walks as well as lively nighttime entertainment and good restaurants. Beyond are the beautiful Potomac plantations, including George Washington's Mount Vernon. In Virginia's Hunt Country, sightseers can enjoy Virginia's traditional historic inns and fine restaurants. Farther south is Manassas, site of the first major battle of the Civil War.

Fredericksburg and the Northern Neck The quaint cobblestone streets and historic houses of Fredericksburg recall America's first heroes—George Washington, James Monroe, John Paul Jones—as does the quiet Northern Neck farmland, where stand the birthplaces of Washington and Robert E. Lee. Military buffs love to explore Fredericksburg's Civil War battlefields.

The Piedmont These rolling hills are "Mr. Jefferson's country." Charlottesville boasts his magnificent estate, Monticello, as well as the University of Virginia, which he designed. From Lynchburg you can visit Popular Forest, his beloved retreat, as well as Patrick Henry's final home at Red Hill and Appomattox Court House, where the Civil War ended when Robert E. Lee surrendered to Ulysses S. Grant.

Shenandoah Valley Some of Virginia's most striking scenery is along the Skyline Drive, which follows the crest of the Blue Ridge Mountains through Shenandoah National Park, where visitors will find a host of hiking paths, including part of the famed Appalachian Trail. Down below, towns like Winchester, Staunton, and Lexington evoke the Civil War, which ebbed and flowed over the rolling countryside of the Shenandoah Valley, the South's breadbasket. Nearby are the famous mineral waters of Warm Springs and Hot Springs.

The Southwest Highlands   The vibrant city of Roanoke is the gateway to the highlands of Virginia's southwestern extremity, a land of untouched forests, waterfalls, and quiet streams. Here sits the state's highest point, Mount Rogers, surrounded by a national recreation area teeming with hiking, mountain-biking, and horse trails. Down in the Great Valley of Virginia, the historic town of Abingdon features the famous Barter Theatre, begun during the Great Depression when its company traded tickets for hams.

Richmond   The state capital has few rivals among U.S. cities for its wealth of historic associations, among them St. John's Church, where Patrick Henry made his famous "Give Me Liberty or Give Me Death" speech. Fine arts and science museums, cafes, lively concerts, and theater add to Richmond's cosmopolitan ambiance. Military buffs can tour the Richmond and Petersburg battlefield sites. And children can get their kicks at nearby Paramount's King's Dominion amusement park.

Colonial Williamsburg, Yorktown, and Jamestown   Coastal Virginia's so-called Historic Triangle is one of the country's most visited areas, and with good reason. Colonial Williamsburg's 173 acres re-create Virginia's colonial capital. Yorktown commemorates the last, victorious battle of the American Revolution. And Jamestown is where America's first permanent English settlers arrived in 1607. Adding to its allure are two theme parks and world-class discount shopping.

Hampton Roads and the Eastern Shore   The great port area of Hampton Roads includes cosmopolitan Norfolk, shipbuilding Newport News, historic Hampton, and Virginia Beach with its 20 miles of white-sand beach, boardwalk, and nearby historic homes. The 17-mile-long Chesapeake Bay Bridge-Tunnel links Norfolk to the Eastern Shore, an unspoiled sanctuary noted for the charming village of Chincoteague and nearby Assateague Island, whose wildlife refuge and national seashore have protected the famous wild ponies and prevented any development on almost 40 miles of pristine beach.

2 Virginia Today

The memory of the state's past still exerts its influence, as it surely must in towns where descendants of America's first patriots still live and where the homes, monuments, and battlefields that shaped the country's history comprise their daily landscape. But Virginia is far from static, and major changes in the 1990s, and those coming up at the close of this century, affect the culture and economy of the state.

Tobacco and Other Industries   Although Colonist John Rolfe is best remembered today for marrying Pocahontas, the tobacco industry he helped found is still important to Virginia's economy, despite its recent troubles.

Besides tobacco, other local farm income is based on the apple orchards of the Shenandoah Valley; livestock, dairy farming, and poultry raising in the Piedmont; and the state's famous Smithfield hams and peanuts from the Tidewater country. Industry continues to grow as well, notably in the manufacturing of clothes, chemicals, furniture, and transportation equipment.

Modern Politics   Prominent in Virginia Tidewater plantation society since the 1600s, the Byrd family dominated the state's politics from World War I until the 1980s. Under their conservative control, the "Mother of Presidents" virtually withdrew from national leadership. The state government vigorously fought federally mandated public school integration in the 1950s, with one county actually closing

❷ Did You Know?

- The only brothers to sign the Declaration of Independence were Richard Henry and Francis Lightfoot Lee.
- Norfolk's innovative recycling program created "Mount Trashmore," a mountain of trash now a children's playground.
- Robert E. Lee's faithful horse, Traveller, is buried just outside the general's crypt on the campus of Washington and Lee University in Lexington.
- More Americans lost their lives in the Civil War than in World Wars I and II combined.
- Over 60% of the Civil War was fought in Virginia.
- Stonewall Jackson acquired his nickname in the first Battle of Manassas, when General Lee, marveling at his persistence in standing his ground, exclaimed, "There stands Jackson, like a stone wall!"
- Playwright George Bernard Shaw, when paid a ham by the Barter Theatre, returned it for spinach because he was a vegetarian.
- There are more miles of trout streams than roads in Virginia.
- Elected in 1912, Woodrow Wilson was the first southern-born president since the Civil War.
- The world's largest office building, the Pentagon contains more than 6.5 million square feet of space and almost 18 miles of corridors.
- Virginia's motto, *Sic Semper Tyrannus,* translated from the Latin means "Thus Always to Tyrants."
- Virginia is known as the "Mother of Presidents" because eight U.S. presidents were born here: George Washington, Thomas Jefferson, James Madison, James Monroe, both William Henry and Benjamin Harrison, John Tyler, and Woodrow Wilson.
- The Norfolk Naval Base is the world's largest naval facility.

its schoolhouse doors rather than admit African-Americans to previously all-white institutions. Today Virginia's politics are about evenly split between Democrats and Republicans, with the statehouse regularly changing hands. Democrat L. Douglas Wilder became the nation's first elected African-American governor in 1989, but Republican George Allen—son of the famous professional football coach—took the mansion back in 1993. Although racial relations have improved, many white Richmonders were incensed when the city council's African-American majority voted

Impressions

To be a Virginian, either by birth, marriage, adoption, or even on one's mother's side, is an introduction to any state in the union, a passport to any foreign country, and a benediction from the almighty God.

—Anonymous

Carry me back to old Virginny, There's where the cotton and the corn and taters grow.

—James A. Bland (1875)

in 1995 to place a statue of tennis star and Richmond native Arthur Ashe among those of Confederate heroes lining Monument Avenue.

3 A Look at the Past

Dateline

- **1607** First permanent English settlement in New World established at Jamestown.
- **1612** John Rolfe begins cultivation of tobacco for export.
- **1619** House of Burgesses—first representative legislative body in New World—meets in Jamestown. First Africans arrive at Jamestown as indentured servants.
- **1624** Virginia becomes a royal colony.
- **1652** Burgesses affirm that only they have right to elect officers of Virginia colony.
- **1682** Tobacco riots protest falling crop prices.
- **1699** Virginia's government moves to Williamsburg.
- **1754** French and Indian War begins as George Washington leads Virginia troops against French in Ohio Valley.
- **1755** Washington takes command of Virginia army on frontier.
- **1765** Patrick Henry protests Stamp Act, saying, "If this be treason, make the most of it."
- **1774** First Virginia Convention meets, sends delegates to Continental Congress.
- **1775** Patrick Henry incites rebellion with his "Liberty or Death" oration at Virginia Convention in Richmond. Washington chosen leader of army by Continental Congress.
- **1776** Patrick Henry elected first governor of self-declared free state of

continues

Virginia's history began on April 26, 1607, when 104 English men and boys arrived at Cape Henry on the Virginia coast after a four-month voyage aboard three small ships: the *Susan Constant,* the *Godspeed,* and the *Discovery.* The expedition—an attempt to compete with profitable Spanish encroachments in the New World—was sponsored by the Virginia Company of London and supported by King James I.

A MODEST BEGINNING   The travelers were lured by promises of wealth. Upon arrival, they were heartened to find, if not streets paved with gold, at least an abundance of fish and game. However, the settlers' optimism was short-lived. The very day of their arrival they were attacked by Native Americans. Fleeing Cape Henry, they started searching for a site that offered greater protection from the Spanish and the Indians. On May 13, the band of English adventurers moored their ships at Jamestown in "six fathom water" and the next day "set to worke about the fortification." Unfortunately, the group's lack of qualifications for the tasks before them soon emerged. Most were gentlemen, unaccustomed to work of any kind and with little inclination or aptitude for it. None of the rest was equipped for survival in a primeval wilderness. As one on-the-scene chronicler described it, "a world of miseries ensewed." An unfamiliar climate, contaminated water, famine, disease, and Native American attacks claimed their victims, and by autumn only 50 remained alive.

Tidewater's Native Americans were ambivalent to the new arrivals. When Capt. John Smith tried to barter for corn and grain, they took him prisoner and carried him to Chief Powhatan. According to legend, they would have killed him, but Powhatan's daughter, the beautiful princess Pocahontas, interceded and saved his life. However, Smith was not much of a diplomat in dealing with natives; he helped sow seeds of dissension that would result in centuries of hostility between the native cultures and European settlers.

In 1613, John Rolfe (who later married Pocahontas) brought from the New World a new aromatic tobacco that proved popular in England.

The settlers had discovered not the glittery gold they expected, but the "golden weed" that would be the foundation of Virginia's fortunes.

The year 1619 was marked by several important happenings: the Virginia Company sent a shipload of 90 women to suitors who had paid their transportation costs; 22 burgesses were elected to set up the first legislative body in the New World; and 20 Africans arrived in a Dutch ship to work as indentured servants, a precursor of slavery.

In 1699, the capital of the colony was moved from Jamestown, which had suffered a disastrous fire, to Williamsburg, and it was from Williamsburg that some of the first strong protests were lodged against Parliament by colonial patriots.

COLONIAL LIFE   By the mid-18th century, the growth of vast tobacco plantations along Tidewater Virginia's rivers brought with it a concurrent increase in the importation of slaves from Africa as the base for the "plantation economy."

The French and Indian War in the 1750s proved to be a training ground for America's Revolutionary forces. When the French built outposts in territory claimed by Virginia, Governor Dinwoody sent George Washington to protect Virginia's claims. In the field, Washington acquitted himself with honor, and after General Braddock's defeat, he was appointed commander-in-chief of Virginia's army on the frontier.

UNREST GROWS   Expenses from the war and economic hardships led the British to increase taxes in the colonies, and protests in Virginia and Massachusetts escalated. The 1765 Stamp Act met with general resistance. Patrick Henry inspired the Virginia General Assembly to pass the Virginia Resolves, setting forth colonial rights according to constitutional principles. The young orator exclaimed, "If this be treason, make the most of it." The Stamp Act was repealed in 1766, but the Revenue Acts of 1767, which included the hated tax on tea, exacerbated tensions.

Ties among the colonies were strengthened when Virginia's burgesses, led by Richard Henry Lee, created a standing committee to communicate their problems in dealing with England to similar committees in the other colonies. When the Boston Post Bill closed that harbor in punishment for the Boston Tea Party, the Virginia Assembly moved swiftly. Although Governor Dunmore had dissolved the legislature, it met at Raleigh Tavern and

Virginia. Thomas Jefferson's wording for Declaration of Independence adopted by Congress.
- 1779 State capital moved to Richmond.
- 1781 Cornwallis surrenders at Yorktown.
- 1787 Washington elected president of Constitutional Convention.
- 1788 Virginia ratifies Constitution.
- 1789 Washington inaugurated as first president. Virginia cedes area to U.S. for seat of government.
- 1801 Thomas Jefferson inaugurated president.
- 1803 Jefferson sends James Monroe to France for purchase of Louisiana Territory.
- 1809 James Madison inaugurated president.
- 1814 President and Dolley Madison flee to Virginia as British enter Washington.
- 1831 Nat Turner's slave rebellion.
- 1832 House of Delegates bill to abolish slavery in Virginia loses by seven votes.
- 1859 John Brown hanged after failed raid on Harper's Ferry Arsenal.
- 1861 Richmond chosen Confederate capital. First battle of Manassas.
- 1862 First ironclad ships, *Monitor* and *Merrimac,* battle in Hampton Roads harbor. Confederate victories at Second Manassas, Fredericksburg.
- 1863 Stonewall Jackson fatally wounded at Chancellorsville.
- 1864 Confederacy wins Battle of the Wilderness at Spotsylvania Court House near Fredericksburg. Grant's siege of Petersburg begins.

continues

- 1865 Richmond evacuated. Lee surrenders at Appomattox.
- 1867 Virginia put under military rule of Reconstruction Act. Confederate president Jefferson Davis imprisoned for treason in Fort Monroe.
- 1870 Virginia readmitted to Union.
- 1900 Legislature passes "Jim Crow" segregation laws.
- 1902 Poll tax in new state constitution effectively keeps African-Americans from voting.
- 1913 Woodrow Wilson inaugurated president.
- 1917 Wilson leads America into war against Germany. Growth of Hampton Roads naval and military installations.
- 1954 Supreme Court school integration ruling leads to school closings to avoid compliance with law.
- 1989 L. Douglas Wilder, nation's first African-American governor, takes office in Richmond.

recommended that a general congress be held annually. Virginia sent seven representatives to the First Continental Congress in 1774, among them Lee, Patrick Henry, and George Washington.

The following year, Patrick Henry made a fiery plea for arming Virginia's militia. He concluded his argument in these now-familiar words, "Is life so dear or peace so sweet as to be purchased at the price of chains and slavery? Forbid it, Almighty God! I know not what course others may take, but, as for me, give me liberty, or give me death!"

Later in 1775, upon hearing news of the battles of Lexington and Concord, the Second Continental Congress in Philadelphia voted to make the conflict near Boston a colony-wide confrontation and chose Washington as commander of the Continental Army. War had begun.

BIRTH OF THE NATION On June 12, 1776, the Virginia Convention, meeting in Williamsburg, adopted George Mason's Bill of Rights and instructed Virginia's delegates to the Continental Congress to propose independence for the colonies. Mason's revolutionary document stated that "all power is vested in, and consequently derived from, the people," and that "all men are created free and independent, and have certain inherent rights . . . among which are the enjoyment of life and liberty, with the means of acquiring and possessing property." He also firmly upheld the right of trial by jury, freedom of the press, and the right of all people to freedom of religion. When the Congress meeting in Philadelphia adopted Thomas Jefferson's Declaration of Independence (based on Mason's bill) on July 4, 1776, the United States of America was born.

The Revolution was a bloody seven-year conflict marked by many staggering defeats for the patriots. Historians believe it was only the superb leadership and pertinacity of Gen. George Washington that inspired the Continental Army (a ragtag group of farmers, laborers, backwoodsmen, and merchants) to continue so long in the face of overwhelming odds.

Victory at Yorktown Although many Virginians were in Washington's army, it was not until the war's final years that the state became a major battleground. The turning point came in March 1781, when British general Lord Cornwallis established a base at the York River.

Two weeks after Cornwallis settled into Yorktown for the winter, General Washington received word from a French admiral, the Comte de Grasse, that he was taking his squadron to the Chesapeake and that his men and ships were at Washington's disposal through October 15. "I shall be obliged to you," wrote de Grasse, "if you will employ me promptly and effectually during that time." After conferring with the Comte de Rochambeau, commander of the French troops in America, Washington decided to march 450 miles to Virginia with the object of defeating Cornwallis.

Meanwhile, on September 5, 1781, a fleet of 19 British ships under Adm. Thomas Graves appeared at the entrance to Chesapeake Bay with the aim of reinforcing Cornwallis's Yorktown entrenchment. They were met by 24 French ships under de Grasse. Though the battle ended in a stalemate, Graves was forced to return to New York to repair his ships. The French remained to block further British reinforcements or the possibility of their escape by water, while the French and American armies under Washington neared Yorktown to block aid or escape by land.

The siege began on September 28 when 17,000 men under Washington occupied a line encircling the town. The allied army, spread out in camps extending 6 miles, dug siege lines and bombarded the redcoats with heavy cannonfire. British defeat was inevitable. On October 17, a cease-fire was called and a British officer was led to American lines, where he requested an armistice. Although the war was not officially over until the Treaty of Paris was signed two years later, Cornwallis's defeat effectively marked the colonists' victory.

Framing the Constitution   The new nation's governmental powers were weak, resting on the inadequate provisions of the Articles of Confederation. To remedy the situation, a Constitutional Convention met in Philadelphia, and Washington was elected president of the Convention. He and fellow Virginian James Madison fought to have the new Constitution include a Bill of Rights and gradual abolition of the slave trade. Although both measures were defeated, the two Virginians voted to adopt the Constitution, feeling that its faults could be amended later.

In 1788, Virginia became the tenth state to ratify the Constitution, and by 1791 the first 10 amendments—the Bill of Rights—had been added. Madison was author of the first nine amendments, Richard Henry Lee the tenth.

The Country's Early Virginian Presidents   Washington was elected president under the new Constitution and took office on April 30, 1789.

As third president of the United States, Jefferson nearly doubled the size of the country by purchasing the Louisiana Territory from Napoleon.

James Madison took office as president in 1809. Unable to maintain Jefferson's peace-keeping efforts in the face of continued provocations by England, Madison was swayed by the popular demand for armed response, and in 1812 Congress declared war. Although some coastal plantations were attacked by British warships, the only suffering Virginia witnessed was the burning of nearby Washington, D.C.

James Monroe followed, having already served Virginia and the nation in many capacities. During his two terms as president, the nation pushed westward, and he faced the first struggle over the slavery question (which resulted in the Missouri Compromise), established the Monroe Doctrine, and settled the nation's boundary with Canada.

A NATION DIVIDES   It was not long before the United States became a nation divided. The issues were states' rights, slavery, and the conflicting goals of an industrial North and an agricultural South. In 1859, John Brown and his small band of followers raided the arsenal at Harper's Ferry (now West Virginia) to obtain arms for a slave revolt he hoped to instigate. Brown was captured and hanged. In the North, his execution rallied support for the abolitionist cause; in the South, people shuddered at the threat of a slave revolt.

The election of 1860 was crucial. The Republicans nominated Abraham Lincoln, whom the South vowed it would not accept, but the Democrats split and Lincoln was elected. Seven states seceded—Texas, Louisiana, South Carolina, Alabama, Georgia, Florida, and Mississippi. At his inauguration, Lincoln declared, "In your hands, my dissatisfied fellow countrymen, and not in mine, is the momentous issue of civil war. You can have no oath registered in heaven to destroy the government, while I have the solemn one to preserve, protect, and defend it."

On April 12, 1861, guns sounded at Fort Sumter in Charleston harbor. Secession had become war.

First Manassas, July 21, 1861   In May 1861, the Confederate capital was transferred to Richmond, only 100 miles from Washington. Virginia was doomed to become the first major battleground of the Civil War. The first of six heavy offensives by the North against Richmond was decisively repulsed on July 21, 1861, at the battle of First Manassas (Bull Run). Union Gen. Irvin McDowell's 35,000 ill-trained federal volunteers marched southward to the cry "Onward to Richmond," and the following Union attacks were successful. Later, however, a stonewall-like stand by the Virginia Brigade of Gen. Thomas J. Jackson swept McDowell's forces back to Washington. In addition to the victory, the South had found a new hero—Stonewall Jackson. Total casualties in this first major engagement of the war: 4,828 men! It was apparent that this would be a long and bitter conflict.

The Peninsula Campaign   The second major offensive against Richmond, the Peninsula Campaign, devised by Union Gen. George B. McClellan, was the setting for the most famous naval engagement in the western hemisphere. On March 9, 1862, two ironclad vessels, the U.S.S. *Monitor* and the C.S.S. *Virginia* (formerly the *Merrimac*) pounded each other with cannon. Although the battle was a draw, the advent of ironclad warships heralded a new era in naval history.

Two months later Yorktown was reduced to rubble and the Union army advanced up the peninsula. The Confederates retreated until they were only 9 miles from Richmond. At that point they fought, and the Confederate leader, General Johnson, was badly wounded. Robert E. Lee, grandson of colonial patriot Richard Henry Lee, was appointed head of the army of Virginia. Personally opposed to secession, Lee had sadly resigned his commission in the U.S. Army when Virginia joined the Confederacy, saying, "My heart is broken, but I cannot raise my sword against Virginia." In a series of victories beginning on June 26, 1862, Lee finally defeated the Union armies. Richmond had again been saved.

Second Manassas, Fredericksburg, and Chancellorsville, 1862–63   The third Union drive against Richmond was repulsed at Manassas, where Gen. Robert E. Lee secured his place in history by soundly defeating 70,000 Union troops under Gen. John Pope with a Confederate army of 55,000 men in 3 days. On December 13, 1862, Gen. Ambrose Burnside, newly chosen head of the Army of the Potomac, crossed the Rappahannock and struck Fredericksburg while Lee's army was scattered in northern Virginia. The federal advance was so slow that by the time the Union armies moved, Lee's forces were firmly entrenched in the hills south of the city. Burnside was unsuccessful, and the fourth Union drive against Richmond was turned back.

Gen. Joseph Hooker took command of the Union army early in 1863, and, once again, federal forces attempted to take Richmond. Fighting raged for four days. The Union army retreated, and the fifth drive on Richmond failed. But Lee's victory was costly. In addition to heavy casualties, Stonewall Jackson was wounded by his own troops and died of complications resulting from the amputation of his arm. Without Jackson, Lee began his second invasion of the North, which would end in the small Pennsylvania town of Gettysburg.

A War of Attrition   In March 1864, Grant was put in command of all federal armies. His plan for victory called for "a war of attrition," total unrelenting warfare that would put constant pressure on all points of the Confederacy. The first great confrontation between Lee and Grant, the Battle of the Wilderness, resulted in a Confederate victory, but the South's casualties were high—11,400. The Richmond campaign was the heaviest fighting of the Civil War. Three times Grant tried and failed to interpose his forces between Lee and Richmond. More than 80,000 men were killed and wounded.

Laying Siege to Petersburg, June 1864–April 1865   Still determined, Grant secretly moved his army across the James River toward Petersburg, an important rail junction south of Richmond. Improvised Southern forces managed to hold the city until Lee arrived. Grant then resorted to ever-tightening siege operations. Blocked in his trenches, Lee could not leave Grant's front. To do so would be to abandon Petersburg and Richmond. Subjected to hunger and exposure, the Confederate will to resist began to wane, and periodic skirmishes further weakened Confederate morale.

Lee, hoping to divert Grant's attention, dispatched a small army under Jubal Early to the menaced Shenandoah Valley. Grant instructed Union Gen. Philip Sheridan: "The Shenandoah is to be so devastated that crows flying across it for the balance of the season will have to bring their own provender." The second valley campaign resulted in the destruction of Early's army and the Shenandoah Valley.

Last Days of the War   Back in Petersburg, Grant's attrition strategy was succeeding. For the army of Northern Virginia, the 10-month siege of that city meant physical hardship, disease, filth, dwindling morale, and tedious waiting for the inevitable onslaught. It came on April 1, 1865, when federal forces smashed through weakened Confederate lines at Five Forks; Petersburg fell, and Richmond was occupied by federal forces. Lee's last hope was to rendezvous with Joe Johnson's army, which was retreating through North Carolina before Sherman's advance. On April 8, however, the vanguard of Grant's army succeeded in reaching Appomattox Court House ahead of Lee, thus blocking the Confederates' last escape route.

On April 9, 1865, the Civil War ended in Virginia at Appomattox, in Wilbur McLean's farmhouse. Grant, so uncompromising in war, proved compassionate in peace. All Confederate soldiers were permitted to return home on parole, cavalrymen could keep their horses, and officers could retain their sidearms. Rations were provided at once for the destitute southerners. Accepting these generous terms, Lee surrendered his 28,000 soldiers, the ragged remnants of the once-mighty Army of Northern Virginia. Lee's farewell was moving in its simplicity: "I earnestly pray that a merciful God will extend to you his blessing and protection. With an unceasing admiration of your constancy and devotion to your country, and a grateful remembrance of your kind and generous consideration for myself, I bid you all an affectionate farewell."

RECOVERY & RENEWAL   To a state devastated by a conflict that pitted brother against brother, recovery was slow. Besides the physical and psychological damages of the conflict, the Reconstruction era brought Virginia under federal military control until 1870.

By the turn of the century, however, Virginia's economic growth was characterized by new railroad lines connecting remote country areas in the west with urban centers. Factories were bringing more people to the cities, and the economy, once based entirely on agriculture, now had a growing industrial base. The great ports enjoyed growing importance as steamship traffic carried an increasing volume of commercial freight. During this period the great scholar, author, and educator Booker T. Washington, who had been born in slavery, studied at Virginia's Hampton Institute and achieved fame as an advisor to presidents.

Virginia-born Woodrow Wilson was serving as governor of New Jersey at the time he was elected president in 1912. Although noted for his peace-loving ideals, Wilson saw the entry of the United States into World War I in 1917. War brought prosperity to Virginia, with new factories and munitions plants and the expansion of military-training camps throughout the state.

World War II brought a population explosion, with men and women of the armed forces flocking to northern Virginia suburbs near Washington, D.C., and the port area of Hampton Roads. Many of these people stayed after the war, and by 1955 the majority of Virginians were urban dwelling. Today the state's population is about 6.5 million.

4 Recommended Books, Films, Videos & Recordings

BOOKS
BIOGRAPHIES & AUTOBIOGRAPHIES

Brodie, Fawn M. *Thomas Jefferson: An Intimate Portrait.* Norton, 1974.

Freeman, Douglas Southall. *George Washington.* 7 vols., 1948–57; abridged 1-vol. edition, Macmillan, 1985.

——————. *Lee.* 4 vols., 1935; abridged 1-vol. edition, Macmillan, 1985.

Malone, Dumas. *Jefferson and His Times.* 6 vols. Little, Brown, 1948–81.

Van Woodward, C., ed. *Mary Chestnut's Civil War.* Yale University Press, 1982. Pulitzer Prize–winning autobiography.

Washington, Booker T. *Up from Slavery.* 1903; reprinted by Doubleday, 1963.

NOVELS

Adams, Richard. *Traveller.* Dell, 1989. About General Lee's horse.

Bontemps, Arna. *Black Thunder.* 1936; reprinted, Beacon, 1968. Based on Gabriel Prosser's slave uprising in Richmond in 1800.

Cather, Willa. *Sapphira and the Slave Girl.* 1940; reprinted by Vintage, 1975.

Crane, Stephen. *Red Badge of Courage.* 1895; Bantam, 1981.

Glasgow, Ellen. *The Voice of the People.* 1900; Irvington, 1972.

Styron, William. *The Confessions of Nat Turner.* 1967; Bantam, 1981.

HISTORY

Dabney, Virginius. *Virginia, The New Dominion.* University Press of Virginia, 1971.

Foote, Shelby. *The Civil War.* 3 vols., 1963–74; Vintage, 3 vols., 1986.

Ward, Geoffrey C., with Ric Burns and Ken Burns. *The Civil War.* Knopf, 1990.

Wheeler, Richard. *Witness to Appomattox.* HarperCollins, 1991.

GENERAL

Dillard, Annie. *Pilgrim at Tinker Creek.* Harper & Row, 1974.

Hume, Ivor Noel. *Martin's Hundred.* Knopf, 1982.

Jefferson, Thomas. *Notes on the State of Virginia.* 1787; reprinted by Norton, 1982.

Loth, Calder. *The Virginia Landmarks Register.* 3rd ed. University Press of Virginia, 1986.

Peters, Margaret T., comp. *A Guidebook to Virginia's Historical Markers.* University Press of Virginia, 1985.

FILMS

Trail of the Lonesome Pine (1937), with Fred MacMurray, Henry Fonda, and Sylvia Sidney, is based on John Fox's romantic tale set in an Appalachian mining village.

Brother Rat (1938), with Jane Wyman and Ronald Reagan, depicting cadet life at the Virginia Military Institute.

Dirty Dancing (1987), with Jennifer Grey and Patrick Swayze; filmed at Mountain Lake Resort.

Silence of the Lambs (1990), with Jodie Foster and Anthony Hopkins; filmed at Quantico, Va.

Sommersby (1993), with Jodie Foster and Richard Gere; filmed in Lexington, Warm Springs, and Bath County.

VIDEOS

The Civil War, PBS Series, Time-Life.
Virginia's Civil War Parks, Finley-Holiday.

RECORDINGS

The Civil War: Its Music and Its Sounds, Philip's Mercury (1991).
Original Sound-Track Recordings: The Civil War, Elektra Nonesuch (1991).

3 Planning a Trip to Virginia

This chapter is devoted to the where, when, and how of your trip to Virginia. Whether you plan to stay a day, a week, two weeks, or longer, there are many choices you'll need to make *before* leaving home. Advice on this, and more, can be found in the sections that follow.

1 Visitor Information

The **Virginia Division of Tourism,** 901 E. Byrd St. (P.O. Box 798), Richmond, VA 23219 (☎ 804/786-2051 or 800/VISIT-VA; fax 804/786-1919), publishes or distributes a host of information that you can request. Included are official state highway maps showing all roads or just the scenic routes; an up-to-date calendar of events; a list of all hotels and motels and another of those that accept pets; a list of country inns and bed-and-breakfast establishments; a state park campground directory; and a list of Virginia wineries and wine festivals.

If you're driving into Virginia, the division operates roadside **Welcome Centers** in Bracey, on I-85 near the North Carolina border (☎ 804/689-2295); Bristol, on I-81 near the Tennessee border (☎ 703/466-2932); Clear Brook, on I-81 near the West Virginia border (☎ 703/722-3448); Covington, on I-64 near the West Virginia border (☎ 703/559-3010); New Church, on U.S. 13 at the Maryland border (☎ 804/824-5000); Fredericksburg, on I-95 southbound (☎ 703/786-8344); Lambsburg, on I-77 (☎ 703/755-3931); Manassas, on I-66 (☎ 703/361-2134); Rocky Gap, on I-77 (☎ 703/928-1873); and Skippers, on I-95 (☎ 804/634-4113).

2 When to Go

Virginia is a gorgeous place in October, when the "Indian summer" weather is at its finest and the leaves blaze orange, red, and yellow across the state. Throngs of visitors mob the mountains to see the autumn foliage during this so-called leaf season. (You can find out when the leaves will be at their peak by calling 804/786-4484.)

Otherwise, Virginia is busiest during summer when the historic sites, theme parks, and beaches draw millions of visitors from around the world—and hotel rates are at their highest. The least crowded—and least expensive—time to visit is in spring. Fortunately, that's when the dogwoods, azaleas, and wildflowers are in a riot of bloom from one end of Virginia to the other.

THE CLIMATE

Virginia enjoys four distinct seasons, with some variations in temperature from the warmer, more humid coastal areas to the cooler climate in the mountains. Wintertime snows usually are confined to northern Virginia and the mountains. In summer, extremely hot and very humid spells can last several weeks, but normally they are short-lived. Spring and autumn are long seasons, and in terms of natural beauty and heavenly climate, they're optimum times to visit. Annual rainfall averages 46 inches; annual snowfall is 18 inches.

Virginia's Average Temperatures

	Jan	Feb	Mar	Apr	May	June	July	Aug	Sept	Oct	Nov	Dec
High (°F)	44	46	56	68	75	84	90	88	81	69	57	47
Low (°F)	26	27	38	45	54	62	66	65	59	48	39	28

VIRGINIA CALENDAR OF EVENTS

January
- **Starvation Ball,** Centre Hill Mansion, Petersburg. Annual reenactment of a post–Civil War ball, with period music, costumes, and "Jeff Davis" punch. New Year's Day.
- **Lee Birthday Celebrations,** Alexandria. Period music, plus house tours at Lee-Fendall House and Lee's Boyhood Home. 4th Sunday. Also, open house at Stratford Hall on the Northern Neck, Lee's birthplace. Feb. 19.

February
- **Antiques Forum,** Williamsburg. Lectures and workshops on 18th-century life. 1st week.
- **Maymont Flower and Garden Show,** Richmond. A breath of spring, with landscape exhibits, vendors, and speakers. Early February.
- ✪ **George Washington Birthday Events.** Black tie or colonial costume Saturday evening dinner, followed by birth-night ball at Gadsby's Tavern, where George and Martha Washington attended balls in 1798 and 1799. On Sunday, Revolutionary War encampment at Fort Ward, featuring a skirmish between British and colonial uniformed troops. Parade on Monday.
  Where: Alexandria. **When:** Washington's Birthday weekend in February. **How:** Phone 703/838-5005 or 703/838-4200 for information.
- **Presidents' Day Celebration,** Fredericksburg. Monday of Washington's Birthday weekend. Reduced rates at attractions.

March
- **James Madison's Birthday,** Montpelier. Ceremony at cemetery and reception at house. March 16.
- **Patrick Henry Speech Reenactment,** St. John's Church, Richmond. "Give me liberty or give me death," he said here. Closest Sunday to March 23.
- **Highland Maple Festival,** Monterey. See maple syrup produced, pour it over pancakes, then see one of the state's largest crafts shows. 2nd and 3rd weekends. ☎ 540/468-2550.

April
- **Thomas Jefferson Birthday Commemoration,** Monticello, Charlottesville. Wreath-laying ceremony at gravesite, fife-and-drum corps, and a speaker. April 13.

✪ **International Azalea Festival.** The brilliant beauty of azaleas in bloom is the back-drop for ceremonies in the Norfolk Botanical Garden saluting NATO countries, including the crowning of a queen who reigns at a parade and other festivities. Also a military display that includes an air show, visiting of ships, and aircraft ground exhibits.

   Where: Norfolk. **When:** 2nd to 3rd week in April. **How:** Call 804/622-2312 for information.

• **Virginia Horse Festival,** Virginia Horse Center, Lexington. All breeds are show-cased with demonstrations, events, seminars, sales, equine art and merchandise. 3rd weekend.

✪ **Historic Garden Week in Virginia.** The event of the year—a statewide celebra-tion with tours of the grounds and gardens of some 200 Virginia landmarks, including plantations and other sites open only during this week.

   Where: Statewide. **When:** Last full week in April. **How:** Contact the Garden Club of Virginia, 12 E. Franklin St., Richmond, VA 23219 (☎ 804/644-7776.

May

✪ **Shenandoah Apple Blossom Festival.** Acres of orchards in blossom throughout the valley, plus 5 days of music, band competitions, parades, coronation of queen, foot races, arts and crafts sale, midway amusements, and a carnival, with a celebrity grand marshal.

   Where: Winchester. **When:** Usually 1st weekend in May. **How:** Contact Festival, 5 N. Cameron St., Winchester, VA 22601 (☎ 540/662-3863).

• **Virginia Gold Cup Race Meet,** Great Meadow Course, The Plains. Everyone dresses to the nines for the state's premier steeplechase event. Call 540/347-2612 for ticket information. 1st Saturday.

• **Seafood Festival,** Tom's Cove, Chincoteague. All you can eat—a seafood lover's dream come true. Must get tickets in advance from Eastern Shore Chamber of Commerce, P.O. Drawer R, Melfa, VA 23410 (☎ 804/787-2460). 1st weekend.

• **George Mason Day,** Gunston Hall, Lorton. All-day celebration with music and costumed role-players portraying his daily life and concern for the Bill of Rights. May 5.

• **Jamestown Landing Day,** Jamestown. Militia presentations and sailing demon-strations to celebrate the first settlers. Early May.

• **New Market Battlefield Historical Park,** New Market. Reenactment of battle. 2nd Sunday.

• **Mother's Day Pageant,** Fredericksburg. A skit portraying George Washington's last visit to his mother is performed at Mary Washington's cottage. Mother's Day, 2nd Sunday.

• **New Market Day,** Virginia Military Institute Campus, Lexington. Annual roll call for cadets who died in the battle. May 15.

• **Oatlands Sheepdog Trials,** Leesburg. Dogs compete in sheepherding contests. Crafts, food, and house and garden tours. Late May.

✪ **Virginia Hunt Country Stable Tour.** A unique opportunity to view prestigious Leesburg, Middleburg, and Upperville horse farms and private estates.

   Where: Loudoun and Fauquier counties. **When:** Memorial Day weekend. **How:** Ticket information at Trinity Church, Upperville (near Middleburg) (☎ 540/592-3711).

June

- **Great Rappahannock Whitewater Canoe Race,** Fredericksburg. Challenging 4.5-mile race. Early June.
- **Vintage Virginia Wine Festival,** Great Meadows Steeplechase Course, The Plains. Taste the premium vintages from 35 wineries. Arts and crafts displays, food, jazz, reggae, and pop music. For information call 540/253-5001. 1st weekend.
- **Harborfest,** Norfolk. Tall ships, sailboat races, air shows, military demonstrations, and fireworks. 1st weekend.
- **Boardwalk Art Show,** Virginia Beach. Works in all media, between 14th Street and 28th Street along the boardwalk. Mid-June.

✪ **James River Festival.** Old fashion "bateaux" boats race from Lynchburg to Richmond. Music at the riverfront, foot races, games, and historic crafts exhibits and demonstrations. The 8-day festival moves along the James, stopping each night at a historic town along the 200-year-old river route.

> **Where:** Lynchburg. **When:** Usually 3rd Saturday in June. **How:** Call 804/847-1811 for a schedule. Call 804/847-1811 for a schedule.

✪ **Ash Lawn-Highland Summer Festival.** James Monroe's home is the setting for opera, musicals, concerts, and traditional bonfire finale.

> **Where:** Charlottesville. **When:** End of June to August. **How:** Tickets from the box office or in town (☎ 804/293-9539).

July

- **Colonial Crafts Festival,** George Washington's Birthplace, Oak Grove. Highlights 18th-century crafts from the time of Washington's youth with demonstrations of handiwork. July 4.
- **Happy Birthday USA,** Staunton. Free concert hosted by Statler Brothers in Gypsy Hill Park. July 4.
- **Stratford Hall Open House.** Honoring Richard Henry Lee and Francis Lightfoot Lee, the only two brothers to sign the Declaration of Independence. July 4.

✪ **Virginia Highlands Festival.** Appalachian Mountain culture showcase for musicians, artists, artisans, and writers. Area's largest crafts show has antiques market and hot-air balloons.

> **Where:** Abingdon. **When:** First 2 weekends. **How:** Call Abingdon Chamber of Commerce (☎ 800/435-3440).

- **Virginia Scottish Games,** Alexandria. Celtic-theme festival with Highland dancing, bagpiping, fiddling competition, and Scottish foods. 4th weekend.

✪ **Pony Swim and Auction.** Famous wild horses swim the Assateague Channel, then are herded to carnival grounds, where they are auctioned off. Return swim to Assateague on Friday.

> **Where:** Chincoteague. **When:** Festival is last 2 weeks of July, swim on last Wednesday. **How:** Call 804/336-6161 for schedule and tickets.

- **Anheuser Busch Golf Classic,** Williamsburg. PGA tour event featuring top professional golfers in competition, at Kingsmill Golf Course. Late July.

August

✪ **Old Time Fiddlers' Convention.** Dating to 1935, one of the largest and oldest such conventions in the world. Fiddlefest street festival coincides. Phone 703/236-8681 for information.

> **Where:** Galax. **When:** Early August. **How:** Call 540/236-8681 for schedule and tickets.

- **Hot Air Balloon Festival and Flying Circus Airshows,** Bealeton. One of the largest regional conventions of hot-air balloons, plus biplanes, barnstorming and open-air cockpit rides. For information call 540/439-8661. Balloon Festival is mid-month; flying circus, weekends May to October.

September

- **Miller Genuine Draft/Autolite Platinum 200 Auto Race,** Richmond. Two-day stock-car event at the International Raceway. Early September.
- **Southwest Blue Ridge Highlands Storytelling Festival,** Historic Crab Orchard Museum and Pioneer Park, Tazewell. You will hear it all here, or learn to spin your own yarn in workshops. Also music for tired ears. Early September.
- **State Fair of Virginia,** Richmond. Rides, entertainment, agricultural exhibits, pioneer farmstead, and flower shows. 10 days in late September.
- **Elizabeth River Blues Festival,** Town Point Park, Norfolk. One of the largest free blues festivals in the east features national, regional, and local artists. 1st Saturday after Labor Day.
- **Apple Harvest Arts & Crafts Festival,** Winchester. Bookend to Winchester's apple festival; the fruits are made into butter, pies, cobblers, but arts and crafts take the spotlight. Square dancing, mountain music, food, too. 3rd weekend.
- **Northern Neck Seafood Extravaganza,** Ingleside Winery, Oak Grove. Oysters, crabs, shrimp, and clams, all washed down with fine vintages. 3rd Saturday.

October

- **International Gold Cup,** Great Meadows Course, The Plains. Fall colors provide a backdrop to one of the most prestigious steeplechase races. For information call 540/253-5001. 3rd Saturday.
- **Chincoteague Oyster Festival,** Chincoteague. A feast of oysters—but for advance ticket-holders only (call 804/336-6161). Early October.
- ✪ **Waterford Homes Tour and Crafts Exhibit.** The tiny Quaker town grows to some 40,000 on this one weekend.
    Where: Waterford Village. **When:** 1st weekend in October. **How:** Call 540/882-3085 for tickets.
- **Yorktown Day.** British surrender in 1781 celebrated with a parade, historic house tours, colonial music and dress, and military drills. October 19.

November

- **The First Thanksgiving,** Charles City. Reenactment at Berkeley Plantation. Early November.
- ✪ **Assateague Island Waterfowl Week.** The only time of the year when visitors can drive to the northern end of Chincoteague National Wildlife Refuge. There are also guided walks for pedestrians.
    Where: Assateague Island. **When:** Thanksgiving week. **How:** Phone 804/336-6577 for schedule.

December

- **Grand Illumination,** Williamsburg. Gala opening of holiday season with fife-and-drum corps, illumination of buildings, caroling, dancing, and fireworks. December.
- **Christmas Candlelight Tour,** Fredericksburg. Early December.
- **Christmas at Point of Honor,** Lynchburg. Early December.
- **Monticello Candlelight Tour,** Charlottesville. Early December.
- **Jamestown Christmas,** Jamestown. 2nd to 4th week.

- **Christmas at Mount Vernon.** One of the few historic sites open 365 days a year. December to January 6.
- **Waterfront New Year's Eve Celebration,** Norfolk. Times Square–style countdown, complete with a silver ball and fireworks at Town Point Park.

3 The Active Vacation Planner

Although Virginia is best known for its multitude of historic sites, it also is home to a host of outdoor activities. Hundreds of miles of mountain trails beckon hikers, mountain bikers, and horseback riders. Backcountry camping possibilities are widespread, especially in Shenandoah National Park and Mount Rogers National Recreation Area. The Chesapeake Bay and its many tributaries are famous for both boating and fishing. In the mountains, the state has more miles of trout streams than it does roads. Depending on the amount of recent rain, the Shenandoah, James, and Maury rivers have white-water rafting, kayaking, canoeing, and tubing. Hunters will find virtually the entire state to be populated with deer, and the Eastern Shore is renowned for goose, duck, and brant. Virginia is not a skiers' paradise, but it does have four resorts with downhill slopes, and many of its hiking trails make for fine cross-country skiing in winter. Virginia also is heavily populated by golf courses, some of them among the nation's finest.

You'll find these and other outdoor activities described in the chapters that follow, but here's a brief overview of the best places to move your muscles, with tips on how to get more detailed information.

BICYCLING & MOUNTAIN BIKING Bicycling is popular throughout Virginia, and with very good reason. Most of the state's scenic highways are open to bicycles: the 105-mile Skyline Drive above the Shenandoah Valley, the 218-mile Blue Ridge Parkway in the Southwest Highlands, and the 22-mile Colonial Parkway between Jamestown and Yorktown, to name the most popular. A bike path follows the scenic George Washington Memorial Parkway for 17 miles along the Potomac River from Arlington to Mount Vernon, the first president's home. Also in Northern Virginia, the Washington & Old Dominion Trail begins in Arlington and ends 45 miles away at Purcellville in the rolling hills of the Hunt Country. Two other rails-to-trails parks follow old railroad beds in the Southwest Highlands: the 55-mile New River Trail near Wytheville, and the 34-mile Virginia Creeper Trail in the Mount Rogers National Recreation Area. They go through some of the state's finest mountain scenery. Even in populous Hampton Roads, bikers can ride their own path along the Virginia Beach boardwalk, then through the natural beauty of First Landing/Seashore State Park and Back Bay National Wildlife Refuge (and even into the heart of the Great Dismal Swamp). Every road on the flat Eastern Shore is bicycling heaven, especially at Chincoteague and Assateague Island.

Statewide, Virginia is crossed by sections of three major bicycling routes: 500 miles of the TransAmerican Bicycle Trail from the Kentucky line to Yorktown; 150 miles of the Maine-to-Virginia route from Arlington to Richmond; 130 miles of the Virginia-to-Florida route from Richmond to the North Carolina line at Suffolk. Parts of these routes make up Interstate Bicycle Routes 1 and 76. For strip maps of these routes, contact Adventure Cycling Association, P.O. Box 8308, Missoula, MT 59807 (☎ 406/721-1776).

Mountain bikers can find plenty of trails, especially in Mount Rogers National Recreation Area and in the George Washington and Jefferson National Forests, which occupy large parts of the Shenandoah Valley and the southwest Highlands. For details about the latter, contact George Washington National Forest, 101 N. Main St. (P.O. Box 233), Harrisonburg, VA 22801 (☎ 540/564-8300), and Jefferson National Forest, 5162 Valleypointe Pkwy., Roanoke, VA 24019 (☎ 540/265-6054). *Mountain Bike Virginia* by Scott Adams (Beachway Press, 1995) is a very handy atlas to Virginia's best trails, with excellent maps.

BIRD-WATCHING   The big bird-watching draws in Virginia are the waterfowl nesting in the flatlands and marshes of the Eastern Shore, all of them on the Atlantic Flyway. Chincoteague National Wildlife Refuge on Assateague Island, the Eastern Shore National Wildlife Refuge (just north of the Chesapeake Bay Bridge-Tunnel), and Back Bay National Wildlife Refuge below Virginia Beach all offer world-class bird-watching.

BOATING, CANOEING, KAYAKING & RAFTING   The Chesapeake Bay and its many tributaries, including the Potomac, Rappahannock, York, and James rivers, offer world-class boating. In fact, one can come away from eastern Virginia with the impression that every other home has a boat and trailer sitting in the yard. Marinas also abound in the region, especially on the Northern Neck and in Hampton Roads. And over on the Eastern Shore, you can rent boats to explore the back bays of Chincoteague and Wachapreague. A detailed map showing public access to the Chesapeake and its tributaries is available from the Virginia Department of Conservation and Recreation, 203 Governor St., Suite 302, Richmond, VA 23219 (☎ 804/786-1712).

Canoeing and kayaking enthusiasts can indulge their passions either on the quiet backwaters of the Eastern Shore or on the swiftly running Shenandoah, James, and Maury rivers. The Southern Fork of the Shenandoah River near Front Royal is the state's most popular venue, with the James and Maury rivers near Lexington a close second. During periods of heavy rain—usually spring and late fall—these rivers also have white-water rafting. In fact, the James River makes Richmond the only city in the country with white water right in town. When the water is low and the weather hot during summer, multitudes cool off by floating down the Shenandoah and other rivers in inner tubes.

FISHING   The same waters that are so great for boating also have just about every species of fresh- and saltwater fish you can imagine. The best rivers for fishing include the South Fork of the Shenandoah for smallmouth bass and redbreast sunfish; the James for smallmouth bass and catfish; the New for wallee, yellow perch, musky, and smallmouth bass; the Rappahannock for smallmouth bass and catfish; and the Chickahominy for largemouth bass, chain pickerel, bluegill, white perch, and channel catfish. Many of these same species are found in reservoirs such as Lake Anna between Richmond and Fredericksburg; Buggs Island on the North Carolina line; Lake Moomaw west of Staunton and Lexington; and Claytor Lake, off I-81 in the Southwest Highlands. The mountains have 2,800 miles of trout streams, many of them stocked annually. From Virginia Beach, Chicoteague, and Wachapreague, you can go on charter and party boats in search of bluefish, kingfish, cobia, sharks, and other saltwater fish.

The Virginia Department of Game and Inland Fisheries, 4010 W. Broad St., Richmond, VA 23230 (☎ 804/367-1000), publishes an annual freshwater-fishing guide and a regulations pamphlet detailing licensing requirements and regulations. Available at most sporting goods stores, marinas, and bait shops, licenses are required except on the first Saturday and Sunday in June, which are free fishing days throughout Virginia. The most comprehensive book on the subject is *Virginia Fishing Guide* by Bob Gooch (University Press of Virginia, 1988, 1993).

GOLF   You can play golf almost anytime and anywhere in Virginia, given the state's mild climate and more than 130 courses. Williamsburg has some of the best, including the Golden Horseshoe, Green, and Gold courses at the Williamsburg Inn, and the links at Kingsmill Resort, home of the annual PGA Anheuser Busch Golf Classic. The Homestead's beautiful course in Hot Springs has the nation's oldest first tee—it's been in continuous use since 1890. Wintergreen Resort near Charlottesville also has one of the nation's best courses.

The free *Golfers' Guide* tabloid newspaper is widely available at tourist information offices throughout the state, or you can request a copy from The Golfers' Guide, Inc., 9616 Sir Barry Court, Richmond, VA 23229 (☎ 804/750-1704). The Virginia Division of Tourism distributes a list of all courses (see "Visitor Information," above).

HIKING   The same trails that make Virginia so popular with bicyclists (see "Bicycling & Mountain Biking," above) also make it a hiker's heaven. Some 450 miles of the Appalachian Trail snake through Virginia, almost climbing Mount Rogers and paralleling in many places the Blue Ridge Parkway and the Skyline Drive. The best backcountry trails are in Shenandoah National Park and Mount Rogers National Recreation Area. The state also has several rails-to-trails paths along old railroad beds, the best of which are the Washington & Old Dominion Trail in northern Virginia, and the Virginia Creeper Trail and the New River Trail, both in the Southwest Highlands.

For information and maps of the Appalachian Trail, contact the Appalachian Trail Conference, P.O. Box 807, Harpers Ferry, WV 25425-0807 (☎ 304/535-6331).

Two recent books give trail-by-trail descriptions. *The Trails of Virginia: Hiking the Old Dominion* by Allen de Hart (University of North Carolina Press, 1995) is the most comprehensive guide to Virginia's trails. *The Hiker's Guide to Virginia* by Randy Johnson (Falcon Press, 1992) is a slimmer, easier-to-carry volume that hits the highlights.

HOT-AIR BALLOONING   The rolling hills of the Hunt Country and the Piedmont are beautiful—especially during leaf season in October—when seen from a basket suspended under a hot-air balloon. Among several operators, United Balloon Ventures in Bealeton (☎ 540/439-8621) operates weekends from May to October. Balloons Unlimited (☎ 540/554-2002) and Rise and Shine Ballooning (☎ 540/729-0055) both fly over the Hunt Country. You can also go up for a quiet ride from Charlottes-ville's Boar's Head Inn. Call the companies well in advance, since reservations are essential, and schedules depend on weather conditions.

HORSEBACK RIDING   Equestrians will find hundreds of miles of public horse trails in Virginia, the majority of them in the Hunt Country of Northern Virginia and in the southwest Highlands. The granddaddy of them all, Virginia Highlands Horse Trail, runs the length of Mount Rogers National Recreation Area, which has campgrounds especially for horse owners. Horses also are permitted on the Virginia Creeper Trail and the New River Trail. You can rent horses at the Mount Rogers National Recreation Area and along the New River Trail. Shenandoah National Park has guided trail rides.

For a list of public horse trails and stables statewide, write the Virginia Horse Council, P.O. Box 72, Riner, VA 24149.

HORSE RACING   The Hunt Country and the Piedmont have 25 steeplechase races from spring to fall. The biggest are the Virginia Gold Cup in May and

International Gold Cup in October, both at The Plains, in the Hunt Country (see "Virginia Calendar of Events," above). For an annual schedule, write the Virginia Steeplechase Association, P.O. Box 1158, Middleburg, VA 22117.

HUNTING   Believe it or not, Virginia's turkey and white-tail deer populations are now larger than when Capt. John Smith hunted them to feed the Jamestown settlers. The state also has squirrel, grouse, bear, bobcat, fox, rabbit, pheasant, and quail, and the marshes of Chincoteague and the Eastern Shore are world famous for their goose, duck, and brant. In other words, you can hunt for something almost anywhere outside Virginia's metropolitan areas. Special seasons even allow hunting with bows and arrows. Licenses are required. Contact the Virginia Department of Game and Inland Fisheries, 4010 W. Broad St., Richmond, VA 23230 (☎ 804/367-1000), for details.

SKIING   You may glide over more man-made snow than the real thing, but Virginia has four downhill ski areas. Two are resorts mentioned in this book: The Homestead in Hot Springs, and Wintergreen near Charlottesville. Two others are condominium developments with golf courses and tennis courts as well as ski slopes: Massanutten, P.O. Box 1227, Harrisonburg, VA 22801 (☎ 540/289-9441); and Bryce Resort, P.O. Box 3, Bayse, VA 22810 (☎ 540/856-2121).

WATER SPORTS   To indulge your passion for surfing, jet skiing, wave running, sailing, or scuba diving, head for Virginia Beach, which has it all in abundance. Jet skis also rip up the waters of Chincoteague's back bays.

PACKAGE TOURS   Among the companies offering outdoor tours to Virginia are the following:

All Adventure Travel, 5589 Arapahoe, Suite 208, Boulder, CO 80303 (☎ 800/537-4025), has cycling and hiking tours to the Shenandoah Valley and the Piedmont.

Atlantic Canoe & Kayak Company, P.O. Box 405, Oakton, VA 22124 (☎ 703/0066, or 800/297-0066), has kayaking packages to the Northern Neck and Assateague Island on the Eastern Shore.

Backroads, 1516 5th St., Suite L101, Berkeley, CA 94710-1740 (☎ 800/462-2848), has 5-day cycling and country inn tours of the Shenandoah Valley.

Highland Adventures, P.O. Box 151, Monterey, VA 24465 (☎ 540/468-2722) has caving, rock climbing, and mountain bike trips to "Virginia's Switzerland," west of Staunton near the West Virginia border.

Hiking Holidays, P.O. Box 750, Bristol, VT 05443 (☎ 802/453-4816) and **New England Hiking Holidays,** P.O. Box 164B, North Conway, NH 03860 (☎ 800/869-0949), both have hiking trips to the Shenandoah National Park and the Blue Ridge Mountains.

4 Health, Insurance & Safety

HEALTH

Malaria may have been a curse of the colonists who settled Virginia, but today the state poses no unusual health threats. Although they don't carry malaria, mosquitoes are still rampant in the Tidewater during summer, especially in the marshes of Chincoteague and the Eastern Shore, so take plenty of insect repellent if you're going there. Hospitals and emergency-care facilities are widespread in the state, so unless you're in the backcountry mountains, help will be close at hand.

INSURANCE

Many travelers buy insurance policies providing health and accident, trip-cancellation and -interruption, and lost-luggage protection. The coverage you need will depend on the extent of protection contained in your existing policies. Some credit card companies also insure their customers against travel accidents if the tickets were purchased with their cards. Read your policies and credit card agreements over carefully before purchasing additional insurance.

Many health insurance companies and health maintenance organizations provide coverage for illness or accidents for their patients while away (don't forget to bring your identification card), but you may have to pay the local provider up front and file for a reimbursement when you get home. You will need adequate receipts, so collect them at the time of treatment.

Trip-cancellation insurance covers your loss if you have made nonrefundable deposits, bought airline tickets that provide no or partial refunds, or if you have paid for a charter flight and for some good reason you can't travel. Trip interruption insurance, on the other hand, provides refunds in case an airline or tour operator goes bankrupt or out of business.

Lost-luggage insurance covers your loss over and above the limited amounts for which the airlines are responsible, and some policies provide instant payment so that you can replace your missing items on the spot.

Your travel agent should know of a company that offers traveler's insurance. Here are some American companies:

Travel Assistance International (TAI) (☎ 202/347-2025 or 800/821-2828). The American agent for Europ Assistance Worldwide Services, Inc.

Travel Guard International (☎ 715/345-0505 or 800/782-5151).

Access America (☎ 804/285-3300 or 800/284-8300).

Health Care Abroad (Wallach & Co., Inc.) (☎ 703/687-3166 or 800/237-6615).

Divers Alert Network (DAN) (☎ 919/684-2948 or 800/446-2671).

SAFETY

Most areas of Virginia are relatively free of street crime, but this is not the case in the downtown areas of Richmond, Norfolk, Roanoke, and other cities. Ask your hotel staff or the local visitor information office whether neighborhoods you intend to visit are safe. Avoid deserted streets and alleys, and always be especially alert at night. Arlington and Alexandria have low crime rates when compared with Washington, D.C., across the Potomac River, but they aren't entirely free of it either. Anywhere you go, it's your responsibility to be on the alert and to safeguard your valuables. Never leave anything of value visible in your parked car; it's an invitation to theft anywhere.

When heading into the great outdoors, keep in mind that injuries often occur when people fail to follow instructions. Believe the experts who tell you to stay on the established ski trails. Hike only in designated areas, follow the marine charts if piloting your own boat, carry rain gear, and wear a life jacket when rafting. Mountain weather can be fickle at any time of the year. And watch out for summer thunderstorms that can send bolts of lightning your way.

5 Tips for Special Travelers

FOR TRAVELERS WITH DISABILITIES

The *Virginia Travel Guide for the Disabled,* published by The Opening Door, Inc., 8049 Ormesby Lane, Woodford, VA 22580 (☎ 804/633-6752), is a 300-page guide for persons with disabilities that is well worth the $5 cost. Its listings provide information on accessible hotels, restaurants, shops, and attractions.

Mobility International USA, P.O. Box 10767, Eugene, OR 97440 (☎ 503/343-1284), is a national nonprofit member organization that provides travel information and referrals to its members and has travel programs for the disabled. Membership includes a quarterly newsletter.

There's no charge for help via telephone (accessibility information and more) from the **Travel Information Service** (☎ 215/456-9600). The **Society for the Advancement of Travel for the Handicapped (SATH),** 347 Fifth Ave., Suite 610, New York, NY 10016 (☎ 212/447-7284), charges $5 for sending requested information.

Amtrak (☎ 800/USA-RAIL) provides special seating arrangements, boarding assistance, and discounts, with 24 hours' notice. Service dogs travel free of charge. Documentation from a doctor or an ID card proving your disability is required. For the hearing-impaired, Amtrak's special reservations and information number for teletypewriters is 800/523-6590.

Greyhound/Trailways (☎ 800/231-2222) allows a disabled person to travel with a companion for a single fare, if you call 48 hours in advance, and it will arrange help along the way.

The **National Park Service** issues "Golden Access Passports," admitting a disabled person and companion into a national park, forest, or wildlife refuge at no charge. The passports are obtainable at park entrances.

FOR SENIORS

Many Virginia hotels, motels, and attractions offer discounts to senior citizens. Always ask about senior discounts when making air or hotel reservations.

The **American Association of Retired Persons (AARP),** 601 E St. NW, Washington, DC 20049 (☎ 202/434-2277), offers members discounts on hotels, car rentals, air travel, and tours. The AARP Travel Service sponsors group worldwide tours and cruises; members must be 50 years or older.

Elderhostel, 75 Federal St., Boston, MA 02110-1941 (☎ 617/426-7788), sponsors vacations on college campuses. Participants must be 55 or older; however, if two people go as a couple, only one has to be of the required age.

The National Park Service issues a **"Golden Age Passport"** to any citizen or person who lives in the United States and is 62 or older, providing free admittance to all national parks. Obtain this lifetime admission permit free at any Park Service property; proof of age is necessary.

FOR FAMILIES

Virginia has a host of activities geared to families with children, from learning American history at Williamsburg to the exciting rides at Paramount's King's Dominion to the annual pony swim and roundup on Chincoteague and Assateague islands. As a consequence, a majority of Virginia hotels and motels are accustomed to hosting families; many offer babysitting services, and most of the resorts have children's programs.

Below are some of the highlights of the state that are particularly good for children.

HISTORIC ATTRACTIONS

Virginia will bring history to life for your kids (and you, too) with myriad associations involving America's first heroes—Washington, Jefferson, Madison, Monroe, and Patrick Henry among them. Be sure to take them to the first English settlement at **Jamestown;** to the picturesque village of **Colonial Williamsburg** and its craft demonstrations, militia reviews, and tours designed especially for kids; and to

Yorktown, where they can climb over the ramparts where Washington defeated Cornwallis. Other possibilities are the presidential homes of **Mount Vernon, Monticello,** and **Ashlawn-Highland. Civil War battlefield** tours portray crucial events with fascinating exhibits, scenic walks and drives, and multimedia programs.

THEME PARKS

Theme parks offer thrills and chills, not to mention food, fun, and entertainment at **Paramount's King's Dominion, Busch Gardens Williamsburg,** and **Water Country USA.**

MUSEUMS

Roanoke's museums, especially the **Museum of Transportation,** with its railroad cars, and **Science Museum,** featuring all sorts of interactive exhibits, rate high with kids. Richmond's **Children's Museum** and the **Science Museum of Virginia** will keep children enthralled with participatory activities and "touch me" exhibits.

Our family favorite is Virginia Beach's **Marine Science Museum,** where computers, exhibits, and the museum's own waterside setting explore the marine environment. Nearby in Norfolk, the new **NAUTICUS** has interactive and "virtual adventures" featuring make-believe U.S. Navy ships. Across the harbor in Hampton, they can see real spaceships at the **Virginia Air and Space Center.**

It's not a museum, but after reading the story of the pony in *Misty of Chincoteague,* kids will adore a chance to see the action themselves at **the wild ponies' swim across Assateague Channel.** The wildlife refuge there also offers hikes, nature programs, and a sandy beach.

THEATER

Theater for young people is sponsored by **TheatreVirginia** in the Virginia Museum of Fine Arts, Richmond. Outdoor theater is appealing to kids of all ages—in Lexington, the **Theatre at Lime Kiln** has folk music and other concerts as well as musicals that kids will enjoy.

6 Getting There

BY PLANE

Most international visitors will arrive at **Washington Dulles International Airport** (☎ 703/661-2700), in Northern Virginia, about 25 miles west of Washington, D.C. Dulles also is a major regional hub for domestic flights.

Also in Northern Virginia, **Washington National Airport** (☎ 703/685-8000), located on the Potomac River midway between Arlington and Alexandria, is the region's busiest airport, but because of space and noise limitations it takes no international flights and only domestic flights originating no farther away than the Mississippi River. Transatlantic and transcontinental flights, therefore, will all arrive at Washington Dulles.

Other major Virginia gateways are **Richmond International Airport** (☎ 804/226-3000); **Norfolk International Airport** (☎ 804/857-3351); **Newport News/Williamsburg Airport** (☎ 804/877-0221); **Charlottesville/Albermarle Airport** (☎ 804/973-8341); and **Roanoke Regional Airport** (☎ 703/362-1999).

The Airlines   Most domestic carriers serve Washington Dulles or Washington National, with many going to both. These include the cut-rate **ValuJet** (☎ 800/825-8538), which has a regional hub at Washington Dulles. Domestic carriers serving other Virginia airports as well as Washington Dulles and Washington National include **American** (☎ 800/433-7300), **Continental** (☎ 800/525-0280), **Delta**

(☎ 800/221-1212), **Northwest** (☎ 800/225-2525), **TWA** (☎ 800/221-2000), **United** (☎ 703/742-4600), and **USAir** (☎ 202/783-4500).

Among the **international airlines** serving Washington Dulles Airport are **Aeroflot** (☎ 800/995-5555, 202/429-4922 in Washington, D.C.), **Air France** (☎ 800/237-2747), **All Nippon Airways** (☎ 800/235-9262), **British Airways** (☎ 800/247-9297), **Japan Airlines** (☎ 800/525-3663), **KLM Royal Dutch Airlines** (☎ 800/374-7747), and **Lufthansa** (☎ 800/645-3880).

Money-Saving Tips   Wherever you're traveling from, always shop the different airlines and ask for the lowest fare. Check travel sections of local and national newspapers for special promotional fares or packages. Contact your travel agent to find out all available options. The cheapest fares are usually advance-purchase, restricted deals (you may have to stay a minimum or maximum number of days and return on a certain day).

BY TRAIN

Amtrak's *Metroliner* and other northeast-corridor trains connect New York to Union Station in Washington, D.C., where riders can board the Metrorail subway to Arlington, Alexandria, and other northern Virginia destinations. All Amtrak trains between New York and Florida stop at Richmond; some also stop at Alexandria, Quantico, and Fredericksburg. Another train runs between New York and Newport News via Williamsburg and Richmond. From Newport News, Amtrak's Thruway bus service is available trainside to Norfolk and Virginia Beach. Some east- and westbound trains to and from Washington stop at Charlottesville, Staunton, and Clifton Forge. From Clifton Forge, a Thruway bus connects to Roanoke.

Call or write Amtrak, Union Station, 60 Massachusetts Ave. NE, Washington, DC 20002 (☎ 800/USA-RAIL), for ticket and schedule information.

BY BUS

Greyhound/Trailways (☎ 800/231-2222) connects many of Virginia's cities and towns with the entire country.

BY CAR

Visitors arriving in Virginia by car from New York and points north and east do so via **I-95,** which runs north-south across the state. From western Maryland and eastern Tennessee, the major highway is **I-81,** which also runs north-south the entire length of the state. Major western entrance points are from West Virginia via **I-77** and **I-64.** The latter runs east-west across the state between Covington and Norfolk. In northern Virginia, **I-66** traverses the state east-west between Arlington and I-81 at Strasberg. For more information about driving in Virginia, contact the **Virginia Department of Transportation**, Administrative Services Division, 1401 E. Broad St., Richmond, VA 23219 (☎ 804/786-2838).

7 Getting Around

BY CAR

If at all possible, see Virginia by car. You'll have optimum flexibility to see the rural beauties of the state, including the plantations and Civil War battlefields. And, of course, two of the state's most scenic attractions, the Skyline Drive and Blue Ridge Parkway, are motoring destinations.

Virginia Driving Times & Distances

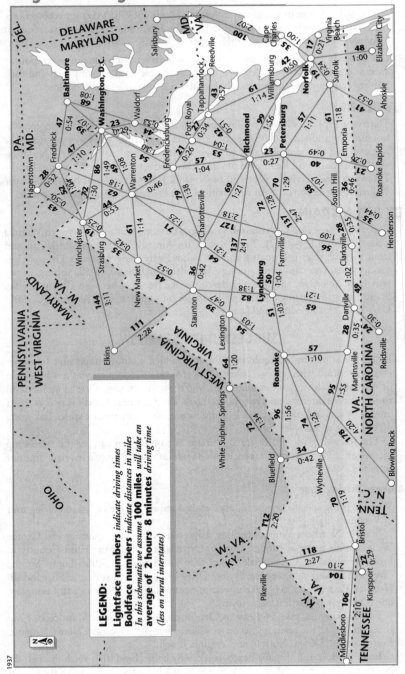

LEGEND:

Lightface numbers *indicate driving times*
Boldface numbers *indicate distances in miles*
In this schematic we assume **100 miles** *will take an average of* **2 hours 8 minutes** *driving time*
(less on rural interstates)

1937

The state maintains a highway helpline (☎ 800/367-ROAD) for emergencies. A free state highway map is available from the Division of Tourism (see "Visitor Information" at the beginning of this chapter).

Car Rentals   Most rental companies operate in Virginia's major metropolitan areas and at all but the smallest of airports. A complete list of companies and their toll-free reservations numbers can be found in the appendix of this book.

BY PLANE

The major airports in Northern Virginia are Washington Dulles and Washington National. Shenandoah Valley and the Virginia Highlands gateways are Roanoke Regional and Shenandoah Valley Regional airports. For central Virginia, Charlottesville, Lynchburg, and Richmond provide scheduled service. In the Hampton Roads/Tidewater area, service is provided by Norfolk International and Newport News/Williamsburg airports. USAir is the airline with the most flights around the state.

BY BUS & TRAIN

Generally, you'll find **Greyhound/Trailways** bus service available between Virginia cities (☎ 800/231-2222). Train service on **Amtrak** is better at getting to and from Virginia than it is getting around, although by using Amtrak's Thruway bus connections, you can travel among Alexandria, Richmond, Williamsburg, Newport News, Norfolk, and Virginia Beach on one line, and between Charlottesville, Staunton, and Clifton Forge, and Roanoke on another. Call Amtrak (☎ 800/USA-RAIL) for schedules and fares.

SUGGESTED ITINERARIES

A grand tour of Virginia could take a month, which is almost impossible for us average Americans with our two paltry weeks of vacation. So unless you're a European or Australian with a glorious month off, you'll have to choose where to go based on time, personal interests, and your pocketbook. Keep in mind that it's very easy to get around by car, and you can cover long distances easily via interstates, which link many of Virginia's scenic splendors.

The following itineraries are *suggestions* as to how you can *see* the state's top attractions. We have not taken into consideration the state's myriad outdoor activities.

A Grand Driving Tour

Without being specific on the number of days required, here's a grand driving tour of Virginia's highlights:

Start in Northern Virginia and see Arlington's National Cemetery and George Washington's home at Mount Vernon. Drive west through the Hunt Country to Front Royal in the Shenandoah Valley, then south on U.S. 340 to Luray. See the caverns there and then take the Skyline Drive through the best part of Shenandoah National Park to U.S. 33. Take it west to Staunton, then I-81 south to Lexington, one of the state's prettiest small towns.

From Lexington, take I-64 east to Charlottesville for a look at Monticello. Keep going on I-64 to Richmond, then on to Williamsburg for a look at Colonial Virginia. Keep going on I-64 to Norfolk and Virginia Beach.

From Norfolk and Virginia Beach, you can fly home, head back north through the Northern Neck and Fredericksburg to northern Virginia, or drive across the Chesapeake Bay Bridge-Tunnel and up the Eastern Shore to Chincoteague and Assateague

Island. From there, U.S. 13 and U.S. 50 combine to bring you back through Maryland and the District of Columbia to Northern Virginia.

If You Have 4 Days (Northern Virginia)

Day 1   Spend a day in Arlington seeing the National Cemetery and nearby attractions. Arlington is a good base if you're combining a visit to Washington, D.C., with northern Virginia sites. Otherwise, you might prefer to stay in Alexandria, which is smaller, has a more diversified selection of hotels, and is also a good center for exploring.

Day 2   Based in either Arlington or Alexandria, head for the major Alexandria attractions—Old Town's museums, historic houses, shops, and restaurants.

Day 3   Again based in Arlington or Alexandria, head south and east about 15 to 20 miles for a day trip to the Potomac plantations—Washington's beloved Mount Vernon and George Mason's Gunston Hall are the premier estates.

Day 4   Leave Arlington or Alexandria and head east to Manassas (about 30 miles). Visit the battlefield, then go north to Hunt Country (about 11 miles). Overnight in Middleburg or Leesburg, take a walking tour of downtown Leesburg, and see the nearby plantations. Civil War buffs can take a 14-mile ride to Harper's Ferry Historic Park, scene of John Brown's raid.

If You Have 5 Days (Richmond & Tidewater)

Day 1   Spend one full day and overnight in Fredericksburg; see the Old Town, and visit one or more of the Civil War battlefields.

Day 2   Head south 45 miles on I-95 to Richmond. Families can spend at least half a day at King's Dominion theme park, about halfway between the two cities. History buffs can go about 10 miles farther south on I-95, then head west for a tour of Scotchtown, Patrick Henry's plantation. If time allows, visit Richmond attractions. Overnight in Richmond.

Day 3   Spend the day in Richmond. Walk around the Court End district, stopping in at the Museum and White House of the Confederacy, the Valentine Museum, the John Marshall House, and the impressive State Capitol building designed by Jefferson, among other attractions. Civil War buffs may choose to go south on I-95 about 14 miles to see Petersburg Battlefield Park. Spend the night again in Richmond.

Day 4   Leave Richmond and take Va. 5 east to Williamsburg, sightseeing along the way at one or more of the James River plantations. Overnight in Williamsburg.

Day 5   After you've explored Williamsburg's many attractions, you'll also want to see Jamestown and Yorktown, both within a 30-mile radius of Williamsburg. Two theme parks—Busch Gardens Williamsburg and Water Country USA—are also within a few minutes of Williamsburg. This area, in itself, could occupy a week.

If You Have 6 Days (Charlottesville, Skyline Drive & Blue Ridge Parkway)

Day 1   Starting at Winchester, the northernmost town of the Shenandoah Valley, see Middletown, Front Royal, and the Skyline Caverns. Overnight in one of the area's charming country inns or B&Bs.

Day 2   Follow the Skyline Drive south, enjoying the superb panoramic views of the Blue Ridge and the valley, to U.S. 211. Head west to visit New Market Battlefield and Luray Caverns. Overnight along the drive in Big Meadows or Skyland Lodge or at a nearby B&B.

Day 3   Continue south on U.S. 11, I-81, or the Skyline Drive (depending on your time frame) to Staunton and Charlottesville, a good overnight stop.

Day 4 You'll have a full day of sightseeing in Charlottesville—here you can see Jefferson's Monticello, Ashlawn-Highland, and the University of Virginia, among other sights. Overnight in Charlottesville.

Day 5 Continue south (U.S. 11, I-81, or the Blue Ridge Parkway) to Lexington. Spend part of the day exploring Lexington's historic sites, but save some time for a drive to Warm Springs on Va. 39, over the Goshen Pass. If the budget allows, spend the night at The Homestead in Hot Springs; for more moderate accommodations, consider the charming inns in nearby Warm Springs or downtown Lexington.

Day 6 Continue south on the Blue Ridge Parkway, enjoying the beautiful scenery, to Roanoke, which has some of the best attractions for children in the state—including the Museum of Transportation and the Science Museum in Market Square.

Those with the time will want to explore the southwest highlands of Virginia, stopping off in the pretty village of Abingdon and exploring the mountain country.

8 Tips on Accommodations

Virginia has a vast array of accommodations, from rock-bottom roadside motels to some of the nation's finest resorts. Whether you spend a pittance or a bundle depends on your budget and your tastes.

MONEY-SAVING TIPS

If you plan carefully, and possess a little knowledge of how the hotel industry works, you can often save a bundle on room rates.

If business is slow, many hotels will accept less than their published "rack" rates, which are their highest regular rates (rack rates are what are quoted in this book). Most rack rates include commissions of 20% or more for travel agents. You might save, therefore, if you make your own reservations and bargain a little.

Most hotels also give discounts to corporate travelers, government employees, senior citizens, automobile club members, active-duty military personnel, and others. They usually don't advertise these discounted rates or even volunteer them at the front desk, but you may be able to take advantage of them by asking politely about any special rates that might apply to you at the time you make your reservation.

Downtown hotels catering to business travelers during the week usually have big discounts on Friday, Saturday, and Sunday nights. If you're staying in a city over a weekend, always ask about a weekend rate or package deal. Weekend rates don't apply in the resort areas such as Virginia Beach, but you should ask there about weekday or week long rates and vacation packages as well as off-season discounts.

Parking fees can run up the cost at downtown hotels, especially for long-term stays. And many hotels jack up the price of long-distance phone calls made from your room. Accordingly, always inquire about the costs of parking, and use a pay phone if the hotel tacks a hefty surcharge on calls.

BED & BREAKFASTS

Bed-and-breakfast inns can be a terrific way to get the flavor and feel of the state, and they often offer added value when you consider that room rates include breakfast and, many times, afternoon tea.

Virginia has far too many first-rate country inns and bed-and-breakfasts to mention them all in this book. We have selected some of the best, but there are many others throughout the state. For a statewide directory, write the **Bed and Breakfast Association of Virginia,** P.O. Box 791, Orange, VA 22960 (☎ 703/672-4893).

The association inspects and approves all of the properties it promotes. In addition, most local visitor information offices will send you a list of bed-and-breakfasts in their locale.

The Virginia Division of Tourism operates a **reservation service** (☎ 800/934-9184) for many country inns and bed-and-breakfast accommodations.

FAST FACTS: Virginia

American Express   To report lost or stolen traveler's checks, call **800/221-7282.** The main office in Richmond is at 1412A Starling Drive (☎ **804/740-2030**); in Roanoke, you'll find it at 22 East Campbell Ave. (☎ **540/982-2200**). Call the main office in Richmond or consult the phone directory for locations in other cities and towns.

Car Rentals   See "Getting Around" earlier in this chapter.

Climate   See "When to Go" earlier in this chapter.

Embassies and Consulates   See Chapter 4, "For Foreign Visitors."

Emergencies   Call **911** (no charge) for police, fire, and ambulance.

Information   See "Visitor Information" earlier in this chapter.

Liquor Laws   In Virginia, many grocery and convenience stores sell beer and wine, but only state-licensed Alcoholic Beverage Control (ABC) stores are permitted to sell bottles of hard liquor. Any licensed establishment (restaurant or bar) can sell drinks by the glass.

Newspapers/Magazines   Each major city in Virginia has its own daily newspaper, and the *Washington Post* is available at newsstands and coin boxes as far south as Richmond, as far west as Lexington.

Pets   Many hotels and motels accept small, well-behaved pets. However, there is often a small fee charged to allow them into guest rooms. Many places, in particular bed-and-breakfast inns, do not allow pets at all. Two good resources for pet owners are *Frommer's On the Road Again with Man's Best Friend: Mid-Atlantic States* and *Frommer's America on Wheels: Mid-Atlantic* (both by Macmillan Travel), which will steer you towards dog-friendly accommodations. Pets are usually restricted in national parks, so check with each park's ranger station before setting out.

Police   To reach the police, dial **911** from any phone (no charge).

Taxes   The Virginia state sales tax is 4.5% for most purchases, and a few local jurisdictions add another .5% to bring the total sales tax to 5%. Hotel taxes vary from town to town; in most communities it is 5%, which makes the total tax on your hotel bill 9.5% or 10%. Some local jurisdictions also add a restaurant tax, bringing the total tax on meal and drink bills to anywhere from 8% to 10%.

Time Zone   Virginia is on Eastern Standard Time (EST), the same as New York and other East Coast cities. When it is 12 noon in Virginia, it is 11am in Chicago, 10am in Detroit, 9am in Los Angeles, 8am in Anchorage, and 7am in Honolulu.

Weather   In Richmond, call **804/268-1212;** in Roanoke, call **540/982-2303.**

4 For Foreign Visitors

Although the United States may seem like familiar territory to foreign visitors au courant with U.S. fads and fashions, there are still many uniquely American situations that you may encounter. In this chapter, we will point out some of the perhaps unexpected differences from what you are used to at home, and explain some of the perhaps more confusing aspects of daily life in the United States.

1 Preparing for Your Trip

ENTRY REQUIREMENTS

DOCUMENT REGULATIONS Immigration laws are a hot political issue in the United States, and the following requirements may have changed by the time you plan your trip. Check at any U.S. embassy or consulate for current information and requirements.

Canadian citizens need only proof of Canadian residence to visit the United States. As we went to press, British subjects and citizens of New Zealand, Japan, and most western European countries traveling on valid passports did not need a visa for holiday or business travel to the United States for less than 90 days, providing that they held a round-trip or return ticket and that they entered the United States on an airline or cruise line participating in the visa-waiver program. Citizens of these visa-exempt countries could then visit Mexico, Canada, Bermuda, and/or the Caribbean islands and re-enter the United States by any mode of transportation, without needing a visa.

Citizens of other countries, including Australia, must have two documents: (1) a valid passport with an expiration date at least six months later than the scheduled end of their visit to the United States, and (2) a tourist visa available from any U.S. embassy or consulate.

To obtain a visa, a traveler must submit a completed application form (either in person or by mail) with a 1¹/₂-inch-square photo and must demonstrate binding ties to a residence abroad. Usually you can obtain a visa at once or within 24 hours, but it may take longer during the summer rush from June to August. If you cannot go in person, contact the nearest U.S. embassy or consulate for directions on applying by mail. Your travel agent or airline office may also be able to provide visa applications and instructions. The U.S. embassy or consulate that processes your application will determine whether you will be issued a multiple- or single-entry visa and any restrictions on the length of your stay.

MEDICAL REQUIREMENTS   No inoculations are needed to enter the United States, unless you are coming from or have stopped over in areas known to be suffering from epidemics, particularly cholera or yellow fever. If you have a disease requiring treatment with medications containing narcotics or drugs requiring a syringe, carry a valid signed prescription from your physician to allay any suspicion that you are smuggling drugs.

CUSTOMS REQUIREMENTS   Every adult visitor may bring free of duty 1 liter of wine or spirits; 200 cigarettes or 100 cigars (but no cigars from Cuba) or 3 pounds of smoking tobacco; $100 worth of gifts. These exemptions are offered to travelers who spend at least 72 hours in the United States and who have not claimed them within the preceding 6 months. It is altogether forbidden to bring into the country foodstuffs (particularly cheese, fruit, cooked meats, and canned goods) and plants (vegetables, seeds, tropical plants, and so on). Foreign tourists may bring in or take out up to $10,000 in U.S. or foreign currency with no formalities; larger sums must be declared to Customs on entering or leaving.

INSURANCE

There is no national health system in the United States, and the cost of medical care is extremely high. Accordingly, we strongly advise every traveler to secure health coverage before setting out.

You may want to take out a comprehensive travel policy that covers (for a relatively low premium) sickness or injury costs (medical, surgical, and hospital); loss or theft of your baggage; and costs of accident, repatriation, or death. Such packages (for example, Europ Assistance Worldwide Services in Europe) are sold by automobile clubs at attractive rates, as well as by insurance companies and travel agencies. The United States agent for Europ Assistance is **Travel Assistance International,** 1133 15th St., NW, Suite 400, Washington, DC 20005 (☎ 202/331-1690 or 800/821-2828).

MONEY

CURRENCY   The U.S. monetary system has a decimal base: 1 American **dollar** ($1) = 100 **cents** (100¢).

Dollar notes ("bills") are all the same size and are green on one side, gray on the other. They come in $1 (a "buck"), $5, $10, $20, $50, and $100 denominations. The six denominations of coins—with their American nicknames—are 1¢ ("penny"), 5¢ ("nickel"), 10¢ ("dime"), 25¢ ("quarter"), 50¢ ("half-buck"), and the rare $1 piece.

CURRENCY EXCHANGE   Foreign-exchange bureaus, so common in Europe, are rare even at airports in the United States and are nonexistent outside major cities. Try to avoid having to change foreign currency or traveler's checks denominated in other than U.S. dollars at small-town banks or even at branches in big cities. In fact, you should change your home currency into U.S. dollars before leaving home.

TRAVELER'S CHECKS   Traveler's checks denominated in U.S. dollars are easily changed in banks and are also accepted at most hotels, motels, stores, and restaurants. Sometimes a passport or other photo identification is necessary.

CREDIT CARDS   The method of payment most widely used in the United States is credit and charge cards: Visa (BarclayCard in Britain, Chargex in Canada), MasterCard (EuroCard in Europe, Access in Britain, Diamond in Japan), American

Express, Diners Club, and Carte Blanche. You must have a credit or charge card to rent a car. It can also be used as proof of identity or as a "cash card," enabling you to draw money from banks that accept it. Automatic teller machines (ATMs) are widespread throughout the United States.

SAFETY

GENERAL   While tourist areas are generally safe, crime is on the increase everywhere, and U.S. urban areas tend to be less safe than those in Europe or Japan. Virginia is generally a safe state, especially in rural areas, but you should be careful in the downtown areas of the larger cities, particularly at night.

As a general rule, visitors should always stay alert. This is particularly true in large U.S. cities. It is wise to ask the city or area's tourist office if you are in doubt about which neighborhoods are safe. Avoid deserted areas, especially at night. Don't go into any city park at night unless there is an occasion that attracts crowds. Generally speaking, you can feel safe in areas where there are many people and many open establishments.

Avoid carrying valuables with you on the street, and don't display expensive cameras or electronic equipment. Hold on to your pocketbook, and place your billfold in an inside pocket. In restaurants, theaters, and other public places, keep your possessions in sight.

Remember also that hotels are open to the public, and in a large hotel, security may not be able to screen everyone entering. Always lock your room door; don't assume that once inside your hotel you are automatically safe and need no longer be aware of your surroundings.

DRIVING   Safety while driving is particularly important. Question your rental agency about personal safety or ask for a brochure on traveler safety tips when you pick up your car. Obtain from the agency written directions or a map with the route clearly marked showing how to get to your destination. And, if at all possible, arrive and depart during daylight hours.

Recently, more and more crime has involved cars and drivers. If you drive off a highway into a doubtful neighborhood, leave the area as quickly as possible. If you have an accident, even on the highway, stay in your car with the doors locked until you assess the situation or until the police arrive. If you are bumped from behind on the street or are involved in a minor accident with no injuries and the situation appears to be suspicious, motion to the other driver to follow you. *Never* get out of your car in such situations. You can also keep a sign in your car: PLEASE FOLLOW THIS VEHICLE TO REPORT THE ACCIDENT. Show the sign to the other driver and go directly to the nearest police precinct, well-lighted service station, or all-night store.

If you see someone on the road who indicates a need for help, do not stop. Take note of the location, drive on to a well-lighted area, and telephone the police by dialing 911.

Park in well-lighted, well-traveled areas if possible. Always keep your car doors locked, whether the car is attended or unattended. Look around you before you get out of your car, and never leave any packages or valuables in sight. If someone attempts to rob you or steal your car, do not try to resist the thief/carjacker; report the incident to the police department immediately.

Also, make sure that you have enough gasoline (petrol) in your tank to reach your intended destination so that you're not forced to look for a service station in an unfamiliar and possibly unsafe neighborhood—especially at night.

2   Getting to the United States

Travelers from overseas can take advantage of the **APEX (advance-purchase excursion) fares** offered by all the major U.S. and European carriers.

Some large American airlines (for example, TWA, American Airlines, Northwest, United, and Delta) offer travelers on their transatlantic or transpacific flights special discount tickets under the name **Visit USA,** allowing travel between any U.S. destinations at minimum rates. Tickets must be purchased before you leave your foreign point of departure. This system is the best, easiest, and fastest way to see the United States at low cost. You should obtain information well in advance from your travel agent or the office of the airline concerned, since the conditions attached to these discount tickets can be changed without advance notice.

The visitor arriving by air, no matter what the port of entry, should cultivate patience and resignation before setting foot on U.S. soil. Getting through immigration control can take as long as two hours, especially on summer weekends. Make very generous allowance for delay in planning connections between international and domestic flights—an average of two to three hours at least.

In contrast, travelers arriving by car or by rail from Canada will find border-crossing formalities streamlined to the vanishing point. And air travelers from Canada, Bermuda, and some places in the Caribbean can sometimes go through Customs and Immigration at the point of departure, which is much quicker.

For further information about travel to and within Virginia, see "Getting There" and "Getting Around" at the end of Chapter 3.

FAST FACTS: For the Foreign Traveler

Automobile Organizations   Auto clubs will supply maps, suggested routes, guidebooks, accident and bail-bond insurance, and emergency road service. **The American Automobile Association (AAA)** is the major club in the United States, with almost 1,000 offices nationwide. Members of some foreign auto clubs have reciprocal arrangements with the AAA and enjoy its services at no charge (inquire with your home club if it has an agreement with AAA). You may be able to join AAA even if you're not a member of a reciprocal club. Check the phone book for local offices. The AAA emergency road service number is 800/336-4357.

Business Hours   Public and private **offices** are usually open Monday through Friday from 9am to 5pm. **Banking** hours vary by establishment in Virginia; most are open Monday to Thursday from 9am to 2pm, with extended hours on Friday. A few banks are open Saturday morning until noon. Most **post offices** are open Monday through Friday from 8:30am to 5pm, Saturday from 8:30am to 12:30pm. **Store** hours are usually Monday through Friday from 10am to 6pm; some shopping centers operate 7 days a week, usually Monday to Saturday from 10am to 9pm, Sunday from noon to 6pm. **Museum** hours vary widely, with many closed Monday.

Currency Exchange   See "Money" under "Preparing for Your Trip," above.

Customs   See "Entry Requirements" under "Preparing for Your Trip," above.

Drinking Laws   Every state has its own laws governing the sale of liquor. The only federal regulation restricts the consumption of liquor in public places to persons aged 21 or over. In Virginia many grocery and convenience stores sell beer and wine, but only state-controlled Alcoholic Beverage Control (ABC) stores are permitted to sell bottles of spirits and other kinds of liquor. Any licensed establishment (restaurant or bar) can sell drinks by the glass, but if you look younger than the legal age, be sure to have a photo ID handy to prove you're at least 21.

Electric Current   The United States uses 110 to 120 volts, 60 cycles, compared to the 220 to 240 volts, 50 cycles, used in most of Europe. In addition to a 100-volt converter, small appliances of non-American manufacture, such as hairdryers and shavers, will require a plug adapter with two flat, parallel pins.

Embassies/Consulates   All embassies are located in the national capital, Washington, D.C.; some consulates are located in major cities (none in Virginia), and most nations have a mission to the United Nations in New York City. Foreign visitors can obtain telephone numbers for their embassies and consulates by calling directory assistance in Washington, D.C. (☎ 202/555-1212).

Emergencies   Call 911 for **fire, police,** and **ambulance.** If you encounter such traveler's problems as sickness, accident, or lost or stolen baggage, call **Traveler's Aid,** an organization that specializes in helping all distressed travelers, whether American or foreign. Check the local telephone directory for the nearest office.

Holidays   The following are legal national holidays when banks, government offices, schools, many stores, and some museums and restaurants are closed: January 1 (New Year's Day), third Monday in January (Martin Luther King Jr. Day), third Monday in February (Presidents' Day), last Monday in May (Memorial Day), July 4 (Independence Day), first Monday in September (Labor Day), second Monday in October (Columbus Day), November 11 (Veterans Day/Armistice Day), last Thursday in November (Thanksgiving), and December 25 (Christmas). Also, the Tuesday following the first Monday in November is Election Day and is a legal holiday in presidential-election years (like 1996).

Mail   You can receive mail at the main post office of the city or region where you expect to be. It should be addressed "c/o General Delivery" and must be picked up in person with proof of identity (passport or driver's license). U.S. mailboxes are found at intersections; they're blue with a red-and-white stripe and carry the inscription U.S. MAIL. A first-class **stamp** costs 32¢.

Newspapers/Magazines   The *New York Times, USA Today,* and *Washington Post* newspapers and *Newsweek* and *Time* magazines cover world news and are widely available throughout Virginia. A few European magazines and newspapers are available in large cities.

Post   See "Mail," above.

Radio/Television   There are many local radio stations throughout Virginia, each broadcasting particular types of talk shows and/or music—classical, country, pop, jazz, and gospel—punctuated at least hourly by news, traffic, and weather updates. Television, dominated by four coast-to-coast networks (ABC, CBS, NBC, and Fox), plays an important role in American life. In recent years, the Public Broadcasting System (PBS) and a growing number of cable channels, notably CNN, have widened program choices.

Safety   See "Safety" under "Preparing for Your Trip," above.

Taxes   There is no VAT (value-added tax) or other indirect tax at a national level in the United States. Every state, and each city in it, has the right to levy its own local tax on all purchases, including hotel and restaurant checks and airline tickets. Virginia adds a 4.5% sales tax to most purchases, and a few local jurisdictions add another .5%, bringing the total sales tax to 5%. Hotel taxes vary from town to town; in most communities it's 5%, which adds a total tax of 9.5% or 10% to your hotel bill. Some local jurisdictions also add a restaurant tax, bringing the total tax on meal and drink bills to 8% to 10%.

Telephone/Fax/Telegraph   Pay phones are located on street corners; in bars, restaurants, public buildings, stores, and service stations; and at highway rest areas. Local calls cost 25¢.

For local **directory assistance** ("information"), dial 411; for long-distance information, dial 1, then the appropriate area code and 555-1212.

For **long-distance or international calls,** stock up with a supply of quarters (the quantity of quarters required for international calls, however, makes this an inconvenient way of paying); the pay phone will instruct you when you should put them in the slot. For long-distance calls in the United States and Canada, dial 1 followed by the area code and the number you want. For direct-dial overseas calls, first dial 011, followed by the country code (Australia, 61; Republic of Ireland, 353; New Zealand, 64; United Kingdom, 44; and so on), the city code (for example, 71 or 81 for London), and the number of the person you wish to call. In Virginia, the country codes and some overseas area codes are given in the front of the White Pages telephone directories (see below).

For reversed-charge or collect calls and for person-to-person calls, dial 0 (zero, not the letter "O") followed by the area code and number you want; an operator will come on the line and assist you. If your operator-assisted call is international, ask for the overseas operator.

There are two kinds of **telephone directories.** The general directory, called the White Pages, lists private and business subscribers in alphabetical order. The inside front cover lists the emergency numbers for police, fire, and ambulance, plus other vital numbers (like the Coast Guard, poison control center, crime-victims hotline, and so on). The first few pages are devoted to community-service numbers, including a guide to long-distance and international calling, complete with country codes and area codes. Government numbers are printed on blue paper.

The second directory, printed on yellow paper (hence its name, Yellow Pages), lists all local services, businesses, and industries by type, with an index at the front or back. The listings cover not only such obvious items as automobile repairs by make of car or drugstores (pharmacies), often by geographical location, but also restaurants by type of cuisine and geographical location, bookstores by special subject and/or language, places of worship by religious denomination, and other information that the tourist might otherwise not readily find. The Yellow Pages also include city plans or detailed area maps, often showing postal ZIP codes and public-transportation routes.

Toll-free numbers are area code 800 throughout the United States. On the other hand, calls to area codes 900, 950, and 960 can involve heavy charges (they are used by dating services, sports-scores reporting services, astrologers, and the like); the companies who operate "900 numbers" are required by law to inform you of their charges as soon as they answer.

Hotel surcharges can double the cost of a call, so before calling from your room you might want to ask the hotel phone operator if there are any telephone surcharges. These are best avoided by using a public phone, calling collect, or using a telephone charge card.

Fax service can be provided by major hotels for a nominal charge or by business service centers found in most towns and cities. You can bring a **telegram** to the nearest Western Union office (there are hundreds across the country) or dictate it over the phone (☎ 800/325-6000). You can also telegraph money, or have it telegraphed to you, very quickly over the Western Union system.

Time   The United States is divided into six time zones. From east to west, these are Eastern Standard Time (EST, 5 hours behind Greenwich Mean Time), Central Standard Time (CST), Mountain Standard Time (MST), Pacific Standard Time (PST), Alaska Standard Time (AST), and Hawaii Standard Time (HST); Virginia is EST. Always keep in mind the changing time zones if you are traveling (or even telephoning) long distances in the United States. For example, noon in New York City (EST) is 11am in Chicago (CST), 10am in Detroit (MST), 9am in Los Angeles (PST), 8am in Anchorage (AST), and 7am in Honolulu (HST).

Daylight Saving Time is in effect in Virginia from 1am on the first Sunday in April until 2am on the last Sunday in October. Daylight Saving Time moves the clock one hour ahead of standard time.

Tipping   Wait staff and taxi drivers are tipped between 15% and 20% (in Virginia, doubling the sales taxes added to restaurant bills will equal the approximate tip). Bellhops should be tipped $1 per bag they carry to your room; airport porters should get at least 50¢ for a small bag, $1 for a larger one.

Toilets   You won't find public toilets (euphemistically referred to as "rest rooms") on the streets in most U.S. cities, but they can be found in hotel lobbies, bars, restaurants, museums, department stores, railway and bus stations, or service stations. Note, however, that restaurants and bars in resort or heavily visited areas may display a notice that TOILETS ARE FOR THE USE OF PATRONS ONLY. You can ignore this sign or, better yet, avoid arguments by paying for a cup of coffee or soft drink, which will qualify you as a patron. Some public places are equipped with pay toilets that require you to insert one or two dimes (10¢) or a quarter (25¢) into a slot on the door before it will open. In rest rooms with attendants, a tip of at least 25¢ is customary.

THE AMERICAN SYSTEM OF MEASUREMENTS

Length

1 inch (in.)			=	2.54cm	
1 foot (ft.)	=	12 in.	=	30.48cm	= .305m
1 yard (yd.)	=	3 ft.		=	.915m
1 mile	=	5,280 ft.			= 1.609km

To convert miles to kilometers, multiply the number of miles by 1.61 (for example, 50 mi. × 1.61 = 80.5km). Note that this conversion can be used to convert speeds from miles per hour (m.p.h.) to kilometers per hour (kmph).

To convert kilometers to miles, multiply the number of kilometers by .62 (example, 25 km × .62 = 15.5 mi.). Note that this same conversion can be used to convert speeds from kilometers per hour to miles per hour.

Capacity

1 fluid ounce (fl. oz.)			=	.03 liter		
1 pint (pt.)	=	16 fl. oz.	=	.47 liter		
1 quart (qt.)	=	2 pints	=	.94 liter		
1 gallon (gal.)	=	4 quarts	=	3.79 liters	=	.83 Imperial gal.

To convert U.S. gallons to liters, multiply the number of gallons by 3.79 (example, 12 gal. × 3.79 = 45.48 liters).

To convert liters to U.S. gallons, multiply the number of liters by .26 (example, 50 liters × .26 = 13 U.S. gal.).

To convert U.S. gallons to Imperial gallons, multiply the number of U.S. gallons by .83 (example, 12 U.S. gal. × .83 = 9.96 Imperial gal.).

To convert Imperial gallons to U.S. gallons, multiply the number of Imperial gallons by 1.2 (example, 8 Imperial gal. × 1.2 = 9.6 U.S. gal.).

Weight

1 ounce (oz.)			=	28.35g				
1 pound (lb.)	=	16 oz.	=	453.6g	=	.45 kg		
1 ton	=	2,000 lb.	=			907kg	=	.91 metric ton

To convert pounds to kilograms, multiply the number of pounds by .45 (example, 90 lb. × .45 = 40.5kg).

To convert kilograms to pounds, multiply the number of kilos by 2.2 (example, 75kg × 2.2 = 165 lb.).

Area

1 acre			=	.41 ha		
1 square mile	=	640 acres	=	2.59 ha	=	2.6 km

To convert acres to hectares, multiply the number of acres by .41 (example, 40 acres × .41 = 16.4ha).

To convert hectares to acres, multiply the number of hectares by 2.47 (example, 20ha × 2.47 = 49.4 acres).

To convert square miles to square kilometers, multiply the number of square miles by 2.6 (example, 80 sq. mi × 2.6 = 208km).

To convert square kilometers to square miles, multiply the number of square kilometers by .39 (example, 150km × .39 = 58.5 sq. mi.).

Temperature

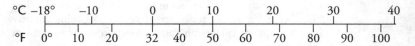

To convert degrees Fahrenheit to degrees Celsius, subtract 32 from °F, multiply by 5, then divide by 9 (example, 85°F–32 × $^5/_9$ = 29.4°C).

To convert degrees Celsius to degrees Fahrenheit, multiply °C by 9, divide by 5, and add 32 (example, 20°C × $^9/_5$ + 32 = 68°F).

5 Northern Virginia

America's past and present meet in northern Virginia. Linked by bridges and three subway lines to the nation's capital, Arlington is very much in Washington's international, cosmopolitan orbit. Yet in nearby Alexandria, the cobblestone streets of the 18th-century Old Town historic district still ring with the footsteps of George Washington, James Monroe, and Robert E. Lee. And south of Old Town on the Potomac, more visitors go through the doors of George Washington's beloved Mount Vernon than of any American home except the White House.

Arlington and Alexandria are part of a vast suburban area stretching west and south from the nation's capital. A boom of high-tech service industries and the arrival of major corporate headquarters have given this region its own economy; no longer are these busy suburbs mere bedrooms for Washington. Wrapping around Arlington and Alexandria, fast-growing Fairfax County now has the largest population of any single jurisdiction in Virginia. If it were incorporated, the Fairfax area known as Tysons Corner, at I-495 and Va. 7, would be one of Virginia's wealthiest cities.

To the west, the suburbs are encroaching on Loudoun and Fauquier Counties, heart of Virginia's renowned Hunt Country. Only when you drive 25 miles out to that lovely region of rolling hills, horse farms, fox hunts, steeplechases, charming country inns, and quaint villages do you get away from the suburbs of Washington, D.C.

1 Arlington

Across the Potomac River from Washington, D.C.; 100 miles N of Richmond

Easy access to Washington, D.C., and its tourist attractions is Arlington's lead card for travelers, although it is also home to northern Virginia's most popular historic site, Arlington National Cemetery, and the Pentagon.

Originally the land now comprising Arlington County was part of the territory ceded to form the nation's new capital district. Unneeded in the final planning, the land was returned to the state of Virginia in 1847. Since the original District of Columbia was a square, Arlington's land boundaries are almost perfectly straight.

The county was named to honor Arlington House, built by George Washington Parke Custis (see "Attractions," below). The beginnings of the national cemetery date from just after the first Battle of Bull Run, when some Union soldiers were buried here.

ESSENTIALS

VISITOR INFORMATION   Contact the **Arlington Visitor Center,** 735 S. 18th St., Arlington, VA 22202 (☎ 703/358-5720 or 800/677-6267), for maps and information about events, accommodations, and restaurants, as well as answers to any questions about the area.

GETTING THERE   By Plane   Washington's **National Airport** (☎ 703/685-8000) is conveniently located on the Potomac River between Arlington and Alexandria. Ground transportation via Washington Flyer Airport Shuttles (☎ 703/685-1400) operates daily from 6am to 10pm to locations in D.C. and northern Virginia. The same company also offers taxi and limousine service. The Washington Metrorail's Yellow and Blue lines serve the airport station.

Dulles International Airport (☎ 703/661-2700) is located about 25 miles west of Washington, D.C. For just $8, Washington Flyer shuttles from Dulles will bring you to the West Falls Church Metro stop, from which you have access to all Metrorail route locations.

By Train   Visitors arriving on Amtrak at Washington's **Union Station,** 50 Massachusetts Ave., NE (☎ 202/484-7540), can easily switch to the Metro stop there for a quick ride to Arlington.

By Bus   Greyhound/Trailways, 3860 S. Four Mile Run Drive, near South Walter Reed Drive (☎ 703/998-6312), has service directly to Arlington.

By Car   From the north, **I-95** and **I-395** are the major highways to Arlington from the north and south. From the north, follow I-95 south to Exit 19, for U.S. 50W. Follow 50W (John Hanson Highway), which will turn into New York Avenue. Follow signs for I-395S/Virginia and cross the 14th Street Bridge, leaving Washington, D.C. In addition, **I-66, U.S. 50,** and **U.S. 29/211** run east-west through Arlington. **U.S. 1** and the **George Washington Memorial Parkway** all pass north-south through the county.

COUNTY LAYOUT   Arlington is a county whose north and east boundaries are the south bank of the Potomac River, across from Washington, D.C. There are no cities in the county, nor is there a single downtown area; its place names—Crystal City and Pentagon City to the south, Clarendon and Ballston to the west, and Rosslyn across the Potomac from Georgetown—denote neighborhoods, not political entities.

The main thoroughfares radiate out from the Potomac River bridges. I-395 runs through the county from the 14th Street Bridge to Alexandria. I-66 begins at the Theodore Roosevelt Bridge and runs from Rosslyn due west. Jefferson Davis Highway (U.S. 1) extends south from the 14th Street Bridge (I-395) through Crystal City to Alexandria. Columbia Pike starts at the Pentagon and goes southwest into Fairfax County. Wilson Boulevard begins at the Key Bridge in Rosslyn and goes west through the neighborhoods of Clarendon and Ballston.

GETTING AROUND   Washington's **Metrorail** subway system offers efficient transport within Arlington and to Washington, D.C. The Orange Line runs from Rosslyn west past Clarendon and Ballston. The Blue Line runs southeast from Rosslyn to Arlington National Cemetery, the Pentagon, Pentagon City, Crystal City,

Arlington

ACCOMMODATIONS:
Americana Hotel **1**
Arlington/Cherry Blossom
    Travelodge **2**
Comfort Inn Ballston **3**
Crystal Gateway
    Marriott **4**
Howard Johnson National
    Airport Hotel **5**
Ritz-Carlton
    Pentagon City **6**
Sheraton National **7**

DINING:
Chez Froggy ◆
Hard Times Cafe ◆
Queen Bee Restaurant ◆
Red Hot & Blue ◆
Ristorante Portofino ◆
Tom Sarris'
    Orleans House ◆

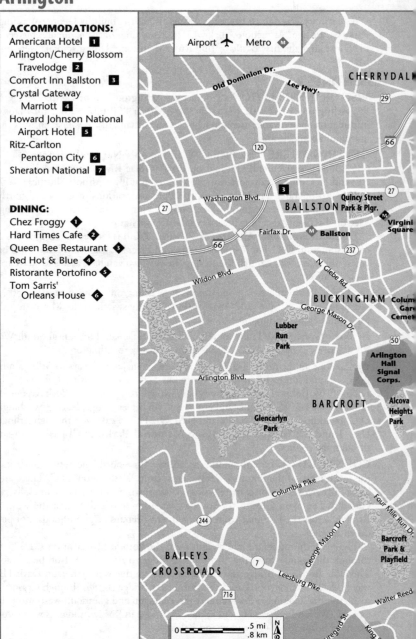

Airport ✈ Metro Ⓜ

CHERRYDALE

Old Dominion Dr.
Lee Hwy.
29
66
120
27
Washington Blvd.
BALLSTON Quincy Street
    Park & Plgr.
Virginia
Square
27
Fairfax Dr. Ⓜ Ballston
66
237
N. Glebe Rd.
Wildon Blvd.
BUCKINGHAM Colum
    Gare
    Cemet
George Mason Dr.
Lubber
Run
Park
50
Arlington
Hall
Signal
Corps.
Arlington Blvd.
BARCROFT Alcova
    Heights
    Park
Glencarlyn
Park
Columbia Pike
Four Mile Run Dr.
244
Barcroft
Park &
Playfield
BAILEYS
CROSSROADS
7
George Mason Dr.
Leesburg Pike
716
Walter Reed
N. Beauregard St.
King St.

0 ___ .5 mi
    .8 km N

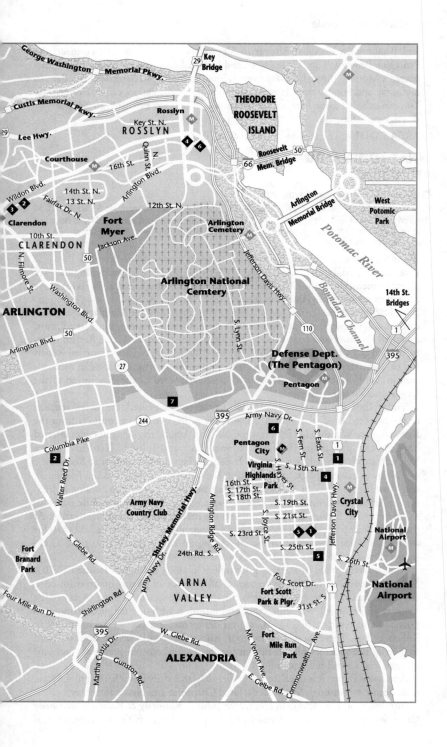

and Washington National Airport to Alexandria. The Yellow Line connects the Pentagon, Pentagon City, Crystal City, and National Airport to Alexandria. Metrorail operates Monday through Friday from 5:30am to midnight, Saturday from 8am to midnight, and Sunday from 10am to midnight. For information, call 202/637-7000. You can call that same number for **Metrobus,** which has extensive 24-hour service throughout Arlington.

AREA CODE   The telephone area code is 703.

WHAT TO SEE & DO
ATTRACTIONS

✪ Arlington National Cemetery

Va. 110 at Memorial Circle. ☎ **703/692-0931.** Free admission. Tourmobile $3 adults, $1.50 children 3–11. April–Sept daily 8am–7pm; Oct–March daily 8am–5pm. Parking $1 per hour first 3 hours, $2 per hour thereafter. Metro: Blue line to Arlington Cemetery. From I-395 or I-66 take Va. 110 to entrance signs.

For more than a century, this famous cemetery on a ridge overlooking the Potomac River and Washington, D.C., has been a cherished shrine commemorating the lives given by members of the U.S. armed forces, but its 612 wooded acres have always figured prominently in American history. In 1778, the "Arlington estate" was purchased by John Parke Custis, son of Martha Washington by her first marriage. Custis died during the siege of Yorktown, and his son, George Washington Parke Custis, inherited the estate and continued to develop it. He erected the Greek Revival structure called the **Custis-Lee mansion** after his daughter Mary Custis married Robert E. Lee, and today it is known as Arlington House. The Lees were residing in the mansion in April of 1861, when General Lee received word of the dissolution of the Union and Virginia's secession.

Today, the national cemetery's seemingly endless graves mark the mortal remains of the honored dead, the known and unknown, who served in conflicts from the Revolutionary War through the Persian Gulf War. Among the many notables interred here are two presidents, William Howard Taft and John F. Kennedy, as are Kennedy's wife, Jacqueline Kennedy Onassis, and his brother Robert F. Kennedy.

This quiet expanse of green overlooking Memorial Bridge, the Lincoln Memorial, and Washington, D.C., is a walker's paradise, but if you're not into hoofing it, head for the **Arlington Cemetery Visitors Center** and purchase a **Tourmobile** ticket for a cemetery tour. Service is continuous, and the narrated commentary interesting. At the Visitor Center you can also purchase Tourmobile combination tickets ($10 for adults, $4.50 for children) that include Arlington and major Washington, D.C., sights, allowing you to stop and then reboard when you're ready.

After it was acquired by the U.S. government in 1883, **Arlington House** (☎ 703/557-0613) was used for several decades as office space and living quarters for cemetery staff. In 1925, however, Congress empowered the secretary of war to restore the house to its pre–Civil War appearance and furnish it with original pieces (insofar as possible) and replicas. In 1955, Congress designated it a permanent memorial to Robert E. Lee. There's a self-guided tour, with volunteers in period dress on hand to give an introductory talk, hand out brochures, and answer questions. Servants' quarters and a small museum adjoin.

Admission is free. It is open from October to March daily from 9:30am to 4:30pm; until 6pm April through September (closed Christmas and New Year's Day).

Just downhill from Arlington House, the **John F. Kennedy & Robert F. Kennedy Gravesites** are marked by an eternal flame. Jacqueline Kennedy Onassis is buried next to her first husband. Nearby stands a simple white cross at the grave of Robert F. Kennedy. Looking north, you'll have a spectacular view of the capital city across the river (during his presidency Kennedy once remarked of this spot, "I could stay here forever"). A few steps below the gravesite is a wall inscribed with JFK quotations, including the one he's most remembered for: "And so my fellow Americans, ask not what your country can do for you, ask what you can do for your country. My fellow citizens of the world, ask not what America will do for you, but what together we can do for the freedom of man."

Watched over by America's most distinguished honor guard, the **Tomb of the Unknowns** is a tribute to all those members of the armed forces who have given their lives for their country in war. The 50-ton white-marble tomb rests above the remains of unidentified combatants slain during World War I. Unknowns from World War II, Korean War, and Vietnam are in the crypts on the plaza in front of it. Plan your visit to coincide with the changing of the guard ceremony—an impressive ritual of rifle maneuvers, heel clicking, and military salutes. It takes place daily every hour on the hour October through March, every half hour the rest of the year.

Adjoining the tomb is the Greek Revival outdoor **Memorial Amphitheater,** used for special holiday services, particularly on Memorial Day when the sitting president or vice-president attends. Free Tourmobile transportation from the Visitor Center parking lot is provided on these occasions.

On the northern periphery of Arlington National Cemetery, just off Va. 110, about 1^1/$_2$ miles north of the Kennedy graves, is the **U.S. Marine Corps War Memorial,** a symbol of the nation's esteem for the honored dead of the U.S. Marine Corps. The tribute is the Iwo Jima statue, recalling the marine invasion of Iwo Jima in February 1945 and the placing of a flag atop Mount Suribachi. News photographer Joe Rosenthal won a Pulitzer Prize for his photo of the flag-raising, and sculptor Felix W. de Weldon, then on duty, was moved to create a sculpture based on the scene Rosenthal had captured.

Born of Vengeance

On April 20, 1861, Robert E. Lee crossed the Potomac River to a meeting at Blair House, opposite the White House in Washington, D.C. There he was offered command of all Union forces that would fight the Civil War. A distinguished career soldier and patriot, Lee nevertheless turned down President Abraham Lincoln and went home to his Custis-Lee mansion across the Potomac River in Arlington. Two days later he left for Richmond, where he took command of his native Virginia's rebel army.

The Union soon turned the Custis-Lee estate into a bivouac area for troops headed to war. Outraged at Lee's inflicting an unexpected defeat on them at the first Battle of Manassas, Quartermaster General Montgomery Meigs ordered that Union dead be buried in the front yard of Lee's mansion. Thus was America's most hallowed national cemetery born of an act of vengeance.

Robert E. Lee never returned to Arlington. It was many years and lengthy litigation later that the U.S. Supreme Court returned ownership to his son. In 1883, George Washington Custis Lee sold the estate to the U.S. government for $150,000. Today you can visit Lee's old home, which has been restored and furnished to reflect its appearance as it was when the Lee family was in residence.

Arlington National Cemetery

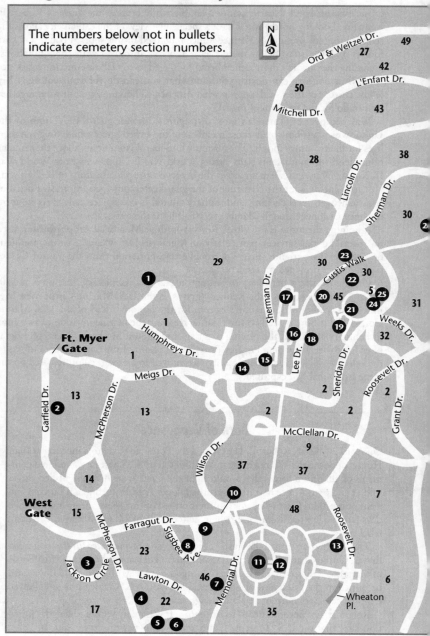

The numbers below not in bullets indicate cemetery section numbers.

N

Ord & Weitzel Dr.
49
27
42
L'Enfant Dr.
50
43
Mitchell Dr.
28
Lincoln Dr.
38
Sherman Dr.
30
2
29
30
23 Custis Walk
22 30
17 **20** 45
5 **25**
24
21
31
Sherman Dr.
19
Weeks Dr.
16 **18**
32
Roosevelt Dr.
2
Sheridan Dr.
1
Humphreys Dr.
1
Ft. Myer Gate
1
14 **15**
Lee Dr.
Meigs Dr.
2
Garfield Dr.
13
2
McClellan Dr.
Grant Dr.
2 13
2
2
9
McPherson Dr.
14
37
37
7
West Gate
15
10
48
Wilson Dr.
Farragut Dr.
9
Roosevelt Dr.
McPherson Dr.
23 **8**
13
3
Sigsbee Ave.
11 **12**
6
Jackson Circle
Lawton Dr.
46 **7**
Wheaton Pl.
17
4 22
Memorial Dr.
35
5 **6**

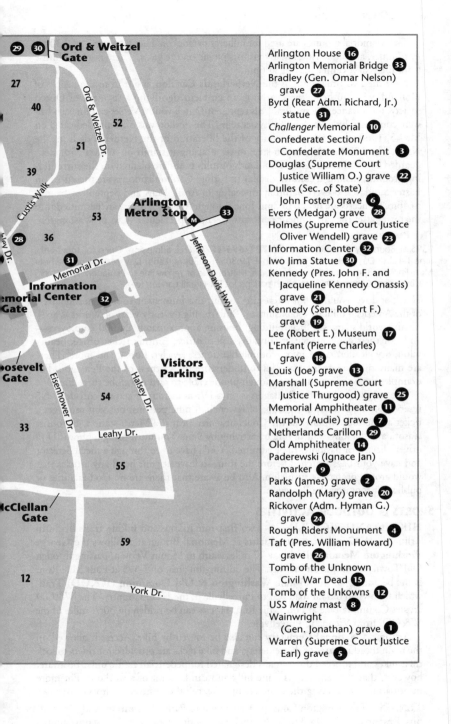

Ord & Weitzel Gate

Ord & Weitzel Dr.

27

40

52

51

39

Curtis Walk

53

Arlington Metro Stop 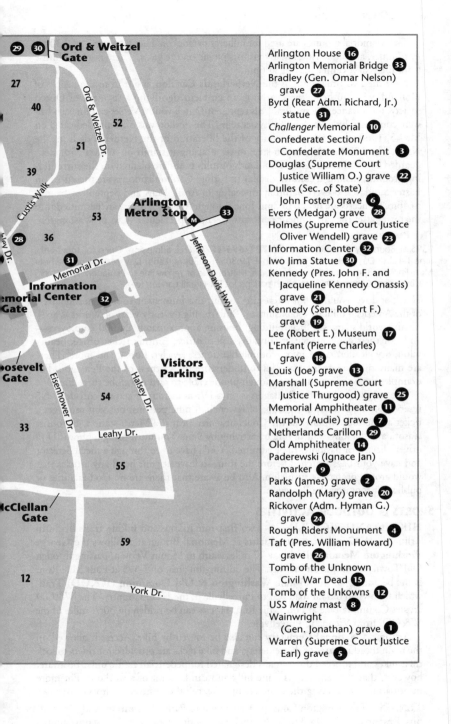 33

28

36

31

Memorial Dr.

Information Memorial Center Gate

32

Jefferson Davis Hwy.

Roosevelt Gate

Eisenhower Dr.

54

Halsey Dr.

Visitors Parking

33

Leahy Dr.

55

McClellan Gate

59

12

York Dr.

The Memorial grounds are used for military parades on Tuesday from 7 to 8:30pm in summer, and at all times many visitors picnic on the grass. There is a free shuttle from the visitor center starting at 6pm.

Near the Iwo Jima statue is the **Netherlands Carillon,** a gift from the people of Holland, with 50 bells, each carrying an emblem signifying a segment of Dutch society; for instance, the smallest bells represent Dutch youth. Verses cast on each bell were composed by poet Ben van Eysselsteijn. The carillon was officially dedicated on May 5, 1960, the 15th anniversary of the liberation of the Netherlands from the Nazis. The 127-foot-high open steel tower housing it stands on a plaza with steps guarded by two bronze lions. Thousands of tulip bulbs are planted on the surrounding grounds, making a colorful display in spring. Carillon concerts are presented on Easter Sunday and every Saturday thereafter in April, May, and September from 2 to 4pm. Concerts are held 6 to 8pm June through August. Visitors are permitted into the tower after the carillonneur performs, to enjoy spectacular views of Washington.

The Pentagon

I-395 at Boundary Channel Drive. ☎ **703/695-1776.** Free admission. Open for tours only, June 1–Labor Day on the half hour Mon–Fri 9:30am–3:30pm; Labor Day–May 31 on the hour Mon–Fri 9am–3pm. Closed federal holidays. Metro: Blue or Yellow line to Pentagon. From I-395 exit Boundary Channel Drive to north parking lot E-1 (small parking fee).

Hawk or dove, you'll find it interesting to tour this immense five-sided headquarters of the American military establishment. Built during the early years of World War II, it's the world's largest office building, housing approximately 24,000 employees— and, for their convenience, it contains a post office, Amtrak ticket office, beauty salon, dry cleaner, two banks, clothing boutiques, jeweler, florist, and more. There are many mind-boggling statistics to underscore the vastness of the Pentagon. For example, the building contains enough phone cable to gird the globe three times!

The only way to see the Pentagon is on a 1 1/2-hour tour of certain corridors. No reservation is necessary for groups of fewer than nine persons, but you must get a ticket at the tour window in the Concourse area near the Metro station. In tourist season, avoid a long wait in line by arriving by 9am. You must bring a photo ID (a driver's license or passport) to be admitted. You'll have to go through a metal detector and have your bags searched before the tour, so leave at your hotel any articles that would arouse protective suspicion. Also be aware that there are no food facilities or public rest rooms at the Pentagon.

SPORTS & OUTDOOR ACTIVITIES

HIKING AND BICYCLING   Two first-rate hiking and biking trails begin in Arlington. A 17-mile paved trail starts at Memorial Bridge and follows the **George Washington Memorial Parkway** 17 miles south to Mount Vernon, passing through Old Town Alexandria on the way. The Shirlington area, on I-395 at Four Mile Run, is the beginning of the 45-mile **Washington & Old Dominion (W&OD) Trail,** which follows an old railroad bed to Purcellville in the Hunt Country. The W&OD crosses Columbia Pike at Four Mile Run. Horses can be ridden on 30 1/2 miles of the W&OD, from Vienna to Purcellville.

Arlington National Cemetery can also be toured by bike. Access is allowed on the main thoroughfares of the cemetery, and bike racks are provided for riders to lock their bikes and proceed down roads designated for pedestrian traffic only. Be aware, however, that the cemetery is quite hilly and can be a bit of a workout. For more information about seeing the cemetery by bike, call the cemetery visitors center.

TENNIS   The Arlington County Department of Parks, Recreation, and Community Resources (☎ 703/358-3320) maintains more than 50 public tennis courts, most of them lighted for night play. Call Monday to Friday from 9am to 5pm for a location near your hotel.

SHOPPING

The suburban sprawl of northern Virginia is mall country. Arlington has two of its own; others are at Tysons Corner, the heavily developed area of Fairfax County due west of Arlington via I-66 and I-495; and in Prince William County, south of Arlington via I-395 and I-95.

Fashion Centre at Pentagon City

1100 S. Hayes St., south of the Pentagon across I-395. ☎ **703/415-2400**. Metro: Pentagon City.

Anchored by Macy's and Nordstrom, this plush four-level shopping complex with more than 150 shops, restaurants, and services is built around a soaring atrium. It adjoins a Ritz-Carlton hotel (see "Where to Stay," below). It features branches of Ann Taylor, Crate & Barrel, Banana Republic, Brentano's, Scribner's, the Disney Store, Record World, Crabtree & Evelyn, Godiva Chocolates, Hoffritz, Laura Ashley, Villeroy & Boch (exquisite china), Victoria's Secret, Lane Bryant, The Limited, the Body Shop, and The Gap. A food court has seating in the atrium. There is a six-screen movie theater, and parking is available in a six-level garage. Across South Hayes Street is another shopping center with a Border's Books, a Best Buy discount electronics and appliance store, a Marshall's discount clothier, a huge Price Club, and two restaurants. The Fashion Centre is open Monday to Saturday from 10am to 9:30pm and Sunday from 11am to 6pm.

☉ Potomac Mills

Dale City, VA, at Exit 143 off I-95. ☎ **703/643-1770** or 800/VA-MILLS.

One of the nation's largest malls, this huge collection of 240 factory outlet and discount shops includes the Swedish retailer Ikea and a large branch of Waccamaw Pottery. Virtually every factory outlet store is represented here, as well as clearance outlets for the likes of Nordstrom, JC Penney, and Levis. The mall is 30 minutes south of Arlington via I-395 and I-95. A shuttle bus runs from the Rosslyn and Crystal City Metro stations Wednesday to Sunday at noon. The return trip leaves the mall at 6pm. Round-trip fare is $10. Call 703/551-1050 for reservations. The mall is open Monday to Saturday from 10am to 9:30pm, Sunday from 11am to 6pm.

Tysons Corner Center

1961 Chain Bridge Rd. at Va. 7, McLean, VA. ☎ **703/893-9400**. Metro: West Falls Church; shuttles run from there every half hour.

Among the 230 shops here are four major department stores—Bloomingdale's, Nordstrom, Lord & Taylor, and Hecht's. Other notable emporia include Laura Ashley, the Nature Company, Williams-Sonoma (kitchenware), The Limited, the Disney Store, Banana Republic, Brooks Brothers, F.A.O. Schwarz, Waldenbooks, Britches of Georgetown, Ann Taylor, Crabtree & Evelyn, the Body Shop, Woolworth's, and The Gap. There are 30 eateries (running the gamut from Auntie Ann's Soft Pretzels to California Pizza Kitchen) and 8 movie theaters. Open Monday through Saturday from 10am to 9:30pm and Sunday from noon to 5pm.

The Galleria at Tysons II

2001 International Dr., McLean, VA. ☎ **703/827-7700** or 800/950-7467. Metro: West Falls Church; shuttles run from there every half hour.

This plush three-level mall offers 120 shops, galleries, restaurants, and services. Anchored by three fine department stores—Macy's, Saks–Fifth Avenue, and Neiman-Marcus—the Galleria also covers the whole shopping spectrum: shoes and clothing for the entire family, jewelry, electronics, home furnishings, gifts, and more. There are five full-service restaurants, as well as a lovely Garden Food Court. Open Monday through Saturday from 10am to 9pm and Sunday from noon to 6pm.

WHERE TO STAY

Generally a room is easy to come by here, even at the last minute, except perhaps during the height of the spring season or during an occasional vast convention. We have arranged the hotels in this section by neighborhood: Crystal City, near Washington National Airport; nearby Pentagon City; Columbia Pike, just off I-395 near the Pentagon; and Ballston, at I-66 and Glebe Road. Crystal City, Pentagon City, and Ballston all have Metro subway stations. Columbia Pike is a 5-minute ride on any number 16 Metrobus from the Pentagon station.

CRYSTAL CITY HOTELS

⑤ Americana Hotel

1400 Jefferson Davis Hwy., Arlington, VA 22202. ☎ **703/979-3772** or 800/548-6261. Fax 703/979-0547. 104 rms. A/C TV TEL. $60–$65 double. Seasonal rates available. AE, DC, DISC, MC, V. Free parking. Entry is on S. Eads St. at S. 15th St. Metro: Crystal City.

A holdover from the days when Crystal City had only roadside motels instead of the high-rises that now make a canyon of Jefferson Davis Highway, this modest well-located hotel is a block from the Metro and Crystal Underground's numerous restaurants and shops. Although the Americana has been around since the 1960s, you'll find it to be extraordinarily well maintained and equipped with all standard hotel features. Complimentary coffee, orange juice, and pastry are served in the lobby each morning. Free shuttle service to National Airport is available.

✪ Crystal Gateway Marriott

1700 Jefferson Davis Hwy. (U.S. 1), Arlington, VA 22202. ☎ **703/920-3230.** Fax 703/979-6332. 700 rms, including 46 suites. A/C TV TEL. $202 double; $239 on concierge level. Children under 18 stay free in parents' room. Weekend and other packages available. AE, CB, DC, DISC, MC, V. Parking $10 per night. Entry is on S. Eads St. at S. 18th St. Metro: Crystal City.

Just 5 minutes from National Airport, this first-rate Marriott is connected by a short passageway under U.S. 1 to a subterranean mall with a Metro stop and some 75 shops, restaurants, and such facilities as a post office, bank, and hair salon. A six-story atrium skylight lobby is adorned with Oriental art objects. Almost up to Ritz-Carlton quality (see below), rooms here have elegant dark-wood furniture, including armoires holding the satellite-fed TVs. The 15th and 16th floors are the concierge level, where a private lounge (closed some weekends) serves a complimentary breakfast and evening cocktails with hors d'oeuvres. A concierge is on duty, and additional in-room amenities include nightly turndown, bathroom scales, electric shoe polishers, and magazines.

Dining/Entertainment: Plushest of the hotel's three restaurants is the romantic Tuscany's, serving northern Italian cuisine under the stars (through the skylight). Not quite as posh is the Terrace, with cushioned wicker furnishings amid lush greenery overlooking the pool. Off the Atrium Lounge, light fare (lunch and dinner) is featured at Teams Sports Bar, equipped with billiard tables and numerous ballgame TVs.

Services: Room service (7am to midnight), nightly turndown on request, free newspaper delivery, concierge, complimentary airport shuttle.

Facilities: Indoor/outdoor pool, Jacuzzi, health spa, saunas, business center, lobby gift shop plus Underground concourse shops.

Howard Johnson National Airport Hotel

2650 Jefferson Davis Hwy., Arlington, VA 22202. ☎ **703/684-7200** or 800/654-2000. 279 rms. A/C TV TEL. $90–$135 double. Weekend rates available. AE, DC, DISC, MC, V. Parking $6 per night. Metro: Crystal City.

Attractively decorated rooms and a good location convenient to the Metro and National Airport make this HoJo a good choice. Its first four floors are used for parking, so the rooms are at least six stories up, and many provide D.C. or Potomac views. Although the midweek rate is moderate to expensive, weekend prices are highly competitive, going down to $69. The restaurant is open daily from 6am to 11pm. An outdoor pool is on site, and there's free airport shuttle service.

PENTAGON CITY HOTELS

✪ Ritz-Carlton Pentagon City

1250 S. Hayes St., Arlington, VA 22202. ☎ **703/415-5000** or 800/241-3333. Fax 703/415-5061. 345 rms, including 41 suites. A/C TV TEL. $210–$250 double, $290–$1,800 suite. Weekend and other packages available. AE, CB, DC, DISC, MC, V. Parking $15 per night. Metro: Pentagon City.

Across from the Pentagon, the Ritz-Carlton is in the upscale Fashion Centre retail-office complex. It's hard to believe that this traditional-looking hostelry—decorated with massive polished china cabinets, graceful wing chairs, plush sofas, Oriental rugs, crystal sconces, and a $2.5-million collection of 18th- and 19th-century paintings and antiques—was built as late as 1990. The impeccable service also harks back to another era. Rooms are spacious and airy, with beautiful mahogany pieces (some have four-poster beds) and every amenity: TVs concealed in armoires, plush terry bathrobes, marble bathrooms (each with extra phone), and in-room safes.

Guests on Club floors have a private lounge where complimentary breakfast, light lunch, afternoon tea, and hors d'oeuvres and cocktails are on tap. Club guests also have a private concierge staff.

Dining/Entertainment: The hotel's highly acclaimed Sunday brunch is served in the Grill, which evokes an English club. A popular luncheon buffet and afternoon tea are served daily in the Lobby Lounge.

Services: 24-hour room service, babysitting, nightly turndown, complimentary shoeshine and airport shuttle, multilingual concierge staff.

Facilities: Fitness and exercise center, indoor pool and Jacuzzi, steam room, sauna, business center, gift shop.

COLUMBIA PIKE HOTELS

Ⓢ Arlington/Cherry Blossom Travelodge

3030 Columbia Pike, Arlington, VA 22204. ☎ **703/521-5570** or 800/578-7878. Fax 703/271-0081. 76 rms. A/C TV TEL. $50–$66 double. Extra person $7. Children under 18 stay free in parents' room. AE, CB, DC, DISC, MC, V. Free parking. Metro: Pentagon, then any No. 16 bus. From I-395, go north on Glebe Road, turn right on Columbia Pike to motel on right.

Set back from the street so there's no traffic noise, this clean, well-run property was recently chosen inn of the year among the Forte chain of hotels. Recently renovated, it offers clean, fairly spacious guest rooms for the money. Rincome, a Thai restaurant open from 11am to 11pm, adjoins the motel. Nearby on Columbia Pike are a number of fast-food and ethnic restaurants, including the excellent Matuba Japanese Restaurant and the very popular Bob & Edith's Diner (the latter open 24 hours).

✪ Sheraton National

900 S. Orme St. (at junction of Columbia Pike & Arlington Boulevard), Arlington, VA 22204. ☎ **703/521-1900** or 800/325-3535. 417 rms, including 17 suites. A/C TV TEL. $102–$135 double. Weekend packages available. AE, CB, DC, DISC, MC, V. Parking $5 per night.

In a small residential neighborhood near the huge Navy Annex office building, this 16-story Sheraton manages to avoid the sterile personality projected by so many large hotels. The two-story lobby is an airy contemporary concourse with lots of plants, cheerful by day with the bright light of skylight windows and lit at night by a rectangular fixture that looks like a modernistic light sculpture. Guest rooms are spacious, and many have fabulous views of the Potomac and Washington, D.C. Concierge-level suites on the 14th floor each come with such luxuries as a separate living room, a wet bar, a refrigerator, two TVs, and a second bathroom, plus a private lounge offering complimentary continental breakfast, afternoon snacks, and an honor bar. All accommodations are handsomely appointed and of exceptional value.

Dining/Entertainment: Stars, an intimate 16th-floor gourmet room that enjoys spectacular nighttime views of the river and Washington, serves fine French cuisine at very reasonable prices Monday to Saturday evenings. A pianist performs nightly in the Stars Lounge, also with great views. Off the lobby, the gardenlike Café Brasserie serves breakfast, lunch, and dinner. Adjoining the cafe, the Quarterdeck Lounge invites relaxation with drinks, light fare, and eight sports TVs.

Services: Room service (7am to 11pm); same-day laundry/valet; complimentary shuttle to airport, Pentagon, and Pentagon City Mall.

Facilities: Rooftop indoor pool and outdoor sundeck with panoramic views; exercise room with sauna; newsstand.

BALLSTON HOTELS

Comfort Inn Ballston

1211 N. Glebe Rd. (at Washington Blvd.), Arlington, VA 22201. ☎ **703/247-3399** or 800/ 228-5150. Fax 703/524-8739. 126 rms. A/C TV TEL. $100–$110 double. Children under 18 stay free in parents' room. Weekend and other packages available. AE, CB, DC, DISC, MC, V. Free parking. Metro: Ballston. From I-66, take Glebe Road exit and turn left.

A pleasant property housed in a three-story redbrick building, this Comfort Inn offers a convenient location off I-66, just 10 minutes from National Airport and a 4-block walk to the Metro and Ballston Common mall. Rooms are exceptionally bright and spacious, with dark polished-wood furnishings and all the standard motel amenities. There are a lobby gift shop and an adjoining Italian restaurant.

DINING

Recent immigrants have given Arlington the most ethnically diverse population in Virginia, and restaurants representing more than 30 nationalities are scattered throughout the county. Two particular areas have a mix of excellent eateries packed into just two blocks, so you can stroll and see which are most appealing to your tastes. One is in Crystal City on South 23rd Street at South Eads Street (a block west of Jefferson Davis Highway). The other is on Wilson Boulevard at the Clarendon Metro station, an area whose plethora of Vietnamese restaurants has given it the nickname Little Saigon—but which also sports a chili parlor, a rib shack, and excellent Japanese and Chinese restaurants.

CRYSTAL CITY RESTAURANTS

Chez Froggy

509 S. 23rd St., at S. Eads St. ☎ **703/979-7676.** Reservations recommended. Main courses $12– $21. CB, DC, DISC, MC, V. Mon–Fri 11am–2pm; Mon–Sat 5:30–10pm. Metro: Crystal City. FRENCH.

The food at this cozy bistro is maintained with consistency by chef Jean-Claude Lelan. In good weather, there's outdoor dining at the sidewalk. Indoors, the decor is pleasant but unpretentious, with lots of ceramic and glass frogs, large and small, scattered around to add a note of whimsy. At dinner, appetizers of homemade duck mousse or half a dozen snails in garlic butter deserve consideration, as does the salad of fresh spinach and chèvre with almonds. You can always get fresh frogs' legs sautéed in butter and garlic. Daily specials include such fresh items as soft-shell crabs with either garlic or almonds. From the regular menu comes veal scallopine in creamy mushroom-and-Calvados sauce, steamed salmon with fresh basil beurre blanc, and roast rack of lamb with garlic and thyme. Potatoes, assorted vegetables, French bread, and sweet butter accompany all entrees. Dessert offerings include *la coupe Froggy* (vanilla ice cream, fresh strawberries, whipped cream, and Curaçao). The lower-priced lunch menu adds salads and omelets.

Ristorante Portofino

526 S. 23rd St., at S. Eads St. ☎ **703/929-8200.** Reservations recommended. Main courses $13.95–$18.95. AE, CB, DC, MC, V. Mon–Fri 11am–2pm; daily 5–10pm. Metro: Crystal City. ITALIAN.

A pretty downstairs garden room is just one of the dining spaces in this bustling Italian restaurant, a family-owned institution here since 1970. The entrance is at the rear of the converted three-story residence, and you'll know when you hear the taped arias of such famous tenors as Enrico Caruso and Luciano Pavarotti that you're in for a home-style Italian meal. The dinner offerings begin with some tasty specialties, including fried calamari, ricotta-filled baked eggplant, and prosciutto with fresh mozzarella. Any of the pastas on the menu can be ordered in a half portion as an appetizer—linguine with green-pesto sauce, fettuccine Alfredo, and spaghetti carbonara are a few of the possibilities. Entrees include veal in all expected guises (parmigiana, piccata, marsala), plus a good variety of chicken and fish dishes. The house special dessert is a wonderful rum cake with whipped cream.

CLARENDON RESTAURANTS

⑤ Hard Times Cafe

3028 Wilson Blvd., at N. Highland St. ☎ **703/528-2233.** Reservations not accepted. Main courses $4–$6.50. AE, MC, V. Mon–Thurs 11:30am–10pm, Fri–Sat 11:30am–11pm, Sun noon–10pm. Metro: Clarendon. TEX-MEX.

A casual, laid-back hangout, the Hard Times Cafe is the kind of chili parlor you'd find in Texas. The bar is always crowded, there's country music on the jukebox, and the "bowls of red" are first rate. The Lone Star State decor features Texas flags, plus a longhorn steer hide and historic photos of the Old West on the walls. Seating is in roomy oak booths. The restaurant cooks up three styles of chili: Texas (ground chuck simmered with secret spices and *no* tomatoes), Cincinnati (with hot and sweet spices, including cinnamon), and vegetarian. All styles are served with homemade cornbread and beans—and cheese, onions, or spaghetti at your request. Sandwiches, burgers, salads, and sides of onion rings and steak fries round out the offerings.

✪ Queen Bee Restaurant

3181 Wilson Blvd., near Washington Blvd. ☎ **703/527-3444.** Reservations not accepted. Main courses $5.50–$8. MC, V. Daily 11am–10pm. Metro: Clarendon. VIETNAMESE.

Locals flock to this friendly and unpretentious eatery that's directly across the street from the Clarendon Metro station. Etched-glass sconces provide soft lighting, and mirrors line one of the walls, adding an illusion of depth to the room. At lunch or dinner, start with the Queen Bee platter, a sampler of appetizers including a spring roll, shrimp tempura, charcoal-grilled pork, and house salad. Among the entrees, specials include steamed rice-flour meat rolls and shrimp cakes. Chicken is prepared in several delicious ways—curried, in ginger sauce, or with lemon grass. Roast duck and quail are also stellar entrees. Vegetarians can choose a mélange of vegetables sautéed in oyster sauce or fresh tofu sautéed with tomato and scallions. Meal-size Vietnamese-style *pho* (noodle soups) are a house specialty.

ROSSLYN RESTAURANTS

✪ Red Hot & Blue

1600 Wilson Blvd., at N. Pierce St. ☎ **703/276-7427.** Reservations not accepted. Main courses $7–$14.50. AE, MC, V. Sun–Thurs 11am–10pm, Fri–Sat 11am–midnight. Metro: Rosslyn. AMERICAN.

Washingtonian magazine calls it "Red Hot & Wonderful," and *Washington Post* food critic Phyllis Richman opines "barbecue worth waiting for." So join the line of hungry diners waiting for tables at this casual, fun-filled, high-energy eatery, or join the crowd at the bar for frosted steins of beer. The late Lee Atwater, chairman of the Republican National Committee, along with a group of Washingtonians transplanted from their native Memphis, opened the restaurant and named it for a hometown radio show. The decor is a jumpy black, white, and red, and seating is in banquettes and at small tables jammed rather close together. But the food is just fine—ribs wet (with sauce) or dry (secret spices), barbecued beef brisket, smoked chicken and ham, and homemade trimmings like beans, coleslaw, potato salad, and fries. For dessert, the warm fudge pie topped with vanilla ice cream packs a sweet wallop. Naturally, the blues come from the speakers, and occasionally nationally known blues artists perform here.

Red Hot & Blue has a **carryout branch** (with tables and counter seating but no table service) at 3014 Wilson Blvd. (☎ 703/243-1510), just east of the Clarendon Metro station. It's open Sunday to Thursday from 11am to 10pm, Friday and Saturday from 11am to 11pm. The menu and prices are the same at both branches.

⊖ Tom Sarris' Orleans House

1213 Wilson Blvd., at N. Lynn St. ☎ **703/524-2929.** Reservations not accepted. Main courses $8–$19. AE, DC, DISC, MC, V. Mon–Fri 11am–11pm, Sat 4–11pm, Sun 4–10pm. Metro: Rosslyn. AMERICAN.

Tom Sarris' has been a local favorite for more than 30 years—and no wonder. A delicious roast prime rib of beef dinner can be had for $8! The menu also features steak, baked chicken, and seafood, but the prime rib, which comes in three cuts—the aforementioned dinner portion (regular, ample for most appetites), Louis XIV ($10), and mammoth ($14)—is what draws the crowds. The meat is tender and well seasoned, served in its own juices. With it you get an oven-roasted potato and offerings from an exceptional salad bar that's decorated like a riverboat. The restaurant is housed in an imposing white pseudo-antebellum building, trimmed in wrought iron. The interior resembles a New Orleans garden, with iron chairs and railings, leaded-glass fixtures, and ceiling fans.

NEARBY DINING

Evans Farm Inn

1696 Chain Bridge Rd., at Dolley Madison Blvd. (Va. 123), McLean, VA. ☎ **703/356-8000.** Reservations recommended. Main courses $15–$25; lunch buffet $12 ($8 for children under 6). AE, CB, DC, DISC, MC, V. Mon–Sat noon–2:30pm and 5–9pm, Sun noon–9pm (Sunday brunch 11am–2pm in the pub). Easiest entry to find is on Dolley Madison Blvd. (Va. 123) about 2 miles east of I-495. AMERICAN.

A 40-acre working farm, complete with horses, goats, pigs, a donkey, and all sorts of fowl, is the setting for the charming Evans Farm Inn, an 18th-century-style building erected in the 1950s with timbers, old bricks, and early glass salvaged from nearby colonial sites. The restaurant has large dining rooms decorated with old farm implements, corner cupboards, carousel horses, and spinning wheels. Downstairs, the Sitting Duck Pub evokes an old Tudor inn with a dart board, Hogarth drawings, copper pitchers, and, in winter, a roaring fireplace. Also on the property are a cookhouse that displays colonial cooking items, a mill and mill pond, a country store and doll shop, and a large duck pond. There's a whole afternoon's entertainment here.

The lunch buffet includes a trip to the bounteous salad bar, an entree, vegetables, and home-baked bread. Dinner entrees, such as roast prime rib, half a chicken, sirloin steak, or barbecued baby back ribs, come with vegetables, spoon bread, and salad bar. The Evans Farm garden provides all the floral decorations and much of the produce used at the inn. On Friday and Saturday nights, there's piano playing and singing in the pub, which also serves Sunday brunch from 11am to 2pm.

ARLINGTON AFTER DARK

On the entertainment scene, Arlington is very much in the orbit of the John F. Kennedy Center for the Performing Arts, the National Theater, and other such first-rate venues across the Potomac in Washington, D.C. The best source of nighttime entertainment information for both Washington and its suburbs is the Friday "Weekend" section of the *Washington Post,* available at newsstands all over northern Virginia. You can also get hints from *Where Washington,* a tourist-oriented magazine available free in many hotel lobbies.

✪ Wolf Trap Farm Park

1624 Trap Rd., Vienna, VA ☎ **703/255-1868.** Seats, $20–$45; lawn tickets, $12–$18. (You'd best arrive early; the lawn opens 90 minutes prior to the performance. Bring a picnic dinner—everyone does.) Metro: West Falls Church. Then take the Wolf Trap Express Shuttle ($3.50); buses run every 30 minutes beginning 2 hours before showtime. Take I-66 west and follow the signs for I-495 north to Dulles Toll Road; stay on local exits (you'll see a sign) until you come to Wolf Trap. Toll is 50¢.

You can buy tickets in advance for the star-studded summer season, from late May to the beginning of September, at the nation's only national park dedicated to the performing arts. In recent years the Boston Pops, the Bolshoi Opera, the Moiseyev Dance Company, B. B. King, Judy Collins, Ray Charles, Willie Nelson, and Bill Cosby have performed here. Talk about eclectic! Performances are held in the 6,900-seat Filene Center II, but many patrons lounge about under the stars on the lawn (the sound system is great, but bring binoculars!). A smaller venue, the Barns of Wolftrap, has various performances indoors during the spring and fall.

2 Alexandria

5 miles S of Washington, D.C.; 95 miles N of Richmond

Founded by a group of Scottish tobacco merchants, the seaport town of Alexandria came into being on a sunny day in July 1749, when a 60-acre tract of land was auctioned off in half-acre lots. Although Alexandria addresses today include a large chunk of nondescript suburbia, George Washington and Robert E. Lee would still recognize the streets of their hometown, now known as **Old Town.** As you stroll the brick sidewalks and cobblestone streets of this highly gentrified historic district, you'll see more than 2,000 18th- and 19th-century buildings. You can visit Gadsby's Tavern, where two centuries ago the men who created this nation discussed politics, freedom, and revolution over tankards of ale. You can stand in the tavern's doorway where Washington reviewed his troops for the last time, visit Lee's boyhood home, and sit in the pews of Christ Church where both men worshipped.

In this "mother lode of Americana," the past is being ever-increasingly restored in an ongoing archaeological and historical research program. And though the present is manifested by an abundance of quaint shops, boutiques, art galleries, and restaurants capitalizing on the volume of tourism (not to mention hordes of young suburbanites just hanging out on Friday and Saturday nights), it's still easy to imagine yourself in colonial times and picture the bustling waterfront where fishermen brought in the daily catch and foreign vessels unloaded exotic cargo.

ESSENTIALS

INFORMATION   The **Alexandria Convention & Visitors Bureau** at Ramsay House, 221 King St., at Fairfax Street (☎ 703/838-4200; 703/838-5005 for 24-hour Alexandria events recording), is open daily from 9am to 5pm (closed Thanksgiving, Christmas, and New Year's Day). Here you can pick up maps and brochures, find out about special events taking place during your visit, and get information about accommodations, restaurants, sights, shopping, and whatever else. If you came by car, get a free **1-day parking permit** here for gratis parking at any 2-hour meter for up to 24 hours.

GETTING THERE   By Plane   Washington's **National Airport** (☎ 703/685-8000) is just 2 miles north of Alexandria. Washington's Metrorail (see below) provides easy transport to Alexandria via its Blue and Yellow lines. Also, Washington Flyer Shuttles (☎ 703/685-1400) has van, taxi, and limo service from the airport.

By Train   The Amtrak passenger **rail station** is at 110 Callahan Dr., near King Street (☎ 703/836-4339).

By Washington Metrorail   From Arlington or Washington, take the Blue or Yellow Lines to the King Street station (it's across the tracks from Amtrak's Alexandria station). From the Metro station, board number AT-2 or AT-5 DASH bus (75¢) to King and Fairfax—right to the door of the Visitors Center. Take a transfer, and you can board any DASH bus for 4 hours. It's a short ride from the station; in fact, you could walk it, but better to save your feet for sightseeing.

By Car   Going south from Washington across the 14th Street Bridge (I-395), take the scenic George Washington Memorial Parkway, which becomes Washington Street, Alexandria's main thoroughfare. A left turn on King Street will take you into the heart of Old Town. I-95 crosses the Potomac River at Alexandria; take Exit 1 (U.S. 1) and go north into Old Town.

CITY LAYOUT   Old Town Alexandria is laid out in a simple grid system. Union to Lee Street is the 100 block, Lee to Fairfax the 200 block, and so on up. The cross streets (more or less going north and south) are divided north and south by King Street. King to Cameron is the 100 block north, Cameron to Queen the 200 block north, and so on. King to Prince is the 100 block south, and so on.

As a glance at your walking-tour map later in this chapter will indicate, Old Town is contained within several blocks. Park your car for the day, don comfortable shoes, and start walking—it's the easiest way.

AREA CODE   The area code for Alexandria is 703.

WHAT TO SEE & DO
ATTRACTIONS

Whenever you come, you're sure to run into some activity or other—a jazz festival, a tea garden or tavern gambol, a quilt exhibit, a wine tasting, or an organ recital. It's all part of Alexandria's *cead mile failte* (100,000 welcomes) to visitors.

The Visitors Bureau at Ramsay House (see above) sells a money-saving **block ticket** for discounted admission to five historic Alexandria properties: Gadsby's Tavern, Lee's Boyhood Home, the Carlyle House, Stabler-Leadbeater Apothecary Shop, and the Lee-Fendall House. The ticket, which can also be purchased at any of the five buildings, costs $12 for adults, $5 for children 6 to 17; under 6 are free. We recommend you visit all these buildings, but you can also buy a block ticket to three sights for $7 adults, $3 children, or to two sights for $6 adults, $2 children.

In planning your schedule, you should be aware that many Alexandria attractions are closed on Monday.

Though it's easy to see Alexandria on your own, you may find your experience enhanced by a comprehensive walking tour. **Doorways to Old Virginia** (☎ 703/548-0100) offers tours Monday to Saturday at 11am and Sunday at 2pm ($3 per person). They leave from the Visitors Bureau at Ramsay House. The company also offers ghost tours weekend evenings from May through October, departing Ramsay House at 9pm. Cost is $4 for adults, $3 for students.

The **Potomac plantations** (described later in this chapter) are just 14 miles south of Alexandria and are most logically visited on day trips from Old Town.

Gadsby's Tavern Museum
134 N. Royal St. ☎ **703/838-4242.** Admission $3 adults, $1 children 6–17. Tues–Sat 10am–5pm, Sun 1–5pm.

Alexandria was at the crossroads of colonial America, and the center of life in Alexandria was Gadsby's Tavern. Consisting of two buildings—a tavern dating to about 1770 and the circa-1792 City Tavern and Hotel—it's named today for a memorable owner, Englishman John Gadsby, whose establishment was a "gentleman's tavern" renowned for elegance and comfort. The rooms have been restored to their 18th-century appearance. The second-floor ballroom with its musicians' gallery was the scene of Alexandria's most lavish parties, and since 1797 George Washington's birthday ball and banquet has been an annual tradition here.

Thirty-minute **tours** depart 15 minutes before and after the hour, with a final tour at 4:15pm. A special tour called Gadsby's Time Travels is offered periodically. To cap off the experience, you can dine at Gadsby's Colonial-style restaurant (see "Dining," below).

Boyhood Home of Robert E. Lee
607 Oronoco St. ☎ **703/548-8454.** Admission $3 adults, $1 children 10–17, free for children under 10. Tours Mon–Sat 10am–3:30pm, Sun 1–3:30pm.

Revolutionary cavalry hero Gen. "Light-Horse Harry" Lee brought his wife, Ann Hill Carter, and five children to this early Federal-style mansion in 1812 when the future commander of the Confederate army was just five years old. A tour of the house, built in 1795, provides a glimpse into the gracious life-style of Alexandria's gentry. George Washington was an occasional guest of earlier occupants, Col. and Mrs. William Fitzhugh. In 1804, the Fitzhughs' daughter, Mary Lee, married Martha Washington's grandson, George Washington Parke Custis, in the drawing room. And the Custises' daughter married Robert E. Lee. General Lafayette, a comrade-in-arms with Light-Horse Harry Lee during the American Revolution, honored Ann Hill Carter Lee with a visit to the house in October 1824. The drawing room today is called the Lafayette Room to commemorate that visit. The furnishings here today are of the Lee period but did not belong to the family.

Lee-Fendall House

614 Oronoco St., at Washington St. ☎ **703/548-1789.** Admission $3 adults, $1 children 10–17, free for children under 10. Tues–Sat 10am–3:45pm, Sun noon–3:45pm.

This handsome Greek Revival–style house is a veritable Lee family museum of furniture, heirlooms, and documents. Light-Horse Harry Lee never actually lived here, though he was a frequent visitor, as was his good friend George Washington. He did own the original lot but sold it to Philip Richard Fendall (himself a Lee on his mother's side), who built the house in 1785. From 1785 to 1903, the house was home to 37 Lees of Virginia. John L. Lewis, the American labor leader, was the last private owner.

Thirty-minute guided **tours** interpret the 1850s era of the home and provide insight into Victorian family life. You'll also see the colonial garden with its magnolia and chestnut trees, roses, and boxwood-lined paths.

Carlyle House

121 N. Fairfax St. ☎ **703/549-2997.** Admission $3 adults, $1 children 10–17, free for children under 10. Tues–Sat 10am–4:30pm, Sun noon–4:30pm.

Not only is Carlyle House regarded as one of Virginia's most architecturally impressive 18th-century homes, but also it figured prominently in American history. Patterned after Scottish/English manor houses, it was completed in 1753 by Scottish merchant John Carlyle for his bride, Sara Fairfax of Belvoir, who hailed from one of Virginia's most prominent families. It was a waterfront property with its own wharf. A social and political center, the house was visited by numerous great men of the time, George Washington among them. But its most important moment in history occurred in April 1755, when Maj. Gen. Edward Braddock, commander-in-chief of His Majesty's forces in North America, met here with five colonial governors and asked them to tax colonists to finance a campaign against the French and Indians. Colonial legislatures refused to comply, one of the first instances of serious friction between America and Britain. Nevertheless, Braddock made Carlyle House his headquarters during the campaign.

The house is furnished in period pieces, and the original large parlor and adjacent study have survived intact. An upstairs room houses an exhibit called "A Workman's View," which explains 18th-century construction methods with hand-hewn beams and hand-wrought nails. **Tours,** taking about 40 minutes, leave every half hour between 10am and 4:30pm.

✪ Christ Church

118 N. Washington St., at Cameron Street. ☎ **703/549-1450.** Free admission. Mon–Fri 9am–4pm, Sat 9am–noon, Sun 2–4:30pm. Closed all federal holidays.

This sturdy redbrick Georgian-style church, in continuous use since 1773, would be an important national landmark even if its two most distinguished members were not Washington and Lee. There have, of course, been many changes since Washington's day. The bell tower, church bell, galleries, and organ were added by the early 1800s, the "wineglass" pulpit during an 1891 restoration. But much of what was changed later has since been unchanged. The pristine white interior with wood moldings and gold trim is colonially correct, though modern heating has obviated the need for charcoal braziers and hot bricks. And, for the most part, the original structure remains, including the hand-blown glass in the windows. The town has grown up around the building that was first called the "Church in the Woods" because of its rural setting.

Christ Church has had its historic moments. Washington and other early members fomented revolution in the churchyard, and Robert E. Lee met here with Richmond representatives, who offered him command of Virginia's army at the beginning of the Civil War. You can sit in the pew where George and Martha sat with her two Custis grandchildren or in the Lee family pew. In 1991, the **Old Parish Hall** was completely restored to its original appearance; it now houses a gift shop and an exhibit on the history of the church. Do walk in the weathered graveyard, Alexandria's first and only burial ground until 1805. The remains of 34 Confederate soldiers are also interred here.

Stabler-Leadbeater Apothecary

105–107 S. Fairfax St. ☎ **703/836-3713.** Admission $2 adults, $1 students 11–17; free for children under 11. Mon–Sat 10am–4pm, Sun 1–5pm. Closed Thanksgiving and Christmas.

When it went out of business in 1933, this landmark drugstore was the second oldest in continuous operation in America. Beginning in 1792, it was run for five generations by the same family, and its early patrons included George Washington and Robert E. Lee, who purchased the paint for Arlington House here. Gothic Revival decorative elements and Victorian-style doors were added in the 1860s.

Today the apothecary shelves are lined with about 900 of the original hand-blown gold-leaf-labeled bottles (the most valuable collection of antique medicinal bottles in the United States, actually), old scales stamped with the royal crown, patent medicines, and equipment for blood letting. Among the shop's documentary records is an 1802 epistle from Mount Vernon: "Mrs. Washington desires Mr. Stabler to send by the bearer a quart bottle of his best Castor Oil and the bill for it."

There are docent **tours** Sundays from 1 to 5pm; other times, a 10-minute recording guides you around the displays.

George Washington Masonic National Memorial

101 Callahan Dr., at King St. ☎ **703/683-2007.** Free admission. Daily 9am–5pm. Guided tours available about every 45 minutes between 9:15am and 3:45pm.

Visible for miles around, this imposing neoclassical shrine is modeled on the design of the lighthouse at Alexandria, Egypt, and dedicated to the most illustrious member and first Worshipful Master of Alexandria Lodge No. 22. It sits atop Shooter's Hill overlooking the city. Emphasizing the panoramic view is an overlook with a wide-angle photograph pinpointing various Civil War battle sites in Alexandria, taken by Matthew Brady during the Civil War. President Coolidge and former president Taft spoke at the cornerstone-laying in 1923. The pink-granite memorial was dedicated in 1932, with President Hoover assisting in the rites.

Visitors enter into the ornate Memorial Hall, dominated by a colossal 17-foot-high bronze of Washington sculpted by Bryant Baker. On either side is a 46-foot-long mural by Allyn Cox: One depicts Washington laying the Capitol cornerstone, the other shows him and his officers in Christ Church, Philadelphia. A stained-glass window in the hall honors 16 patriots associated with Washington. A fourth-floor museum displays many valuable items, including the Washington family bible, the bedchamber clock stopped by Washington's physician at 10:20pm (the time of his death), and a key to the Paris Bastille presented to the lodge by the Marquis de Lafayette. On the ninth floor is an observatory parapet where the 360-degree view takes in the Potomac, Mount Vernon, the Capitol, and the Maryland shore.

Old Presbyterian Meeting House

321 S. Fairfax St. ☎ **703/549-6670.** Free admission. Mon–Fri 9am–4pm; services Sun at 8:30 and 11am.

Presbyterian congregations have worshipped in Virginia since Jamestown days when the Rev. Alexander Whittaker converted Pocahontas. This brick church was established by Scottish pioneers in 1774. Though it wasn't George Washington's church, the Old Meeting House bell tolled continuously for four days after his death in December 1799, and memorial services were preached from the pulpit here by Presbyterian, Episcopal, and Methodist ministers.

Many famous Alexandrians are buried in the church graveyard: John and Sara Carlyle; Dr. James Craik (the surgeon who treated Washington, dressed Lafayette's wounds at Brandywine, and ministered to the dying Braddock at Monongahela); and William Hunter Jr., founder of the St. Andrew's Society of Scottish descendants (bagpipers pay homage to his grave the first Saturday of each December). It is also the site of the Tomb of an Unknown Revolutionary Soldier. The original parsonage, or manse, is still intact. There's no guided tour, but there are recorded narratives in the church and graveyard.

The Athenaeum

201 Prince St., at Lee St. ☎ **703/548-0035.** Free admission (donations appreciated). Wed–Sat 11am–4pm, Sun 1–4pm. Gallery shows Sept–June.

A handsome Greek Revival building with a classic portico and unfluted Doric columns, the Athenaeum is home to the Northern Virginia Fine Arts Association. Art exhibits here run the gamut from Matisse lithographs to shows of East Coast artists. The building dates from 1851, and originally it contained the Bank of the Old Dominion. The bank's operations were interrupted by the Civil War, when Yankee troops turned the building into a commissary.

The Lyceum

201 S. Washington St. ☎ **703/838-4994.** Free admission. Mon–Sat 10am–5pm, Sun 1–5pm.

Another distinguished Greek Revival building, the Lyceum is a museum focusing on Alexandria's history from colonial times through the 20th century. It features changing exhibits and an ongoing series of lectures, concerts, and educational programs. An adjoining nonprofit shop carries 18th-century reproductions and crafts.

But even without its manifold offerings, the brick-and-stucco Lyceum itself merits a visit. Built in 1839, it was designed in the Doric temple style (with imposing white columns) to serve as a lecture, meeting, and concert hall. The first floor originally contained the Alexandria Library and various natural-science and historical exhibits. It was an important center of Alexandria's cultural life until the Civil War, when Union forces took it over for use as a hospital.

Friendship Firehouse

107 S. Alfred St. ☎ **703/838-3891** or 703/838-4994. Free admission. Thurs–Sat 10am–4pm, Sun 1–4pm.

Alexandria's first fire-fighting organization, the Friendship Fire Company, was established in 1774. As the city grew, the company attracted increasing recognition, not only for its fire-fighting efforts but also for its ceremonial and social presence at parades and other public occasions. In 1855, Friendship's building at 107 S. Alfred St. was destroyed by fire, and a new brick building (today the restored museum) in the fashionable Italianate style was erected on the same spot. A strong local tradition centers on George Washington's involvement with the firehouse as a founding member, active firefighter, and purchaser of its first fire engine, although extensive research does not bear out these stories. This interesting museum not only exhibits fire-fighting paraphernalia dating back to the 18th century but also documents the Friendship Company's efforts to claim Washington as one of their own.

Fort Ward Museum and Historic Site

4301 W. Braddock Rd. ☎ **703/838-4848.** Free admission. Park, daily 9am–sunset; museum, Tues–Sat 9am–5pm, Sun noon–5pm. From Old Town, follow King Street west, go right on Kenwood Street, then go left on West Braddock Road. Continue for three-quarters of a mile to the entrance on the right.

A short drive from Old Town is a 45-acre museum, park, and historic site that takes you a leap forward in Alexandria history to the Civil War. The action here centers, as it did in the early 1860s, on an actual Union fort that Lincoln ordered erected as part of a system called the Defenses of Washington. About 90% of the earthwork walls are preserved, and the Northwest Bastion has been restored, with 6 mounted guns (there were originally 36) facing south waiting for the Confederates who never came. Visitors can explore the fort and replicas of the Ceremonial Entrance Gate and an officer's hut. A museum on the premises houses Civil War memorabilia. **Tours** of the fort are given by guides in Union soldier costumes on selected Sundays.

There are picnic areas with barbecue grills in the park surrounding the fort, and concerts are presented on selected June through mid-September evenings in the outdoor amphitheater.

The Torpedo Factory

105 N. Union St. ☎ **703/838-4565.** Free admission. Shops and galleries daily 10am–5pm; archaeology exhibits Tues–Fri 10am–3pm, Sat 10am–5pm, Sun 1–5pm.

Studio space for some 160 artists and craftspeople, who create and sell their own works on the premises, is contained in this block-long three-story building. Here you can see artists at work—potters, painters, printmakers, photographers, sculptors, and jewelers, among others.

In addition, on permanent display are exhibits on Alexandria history provided by **Alexandria Archaeology** (☎ 703/838-4399), headquartered here and engaged in extensive city research.

And the building itself is of historic interest. It's a converted torpedo shell-case factory built by the U.S. Navy in 1918 and operated as such through the early 1950s. Later, the Smithsonian used it to store various and sundry, including dinosaur bones.

The Schooner *Alexandria*

Waterfront Park, foot of Prince St. ☎ **703/549-7078.** Free admission (donations appreciated). Spring–fall, Sat–Sun noon–5pm, when it's in port.

The Alexandria Seaport Foundation, an organization devoted to maritime heritage, acquired the Scandinavian schooner *Alexandria* (formerly the *Lindoø*) in 1983, and when it's in port (sometimes it's elsewhere participating in tall-ship festivals), it's docked at Waterfront Park. A red-sail Baltic trader vessel built in 1929, the ship was remodeled for passenger use in the 1970s.

Alexandria Black History Resource Center

638 N. Alfred St. ☎ **703/838-4356.** Free admission. Tues–Sat 10am–4pm.

In a 1940s building that originally housed the black community's first public library, the Black History Resource Center exhibits historical objects, photographs, documents, and memorabilia relating to African-Americans in Alexandria from the 18th century forward. In addition to the permanent collection, the museum presents rotating exhibits.

POTOMAC RIVER CRUISES

"Alexandria by Water" and "Washington by Water" sightseeing cruises of both the Alexandria and Washington, D.C., waterfronts aboard the **Admiral Tilp** and the **Matthew Hayes** depart from the city pier behind the Torpedo Factory Art Center, 105 N. Union St. (☎ 703/548-9000). Tour guides provide an entertaining commentary on the cities' history, legends, and sights. There are snack stands on the passenger boats, or you can bring your own lunch. The schedules change from year to year and season to season, so call for information and reservations. Price is $13 for adults, $10 for seniors, and $6 for children 2 to 12.

The **Dandy,** a 100-ton restaurant cruise ship berthed at the foot of Prince Street (☎ 703/683-6090), sails up the Potomac to Washington, D.C., affording passengers super views of the city and its monuments on 2¹/₂-hour luncheon and 3-hour dinner cruises. Reservations are imperative, since you'll choose your entree when you call. Lunches have three courses. Dinner is a multicourse affair. Cost for lunch is $26 from Monday to Friday, $28 on Saturday; dinner is $48 from Sunday to Thursday, $50 on Friday, and $56 on Saturday. Sunday champagne brunch cruises cost $30. Prices do not include bar drinks, coffee, or gratuities. There are soft music and a small dance floor to round out the dinner cruise. The *Dandy* also offers midnight cruises.

WALKING TOUR
Old Town Alexandria

Start: Ramsay House Visitors Center, King Street and Fairfax Street.
Finish: Torpedo Factory, Waterfront at Cameron Street.
Time: Allow approximately 2¹/₂ hours, not including museum and shopping stops.
Best Time: Anytime.
Worst Time: Monday, when many historic sites are closed.

You'll feel as though you've stepped back into the 18th century as you stroll Alexandria's brick-paved sidewalks, lined with Colonial residences, historic houses and churches, museums, shops, and restaurants. This walk ends at the waterfront, no longer a center of commercial shipping but now home to a vibrant arts center along the Potomac riverfront park.

Begin your walk at the:

1. **Ramsay House Visitors Center,** 221 King St., at Fairfax Street, in the heart of the Historic District. It's a historic structure itself, with a Dutch barn roof and an English garden. After perusing the wealth of information offered here about Alexandria, go north on Fairfax to:

2. **Carlyle House,** an elegant 1753 manor house set off from the street by a low wall. Continue north on Fairfax to the corner. Turn left on Cameron, past the back of the old city hall, to the redbrick buildings across Royal Street, known as:

3. **Gadsby's Tavern.** The original 18th-century tavern now houses a museum of 18th-century antiques, while the hotel portion is an Early American–style restaurant.

☕ **TAKE A BREAK**   If you're ready for lunch, the 18th-century atmosphere at Gadsby's Tavern is the perfect place for a sandwich or salad.

From here, continue west on Cameron Street to St. Asaph Street. Turn right onto it. At Queen Street, you can see:

Walking Tour—Old Town Alexandria

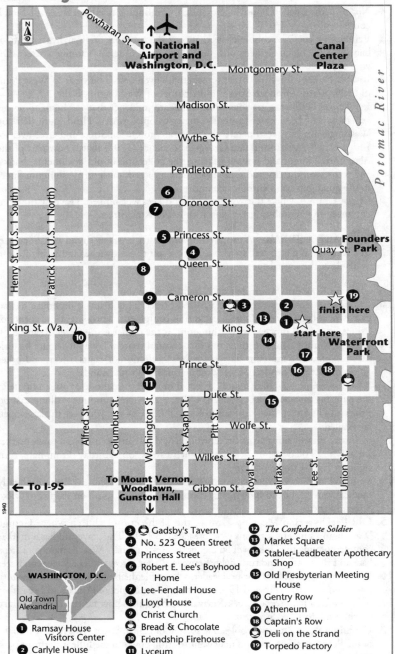

Powhatan St.

To National Airport and Washington, D.C.

Montgomery St.

Canal Center Plaza

Potomac River

Madison St.

Wythe St.

Pendleton St.

⑥
⑦ Oronoco St.

⑤ Princess St.

④ Queen St. **Founders Park**

Quay St.

Henry St. (U.S. 1 South)

Patrick St. (U.S. 1 North)

⑧

⑨ Cameron St.
🌀 ③ ② ⑲ **finish here**

⑬ ① ⭐ **start here**

King St. (Va. 7) 🌀 King St. ⑭ **Waterfront Park**

⑩

⑰

⑫ Prince St. ⑯ ⑱ 🌀

⑪

Duke St.

⑮

Alfred St.

Columbus St.

Washington St.

St. Asaph St.

Pitt St.

Wolfe St.

Wilkes St.

Royal St.

Fairfax St.

Lee St.

Union St.

← To I-95

To Mount Vernon, Woodlawn, Gunston Hall

Gibbon St.

1940

WASHINGTON, D.C.

Old Town Alexandria

① Ramsay House Visitors Center

② Carlyle House

③ 🌀 Gadsby's Tavern

④ No. 523 Queen Street

⑤ Princess Street

⑥ Robert E. Lee's Boyhood Home

⑦ Lee-Fendall House

⑧ Lloyd House

⑨ Christ Church

🌀 Bread & Chocolate

⑩ Friendship Firehouse

⑪ Lyceum

⑫ *The Confederate Soldier*

⑬ Market Square

⑭ Stabler-Leadbeater Apothecary Shop

⑮ Old Presbyterian Meeting House

⑯ Gentry Row

⑰ Atheneum

⑱ Captain's Row

🌀 Deli on the Strand

⑲ Torpedo Factory

4. **No. 523,** the smallest house in Alexandria. Continuing north on St. Asaph, you'll come to:

5. **Princess Street.** The cobblestones that pave the street are original; heavy traffic is banned. One block farther north on St. Asaph, turn left at Oronoco Street. On your right is:

6. **Robert E. Lee's Boyhood Home,** where he lived before he went to West Point in 1825. Across Oronoco Street, at the corner of Washington, is the:

7. **Lee-Fendall House,** a gracious white clapboard residence that was home to several generations of Lees. Enter through a pretty colonial garden. Head south (left) on Washington, a busy commercial thoroughfare, to Queen Street and cross over to:

8. **Lloyd House,** a beautiful late-Georgian residence (1797) that is now part of the Alexandria Library and houses a fascinating collection of old documents, books, and records on the city and state. From here, proceed south on Washington Street to the quiet graveyard entrance behind:

9. **Christ Church,** where the Washingtons and Lees worshiped. Leave by the front entrance, on Columbus Street, and turn left to King Street.

☕ **TAKE A BREAK**   A cappuccino-and-pastry break at **Bread & Chocolate,** 611 King St., is guaranteed to revive flagging spirits. Sandwiches and salads are also available at this casual spot.

From King Street, turn left on Alfred Street, to the:

10. **Friendship Firehouse,** on South Alfred Street. This historic firehouse has an extensive collection of antique fire-fighting equipment. Turn left at the corner of Prince Street and proceed to Washington. At the corner is the Greek Revival:

11. **Lyceum,** built in 1839 as the city's first cultural center. Today it's a city historical museum. The museum shop has a lovely selection of crafts, silver, and other gift items. At the intersection of Washington and Prince stands:

12. *The Confederate Soldier,* a sadly dejected bronze figure modeled after a figure in the painting *Appomattox* by John A. Elder. From here, continue walking east on Prince to Pitt Street, then turn left to King. Turn right and you'll see the large open area called:

13. **Market Square,** along King Street from Royal to Fairfax, used as a town market since 1749. Today the market is held once a week, on Saturday. From here, turn right on Fairfax to the quaint:

14. **Stabler-Leadbeater Apothecary Shop,** housing a remarkable collection of early medical ware and hand-blown glass containers. Proceed south on Fairfax to Duke Street, to the:

15. **Old Presbyterian Meeting House,** the 18th-century church where George Washington's funeral sermons were preached in 1799. The graveyard has a marker commemorating the Unknown Soldier of the Revolutionary War. Retrace your steps back to Prince Street and turn right. Between Fairfax Street and Lee Street you'll see:

16. **Gentry Row,** named for the local leaders who made their homes in these three-story town houses in the 18th and 19th centuries. At the corner of Prince and Lee is the:

17. **Atheneum,** a handsome Greek Revival structure that now houses contemporary art shows. Cross Lee Street to:

18. **Captain's Row,** a pretty cobblestone section of Prince Street. You're now in sight of the Potomac riverfront and may want to stroll down to the little waterfront park at the foot of Prince Street for a panoramic view of the river.

☕ **TAKE A BREAK**   The **Deli on the Strand,** on Union Street between Prince and Duke, has delicious salads and sandwiches you can eat at picnic tables on their porch or carry out to the park.

Continue north on Union Street to the:

19. Torpedo Factory, an arts-and-crafts center where studios and galleries are open to the public.

SHOPPING

Old Town has hundreds of charming boutiques, antiques stores, and gift shops selling everything from souvenir T-shirts to 18th-century reproductions. Plan to spend a fair amount of time browsing between visits to historic sites. A guide to antiques stores is available at the Visitor Center. Here are some suggestions to get you started.

ON KING STREET

The Winterthur Museum Store
207 King St. ☎ **703/684-6092.**

Appropriately located in a restored 1810 brick town house, this off-site venture of the renowned museum of decorative arts on the magnificent country estate of horticulturist Henry Francis du Pont, in Delaware's Brandywine Valley, is a delightful browse, including the back garden, which features all sorts of garden plants and ornaments. You'll come across fine reproductions from the Winterthur collections, including lamps, prints, ceramics, brassware, jewelry, garden furniture, and statuary.

The Pineapple, Inc.
132 King St., at S. Lee St. ☎ **703/836-3639.**

Pineapple's two floors of gorgeous things for the home bring out our most poignant material instincts. We would love to blow a few thousand dollars on the exquisite door handles and knobs, handmade antique quilts, period reproduction furnishings, candlesticks, hurricane lamps, picnic baskets, and the like.

ON CAMERON STREET

Granny's Place
303 Cameron St. ☎ **703/549-0119.**

This store specializes in imported (France, Italy) and domestic children's clothing (up to size 10 for boys and girls) and wooden toys. You'll also find teddy bears, beautiful dolls and stuffed animals, puppets, imported toys, stick horses, and swing sets. Many excellent gifts for toddlers, too.

La Cuisine
323 Cameron St. ☎ **703/836-4435.**

A delight for those who can pore endlessly over copperware, cookbooks, terrines, cooking implements, and hard-to-find ingredients.

Gossypia
325 Cameron St. ☎ **703/836-6969.**

Gossypia carries Mexican and Latin American fold art—masks, textiles, nativity scenes, and jewelry. Some clothing here as well.

ON SOUTH UNION STREET

The Christmas Attic
125 S. Union St., at Prince St. ☎ **703/548-2829.**

It's always the holiday season here, complete with toy train sets choo-chooing along a track overhead and 20 or more decorated trees. Christmas decorations, gifts, toys, and ornaments are sold year-round, festive items for other holidays in their proper months.

Carriage House
215 S. Union St., between Prince and Duke Sts.

Two shops share the premises here: **Rocky Road to Kansas** (☎ 703/683-0116) has more than 200 vintage patchwork quilts on display, patchwork dolls, antiques, gift items, and collectibles. **Olde Town Coffee, Tea & Spice** (☎ 703/683-0856) has about 50 kinds of coffee and 175 kinds of tea, as well as gourmet imports like German cornichons, Dundee preserves from Scotland, and imported cheeses and pâtés. Accessories such as teapots and cosies and coffee pots here, too.

ON NORTH LEE STREET BETWEEN CAMERON & QUEEN STREETS

Crilley Warehouse Mall
218 N. Lee St.

This mini-mall houses about eight shops on two levels in a turn-of-the-century bakery. In later years the building served as a storehouse, hence the name. Noteworthy is **Monday's Child** (☎ 703/548-3505), featuring lovely imported and domestic clothing for children. **Hunt's III** (☎ 703/548-1111) has three showrooms filled with antiques and collectibles—furniture, Herend hand-painted porcelain china and figurines, silver, jewelry boxes, crystal, and more.

Teacher's Pet/Trojan Antiques
210 N. Lee St. ☎ **703/549-9766.**

These two fine shops share space and a phone number in the Antique Mall—another of Alexandria's many rabbit-warren-of-shops complexes. Together they offer a highly browsable mix of beautiful collectible dolls and stuffed animals, hand-painted birdhouses, antique and reproduction furnishings, antique silver, old books and post cards, and much more. When you're here, peek into two antiques/collectibles shops—**Time Juggler** (☎ 703/836-3594) and **Old Town Antiques** (☎ 703/519-0009).

ON PRINCE STREET

Olde Towne Gemstones
6 Prince St., between S. Union and Strand Sts. ☎ **703/836-1377.**

Rock and fossil enthusiasts Pat, Mike, and Marvin Young offer fossils up to 500 million years old. There's also a wide-ranging collection of minerals, gemstones, petrified wood, and objets d'art and jewelry made from them. Banded-agate clocks are a big item.

ACCOMMODATIONS
VERY EXPENSIVE

✪ Morrison House
116 S. Alfred St., Alexandria, VA 22314. ☎ **703/838-8000** or 800/367-0800. Fax 703/684-6283. 45 rms, including 3 suites. A/C TV TEL. $150–$240 double; $295 suite. Weekend and holiday packages available. AE, CB, DC, MC, V. Parking $10 per night.

Old Town Alexandria Accommodations & Dining

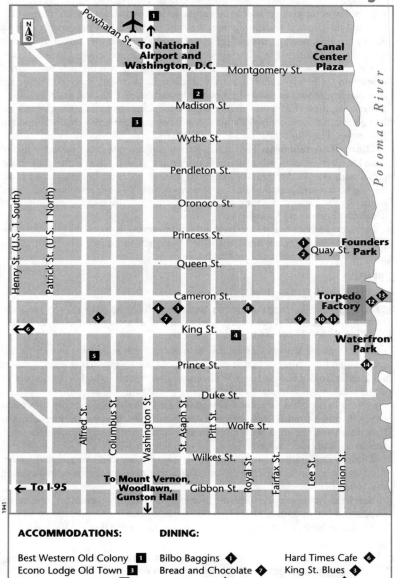

ACCOMMODATIONS:

Best Western Old Colony **1**
Econo Lodge Old Town **3**
Holiday Inn Old Town **4**
Morrison House **5**
Sheraton Suites **2**

DINING:

Bilbo Baggins ◆**1**
Bread and Chocolate ◆**7**
Chart House ◆**13**
Deli on the Strand ◆**14**
East Wind ◆**5**
Fish Market ◆**11**
Gadsby's Tavern ◆**8**

Hard Times Cafe ◆**6**
King St. Blues ◆**3**
La Bergerie ◆**2**
Landini Brothers ◆**10**
Le Refuge ◆**4**
Radio Free Italy ◆**12**
Two–Nineteen ◆**9**

Designed after the grand manor houses of the Federal period, Morrison House, in the heart of Old Town, is enchanting from the moment you ascend the curving staircase to its white-columned portico, where a butler greets guests at the door of the marble foyer. The residential-style lobby divides into a series of beautifully appointed, cozy rooms: a mahogany-paneled library, a formal parlor, and two intimate restaurants. Afternoon tea is served daily from the sideboard in the library. Guest rooms are charmingly furnished in fine Federal-period reproductions, including mahogany four-poster beds, brass chandeliers, and decorative fireplaces. In-room amenities include two phones, a remote-control TV housed in an armoire, fresh flowers, and imported terry robes. The plush Italian marble baths are equipped with hairdryers.

Dining/Entertainment: The Dining Room, with antique prints on the walls and fresh bouquets on every table, serves all three meals. The Elysium is the inn's show-piece, with fine Mediterranean-influenced cuisine; it has an English clubby look. Serving both restaurants, the Grill bar offers more than 20 different wines and cham-pagnes by the glass. A resident pianist performs on the baby grand in the lounge on Thursday, Friday, and Saturday.

Services: 24-hour butler, concierge, and room service; indoor valet parking; com-plimentary shoeshine; free newspaper delivery; nightly turndown.

Facilities: Privileges at nearby health club.

EXPENSIVE

✪ Holiday Inn Select Old Town

480 King St., Alexandria, VA 22314. ☎ **703/549-6080** or 800/368-5047. Fax 703/684-6508. 227 rms. A/C TV TEL. $140–$160 double. Weekend and other packages available. AE, CB, DC, DISC, MC, V. Parking $6 per night.

A block from the Visitors Center, this six-story redbrick building is one of the fin-est of all Holiday Inns; in fact, it even feels more like an inn than a hotel. Entered via a quiet brick courtyard and Williamsburg-look lobby, the hotel occupies an entire block. Complimentary morning coffee and Danish and afternoon English tea are served in the lamp-lit lobby. Guest rooms are Colonial in feel, many with green rugs, off-white patterned wallpaper, and dark furnishings. Rooms with king-size beds have small seating areas with couches and coffee tables; all rooms offer safes, hairdryers, and clock radios.

Dining/Entertainment: 101 Royal Restaurant features seafood and steaks. Annabelle's, an intimate lounge off the courtyard, is open for afternoon and evening drinks and light snacks.

Services: Room service (6:30am to midnight), nightly turndown, concierge, airport and Metro shuttle, same-day valet.

Facilities: Heated indoor pool, exercise room, sauna, gift shop, beauty salon.

Sheraton Suites

801 N. St. Asaph St., Alexandria, VA 22314. ☎ **703/836-4700** or 800/325-3535. 249 suites. A/C TV TEL. $180 double. Weekend and holiday packages available. AE, CB, DC, DISC, MC, V. Parking $7 per night.

This very hospitable all-suite hotel provides a luxurious residential atmosphere. Each spacious suite has a full living room, with a wet bar and fridge, an extra phone on the desk (equipped with call waiting), a comfortable convertible sofa, and a big con-sole TV (with remote). Bedrooms, set off from the living rooms by curtained French doors, are furnished in traditional dark mahogany pieces. Most have king-size beds. Other in-room amenities are coffeemakers and hairdryers.

Dining/Entertainment: There is a surf-and-turf restaurant, and breakfast is served buffet-style in the lobby.

Services: Room service (6:30am to 11pm), concierge, complimentary newspaper and airport shuttle, same-day laundry/valet.

Facilities: Indoor pool, health club, Jacuzzi, gift shop.

MODERATE

Best Western Old Colony

615 First St., Alexandria, VA 22314. ☎ **703/739-2222** or 800/528-1234. Fax 703/549-2565. 151 rms. A/C TV TEL. $89 double. Rates include continental breakfast. AE, DC, DISC, MC, V. Free parking.

Encompassing some 7 acres, this Best Western is at the corner of 1st and Washington streets on the northern edge of Old Town, a 15-minute walk from the prime attractions. It's a rambling two-story redbrick motel built in 1958 but greatly improved over the years. Although the grounds are predominately parking lots, ivy and large shade trees break up the black-top and lend a colonial ambiance. The rooms are spacious, although the baths are dated and small. Limited facilities include an outdoor pool, but the adjoining Holiday Inn Hotel & Suites (until recently part of this Best Western) has a restaurant, indoor pool, and fitness center.

INEXPENSIVE

Econo Lodge Old Town

700 N. Washington St., Alexandria, VA 22314. ☎ **703/836-5100** or 800/424-4777. 39 rms. A/C TV TEL. $50–$65 double. Extra person $5. AE, DISC, MC, V. Free parking.

Part of the well-run budget chain whose motto is "Spend a night, not a fortune," this very plain but clean Econo Lodge is just a few blocks from the center of Old Town activity. Rooms in the two-story building face a small parking lot. The motel offers good-sized rooms and a free shuttle service to National Airport.

BED & BREAKFAST ACCOMMODATIONS

Thirty private homes, all historic properties (1790–1895) in Old Town Alexandria, offer B&B accommodations under the aegis of Mr. E. J. Mansmann of **Princely Bed & Breakfast Ltd.,** 819 Prince St., Alexandria, VA 22314 (☎ 703/683-2159). The best time to call for reservations is Monday through Friday between 10am and 6pm. Rooms are nicely furnished, most with antiques and fireplaces, and cost $75 to $90, plus tax, per room per night. There's a $20 surcharge on those rates if you stay only one night.

DINING
EXPENSIVE

Chart House

1 Cameron St., on the Potomac River. ☎ **703/684-5080.** Reservations advised. Main courses $15.50–$26; Sun brunch $17–$19. AE, CB, DC, DISC, MC, V. Mon–Thurs 5–10:15pm, Fri–Sat 5–11pm, Sun 11am–2:30pm and 5–10pm. AMERICAN.

The Chart House, on Alexandria's waterfront, enjoys a unique perch on the dock, giving diners a view of the Potomac (and al fresco riverside dining in good weather). Under a soaring cathedral ceiling, the interior is decidedly tropical, sparked by brilliant hues of green, turquoise, pink, and purple, with rattan furniture, potted palms, and a copper-covered salad bar. Straightforward American fare includes steaks, prime rib, and seafood, supplemented by daily specials. All entrees come with freshly baked squaw and sourdough breads and unlimited salad-bar selections. For dessert, try the house specialty—mud pie, which is Kona coffee ice cream in an Oreo cookie crust that's topped with fudge, whipped cream, and diced almonds.

La Bergerie

218 N. Lee St., in Crilley Shops. ☎ **703/683-1007.** Reservations required. Main courses $15–$24. AE, CB, DC, DISC, MC, V. Mon–Sat 11:30am–2:30pm and 6–10pm. FRENCH.

Alexandria's fanciest restaurant features Basque specialties in a fittingly provincial setting with crystal chandeliers and oil paintings of the Pyrenees countryside on exposed-brick walls. White-linened tables, each adorned with a pink rose in a silver vase, add an elegant note. Exquisite desserts and a large floral arrangement grace an antique dresser up front, and there are many hanging and potted plants. Owner-chef Jean Champagne-Ibarcq's lunch fare includes hors d'oeuvres of pâté, escargots, and avocado stuffed with crabmeat, plus main courses of chicken in white wine and filet of fresh sole sautéed with apples. His dinner entrees include wine-braised salmon, swordfish with tomato and basil over pasta, or roast duck. Fresh raspberry soufflé is a delicious finish.

Landini Brothers

115 King St., between Lee and Union Sts. ☎ **703/836-8404.** Reservations recommended. Main courses $12.50–$24.50. AE, CB, DC, DISC, MC, V. Mon–Sat 11:30am–11pm, Sun 4–10pm. NORTHERN ITALIAN.

The classic, delicate cuisine of Tuscany is featured at this rustic, almost grottolike restaurant with stone walls, a flagstone floor, and rough-hewn beams overhead. It's especially charming at night by candlelight. There's additional seating in a lovely upstairs dining room. Everything is homemade—the pasta, the desserts, and the crusty Italian bread. Things might get underway with prosciutto and melon or shrimp sautéed in garlic with tangy lemon sauce, followed by prime aged beef tenderloin médaillons sautéed with garlic, mushrooms, and rosemary in a Barolo wine sauce. Dessert choices include tiramisù and custard-filled fruit tarts.

Two-Nineteen

219 King St. ☎ **703/549-1141.** Reservations suggested, especially for dinner in the formal dining rooms. Main courses $15–$24. AE, DC, DISC, MC, V. Mon–Thurs 11am–10:30pm, Fri–Sat 11am–midnight Sun. 10am–4pm and 5–10:30pm. AMERICAN/CREOLE.

Two-Nineteen is comprised of three formal Victorian-style dining rooms, a covered sidewalk patio, and the Bayou Room, a basement Ratskeller. Crystal chandeliers, rose-velvet upholstery, and a floral-patterned carpet highlight the elegant dining rooms. New Orleans cuisine is featured. Begin with oysters Bienville (baked in cream sauce with shrimp and crab) or crabmeat royale (with artichoke bottoms and hollandaise sauce). Seafood entrees include blackened gulf fish with blue crab claws, *poisson en papillote* (fish baked in parchment paper), and seafood-stuffed rainbow trout. The covered patio, reminiscent of a New Orleans courtyard, is a delightful alternative in warm weather.

In the Bayou Room, you'll find many of the same items featured upstairs, plus sandwiches and salads. The setting is highly atmospheric, with stone and brick walls, oak beams, a bar of leaded glass and oak, and a ceiling that's plastered with a collection of business cards from all over the country.

MODERATE

✪ Bilbo Baggins

208 Queen St. ☎ **703/683-0300.** Reservations suggested, especially for dinner on weekends. Main courses $12–$16. AE, CB, DC, DISC, MC, V. Mon–Sat 5:30–10:30pm, Sun 4:30–9:30pm. AMERICAN.

Named for a character in Tolkien's *The Hobbit*, this charming two-story restaurant offers fresh homemade fare. The downstairs area has rustic wide-plank floors, wood-paneled walls, oak tables, and a brick oven centerpiece. Upstairs is another dining room with stained-glass windows and seating on old church pews. It adjoins a skylit wine bar with windows overlooking Queen Street treetops. Candlelit at night, it becomes an even cozier setting. The eclectic menu changes daily to reflect seasonal specialties, but lunch entrees usually include quiche Lorraine, gnocchi pesto, and spinach salad. At dinner, we've enjoyed entrees like salmon topped with crabmeat and red and black caviar, and lamb chops brushed with Dijon mustard and sautéed in bread crumbs. An extensive wine list is available (more than 30 boutique wines are offered by the glass and another 150 by the bottle), as are all bar drinks and excellent homemade desserts like steamed dark-chocolate bread pudding topped with sliced bananas.

Ⓢ Fish Market

105 King St., at Union Street. ☎ **703/836-5676.** Reservations not accepted. Main courses $9–$17. AE, DC, MC, V. Sun–Thurs 11:15am–1am, Fri–Sat 11:15am–2am (kitchen closes at midnight). SEAFOOD.

So popular is the Fish Market that its original seven dining rooms were expanded to include the building next door. The original corner location is a 200-year-old-plus warehouse, with heavy beams, terra-cotta tile floors, exposed-brick and stucco walls adorned with nautical antiques, copper pots suspended over a fireplace, copper-topped bars, and saloon doors. The newer Sunquest Room is bright, with light streaming in through floor-to-ceiling windows; its white walls are graced with musical instruments. At lunch you might have a crab cake sandwich, seafood stew, or a platter of fried oysters. The same menu is available at dinner, when platters cost $2 or $3 more. On weekends there's live entertainment—guitar and ragtime piano in the upstairs Main Dining Room and the Sunquest Room.

Gadsby's Tavern

138 N. Royal St., at Cameron Street. ☎ **703/548-1288.** Reservations advised. Main courses $15–$23. CB, DC, DISC, MC, V. Mon–Sat 11:30am–3pm, Sun 11am–3pm; daily 5:30–10pm. AMERICAN.

In the spirit of history, pass through the portals where Washington reviewed his troops for the last time and eat at the famous Gadsby's Tavern, where the period furnishings, wood-plank floors, fireplace, and gaslight-style lamps re-create an authentic Colonial atmosphere. You'll dine off the same kind of pewter and china plates our ancestors used and be served by appropriately costumed waiters and waitresses. The coachyard serves as an outdoor dining area. All the fare is homemade, including the Sally Lunn bread baked daily. Lunch might consist of an appetizer of shrimp and clams in puff pastry, chicken roasted on an open fire and served with fried potatoes, and a dessert of buttermilk pie. In winter, warm yourself with drinks like hot buttered rum and Martha's Remedy—coffee, cocoa, and brandy. Dinner entrees usually include roast turkey, crabcakes, stuffed flounder, and Colonial game pie. Entertainers perform 18th-century style during dinner and at Sunday brunch.

Ⓢ Le Refuge

127 N. Washington St. ☎ **703/548-4661.** Reservations recommended, especially at dinner. Main courses $14–$20; early-bird dinner $20. AE, CB, DC, MC, V. Mon–Sat 11:30am–2:30pm and 5:30–10pm (early-bird dinner, Mon all evening, Tues–Thurs 5:30–7pm). FRENCH.

There's a wicker model of the Eiffel Tower in the bowfronted window of this charming little restaurant, one of the best-kept dining secrets in Alexandria. The intimate setting is typically French—bentwood chairs, black-leather banquettes, and tables covered with beige-and-brown napery. The three-course early-bird dinner is a great buy: It includes soup or salad; fresh catch of the day, leg of lamb, or calf's liver; and crème brûlée or peach Melba for dessert. There's a lunch version for $10. Regular house specialties include bouillabaisse, classic rack of lamb, and salmon in a crust with champagne-cream sauce, and nightly specials feature produce fresh from the market.

INEXPENSIVE

Bread And Chocolate
611 King St., between Washington and St. Asaph Sts. ☎ **703/548-0992**. Breakfast $2.50–$6; main courses $5.50–$9. AE, DISC, MC, V. Mon–Sat 7am–7pm, Sun 8am–6pm. CONTINENTAL.

Modeled after a Swiss *Konditorei,* this cheerful place has a counter up front displaying an array of fresh-baked breads, croissants, napoleons, cakes, Bavarian fruit tarts, and other goodies. The interior features a changing art show on white walls lit by gallery lights. At breakfast, you can get a café mocha and an almond croissant or opt for a three-minute egg with a selection of cheeses and a basket of bread. The rest of the day, entrees like spinach quiche, a salad of grilled portobello mushrooms with baby greens in blue cheese dressing, and a fresh fruit plate with raspberry-yogurt sauce are served with fresh breads.

East Wind
809 King St. ☎ **703/836-1515**. Reservations suggested. Main courses $10–$16. AE, CB, DC, DISC, MC, V. Mon–Fri 11:30am–2:30pm; Mon–Thurs 6–10pm, Fri–Sat 5:30–10:30pm, Sun 5:30–9:30pm. VIETNAMESE.

The decor of this Vietnamese restaurant is very appealing: Sienna stucco and knotty-pine-paneled walls are adorned with works of talented Vietnamese artist Minh Nguyen. There are planters of greenery, a lovely floral arrangement on each table, and a large floral display up front. An East Wind lunch might begin with an appetizer of *cha gio* (delicate Vietnamese egg rolls). One of our favorite entrees is *bo dun*—beef tenderloin strips marinated in wine, honey, and spices; rolled in fresh onions; and broiled on bamboo skewers. Also excellent are the grilled lemon chicken, and the charcoal-broiled shrimp and scallops served on rice vermicelli. Vegetarians will find many selections here.

Ⓢ Hard Times Cafe
1404 King St., near S. West St. ☎ **703/683-5340**. Main courses $4.50–$6. MC, V. Mon–Thurs 11am–10pm, Fri–Sat 11am–11pm, Sun 4–10pm (extended hours in summer). AMERICAN SOUTHWEST.

Like its Arlington counterpart, this authentically Texas-style chili parlor features award-winning "bowls of red." At lunch or dinner, you can get a big bowl of Texas, Cincinnati, or vegetarian chili with or without beans and including a big hunk of cornbread. Available extras are cheese (parmesan or Cheddar), chopped onions, and side dishes of steak fries cooked with the skins and fried onion rings. For dessert, there's pecan-walnut or apple-crumb pie. The ambiance is Old Southwest, with roomy oak booths, country music on the jukebox, and a laid-back young staff in jeans and T-shirts.

✪ King Street Blues
112 N. St. Asaph St. ☎ **703/836-8800**. Reservations not accepted. Main courses $7–$11.75. AE, DC, DISC, MC, V. Mon–Thurs 11:30am–10:30pm, Fri–Sat 11:30am–11:30pm; Sun 10:30am–10pm; bar stays open later. AMERICAN/SOUTHERN.

King Street Blues is one of Alexandria's most charming eateries, a re-creation of a Virginia roadhouse. It's easy to find, for it occupies all three floors of a small brick building with windows painted on its exterior brick wall and whose blue entrance canopy is adorned with a pig trumpeting the words GOOD FOOD. Blue neon out-lines the real window panes. Brian McCall, a local artist whose studio (called The Barking Dog) is in the Torpedo Factory, has covered almost every inch of the interior walls with papier-mâché figures and murals. His colorful work reminded us of Red Grooms constructions, created with a sly tongue-in-cheek good humor. Locals flock here at lunch for the house beef stew (the accompanying garlic mashed potatoes are memorable), chili salad, and barbecued chicken. At dinner, there are more all-American favorites, like southern-fried catfish filet; baked meatloaf; and house-smoked baby-back ribs served with barbecue sauce, "peppa" slaw, and road-house toast. The daily blue-plate special, served at both lunch and dinner for $4.95, is an excellent value.

Radio Free Italy

5 Cameron St., behind the Torpedo Factory. ☎ **703/683-0361.** Reservations accepted for large parties only. Main courses $5.50–$11. AE, DC, DISC, MC, V. Daily 11:30am–midnight. CONTEMPORARY.

Anchor of the Torpedo Factory's Food Pavilion, a pleasant riverfront dining complex, Radio Free Italy has a downstairs carry-out counter and a fancier dining area on the mezzanine, which enjoys great views of the boat-filled marina. Both levels offer outdoor waterfront seating in good weather. A marvelous salad of chilled seafood marinated in lemon and olive oil leads the appetizers, while oak-fired pizzas have California-style toppings such as grilled chicken, goat cheese, spinach, and marinara. A good entree choice is fresh fettuccine tossed with pesto, sun-dried tomatoes, garlic-roasted mushrooms, and paper-thin slices of oak-roasted, peppercorn-studded sirloin. There's a full bar, with Italian wines available by the glass.

PICNIC FARE

Buy the fixings for a picnic at the **Deli on the Strand,** 211 The Strand (☎ 703/548-7222), a pleasant establishment a block south of King Street. They bake bread on the premises, so the aroma is divine, and you can get reasonably priced cold-cut sandwiches, as well as croissants, muffins, and, on weekends, bagels. Also available are luscious homemade salads, cheeses, beer, and wine. There are a few picnic tables outside. Open daily from 8am to 6pm, until 7pm in summer.

ALEXANDRIA AFTER DARK

Like Arlington, Alexandria falls under the aegis of Washington, D.C., when it comes to the performing arts (see "Arlington After Dark," above).

King Street restaurants are the center of Alexandria's on-going club and bar scene. Especially noteworthy are **Two-Nineteen,** 219 King St. (☎ 703/549-1141), which features live jazz every night in the Basin Street Lounge; **Murphy's,** 713 King St. (☎ 703/548-1717), where live bands lead Irish and Welsh sing-alongs on weekends; and the **Fish Market,** 105 King St. (☎ 703/836-5676), with either a pianist or guitarist from Thursday to Saturday nights.

For bluegrass, country, and folk, head out to **The Birchmere,** 3901 Mount Vernon Ave. (☎ 703/549-5919), a showcase for nationally known stars. The Birchmere is just south of Glebe Road on Mount Vernon Avenue.

The **Laughing Lizard Lounge Comedy Club,** 1322 King St. (☎ 703/548-CLUB), highlights improv comedy, with open-mike nights and scheduled performers in the nightclub; there's music in the bar and out on the patio.

3 Mount Vernon & the Potomac Plantations

Mount Vernon: 8 miles S of Alexandria

It's easy to picture Scarlett O'Hara saying "fiddle-dee-dee" to Rhett Butler on the spacious lawns of the Potomac River plantations at Mount Vernon, Woodlawn, and Gunston Hall. Dating from Colonial times, these are the homes of the men who shaped our government and its institutions. To visit them is an education in early American thought, politics, sociology, art, architecture, fashion, and the decorative arts.

ESSENTIALS

GETTING THERE You will need a car to get to Woodlawn and the other attractions south of Mount Vernon, but you can get to the first president's home by public transportation.

By Tourmobile From Arlington National Cemetery or the Washington Monument in Washington, D.C., you can take the Tourmobile (☎ 202/554-5100) to Mount Vernon from April to October daily at 10am, noon, or 2pm. Fares are $17 for adults and $8.25 for children 3 to 11; under 3, free. The trips take about 4 hours and reservations are required in person at least 30 minutes before each departure. Call for off-season departure times.

By Boat From early March through December, the *Spirit of Washington* (☎ 202/554-8000) travels down the Potomac to Mount Vernon from Pier 4, 6th and Water Streets SW in Washington, D.C. The fare, including round-trip cruise and entrance to Mount Vernon, is $21.50 for adults, $19.25 for seniors, $12.75 for children 6 to 11, free for 5 and under. Call for detailed information and reservations.

By Car It's a pleasant drive 8 miles south of Alexandria via the George Washington Parkway/Mount Vernon Memorial Highway. The same highway connects to U.S. 1 and the nearby attractions.

By Metro and Bus Take the Blue or Yellow Metro lines to Huntington and catch the 11P bus to the entrance gate to Mount Vernon. Call 703/637-2437 for departure times and fares.

WHAT TO SEE & DO

✪ Mount Vernon

End of George Washington Parkway, 8 miles S of Old Town Alexandria and I-95. ☎ **703/780-2000.** Admission $8 adults, $7.50 senior citizens, $4 children 6–11. April–Aug daily 8am–5pm; March, Sept, and Oct daily 9am–4pm; Nov–Feb daily 9am–4pm.

In 1784, George Washington wrote the Marquis de Lafayette, "I am become a private citizen on the banks of the Potomac, and under the shadow of my own Vine and my own Fig-tree, free from the bustle of a camp and the busy scenes of public life . . . I am not only retired from all public employments, but I am retiring within myself; and shall be able to view the solitary walk, and tread the paths of private life with heartfelt satisfaction."

Alas, Washington's announcement of retirement to his beloved ancestral plantation home was premature. In 1787, he once again heeded the call to duty, presiding over the Constitutional Convention in Philadelphia. In 1789, he became the first president of the United States and managed to visit Mount Vernon only once or twice a year during his eight-year term. It wasn't until 1797, two years before his death, that Washington was finally able to devote himself fully to the "tranquil enjoyments" of Mount Vernon.

The home and final resting place of George and Martha Washington has been one of America's most-visited shrines since 1858, when a group of women, led by Ann Pamela Cunningham, banded together to raise money to rescue the sadly deteriorated mansion. The organization they formed, the Mount Vernon Ladies Association of the Union, purchased the estate from Washington's great-grandnephew, John Augustine Washington Jr., and continues to own and maintain the mansion and its beautifully kept grounds. For more than 100 years there's been an ongoing effort to locate and return the estate's scattered contents and memorabilia, thus enhancing its authentic appearance circa 1799.

There's no formal tour of Mount Vernon, but attendants stationed throughout the house and grounds provide explanatory commentary that provides a unique glimpse into 18th-century plantation life.

The house itself—an outstanding example of Georgian architecture—is constructed of beveled pine painted to look like stone. You'll enter by way of the "large dining room," which contains many of the original chairs, Hepplewhite mahogany sideboards, and paintings. Step outside and enjoy the view that prompted Washington to declare, "No estate in United America is more pleasantly situated than this."

A key to the Paris Bastille that Lafayette presented to Washington in 1790 via messenger Thomas Paine hangs in the central hall, which was the social center of the house in Washington's day. The "little parlor" contains the English harpsichord of Martha Washington's granddaughter, Nelly Custis. Martha's china tea service is laid out on the table in the "west parlor." In the "small dining room," the sweetmeat course set up on the original mahogany dining table is based on a description of an actual Mount Vernon dinner in 1799. The "downstairs bedroom" was used to accommodate the many overnight guests Washington mentions in his diary. Washington's study contains its original globe, desk, and dressing table.

Upstairs are five bedchambers, including the "Lafayette Room," named for its most distinguished occupant, and George and Martha's bedroom, in which Washington died.

After leaving the house, you can tour the outbuildings, including the kitchen, smokehouse, overseer's and slave quarters, and the Washingtons' graves. A museum on the property contains many interesting exhibits and memorabilia, and a four-acre exhibition area focuses on Washington's accomplishments off the battlefield and outside the government.

Allow at least two hours to tour the entire house and grounds. A detailed map is provided at the entrance. The best time to visit is off-season, when the crowds are sparser. If you must visit in spring or summer, come early on weekends and holidays or you may encounter long lines. On Washington's Birthday, by the way (the federal holiday, not the actual date), admission is free and a wreath-laying ceremony is held at his tomb.

Note: There's an ongoing schedule of special activities at Mount Vernon, especially in summer. These run the gamut from special garden and history tours to Colonial craft demonstrations and treasure hunts for children. Call to find out what's going on during your visit.

Where to Eat Near Mount Vernon: A **snack bar** at the entrance serves light fare daily. There are picnic tables outside. If you pack your own picnic, consider driving about a mile north on the George Washington Memorial Parkway to **Riverside Park,** where picnic tables overlook the Potomac.

The **Mount Vernon Inn** (☎ 703/780-0011), to the right of the gift shop at the entrance to the plantation, is a quaintly charming Colonial-style restaurant complete with wait staff in 18th-century costumes, period furnishings, working fireplaces, and a menu that includes Virginia peanut-and-chestnut soup and Colonial pye (a crock of meat or fowl and garden vegetables with a puff-pastry top). There's a full bar, and premium Virginia wines are offered by the glass. A fixed-price dinner costs $14, including a soup or salad, entree, homemade breads, and dessert. Reservations are suggested at dinner. Main courses cost $5.25 to $7.25 at lunch, $12 to $24 at dinner. American Express, Discover, MasterCard, and Visa accepted. Open Monday to Saturday from 11am to 3:30pm, Sunday from 11:30am to 4pm; and for dinner, Monday to Saturday from 5 to 9pm.

Woodlawn Plantation

9000 Richmond Hwy. (U.S. 1), at Mount Vernon Memorial Pkwy. (Va. 235). ☎ **703/780-4000.** Admission $6 adults, $4 students and seniors, under 5 free. Admission may be higher during special events. March–Dec daily 9:30am–4:30pm; Jan–Feb Sat–Sun 9:30am–4:30pm. Tours on the half hour. Closed New Year's Day, Thanksgiving, and Christmas. From Mount Vernon, drive 2 miles west on Mount Vernon Memorial Parkway (Va. 235) to U.S. 1.

Originally a 2,000-acre part of the Mount Vernon estate (today some 130 acres remain), Woodlawn was a wedding gift from George Washington to his adopted daughter (and Martha's actual granddaughter), the beautiful Eleanor "Nelly" Parke Custis, and his nephew, Maj. Lawrence Lewis, who married in 1799. Three years later they moved into the house designed by William Thornton, first architect of the Capitol, and furnished it primarily with pieces from Mount Vernon.

Under the auspices of the National Trust for Historic Preservation, the restored mansion and its elegant formal gardens reflect many periods of history. Post-Lewis occupants included antislavery Quaker and Baptist settlers from the North (1846–89); New York City playwright Paul Kester (1901–05); and Elizabeth Sharpe of Pennsylvania (1905–25), who commissioned noted architect Waddy Wood to restore the house to a semblance of its original appearance. Finally, Sen. Oscar Underwood of Alabama and his wife, Bertha, retired here in 1924. The Underwood family occupied the house through 1948, retaining Waddy Wood to continue its restoration. With nature trails designed by the National Audubon Society, the grounds are representative of many periods in the estate's history and include the largest East Coast collection of 19th-century species of roses.

Allow at least an hour to see the house and grounds, including a 30-minute guided tour.

Also on the premises are two other houses: **Grand View,** built about 100 yards from the mansion in 1858, and Frank Lloyd Wright's **Pope-Leighey House,** designed in 1940 for the Loren Pope family of Falls Church. The Pope-Leighey House was rescued from highway construction and moved to the Woodlawn grounds in 1964. Built of cypress, brick, and glass, the house was created as a prototype of well-designed architectural space for middle-income people. "The house of moderate cost," said Wright in 1938, "is not only America's major architectural problem but the problem most difficult for her major architects." In 1946, the house was purchased by the Robert A. Leigheys—hence, the double name. After living in the house for 17 years, the Leigheys donated to the National Trust both the house and the money to dismantle and move it.

Woodlawn and the Pope-Leighey House have the same opening hours and can be seen via a combination ticket. Grand View is not open to the public.

Gunston Hall

10709 Gunston Rd. (Va. 242). ☎ **703/550-9220.** Admission $5 adults, $4 seniors, $1.50 students through 12th grade, under 6 free. Daily 9:30am–5pm. Closed Thanksgiving,

Christmas, New Year's Day. From Woodlawn, drive 6 miles south on U.S. 1, turn left on Gunston Road (Va. 242).

Yet another meticulously restored 18th-century plantation awaits exploration if you continue south on U.S. 1 to Va. 242. Some 550 acres remain of the original 5000 acres belonging to George Mason (1725–92), a statesman and political thinker who, while shunning public office, played an important behind-the-scenes role in founding our nation. Mason drafted the Virginia Declaration of Rights, model for the Bill of Rights. Thomas Jefferson based the famous sentence of the Declaration of Independence on Mason's statement that "all men are by nature equally free and independent and have certain inherent rights . . . namely, the enjoyment of life and liberty, with the means of acquiring and possessing property, and pursuing and obtaining happiness and safety." A staunch believer in human rights, Mason refused to sign the Constitution (which he helped write) because it didn't abolish slavery or, initially, contain a Bill of Rights.

At the reception center an 11-minute film introduces visitors to Mason and his estate. En route to the house you'll pass a small museum of Mason family memorabilia. And inside the house a guide is on hand to answer questions.

A highlight is the Palladian Room, the chef d'oeuvre of Gunston Hall's brilliant young creator, an indentured English craftsman in his early 20s named William Buckland, who worked here from 1755 to 1759. The room's intricately carved woodwork was inspired by the 16th-century Italian architect Andrea Palladio. Another room has chinoiserie interior, the latest London rage in the mid-18th century. In Mason's library and study is the writing table on which he penned the Virginia Declaration of Rights.

Containing only plants found in colonial days, the formal gardens focus on the 12-foot-high English boxwood allée planted by Mason. A nature trail leads down the Potomac past the deer park and woodland area. Also on the premises is the family graveyard where George and Ann Mason are buried.

Gunston Hall borders Pohick Bay Regional Park (see below).

George Washington's Grist Mill

Mount Vernon Memorial Parkway (Va. 235), 1 mi. west of Mount Vernon. ☎ **703/780-3383.** Admission $1.25 adults, $1 children 7 to 12, under 7 free. Memorial Day–Labor Day Thurs–Mon 9am–5pm.

The Woodlawn part of Mount Vernon contained a grist mill used by neighboring farmers to grind corn and wheat. In 1932, the Virginia Conservation Commission purchased part of the property, known as Dogue Run Farm, on which the mill and other buildings had been located. The site was excavated, and part of the original water wheel, the bearings for the wheel, part of the trundlehead, complete wheel buckets, and other articles were found.

Pohick Church

9301 Richmond Hwy. (U.S. 1). ☎ **703/339-6572.** Free admission. Daily 9am–4pm. From Woodlawn, drive 5 miles south on U.S. 1.

Located about 4^1/2 miles south of the grist mill, Pohick Church was built in the 1770s from plans drawn up by George Washington. The interior was designed by George Mason, owner of Gunston Hall (see above), with box pews like those prevalent in England at the time. During the Civil War, Union troops stabled their horses in the church and stripped the interior. The east wall was used for target practice. Today the church is restored to its original appearance and has an active Episcopal congregation.

Pohick Bay Regional Park

6501 Pohick Bay Dr., off Gunston Rd. (Va. 242). ☎ **703/339-6104.** Admission $4 per car; use of pool $3.25 adults, $2.75 seniors and children 2–11, under 2 free. Park daily 8am–dark; pool Memorial Day–Labor Day daily 10am–8pm.

Close to Gunston Hall, this 1,000-acre park focusing on water-oriented recreations occupies a spectacular bayside setting on the historic 100,000-acre Mason Neck peninsula. It offers one of the largest swimming pools on the East Coast; boat access to the Potomac (sailboat and paddleboat rentals are available); 200 campsites available on a first-come, first-served basis; a 4-mile bridle path; scenic nature trails; an 18-hole golf course and pro shop; miniature golf; and sheltered picnic areas with grills. It's the perfect place to refresh yourself after a morning spent traipsing around old plantations.

4 The Hunt Country

Leesburg: 35 miles NW of Washington, D.C.; 115 miles NW of Richmond. Middleburg: 45 miles W of Washington, D.C.; 95 miles NW of Richmond

The colonial tradition of foxhunting continues today in Virginia's Hunt Country, the rolling hills between the Washington, D.C., metropolitan area and the Blue Ridge Mountains. The Hunt Country is studded with expansive horse farms bordered by stone fences, plantations with elegant manses, picturesque villages, historic country inns, and fine restaurants. You could see the rich and famous strolling the streets or having a bite of lunch in picturesque Leesburg and Middleburg, for some of the world's wealthiest people keep their thoroughbreds here.

In addition to attracting horse lovers, the area's picturesque back roads and the 45-mile Washington & Old Dominion Railroad (W&OD) Trail bring bicyclists from all over the mid-Atlantic states. Horses also can be ridden on the W&OD Trail, which follows an old railroad bed through the Horse Country, crossing South King Street in downtown Leesburg.

ESSENTIALS

VISITOR INFORMATION   For information about **Leesburg** and **Loudoun County,** contact the Loudoun Tourism Council, 108-D South St. SE, Leesburg, VA 20175 (☎ 703/777-0519 or 800/752-6118). The Leesburg tourist office is on Loudoun Street in Market Station, a renovated complex of shops and restaurants. It's open daily from 9am to 5pm.

Middleburg has an information center in the Pink Box, 12 Madison Street, Middleburg, VA 20117 (☎ 540/687-8888). It's open Monday to Friday from 11am to 3pm, Saturday and Sunday from 11am to 4pm.

GETTING THERE   By Plane   Washington Dulles Airport is on the eastern edge of the Hunt Country, 14 miles east of Leesburg and 21 miles east of Middleburg.

By Car   Leesburg: There are 2 routes from the Capital Beltway (I-495) to Leesburg. The free but slow route is Va. 7 to Leesburg. The fast way is via the Dulles Toll Road (Va. 267), between both I-495 and I-66 and Washington Dulles Airport; it feeds into the Dulles Greenway, a privately financed toll expressway connecting Dulles to Leesburg. The total toll from I-495 to Leesburg is $2.25. **Middleburg:** From Arlington or I-495, follow I-66 west to Va. 28 north to U.S. 50 west into town. U.S. 15 south from Leesburg intersects with U.S. 50 westbound 10 miles east of Middleburg.

Hunt Country

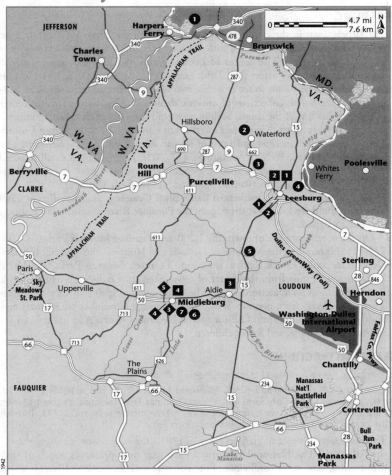

ACCOMMODATIONS:
Laurel Brigade Inn **1**
Little River Inn **3**
Norris House Inn **2**
Red Fox Inn &
   Mosby's Tavern **4**

DINING:
Black Walnut **5**
Coach Stop Restaurant **4**
The Green Tree **1**
Tuscarora Mill **2**
Upper Crust Bakery **3**

ATTRACTIONS:
Ball's Bluff Cemetery **4**
Harpers Ferry National
   Historical Park **1**
Meredyth Vineyard **6**
Morven Park **3**
Oatlands **5**
Piedmont Vineyards **7**
Waterford Village **2**

LEESBURG

The largest town in the Hunt Country, Leesburg is a good base for exploring the region. It has considerable charm, with architecture ranging from pre-Revolutionary to late 19th century. The center of Leesburg and its historic district is at the intersection of Market Street (Va. 7 Business) and King Street (U.S. 15 Business). Everything you will want to see is within two blocks of this key crossroads, including one of the largest collections of **antique dealers** in Virginia. The visitor center (see above) has lists of the shops, both in town and throughout the Hunt Country.

At the Market Street–King Street intersection stands the brick **Loudoun County Court House,** built in 1894 and a mix of Roman Revival and classical elements. The **Loudoun Museum,** 16 W. Loudoun St. (☎ 703/777-7427), is a small regional museum housing memorabilia about the county from pioneer days. It's open Monday through Saturday from 10am to 5pm and Sunday from 1 to 5pm.

The little circle of stone markers in **Ball's Bluff Cemetery** and the adjacent **Civil War battlefield** are located at the edge of the Potomac River in northeast Leesburg, off U.S. 15 Bypass.

On the northwest edge of town, the 1,200-acre estate of **Morven Park** (☎ 703/777-2414) is home to the Museum of Hounds and Hunting, the Winmill Carriage Collection, and a Greek Revival mansion. To reach Morven Park, take Va. 7 Business west 1 mile from the center of town, then turn right onto Morven Park Road, left onto Old Waterford Road. The estate is open April 1 to October 31 on Tuesday to Friday from noon to 5pm, April 1 through November on Saturday and Sunday from 10am to 5pm. Call for special December hours. Admission is $6 for adults, $5 for seniors, and $3 for children.

NEARBY ATTRACTIONS

✪ Harpers Ferry National Historical Park

Harpers Ferry, WV. ☎ **304/535-6298.** Admission $5 per car, $3 per pedestrian, bicyclist, and bus passenger 17–61. Daily 8am–5pm. Closed Christmas. From Leesburg, it's about 12 miles to Harpers Ferry. Take Va. 7 west, turn right at Va. 9. Take another right at C.R. 671. Turn left at the intersection of U.S. 340 and go west to Harpers Ferry.

Thomas Jefferson wrote of Harpers Ferry in 1783, "the view is worth a voyage across the Atlantic." The National Historical Park that now preserves much of that breathtaking view at the confluence of the Potomac and Shenandoah Rivers is worth a visit from anyone interested in discovering a wealth of American history—and not just John Brown's famous raid against slavery in 1859, for Harpers Ferry also saw the arrival of the first successful American railroad, the first application of interchangeable parts, the largest surrender of Union troops during the Civil War, and the education of former slaves in one of the earliest integrated schools in the United States.

Nevertheless, Harpers Ferry is best remembered for John Brown's Raid, which presaged the Civil War. After his friend, abolitionist editor Elijah Lovejoy, was murdered by a mob in 1837, Brown dedicated his life to the destruction of slavery. When the Supreme Court decreed in its infamous Dred Scott decision that Congress could not deprive slave owners of their human property, Brown led a raid into Missouri and freed 11 slaves. Seeking weapons, he captured the federal arsenal at Harpers Ferry on October 16, 1859. The next day, 90 U.S. Marines under the command of Col. Robert E. Lee surrounded the arsenal, and Col. J. E. B. Stuart twice delivered surrender demands to Brown. When he refused, a party of 12 marines smashed the door and captured Brown and the surviving raiders. Brown was tried for treason and hanged in Charles Town on December 2.

You can hop a free shuttle bus from the **Visitors Center** and parking lot to the Historic Area, a half-mile away, where the **John Brown Museum** vividly recounts the story with photographs, documents, and a slide show. Many original stone buildings are open, including a restored dry-goods store, a blacksmith shop, and an armorer's house. In addition, the area is a terrific place for **hiking,** since several scenic walking tracks—including the Appalachian Trial—lead to less congested areas of the park.

Oatlands

U.S. 15, 6 miles south of Leesburg. ☎ **703/777-3174**. Admission $6 adults, $5 seniors and children 12–16, under 12 free. Apr–Dec, Mon–Sat 10am–4:30pm, Sun 1–4:30pm.

An 1803 Greek Revival mansion with a Corinthian portico and beautiful gardens, Oatlands hosts numerous events, such as the Hunt Country Antiques Show in January, annual sheep dog trials in May, a Celtic festival in June, and a Civil War weekend in August. It's open to the public from early April to late December, when it is all decked out in Edwardian-era Christmas decorations.

Sully Plantation

Va. 28, Chantilly. ☎ **703/437-1794.** Admission $4 adults, $2 seniors and children under 16. Mar–Dec, Wed–Mon 11am–4pm; Jan–Feb, Sat–Sun 11am–3:30pm. Closed Thanksgiving, Christmas, and New Year's Day. Sully is on Va. 28, three-quarters of a mile north of U.S. 50, 9 miles south of Va. 7.

Sully Plantation, a 2^1/$_2$-story farmhouse, was built in 1794 by Richard Bland Lee (brother of Light-Horse Harry Lee and Northern Virginia's first congressman) for his wife, Elizabeth Collins. The original plantation was situated on more than 3,000 acres and consisted of a main house, a dairy, a smokehouse, a kitchen building, and slave quarters.

Today the house is furnished with antiques of the Federal period and looks much as it would have during the 1795–1842 era. Mahogany furniture, Wilton carpets, and imported silver approximate the style in which the Lees lived. Living-history programs further re-create the era.

✪ Waterford Village

☎ **540/882-3018.** Free admission. Daily 24 hours. From Leesburg, take Va. 7 west, turn right onto Va. 9, then follow C.R. 662 (right turn) into Waterford.

This is one of the most scenic drives in the area. The enchanting hamlet of Waterford, with numerous 18th- and 19th-century buildings, is a National Historic Landmark. Surrounded by a lush landscape of 1,420 acres, it offers vistas of farmland and pasture that unfold behind barns and churches. You'll feel as though you've entered an English country scene painted by Constable. A Quaker from Pennsylvania, Amos Janney, built a mill here in the 1740s. Other Quakers followed, and by 1840, most of the buildings now on Main Street and Second Street were in place. In 1870, the railroad bypassed Waterford, and because the pace of change slowed, much of the town was preserved. The population swells to some 40,000 on the first weekend in October, however, when local residents stage the annual **Waterford Arts and Crafts Fair,** one of the best in the region.

ACCOMMODATIONS

Norris House Inn

108 Loudon St., Leesburg, VA 20175. ☎ **703/777-1806** or 800/644-1806. Fax 703/771-8051. 6 rms (none with bath). $55–$140 single or double. Rates include breakfast. AE, DC, DISC, MC, V.

A charming 2^1/$_2$-story redbrick 1760 home, Norris House was renovated in the Eastlake style in the Victorian era. Its facade is bedecked with green shutters and a white-columned entrance porch, the whole capped by three pedimented dormer windows. The common rooms include a parlor and library, the former with an oak fireplace. A full breakfast is served in the formal dining room. The breakfast might feature fresh fruit or juice, quiche, and home-baked muffins. Guest-room furnishings are a charming mix of antiques. All share three baths and have fireplaces, stenciled fireplace surrounds, four-poster beds (some with lace canopies), rockers, and framed botanical prints on the walls.

⑤ Laurel Brigade Inn

20 W. Market St., Leesburg, VA 20176. ☎ **703/777-1010.** 8 rms. A/C. $50–$75 double. No credit cards.

To secure a room at this very popular inn, reserve at least 4 to 6 weeks in advance for weekends, 7 to 10 days otherwise. The history of this two-story Federal period charmer goes back to 1766, when town records show that a tavern operator named John Miller became the owner of an "ordinary" on this lot. In 1817, the hotel was purchased by Eleanor and Henry Peers, and it became Peers Hotel. The hotel's kitchen was so highly regarded it was chosen to prepare the food for the collation on the courthouse green when Lafayette visited Leesburg in 1825. In 1949, the building became Laurel Brigade Inn, named for the Civil War brigade led by local Col. Elijah V. White. Rooms today are pleasantly furnished with wing chairs, chenille spreads, and hooked rugs, and some have fireplaces. Although there are no phones in the rooms, a pay phone is in the lobby. Rooms facing the back overlook a lovely garden stretching back to a gazebo that's been the setting for weddings.

Dining/Entertainment: The Laurel Brigade Restaurant is open for lunch and dinner. The price of the entree ($10.75 to $14.50) brings you a full meal at lunch: appetizer, an entree (perhaps chicken pot pie, crabcakes, or grilled pork chop with spiced apple), vegetable and hot rolls, a dessert such as apple dumpling with hard sauce, and coffee or tea. Or you can order an à la carte soup, sandwich, or salad at lunch. Dinner is fixed price ($12.50 to $25), featuring entrees like crab imperial, baked scallops, and strip steak.

DINING

Tuscarora Mill

203 Harrison St., in Market Station, Leesburg, VA ☎ **703/771-9300.** Reservations recommended, especially at dinner. Main courses $12–$22. AE, MC, V. Daily 11:30am–2:30pm and 5:30–9:30pm; cafe serves light fare until 11pm Sun–Thurs, until midnight Fri–Sat. AMERICAN.

Housed in a renovated turn-of-the-century mill, one of the six historic buildings renovated in 1985 to make up the Market Station shopping and dining complex, this simpatico restaurant has a casual ambiance—a combination of light jazz music and a decor utilizing flourishing plants suspended from wood-beamed high ceilings, skylights, pretty floral tablecloths, fresh bouquets, and black wrought-iron street lamps. Its red-metal exterior siding, grain bins, old belts and pulleys, and a grain scale evoke the mill's past. Local businesspeople and visiting Washingtonians fill the tables at lunch, both in the cozy cafe at the front of the restaurant and in the sunny, spacious back room. Delicious luncheon fare ($7 to $13) includes sandwiches, omelets, and hot entrees like sautéed shrimp over angel-hair pasta. A dinner appetizer might be calamari with black olives, tomatoes, and capers over sourdough bruschetta. For the main course, the house-smoked chicken with mushrooms, brandy, and cream over fettuccine or Basmati-crusted yellowfin tuna with salsa of red curry and pineapple are both standouts. À la carte vegetables such as braised endive and garlic mashed potatoes are tempting extras. For dessert, warm strawberry napoleon with zabaglione is a seasonal favorite; chocoholics may opt for the double-chocolate torte with raspberry sauce.

The Green Tree

15 S. King St., Leesburg, VA. ☎ **703/777-7246.** Reservations recommended, especially for dinner on weekends. Main courses $9.25–$17. AE, CB, DC, DISC, MC, V. Mon–Thurs 11:30am– 9:30pm, Fri–Sat 11:30am–10pm, Sun 11:30am–4pm. COLONIAL AMERICAN.

Not only is the decor colonial at this downtown restaurant, but most of the dishes are made from faithfully reproduced 18th-century recipes gathered from the Library of Congress and the National Archives. Recipes for green-herb soup, Sally Lunn bread, roast prime rib with Yorkshire pudding, and rum-and-black-walnut pie are among the stellar results of this research. Both dining rooms have wide-plank floors, harvest dining tables, ladderback chairs, brass chandeliers, working fireplaces, and walls hung with hunting prints. Servers are in period dress as well. A full dinner could start with cabbage pie or a sampling platter of smoked-sausage pie, seafood, mushroom canapés, pâté with rusks, and English beer cheese. Among the entrees are rabbit fricassee, crab, roast chicken, and broiled brook trout.

MIDDLEBURG

One of Virginia's most beautiful small towns, Middleburg likes to call itself the unofficial capital of the Hunt Country. Indeed, jodhpurs and riding boots are *de rigeur* in this town that is home to those interested in horses, and horse breeding, steeplechase racing, and fox hunting.

Middleburg is included on the National Register of Historic Villages, and it's about the same size today as when it was settled in 1731. You can't get lost here, for the entire town occupies just 6 blocks along Washington Street (U.S. 50). Park anywhere on Washington Street and buy a copy of a walking-tour brochure for $1 from the **Pink Box Visitor Information Center,** 12 N. Madison St. (☎ 540/687-8888). Then stroll along Middleburg's brick sidewalks, poke your head into upscale shops with names like The Finicky Filly which sell "home embellishments," have lunch at one of several fine restaurants, or stop for a cone at Scruffy's Ice Cream Parlor. Note the small Gothic Revival **Emmanuel Episcopal Church** (1842) at Liberty Street; it was the first example of mid-19th-century architecture in the village.

NEARBY ATTRACTIONS

Adding to the area's interest are a number of wineries. Just 5 minutes south of Middleburg is the **Meredyth Vineyard,** on C.R. 628 (☎ 540/687-6277). A beautiful setting in the Bull Run Mountains distinguishes the 58 acres of this farm winery. There are tours daily from 10am to 4pm (except New Year's Day, Thanksgiving, and Christmas). There are a picnic area (see Black Walnut and Upper Crust food shops described below for picnic fare) and gift shop. **Piedmont Vineyards,** on C.R. 626 about 3 miles south of town (☎ 540/687-5528), was formerly a dairy farm; its barn now houses a winery, tasting room, and gift shop. Tours are given daily from 10am to 4pm (open major Monday holidays).

✪ Manassas National Battlefield Park

6511 Sudley Rd. (Va. 234), Manassas, VA. ☎ **703/361-1339.** Admission $2 adults, free for children under 17. Summer, daily 8:30am–6pm; winter, daily 8:30am–5pm. From Middleburg (about 11 miles), take U.S. 50 east, turn right onto U.S. 15 south, turn left at Va. 234, and continue southeast to Manassas. From I-66, take Exit 47B and go ¹/₂ mile north on Va. 234.

The first massive clash of the Civil War took place here on July 21, 1861. A well-equipped but poorly trained Union army of 35,000 under Gen. Irvin McDowell had marched from Washington, where cheering crowds expected them to return victorious within several days. Most of the men were 90-day volunteers who had little knowledge of what war would mean. Their goal was Richmond, and to meet the oncoming army, Gen. P. G. T. Beauregard deployed his Confederate troops along a stream known as Bull Run to the north and west of the important railroad junction of Manassas. The 10 hours of heavy fighting on the first day stunned soldiers on both sides as well as on-lookers who had ridden out from Washington to watch the fray. And a surprise Confederate victory shattered any hopes that the war would end quickly. Historians later conjectured that had the Confederates not been too disorganized to follow the fleeing Union troops, an even more decisive victory perhaps could have ended the war, with the South victorious.

Union and Confederate armies met here again on August 28–30, 1862. The Second Battle of Manassas secured Gen. Robert E. Lee's place in history as his 55,000 men soundly defeated the Union army under Gen. John Pope.

The two battles are commemorated at the 5,000-acre battlefield park. Start your tour here at the visitors center, where a museum, a 13-minute slide show, and a battle map program tell the story of the battle. There are a number of self-guided walking tours that highlight Henry Hill, Stone Bridge, and the other critical areas of the two battles. A 12-mile driving tour covers the sites of Second Manassas, which raged over a much larger area.

ACCOMMODATIONS

Red Fox Inn & Mosby's Tavern

2 E. Washington St. (P.O. Box 385), Middleburg, VA 20118. ☎ **540/687-6301** or 800/223-1728. Fax 540/687-6053. 23 rms and suites. A/C TV TEL. $135–$225 single or double. Rates include continental breakfast. AE, DC, MC, V.

The historic Red Fox Inn in the center of Middleburg maintains the romantic charm of early Virginia in its original 1728 stone structure. Later additions include the Stray Fox Inn building, so called because a misfired cannon ball struck its foundation in the Civil War, and the McConnell House Inn building. In the Red Fox are three rooms and three suites, all with wide-plank floors and 18th-century furnishings; several have working fireplaces. Rooms in the Stray Fox and McConnell also preserve a traditional character with hand-stenciled floors and walls, canopy beds, hooked rugs, and original fireplace mantels. Continental breakfast is served in the rooms, and terry bathrobes, bedside sweets, fresh flowers, and a morning Washington newspaper are extra amenities.

Dining/Entertainment: The Red Fox Inn restaurant occupies the first floor of the inn. It features a Hunt Country ambiance—low beamed ceilings, pewter dishes, and equestrian prints lining the walls. The seasonal menu runs the gamut from creative pastas to dinner entrees ($16.50 to $19.50) like chicken breast stuffed with Boursin cheese. Mosby's Tavern serves Mexican lunch/brunch and dinner.

Nearby Accommodation

✪ Little River Inn

U.S. 50 (P.O. Box 116), Aldie, VA 20105. ☎ **703/327-6742.** 5 rms (2 with bath), 3 cottages (with bath). A/C. $80–$210 double. Rates include breakfast. AE, MC, V. Aldie is 5 miles east of Middleburg on U.S. 50.

The peaceful setting of this country inn is so appealing it's almost worth coming to Aldie just to stay here. Farm animals, a small garden, and a patio are behind the main house, an early 19th-century farmhouse. The living room has polished wide-plank floors; in front of the fireplace are two antique wing chairs and a sofa, all upholstered in colonial-print fabrics. Fresh flowers, a basket of magazines, and a few decorative pieces of china add warmth to the setting. Accommodations range from one room to a cottage of your own. The main house has five bedrooms, all charmingly furnished with antique pieces and pretty quilts; one has a working fireplace. Three small houses are also on the property, one a log cabin with a working stone fireplace; another, the Patent House, a small late-1700s domicile, also with a working fireplace. Hill House (ca. 1870) sits on two acres of landscaped gardens and can be rented in its entirety, or the two bedrooms may be rented separately. Breakfast includes such home-baked goodies as poppy seed muffins and giant popovers filled with cooked apples, raisins, and cinnamon sauce.

DINING

You may want to buy the fixings for a gourmet picnic before you set out on a day's excursion in Hunt Country. Try **Black Walnut,** 20 E. Washington St. (☎ 540/687-6833), or the **Upper Crust Bakery,** 2 N. Pendleton St. (☎ 540/687-5666).

Coach Stop Restaurant

9 E. Washington St., Middleburg, VA. ☎ **540/687-5515.** Reservations not necessary. Main courses $12–$17. AE, CB, DC, MC, V. Mon–Sat 7am–9pm, Sun 8am–9pm. AMERICAN.

Locals flock here for good old-fashioned American fare—everything from a delicious breakfast of Virginia country ham and eggs or creamed chipped beef to a dinner of honey-dipped fried chicken. Seating is at the counter, tables, and booths set with hunting-themed place mats and green napkins. Ceiling fans keep the breezes moving as you tuck into a hearty meal. Lunchtime sandwiches, including turkey, bacon, and avocado or a grilled Reuben, are served with french fries or pasta salad. Dinner entrees—comfort foods like roast turkey with stuffing and gravy or pork chops—are served with two vegetables.

6 Fredericksburg & the Northern Neck

Like other early Virginia towns, Fredericksburg is steeped in American history, with a heritage spanning three centuries of colonial, Revolutionary, and Civil War events. It came into being in 1728 as a 500-acre frontier settlement on the banks of the Rappahannock River. George Washington, James Monroe, Thomas Jefferson, and George Mason are among the great names who walked Fredericksburg's cobblestoned streets. And during the Civil War, military heroes such as Stonewall Jackson fought one major battle in the town and three others nearby. Remarkably, Fredericksburg survived, though the scars of war are still visible; a 40-block area of the town has been designated a National Register Historic District. And each year hundreds of thousands of visitors come to the battlefields, now part of a national military parks.

Both George Washington and Robert E. Lee were born east of Fredericksburg on the bucolic Northern Neck, a peninsula set apart by the broad Potomac on one side and the winding Rappahannock River on the other. At the end of the peninsula sits the Tides Inn, one of Virginia's finest resorts, and the tiny fishing village of Reedville, built in the Victorian era and still making its living from the Chesapeake Bay. Large and small creeks crisscross the neck, and bald eagles, blue heron, flocks of waterfowl, and an occasional wild turkey inhabit the unspoiled marshland.

1 Fredericksburg

50 miles S of Washington, D.C.; 45 miles S of Alexandria; 50 miles N of Richmond

Though George Washington always called Alexandria his hometown, he spent his formative years in the Fredericksburg area at Ferry Farm (where he supposedly never told a lie about chopping down the cherry tree). His mother later lived in a house he bought her on Charles Street, and she is buried on the former Kenmore estate, home of his sister, Betty Washington Lewis.

The town was a hotbed of revolutionary zeal in the 1770s. Troops drilled on the courthouse green on Princess Anne Street, and it was in Fredericksburg that Thomas Jefferson, George Mason, and other founding fathers met in 1777 to draft what later became the Virginia Statute of Religious Freedoms, the basis for the First Amendment

Old Town Fredericksburg

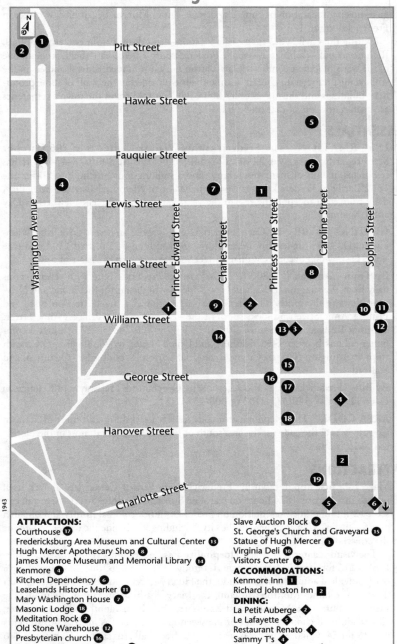

ATTRACTIONS:
Courthouse 🄯
Fredericksburg Area Museum and Cultural Center 🄭
Hugh Mercer Apothecary Shop 🄼
James Monroe Museum and Memorial Library 🄮
Kenmore 🄬
Kitchen Dependency 🄰
Leaselands Historic Marker 🄫
Mary Washington House 🄰
Masonic Lodge 🄲
Meditation Rock 🄫
Old Stone Warehouse 🄬
Presbyterian church 🄰
Religious Liberty Monument 🄫
Rising Sun Tavern 🄯

Slave Auction Block 🄰
St. George's Church and Graveyard 🄯
Statue of Hugh Mercer 🄯
Virginia Deli 🄰
Visitors Center 🄯

ACCOMMODATIONS:
Kenmore Inn 🄫
Richard Johnston Inn 🄬

DINING:
La Petit Auberge 🄬
Le Lafayette 🄯
Restaurant Renato 🄫
Sammy T's 🄰
Sophia Street Station 🄰
Southwestern Grill 🄯

1943

guaranteeing separation of church and state. James Monroe began his law career in Fredericksburg in 1786.

During the Civil War, its strategic location—equidistant from two rival capitals, Richmond and Washington—made Fredericksburg a fierce battlefield, scene of one of the war's bloodiest conflicts. Clara Barton nursed wounded Federal soldiers in the still-extant Presbyterian church. Cannonballs embedded in the walls of some prominent buildings and the graves of 17,000 Civil War soldiers in the town's cemeteries are grim reminders of that tragic era.

ESSENTIALS

INFORMATION   The **Fredericksburg Visitor Center** is at 706 Caroline St., Fredericksburg, VA 22401 (☎ 540/373-1776 or 800/678-4748). It has free maps, menus of many restaurants, and a walking tour brochure following the 1862 Battle of Fredericksburg. The center is open Memorial Day to Labor Day, daily from 9am to 7pm; the rest of the year, 9am to 5pm (except New Year's Day and Christmas).

GETTING THERE   By Car   Fredericksburg is about an hour's drive from Washington, D.C.; a little less from Alexandria. Go south on I-95 to Exit 130A and take Va. 3 East, which becomes William Street and takes you to the heart of town.

By Train   Amtrak (☎ 800/872-7245) serves Fredericksburg with several trains daily from Washington, D.C., and New York City to the north, Richmond and Newport News to the south. The Fredericksburg station is at Lafayette Boulevard and Princess Anne Street, 3 blocks south of the visitors center at Princess Anne Street. **Virginia Railway Express** (☎ 703/497-7777 or 800/743-3843) operates a commuter rail link between Fredericksburg and Union Station in Washington, D.C., with stops at Arlington (Crystal City), Alexandria, Lorton, Woodbridge, Quantico, and Stafford.

By Bus   Fredericksburg is also accessible by **Greyhound/Trailways,** 1400 Jefferson Davis Hwy. (☎ 540/373-2103 or 800/231-2222).

AREA CODE   The telephone area code for Fredericksburg and most of Stafford County is 540; the code for the area south of Fredericksburg and most of the Northern Neck is 804.

ATTRACTIONS

Make your first stop in town the **Fredericksburg Visitor Center** (see above), itself housed in a historic 1824 house on Caroline Street at Charlotte Street. Here you can see a 12-minute slide presentation on Fredericksburg's colonial history and obtain a pass for free parking anywhere in the city (including lots beside the center and across the street).

The visitor center also sells a **Hospitality Pass** ticket for seven main attractions. It costs $16 for adults, $6 for students 6 through 18; for adults, that's a saving of 30% over individual admissions. It includes the Hugh Mercer Apothecary, the Rising Sun Tavern, the James Monroe Museum, the Mary Washington House, Belmont, the Fredericksburg Area Museum, and Kenmore. **Pick Four,** another discount ticket, allows adults to choose any four of the seven main attractions for $11.50, students 6 to 18 for $4. Children under 6 are admitted free to all attractions. (Tickets can also be purchased at any of these attractions.)

Note: The seven block-ticket attractions listed below are closed New Year's Day, Thanksgiving, and December 24, 25, and 31. All these attractions except Belmont are within walking distance of the visitor center.

The visitor center also sells tickets for **Trolley Tours of Fredericksburg** (☎ 540/ 898-0737), an easy way to see 35 historic sights. The 1¼-hour tours leave the visitor center at 10am, noon, 1:30pm, and 3:30pm from June through October. During April and May, they depart at 10:30am and 1:30pm. Fares are $7 for adults, $3 for children 6 to 12, free for kids under 6.

THE BLOCK-TICKET ATTRACTIONS

✪ Kenmore

1201 Washington Ave., between Lewis and Fauquier streets. ☎ **540/373-3381.** Admission (without block ticket) $5 adults, $2.50 children (under 6, free). Mar–Dec, Mon–Sat 10am–5pm, Sun noon–5pm; Jan–Feb, Mon–Fri by reservation only, Sat and Presidents' Day 10am–4pm, Sun noon–4pm.

This stately Georgian mansion was built in the 1770s for Betty Washington (George's sister) and her husband, Fielding Lewis, one of the wealthiest planters in Fredericksburg. According to legend, George involved himself considerably in the building, decoration, and furnishings of the estate. During the Revolution, Lewis financed a gun factory and built vessels for the Virginia navy. As a result of his large expenditures in the cause of patriotism, he eventually had to sell Kenmore to liquidate his debts. He died soon after the victory at Yorktown.

Today the house is meticulously restored to its Colonial appearance. The original exquisitely molded plaster ceilings and cornices are its most outstanding features. Most of the floors and all the woodwork and paneling are also original, and the authentic 18th-century English and American furnishings contain several Lewis family pieces.

After touring the house, take a walk through the famous boxwood gardens, the Wilderness Walk, and the cutting garden, all restored and maintained according to the original plans by the Garden Club of Virginia. A museum shop is also on the premises.

Mary Washington House

1200 Charles St. at Lewis St. ☎ **540/373-1569.** Admission (without block ticket) $3 adults, $1 ages 6–18 (under 6, free). Mar–Nov, daily 9am–5pm; Dec–Feb, daily 10am–4pm. Closed Thanksgiving, Dec 24–25, and Jan. 1.

George Washington purchased this house for his mother, Mary Ball Washington, in 1772 and added a two-story extension. She was then 64 years old and had been living at nearby Ferry Farm since 1739. Lafayette visited during the Revolution to pay respects to the mother of the greatest living American. And Washington came in 1789 to receive her blessing before going to New York for his inauguration as president. He did not see her again; she died later that year. Thirty-minute **tours** are given by hostesses in Colonial garb throughout the day.

James Monroe Museum and Memorial Library

908 Charles St., between William and George streets. ☎ **540/654-1043.** Admission (without block ticket) $3 adults, $1 ages 6–18 (under 6, free). Mar–Nov, daily 9am–5pm; Dec–Feb, daily 9am–4pm.

James Monroe came to Fredericksburg in 1786 to practice law and went on to be a senator; minister to France, England, and Spain; governor of Virginia; secretary of state; secretary of war; and fifth president of the United States. His shingle hangs outside. Within, all the furnishings are from the Monroes' White House years or their retirement home.

In a cozy office much like one Monroe might have used, you can peruse correspondence from Thomas Jefferson (a letter partially in code), James Madison, and Benjamin Franklin. Here, too, are the gun and canteen Monroe used in the American

Revolution. Other than Washington, he was the only president actually to fight in the war for independence, and he shared the grim winter at Valley Forge.

Also on display are two Rembrandt Peale portraits of Monroe, the outfits the Monroes wore at the court of Napoleon, silhouettes of the Monroes by Charles Willson Peale, his wife's teensy wedding slippers, his dueling pistols, and other memorabilia. The library of some 10,000 books is a reconstruction of Monroe's own personal collection.

Thirty-minute **tours** are given throughout the day.

The Rising Sun Tavern
1306 Caroline St., at Fauquier St. ☎ **540/371-1494.** Admission (without the block ticket) $3 adults, $1 ages 6–18 (under 6, free). Mar–Nov, daily 9am–5pm; Dec–Feb, daily 10am–4pm.

The Rising Sun was originally a residence, built in 1760 by Charles Washington, George's youngest brother, but it served as a tavern for some 30 years, beginning in the early 1790s. The building is preserved, not reconstructed, though the 17th- and 18th-century furnishings are not all originals. Thirty-minute tours are led by a tavern wench—an indentured servant sentenced to seven years for stealing a loaf of bread in England. The Rising Sun Tavern was a proper high-class tavern, she explains, not for riffraff. The gentlemen congregated over Madeira and cards in the Great Room, or had a rollicking good time in the Taproom over multicourse meals and numerous tankards of ale (the tavernkeeper's son will serve you wassail—a delicious spiced drink—during the tour). Meanwhile, ladies were consigned to the Retiring Room, where they would spend the entire day gossiping, doing needlework, and reading the Bible (novels were verboten).

Hugh Mercer Apothecary Shop
1020 Caroline St. at Amelia St. ☎ **540/373-3362.** Admission (without block ticket) $3 adults, $1 ages 6–18 (under 6, free). Mar–Nov, daily 9am–5pm; Dec–Feb, daily 10am–4pm.

Dr. Hugh Mercer practiced medicine and operated this shop from 1761 to 1776. A much-admired patriot and scholar, he followed his close friend George Washington into the Revolution as a brigadier-general. His soldiering career was short-lived, for he met a violent death at the Battle of Princeton in 1776. The warrior tradition continued in his family, however—Gen. George S. Patton was his great-great-great-grandson. A fascinating **tour** is given by a hostess in colonial dress, who explains how the doctor treated patients in those days.

Belmont
Washington St. (C.R. 1001), Falmouth, VA. ☎ **540/654-1015.** Admission (without block ticket) $3 adults, $1 ages 6–18 (under 6, free). Mar–Nov, Mon–Sat 10am–5pm, Sun 1–5pm; Dec–Mar, Mon–Sat 10am–4pm, Sun 1–4pm. From the visitors center, take U.S. 17N across the Falmouth Bridge, turn left at the traffic light in Falmouth, and go ¹/₄ mile up the hill; turn left on Washington Street (C.R. 1001) to Belmont.

Situated on 27 hillside acres overlooking the falls of the Rappahannock River, Belmont began as an 18th-century farmhouse (the central six rooms of the house date to the 1790s) and was enlarged to a 22-room estate by a later owner. The house is furnished with the art treasures, family heirlooms, and European antiques of famed American artist Gari Melchers, who lived here from 1916 until his death in 1932. His wife, Corinne, gave Belmont to the Commonwealth of Virginia in 1955. In addition to Melchers's own works, there are many wonderful paintings in the house—a watercolor sketch by Jan Brueghel, 19th-century paintings by Morisot, and works by Rodin. **Tours** (about an hour long) are given on the hour and half hour. They begin in the Stroh Visitor Center (Melchers's former carriage house), where you can view an orientation video.

Little Shop of Horrors

You've only to visit Dr. Hugh Mercer's Apothecary Shop to realize the ghastliness of getting sick in the 18th century.

Patients didn't read magazines while waiting to see this doctor, for Mercer's waiting room doubled as his operating room. Since opium, the only known anesthesia, was too expensive and too difficult to obtain, those waiting for treatment were often put to work holding down the screaming wretch under the knife. And even minor treatment seems ghoulish by today's standards, as displays in Mercer's shop attest. Leeches and other devices were used to bleed patients (George Washington may well have bled to death while undergoing treatment in his final days). A heated cup removed boils and carbuncles, a knife cut out cataracts, and an ominous-looking key extracted teeth (Dr. Mercer did it all). You can also see Mercer's saw, used to amputate limbs. Such instruments gave rise to the early slang name for doctors: sawbones.

Though he suffered a violent death at the Battle of Princeton in 1776, you can't help but feel that the doctor gave as good as he got.

Fredericksburg Area Museum and Cultural Center

907 Princess Anne St., at William St. ☎ **540/371-5668.** Admission (without block ticket) $3 adults, $1 ages 6–18 (under 6, free). Mar–Nov, Mon–Sat 9am–5pm, Sun 1–5pm; Dec–Feb, Mon–Sat 10am–4pm, Sun 1–4pm.

This municipal museum and cultural center occupies the 1816 Town Hall located in Market Square. In existence since 1733, Market Square for over a century was the center of trade and commerce in Fredericksburg, while Town Hall served as the city's social and legal center. Lafayette was entertained at Town Hall in 1824 with lavish parties and balls, and the building continued in its original function until 1982.

The first level is a changing exhibit area for displays relating to regional and cultural history. The second floor houses permanent exhibits on Native American settlements and pre-English explorers (the earliest years); natural history; Colonial settlement; the Revolution and Federal Fredericksburg, including architectural and decorative aspects of the period; the antebellum period (1825–61), focusing on the development of canals, early industry, railroads, and the cholera epidemic of 1833; the Civil War and its aftermath, graphically depicting the reality of the war as experienced by the local citizenry; Fredericksburg's evolution from town to city (1890–1920); and, finally, 20th-century Fredericksburg. Exhibits are enhanced by audiovisual presentations, crafts demonstrations, and symposiums. On the third floor, the hall's 19th-century Council Chamber is another area used for changing exhibits.

OTHER TOP ATTRACTIONS

Masonic Lodge No. 4

803 Princess Anne St. at Hanover St. ☎ **540/373-5885.** Admission $2 adults, $1 students, 50¢ children under 13. Mon–Sat 9am–4pm, Sun 1–4pm.

Not only is this the mother lodge of the father of our country, it's also one of the oldest Masonic lodges in America, established, it is believed, around 1735. Though the original building was down the street, Masons have been meeting at this address since 1812. On display are all kinds of Masonic paraphernalia and memorabilia, among them the Masonic punchbowl used to serve Lafayette, a Gilbert Stuart portrait of Washington in its original gilt Federalist frame, and the 1668 Bible on which Washington took his Masonic obligation (oath). **Tours** are given throughout the day.

Chatham

120 Chatham Lane. ☎ **540/373-4461.** Free admission. Daily 9am–5pm. Closed New Year's Day and Christmas. Take William Street (Va. 3) east across the river and follow the signs.

This pre-Revolutionary mansion built between 1768 and 1771 by wealthy planter William Fitzhugh has figured prominently in American history. Fitzhugh was a fourth-generation American who supported the Revolution both politically and financially. In the 18th century, Chatham was a center of southern hospitality, often visited by George Washington. During the Civil War the house, then belonging to J. Horace Lacy, served as headquarters for federal commanders and as a Union field hospital. Lincoln visited the house twice, and Clara Barton and Walt Whitman nursed the wounded here. Exhibits on the premises tell about the families who've owned Chatham and detail the role the estate played during the war. Plaques on the grounds identify battle landmarks. Five rooms and the grounds can be viewed on a self-guided tour, with National Park Service employees on hand to answer questions. A picnic area is on the premises.

MORE ATTRACTIONS

St. George's Episcopal Church

Princess Anne St. between George and William streets. ☎ **540/373-4133.** Free admission. Mon–Sat 9am–5pm (unless a wedding is taking place Sat), Sun services Labor Day–May at 8 and 11am, June–Labor Day at 10am.

Martha Washington's father and John Paul Jones's brother are buried in the graveyard of this church, and members of the first parish congregation included Mary Washington and Revolutionary War generals Hugh Mercer and George Weedon. The original church on this site was built in 1732, the current Romanesque structure in 1849. During the Battle of Fredericksburg the church was hit at least 25 times, and in 1863 it was used by General Lee's troops for religious revival meetings. In 1864, when wounded Union soldiers filled every available building in town, it served as a hospital. Do note the three signed Tiffany windows.

Presbyterian Church

George and Princess Anne streets. ☎ **540/373-7057.** Free admission. Sun service Labor Day–May at 11am, June–Labor day at 10am (go to church office at other times).

This Presbyterian church dates to the early 1800s, though the present Greek Revival building was completed in 1855—just in time to be shelled during the Civil War and, like St. George's, to serve as a hospital where Clara Barton nursed Union wounded. Cannonballs in the front left pillar and scars on the walls of the loft and belfry remain to this day. The present church bell replaced one that was given to the Confederacy to be melted down for making cannons.

The Courthouse

Princess Anne and George streets. Free admission. Mon–Fri 9am–4pm.

Those of you interested in architecture should be sure to look at the Gothic Revival courthouse, built in 1853. Its architect was James Renwick, who also designed New York's St. Patrick's Cathedral and, in Washington, D.C., the original Smithsonian "Castle" and Renwick Gallery. Exhibits in the lobby include copies of Mary Ball Washington's will and George Washington's address to the city council in 1784.

Washington Avenue

Washington Avenue, just above Kenmore, is the site of several notable monuments. A brochure detailing its historic buildings is available at the visitor center. Mary Washington is buried at **Meditation Rock,** a spot where she often came to pray and meditate; there's a monument in her honor. Just across the way is the **Thomas Jefferson Religious Freedom Monument,** commemorating Jefferson's Fredericksburg meeting with George Mason, Edmond Pendleton, George Wythe, and Thomas Ludwell Lee in 1777 to draft the Virginia Statute of Religious Freedom. The **Hugh Mercer Monument,** off Fauquier Street, honors the doctor and Revolutionary War general.

ACCOMMODATIONS

Chain lodgings are well represented in the area. You'll find a **Best Western, Hampton Inn, Econo Lodge,** and **Super 8** at I-95 and Va. 3 (Exit 130). This is Fredericksburg's major suburban shopping area, with the Spotsylvania Mall and several chain family restaurants. The following inns are in Old Town.

⑤ Fredericksburg Colonial Inn

1707 Princess Anne St., Fredericksburg, VA 22401. ☎ **540/371-5666.** Fax 540/371-5697. 30 rms, 10 suites. A/C TV. $55 double; $65 two-room family unit for four. Rates include morning coffee and doughnuts. AE, MC, V. Free parking.

Victorian furnishings of the Civil War era make this attractive spot a natural hub for Civil War buffs, and people participating in local Civil War reenactments often drop by; don't be surprised to see musket-toting Blues and Grays in the lobby. In the Conference Room there's a display of Civil War weaponry and Confederate dollars. The rooms are furnished with antiques (owner Alton Echols Jr. is an avid collector). Perhaps you'll draw a marble-top walnut dresser, a rag rug, a canopied bed, a bowl and pitcher, a Victorian sofa, or a bed that belonged to George Mason's son. The spacious lobby is comfortably furnished with wicker rocking chairs, and there's a player piano.

⊘ Kenmore Inn

1200 Princess Anne St., Fredericksburg, VA 22401. ☎ **540/371-7622** or 800/437-7622. Fax 540/371-5480. 14 rms, including 1 suite. A/C TEL. $95–$125 double, $150 suite. Rates include continental breakfast. Extra person $10. Packages available. AE, DC, MC, V. Street parking with free card from visitors center.

An elegant white pediment supported by fluted columns and a front porch with wicker chairs welcome you to this late-1700s mansion in Old Town on property originally owned by George Washington's brother-in-law, Fielding Lewis. Crystal chandeliers, Oriental rugs, polished Georgian side tables, and an enormous gold-framed mirror enhance the foyer. A sweeping staircase leads to the guest rooms— a handsome assortment of both cozy and spacious accommodations furnished with a mix of antiques, many in Regency style. Expect to find four-poster beds with pretty coverlets and lacy canopies, draperies framing louver-shuttered windows, antique chests, and walls hung with botanical prints and engravings. The house has eight working fireplaces, four in the bedrooms.

The inn serves lunch and afternoon tea Tuesday through Saturday and dinner daily. On Sunday there's brunch from 11:30am to 2:30pm. The Pub, a convivial spot, offers live music Friday and Saturday nights.

Richard Johnston Inn

711 Caroline St., Fredericksburg, VA 22401. ☎ **540/899-7606.** 7 rms, 2 suites. A/C. $90–$130 double. Rates include continental breakfast. Extra person $10. AE, MC, V. Free parking.

Two 18th-century brick row houses have been joined to form this elegantly restored inn directly across the street from the visitors center. The downstairs sitting rooms and dining room, where continental breakfast is served, are invitingly furnished. The mahogany furniture and Oriental rugs in the second-floor rooms in one house are more formal than in the other, where braided rugs, rockers, oak dressers, and four-poster beds lend a country charm. Third-floor dormer rooms are cozy, with low ceilings. The inn's original summer kitchen exudes rural charm, with brick floors, two antique beds, and a private entrance off the courtyard. The spacious and comfortable suites each offer a private courtyard entrance as well as a separate living room with TV, wet bar, and refrigerator. The owners have dogs in the house, but your pets aren't allowed.

DINING
EXPENSIVE

Le Lafayette
623 Caroline St., at Charlotte St. ☎ **540/373-6895.** Reservations recommended. Main courses $13–$22.50, Sunday brunch $20. AE, DC, DISC, MC, V. Tues–Thurs 11:30am–3pm and 5–9pm, Fri–Sat 11:30am–2:30pm and 5–10pm, Sun 11:30am–3pm and 5:30–9pm. FRENCH.

Owners Pierre and Edith Muyard have restored a Georgian-style private home, once called The Chimneys, to create an elegant restaurant named for the famed French marquis. The interior retains much of its period character, with original wide-plank flooring, paneling, and dining-room fireplaces. Tables are set with white cloths, gleaming china, and silver. During the day, sunlight pours in through the many-paned windows; at night, lamps on each table glow in crystal holders. Traditional French cuisine dominates the menu, but you'll also note many nouvelle innovations. Dinner might start with hearty onion soup gratinée, luscious curried backfin crab with endive, or savory duck-liver pâté with pistachios and Canadian bacon. Specialties among the entrees are poached salmon filet with sea scallops in lobster bouillon; fresh trout sautéed with shrimp, tomatoes, and toasted almonds; and sautéed veal scallopine with morel and dry-sherry cream sauce. There is an extensive wine list with both French and domestic offerings. The homemade desserts vary but usually include a delectable chocolate mousse cake. Sunday brunch offers a bountiful buffet and made-to-order omelets.

MODERATE

La Petite Auberge
311 William St., between Princess Anne and Charles streets. ☎ **540/371-2727.** Reservations recommended, especially at dinner. Main courses $10–$19; early-bird dinner $13. AE, CB, DC, MC, V. Mon–Fri 11:30am–2:30pm; Mon–Sat 5:30–10pm (early-bird dinner Mon–Thurs 5:30–7pm). FRENCH.

The delightful La Petite Auberge was designed to look like a garden, an effect enhanced by white latticework and garden furnishings. Unpainted brick walls are hung with copper pots and cheerful oil paintings, and candlelit tables are adorned with fresh flowers. A cozy lounge adjoins.

The menu changes daily. A recent visit included a salade niçoise, tortellini in cream sauce, *poulet aux champignons*, and avocado stuffed with curried chicken salad. The early-bird dinner here is an attractive offering—soup, salad, a choice of seven entrees from the regular dinner menu, and homemade ice cream.

Ristorante Renato
422 William St., at Prince Edward St. ☎ **540/317-8228.** Reservations recommended, especially on weekends. Main courses $10–$22 (most under $16); lunch special $6; early-bird

dinner $11. AE, MC, V. Mon–Fri 11:30am–2pm, daily 4:30–10pm (early-bird dinner Mon–Fri 4:30–7pm). ITALIAN.

The decor of this very good and very reasonably priced Italian eatery is homey— candlelit (at night) white-linened tables adorned with fresh flowers, ceramic candelabra chandeliers, oil paintings of Italy lining the walls, and a working fireplace. A small room to one side with booths is especially cozy. In addition to its regular menu, Renato offers a complete luncheon featuring salad, homebaked bread, and a choice of such entrees as eggplant parmigiana, fettuccine Alfredo, or steamed mussels in white sauce. A similar early-bird dinner adds dessert and a demicarafe of wine.

Smythe's Cottage

303 Fauquier St., at Princess Anne St. ☎ **540/373-1645.** Reservations suggested on weekends. Main courses $10–$15. DISC, MC, V. Mon and Wed–Thurs 11am–9pm, Fri–Sat 11am–10pm, Sun noon–9pm. TRADITIONAL SOUTHERN.

At quaintly charming Smythe's Cottage you can dine on traditional Virginia fare on the site of a blacksmith's stable once operated by George Washington's brother. The current building, dating from 1840, was once a blacksmith's stable. The original owner hailed from an old Virginia family, hence the photograph of General Grant upside down next to a photo of her great-great-grandfather, who was hanged by the Union army in the Civil War. The low-ceilinged interior is extremely cozy, with Colonial-style furnishings and old oil portraits and family memorabilia hung on the walls. In summer there's al fresco dining in a flower-bordered garden.

The innlike ambiance is enhanced by a menu featuring dinner items like peanut soup, Brunswick stew, and delicious chicken pot pie. The entrees are served with a basket of oven-fresh bread, soup or salad, and vegetable. The homemade desserts include hot cherry or apple turnovers. Lunch here is very reasonably priced.

Sophia Street Station

503 Sophia St., at Lafayette Blvd. ☎ **540/371-3355.** Reservations recommended for the River Room, especially on weekends. Main courses $8–$15; Sun brunch $10, $4 for children 6–12, under 6 free. AE, DISC, MC, V. Mon–Thurs 11:30am–11pm, Fri–Sat 11:30am–midnight, Sun 10am–10pm (brunch 10am–2pm). AMERICAN.

Sophia Street Station, on the Rappahannock River, can offer a festive evening's entertainment with music in the clubby front room or a more sedate ambiance in the formal River Room, which has a dining terrace overlooking the river. Appetizers and snacks range from shrimp cocktail and Buffalo chicken wings to a giant nacho platter. Main dishes—like New York strip steak, filet mignon wrapped with bacon and topped with béarnaise sauce, or shrimp and scallops over linguine—are served with vegetable, baked potato or rice, and soup or house salad. There's a special raw bar Thursday from 5 to 8pm with live jazz. There are croissant sandwiches and burgers, including a blackened one with Cajun spices, anytime. The lavish Sunday brunch buffet features omelets and crêpes made to order, salads, hot roast beef, curried chicken, and much more.

INEXPENSIVE

Sammy T's

801 Caroline St., at Hanover St. ☎ **540/371-2008.** Reservations not accepted. Sandwiches $2.50–$5.50; main courses $4.50–$8. DISC, MC, V. Mon–Sat 7am–midnight, Sun 11am–9pm. AMERICAN/NATURAL FOOD.

Sammy T's is one of the most popular pubs in town and offers a relaxed, tasteful setting and a creative health-food orientation. It has a rustic feel, with large overhead fans, a pressed-tin ceiling, roomy knotty-pine booths, a long oak bar, and painted wood walls adorned with framed art posters. Everything on the menu is made from scratch, with an emphasis on natural ingredients. Breakfast, served until 11am, features Belgian waffles and buckwheat pancakes with a choice of toppings, ham or sausage, biscuits, and a fresh fruit bowl with yogurt and granola. The lunch and dinner menu has many vegetarian items, such as a baked potato stuffed with mushrooms, tomatoes, walnuts, sunflower seeds, three cheeses, and sprouts, all topped with sour cream and served with soup. Entrees like broiled salmon steak, vegetarian lasagna, and chicken parmesan over fettuccine are other enticing possibilities.

2 The Civil War Battlefields

Fredericksburg has never forgotten its Civil War victories and defeats. In **Fredericksburg and Spotsylvania National Military Park** you can take all or part of a 75-mile-long self-guided auto tour of 16 important sites relating to 4 major battles.

Starting point is the **Fredericksburg Battlefield Visitor Center,** 1013 Lafayette Blvd. (U.S. 1 Business), at Sunken Road (☎ 540/373-6122), where you can get detailed tour brochures and rent 2^{1}/$_{2}$-hour-long auto-tour tapes ($2.75 per battlefield for cassette player and tape, $4.25 to buy each tape). We strongly recommend the tapes, since they definitely enhance the experience, and renting a player along with them will allow you to get out of your car and still hear the informative commentary. The center offers a 12-minute slide-show orientation and related exhibits. Open daily from 9am to 5pm, with extended hours in summer determined annually. There were no entrance fees when we recently visited the battlefields, but this could change.

For advance **information,** write to the Superintendent, Fredericksburg and Spotsylvania National Military Park, 120 Chatham Lane, Fredericksburg, VA 22405.

BATTLE OF FREDERICKSBURG

Lee used the Rappahannock River as a natural line of defense for much of the war, while the Union army's goal was to cross it and head for Richmond. The Battle of Fredericksburg took place from December 11 to 15, 1862, when the Union army under Gen. Ambrose E. Burnside crossed the river into Fredericksburg via pontoon bridges. Burnside made a major mistake when he sent the main body of his 100,000 men uphill against Lee's 75,000 troops, most of whom were dug in behind a stone wall along Sunken Road at the base of Marye's Heights. Then open space, the ground below the heights became a bloody killing field as Lee's cannon, firing from the hill, mowed down the Yankees like shooting ducks in a barrel. The stone wall—some parts original, some reconstructed—stands beside the visitor center at the base of Marye's Heights. The driving tour begins here at the visitor center, but before you go, examine the wall and climb up the heights for a fine view over the town.

BATTLE OF CHANCELLORSVILLE

President Lincoln fired Burnside after the Marye's Heights massacre. Under his replacement, Gen. Joseph Hooker, the Union forces crossed the river above Fredericksburg in late April, 1863, and advanced to Chancellorsville, a crossroads 10 miles west of Fredericksburg on the Orange Turnpike (now Va. 3). When Lee rushed westward to meet him, Hooker dug in. In a surprise attack, Stonewall Jackson flanked Hooker's line on May 2 and won a spectacular victory. Unfortunately, Jackson was inadvertently shot by his own men that same night. Field surgeons amputated his left arm and moved him to Guinea Station, 27 miles away, where he could be evacuated by train. Pneumonia set in, however, and Jackson died there on May 10. By then, Lee had driven the Union army back across the Rappahannock.

The **Chancellorsville Visitor Center** is on Va. 3 (☎ 540/786-2880). Stop there to see another 12-minute audiovisual orientation and related exhibits. Once again, an auto-tour tape is available. The center is open daily from 9am to 5pm.

Now part of the park, the **Jackson Shrine** where the general died is at the junction of C.R. 606 and C.R. 607, about 27 miles southeast of Chancellorsville. From I-95, take Exit 118 at Thornburg and follow the signs east on C.R. 606.

BATTLE OF THE WILDERNESS

A year later and now under the aggressive Ulysses S. Grant, the Union once again crossed the Rappahannock and advanced south to Wilderness Tavern, 5 miles west of Chancellorsville near what is now the junction of Va. 3 and Va. 20. Lee advanced to meet him, thus setting up the first battle between these two great generals. For the two days of May 5 and 6, 1864, the protagonist armies fought in the tangled thickets of the Wilderness. The battle was a stalemate, but instead of retreating as his predecessors had done, Grant backed off and then went around Lee toward his ultimate target, Richmond.

BATTLE OF SPOTSYLVANIA COURT HOUSE

Lee next tried to stop Grant on May 12 at Spotsylvania Court House, on the shortest road south (now Va. 208). Taking advantage of thick fog and wet Confederate gunpowder, Union troops breached the Southerners' line. When Lee's reinforcements arrived, the two sides spent 20 hours in the war's most intense hand-to-hand combat at a site known as Bloody Angle. During the fighting, Lee built new fortifications to the rear, which he successfully defended. Instead of pushing the fight to the finish, however, Grant again backed off and moved his entire army around Lee's toward Richmond. It was the end of major fighting in the Fredericksburg area, as the war moved progressively south to its ultimate conclusion 11 months later at Appomattox.

3 The Northern Neck

A long, narrow strip of land stretching east from Fredericksburg, the Northern Neck is bounded by the Potomac and Rappahannock rivers and Chesapeake Bay. This picturesque country is a blend of venerable colonial history and saltwater vitality. The Pope's Creek Plantation, site of George Washington's birthplace, and Stratford Hall, the magnificent ancestral home of the Lee family, are both on the Potomac riverfront. Nearby, the Ingleside Plantation Winery offers tours and tastings.

In the riverfront town of Irvington is the Tides Inn, one of the premier resorts in the country. Nearby stands Christ Church, which has been described as the most perfect example of Colonial church architecture in the United States. And from Victorian Reedville, you can go fishing or depart on cruises to remote Tangier Island out in the Chesapeake.

ESSENTIALS

VISITOR INFORMATION   For **information,** contact the **Northern Neck Travel Council,** P.O. Box 312, Reedville, VA 22539 (☎ 800/453-6167, fax 804/453-3915).

GETTING THERE   By Car   From Fredericksburg, take Va. 3 East, which traverses the length of the peninsula. From Fredericksburg, Washington Birthplace is 40 miles; Irvington, 95 miles. You can make a scenic loop tour of the peninsula by taking Va. 3 to Irvington, Va. 200 to Reedville, then U.S. 360, Va. 202, and

Va. 3 back to Fredericksburg. Alternatively, you can drive directly west to Richmond via U.S. 360.

AREA CODE   The telephone area code for most of the Northern Neck is 804 (Fredericksburg and its suburbs are in 540).

WHAT TO SEE & DO
ATTRACTIONS

◎ George Washington Birthplace National Monument

Va. 204, off Va. 3, Washington's Birthplace, VA. ☎ **804/224-1732.** Admission $2; free for children under 17. Daily 9am–5pm. Closed New Year's Day and Christmas.

Encompassing some 500 acres along a tributary of the Potomac, Popes Creek Plantation is a living-history display, complete with a charming re-creation of George Washington's first home, costumed guides, and crafts demonstrations. The first child of Augustine and Mary Ball Washington, the first president was born on February 22, 1732, and lived here until he was 3¹/₂, when the family moved to the Mount Vernon estate. The land was first settled by Washington's great-grandfather, John, in the mid-17th century. The farmhouse burned down in 1779 and was never rebuilt. The re-created building we see today is called Memorial House. There are no historic records detailing what the house looked like, so this memorial, operated by the National Park Service, is a representation of a typical farmhouse of Washington's childhood, with antique furnishings appropriate to the period.

At the visitors center, a 14-minute film called *A Childhood Place* evokes life at the plantation. There is an uphill walk of some 300 yards to the historic area; transportation is provided for those unable to walk that distance. In the historic area are the birthplace site, an herb garden, a separate building housing the plantation's kitchen (cooking demonstrations are often in progress here), and a weaving room. Graves of some Washington family members, including George's father, are in a small burial ground on the property.

Tours are offered throughout the day. Children will enjoy particularly the Colonial farm, with horses, chickens, and cows. A picnic area is available but no refreshments, except for soda and vending-machine snacks, are sold at the park.

Ingleside Plantation Winery

Oak Grove. ☎ **804/224-8687.** Free admission. Mon–Sat 10am–5pm, Sun noon–5pm. Closed major holidays. Traveling east from Fredericksburg on Va. 3, turn right in Oak Grove on C.R. 638 and continue about 2¹/₂ miles south.

The rich soil and mild climate of the Northern Neck provide ideal grape-growing conditions for this 2,500-acre plantation winery. In addition to winery tours, tastings, and a gift shop selling wine-related items, Ingleside has a small exhibit area displaying Colonial wine bottles, Chesapeake waterfowl carvings, and Native American artifacts.

◎ Stratford Hall Plantation

Va. 214, 2 mi north of Va. 3, Stratford. ☎ **804/493-8038.** Admission $7 adults, $6 seniors, $3 children 6–18, free for children under 6. Daily 9am–4:30pm. Closed Thanksgiving, Christmas, New Year's Day.

This is one of the great houses of the South, magnificently set on 1,600 acres above the Potomac. It is renowned not only for its distinctive architectural style but also for the illustrious family who lived there. Thomas Lee (1690–1750), a planter who later served as governor of the Virginia colony, built Stratford in the late 1730s. Five of his sons played major roles in the forming of the new nation, most notably

Richard Henry Lee, who made the motion for independence in the Continental Congress in 1776. He and Francis Lightfoot Lee were the only brothers to sign the Declaration of Independence. Gen. Henry "Light-Horse Harry" Lee, a cousin and hero of the Revolution, married into this family. He was a friend of George Washington and father of the most famous Lee child born at Stratford—Robert E.

The H-shaped manor house, its four dependencies, its coach house, and its stables have been brilliantly restored. On approaching the imposing two-story-high stone entrance staircase, you'll meet a costumed guide who will point out one of the mansion's most striking features—the brick chimney groupings that flank the roofline.

The paneled Great Hall, one of the finest rooms to have survived from Colonial times, runs the depth of the house and has an inverted tray ceiling. On the same floor are bedrooms and a nursery, where you can see Robert E. Lee's crib.

Tours conclude in the kitchen and estate offices. You can then stroll the meadows and gardens of this 1,600-acre estate, still operated as a working farm.

Also on the estate is a rustic log-cabin-style public dining room with a screened in terrace; it offers breakfasts, light snacks, a plantation lunch with fried chicken, crabcakes, or ham ($8 adults, $4 children), and its own vintage chardonnay and cabernet sauvignon wines.

Fishermen's Museum

Main Street, Reedville. ☎ **540/453-6529.** Admission by donation. May 1–Oct 31, daily 10:30am–4:30pm; Nov 1–Dec 23 and Feb 15–Apr 30, Sat–Sun 1–3pm. Closed Dec 24–Feb 15. From Va. 3 east, take U.S. 360 east to Reedville.

The small village of Reedville on Cockrell's Creek, an inlet of Chesapeake Bay, provides a living image of the past with its Victorian mansions and seafaring atmosphere. The Fishermen's Museum consists of the 1875 William Walker House, restored to appear as it did in 1900, and the Covington Building, which houses a permanent collection and special exhibits. It commemorates the watermen who participate in the town's leading industry, based on a small, toothless fish, the menhaden, which is of little use for human consumption but extremely valuable for its by-products: meal, oil, and protein supplements used in animal feeds. Capt. Elijah Reed, who came to this area from Maine in 1874, built a menhaden factory, a steamboat wharf, and a home.

✪ Historic Christ Church

C.R. 646, off Va. 200, 2 mi north of Irvington. ☎ **804/438-6855.** Free admission. Church, daily 9am–5pm. Carter Reception Center, Apr–Thanksgiving, Mon–Fri 10am–4pm, Sat 1–4pm, Sun 2–5pm. Closed Christmas.

Elegant in its simplicity and virtually unchanged since it was completed in 1735, Christ Church, listed on the National Register of Historic Places, was the gift of Robert "King" Carter. Carter offered to finance the building of the church if his parents' graves remained in the chancel. In the chancel today are interred the bodies of John Carter, four of his five wives, and two infant children. Robert Carter's tomb is on the church grounds. Among the descendants of the Carters are eight governors of Virginia; two presidents of the United States (the two Harrisons); Gen. Robert E. Lee; and Edward D. White, a chief justice of the U.S. Supreme Court.

The building is cruciform in shape, its brick facade laid in a pleasing Flemish bond pattern, with a three-color design that saves the expanse of brick from monotony. Inside, the three-decker pulpit is in excellent condition, and all 26 original pews remain. The building has no artificial heat or light and is now used for services only during the summer.

A CRUISE TO TANGIER ISLAND

Out in the Chesapeake Bay lies quaint and still relatively remote Tangier Island, whose inhabitants own no cars and still speak with the Elizabethan brogue of their colonial ancestors. **Tangier Island Cruises** (☎ 804/453-2628) leave from Buzzards Point Marina, off U.S. 360 near Reedville, at 10am daily from May to October 15. The voyage takes 90 minutes each way, and passengers are treated to a narrated tour of Tangier once they get there (see the Hampton Roads & Eastern Shore chapter later in this book for more information about the island). Fares are $18.50 adults, $9.25 children 4 to 13, free for kids 3 and under.

SPORTS & OUTDOOR ACTIVITIES

CHARTER FISHING   With two rivers and the Chesapeake Bay surrounding the Northern Neck, it's little wonder that the area is a favorite destination for fishing. Most folks trailer their own boats to the Neck, but several "party" boats are available for charter from May to December. From Reedsville on the bay, you can go out with **Pittman's Charters** (☎ 804/453-3643), which operates the *Mystic Lady,* or on Capt. Fred Biddlecomb's *Dudley* (☎ 804/453-3568). **Capt. Billy's Charters** (☎ 804/ 580-7292) offers both fishing trips and sightseeing cruises from Heathville, near Reedsville. Rates are about $350 a day per boat. Reservations are essential, so call ahead.

CANOEING   A full-service canoe livery based in Walkerton, **Tidewater River Adventure** (☎ 804/769-1602) has guided trips, excursions, and expeditions on the area's rivers and broad creeks.

GOLF   In addition to the courses shared by guests of The Tides Inn and The Tides Lodge (see below), the area has other links: **Bushfield Golf Course** in Mt. Holly (☎ 804/472-2602); **Cameron Hills Golf Links** in King George (☎ 540/ 775-4653); **Quinton Oaks Golf Course** (☎ 804/529-5367) and **Village Green Golf Club** (☎ 804/529-6332), both in Callao; and **Windjammer Golf Course** at Windmill Point Marine Resort (☎ 804/435-1166). The latter two have 9 holes.

ACCOMMODATIONS

✪ The Tides Inn

King Carter Drive (P.O. Box 480), Irvington, VA 22480. ☎ **804/438-5000** or 800/TIDES INN. 110 rms. A/C TV TEL. $125–$189 per person double. Family rate for two rooms $400 per couple (no charge for children under 4), $43 for children 4–15, $53 for children 16 and over. Rates include breakfast and dinner daily. Golf packages available. Pets $8 per animal (in some rooms). AE, MC, V. Closed early Jan to mid-Mar. Free parking. From Va. 3, take Va. 200 south 2 miles to Irvington, turn right at the sign to end of King Carter Drive.

Recently rated one of America's top 20 resorts by Condé Nast's *Traveler* magazine, The Tides Inn has maintained a tradition of gracious service under the auspices of the Stephens family since 1947. The sprawling resort complex consists of several low-rise buildings encircling a nicely landscaped entrance. Guests can choose accommodations in the Main Building, where the dining room and gift shop are located, or in the Windsor or Lancaster House, where the rooms are more spacious and have dressing rooms, living areas, and, in some cases, balconies overlooking Carter's Creek. The sports facilities are extensive here, with no fewer than three golf courses and many boating and watersports opportunities.

Dining/Entertainment: For the duration of their stay, guests are assigned a table in the lovely main dining room, which overlooks the creek. Food is also available at Cap'n B's at the Golden Eagle golf course, and at Commodore's, an airy glass-enclosed room serving informal buffet luncheons adjacent to the pool. Menus feature seafood items like soft-shell crabs and fried-oyster sandwiches, along with prime rib and pork tenderloin. The Chesapeake Club lounge, adjacent to the dining room, has exquisite wood paneling, panoramic views, music, and dancing.

Services: Nightly turndown, morning newspaper, no surcharge for local or long-distance phone calls.

Facilities: Yacht cruises; heated saltwater pool; unlimited tennis, sailing, paddleboating, canoeing, bicycling, croquet; playroom with Ping Pong, billiards, electronic games, shuffleboard; complimentary nearby health club with aerobics classes, weights, sauna, racquetball; two 18-hole golf courses, and one 9-hole par-three course plus driving range and putting green; gift and resort-wear shops.

The Tides Lodge

P.O. Box 309, Irvington, VA 22480. ☎ **804/438-6000** or 800/248-4337. Fax 804/438-5950. 60 rms, 1 cottage. A/C TV TEL. $100–$130 double (room only), $90–$105 per person double occupancy (including breakfast and dinner); $200–$250 cottage. $12 per person daily service charge in lieu of tipping. Golf and other packages available. AE, MC, V. Free parking. From Va. 3, take Va. 200 south 2 miles to Irvington, follow signs.

Another branch of the Stephenses operates this less charming but also less expensive version of the family's Tides Inn across Carter's Creek. A Scottish motif prevails in both the public areas and in the comfortable, motel-style rooms, whose walls are adorned with hunting and fishing scenes. Men must wear jackets with or without ties at dinner in the Royal Stewart Dining Room, but they can get away with collars only in the casual Binnacle Restaurant, which overlooks the creek. There's also a Sandwich Bar beside a saltwater swimming pool. The Royal Stewart has dancing three nights a week, and McD's Pub has weekend entertainment. Guests here can share The Tides Inn golf courses and cruises, but they have their own pool, tennis courts, and exercise room.

Cedar Grove Bed & Breakfast Inn

Fleeton Road and Route 1, Box 2535, Reedville, VA 22539. ☎ **804/453-3915.** 3 rms. $65–$90 double. Rates include full breakfast. MC, V. Free parking. From Reedville, follow Fleeton Road (C.R. 657) approximately 3 miles, to Cedar Grove.

Surrounded by farm fields, Cedar Grove is a stately 1913 Colonial Revival house that looks out over Chesapeake Bay and the lighthouse at the mouth of the Great Wicomico River. Arctic swans spend the winter here in the coves and marshes of the bay, and ospreys nest on nearby Big Fleet's Pond. In this tranquil setting, hosts Susan and Bob Tipton run an appealing B&B, with three spacious guest rooms boasting white wicker and Victorian pieces. One room has a private balcony. Downstairs, the formal parlor features Oriental rugs and Victorian Eastlake furnishings. The sun room is a pleasant spot to read or watch TV. Outdoors are a tennis court and croquet, and bicycles are available for touring the area. Less active types can kick back in a hammock or the rocking chairs on the porch.

7

Charlottesville & Lynchburg: The Piedmont Area

With the serene Blue Ridge Mountains on the horizon to the west, the rolling hills of the Piedmont reveal a scenic pastoral landscape. No wonder Peter Jefferson, coming here to survey the land, decided to settle and amassed hundreds of acres. His son Thomas Jefferson, America's third president, inherited not only his father's property but also an abiding attachment to the land where he, too, spent much of his life associating with two other presidents, James Madison and James Monroe.

Today Charlottesville is a lively town, filled with visitors drawn by the monuments to Thomas Jefferson's genius and the University of Virginia he founded. The historic tobacco town of Lynchburg, on the James River, has interesting sights of its own, including Jefferson's beloved country retreat and the tiny village of Appomattox Court House, where Robert E. Lee surrendered to Ulysses S. Grant.

1 Charlottesville

72 miles W of Richmond; 120 miles SW of Washington, D.C.

It was in Charlottesville that Thomas Jefferson, one of America's most passionate believers in freedom and human rights, built his famous mountaintop home, Monticello; selected the site for and helped plan James Monroe's Ash Lawn-Highland; designed his "academical village," the University of Virginia; and died at home. "All my wishes end where I hope my days will end," he wrote, "at Monticello."

Established in 1762 as the county seat for Albemarle, the town had its Court Square complete with Court House, jail, whipping post, pillory, and stocks to keep fractious citizens in line. The Court House doubled as marketplace in those early days and served as a church with rotating services for different denominations (Jefferson called it the "Common Temple"). Elections were held in Court Square followed by raucous political celebrations. The taverns across the street were well patronized.

Along with neighbor James Madison, Jefferson and Monroe were instrumental in developing the emerging nation. In addition to writing the Declaration of Independence, Jefferson advocated freedom of religion, public education, and the abolition of slavery. Madison was instrumental in developing the Constitution and its Bill of

Charlottesville

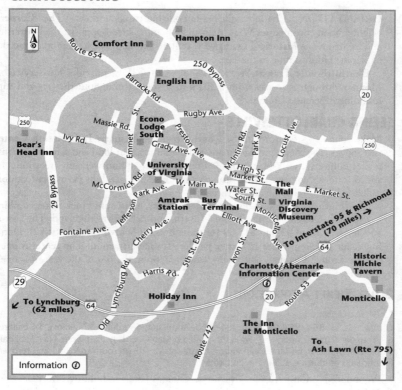

Rights. One of the two American presidents actually to fight in the Revolution, Monroe nearly doubled the new nation's size by negotiating the Louisiana Purchase, and he kept Colonial powers out of the Americas by declaring the Monroe Doctrine.

Though today's Charlottesville is a cosmopolitan center, it is still sufficiently unchanged and pastoral for visitors to imagine themselves back in Colonial times when Jefferson would ride 2 miles on horseback to visit his friend Monroe.

ESSENTIALS

VISITOR INFORMATION   The **Charlottesville/Albemarle Information Center,** P.O. Box 161, Charlottesville, VA 22902 (☎ 804/977-1783), is in the Thomas Jefferson Visitor Center on Va. 20, at exit 121 off I-64 (☎ 804/977-1783). Open daily from 9am to 5:30pm.

GETTING THERE   **By Plane**   USAir, Delta, and United fly to **Charlottesville-Albemarle Airport,** 201 Bowen Loop (☎ 804/973-8341).

By Car   Charlottesville is immediately accessible by I-64 from east or west and by U.S. 29 from north or south. I-64 connects with I-81 at Staunton and with I-95 at Richmond.

By Train   **Amtrak** (☎ 804/296-4559, or 800/872-7245) has daily service to points north and south. The station is at 810 W. Main St.

By Bus   The **Greyhound/Trailways Bus Terminal** is at 310 W. Main St. (☎ 804/295-5131 or 800/231-2222).

ORIENTATION Charlottesville has not one but two downtowns: **The "Corner"** neighborhood encompasses West Main and adjoining streets opposite the University of Virginia, while **historic downtown** is centered around a pedestrian mall and the old Court House a mile to the east.

Charlottesville Transit Service (☎ 804/296-RIDE) provides bus service on Monday through Saturday from 6:30am to 6:30pm throughout the city and surrounding Albemarle County.

SEEING CHARLOTTESVILLE

Make your first stop in town the **Charlottesville/Albemarle Information Center** (see above). The center provides maps and literature about local and state attractions, makes same-day, walk-in hotel/motel reservations, and answers any questions. In addition to welcoming visitors, the center houses a marvelous permanent exhibit called "Thomas Jefferson at Monticello."

The information center sells a **Presidents' Pass,** a discount block ticket combining admission to Monticello, Michie Tavern, and Ash Lawn-Highland. The cost is $17 for ages 12 to 59 and $15.50 for those over 59 (a savings of about $2). Don't buy it for children under 12—they pay less at each attraction. The center is open March through October, daily from 9am to 5:30pm; the rest of the year, it is open until 5pm.

BLOCK-TICKET ATTRACTIONS

✪ Monticello

Off Va. 53. ☎ **804/984-9822** or 984-9800. Admission $8 adults, $7 seniors, $4 children 6–11, under 6 free. 25-minute guided tours offered Mar–Oct, daily 8am–5pm; Nov–Feb, daily 9am–4:30pm. From the Monticello Visitors Center on Va. 20, go south to Va. 53 and turn left; Monticello's entrance is about 2 miles farther.

Pronounced "Mon-ti-*chel*-lo," the home Thomas Jefferson built over 40 years from 1769 to 1809 is considered an architectural masterpiece. Is was the first Virginia plantation to sit atop a mountain rather than beside a river. Rejecting the Georgian architecture that characterized his time, Jefferson opted instead for the 16th-century Italian style of Andrea Palladio. Later, during his five-year term as minister to France, he was influenced by the homes of nobles at the court of Louis XVI, and after returning home in 1789, he enlarged Monticello, incorporating features of the Parisian buildings he so admired.

Today the house is restored as closely as possible to its appearance during Jefferson's retirement years. Nearly all its furniture and other household objects were owned by Jefferson or his family. The garden has been extended to its original 1,000-foot length, and Mulberry Row—where slaves and free artisans lived and labored in light industrial shops such as a joinery, smokehouse-dairy, blacksmith shop-nailery, and carpenter's shop—has been excavated. Guided tours of the gardens and Mulberry Row are available from April through October.

Jefferson's grave is in the family burial ground (still in use). After visiting the graveyard, you can take a shuttle bus back to the visitor parking lot or walk through the woods via a delightful path. There is a lovely wooded picnic area with tables and grills on the premises, and, in summer, lunch fare can be purchased.

It's best to avoid weekends, when the tourist traffic is heaviest; the 8am tour is advised during summer.

Historic Michie Tavern

683 Thomas Jefferson Pkwy. (Va. 683). ☎ **804/977-1234.** Admission $5.50 adults, $5 seniors, $2 children 6–11, under 6 free. Self-guided tour with recorded narratives, daily 9am–5pm.

Jefferson Survives

The phrase "Renaissance man" might have been coined to describe Thomas Jefferson. Perhaps our most important founding father, he was a lawyer, an architect, a scientist, a musician, a writer, an educator, a horticulturist, and one of our young country's first gourmets.

After writing the Declaration of Independence, Jefferson served as governor of Virginia, ambassador to France, secretary of state, and two terms as president, during which he nearly doubled the size of the United States by engineering the Louisiana Purchase from France. He also helped found one of America's first political parties.

Yet despite all his national and international achievements, Jefferson ordered that his gravestone be inscribed: "Here Was Buried Thomas Jefferson/Author Of The Declaration Of American Independence/Of The Statute Of Virginia For Religious Freedom/And Father Of The University Of Virginia."

Jefferson was 83 when he died at Monticello on July 4, 1826, exactly 50 years to the day after his Declaration of Independence was signed at Philadelphia. Ironically, his fellow revolutionary—but later heated political enemy—John Adams, lay on his own deathbed in Massachusetts. Unaware that Jefferson had died a short time earlier, Adams's last words were: "Jefferson survives."

Closed New Year's Day and Christmas. From the Visitors Center on Va. 20, go south to Thomas Jefferson Parkway (Va. 683) and turn left; Michie Tavern is about 1 mile farther.

In 1746, Scotsman "Scotch John" Michie (pronounced "Mickey") purchased 1,152 acres of land from Patrick Henry's father, and in 1784 Michie's son, William, built this historic tavern on a well-traveled stagecoach route at Earlysville, 17 miles northwest of Charlottesville. A wealthy businesswoman, Josephine Henderson, saw its value as a historic structure and in 1927 had it moved to its present location and painstakingly reconstructed. Michie Tavern stands today as a tribute to early preservationists.

Behind the tavern are reproductions of the "dependencies"—log kitchen, dairy, smokehouse, ice house, root cellar, and "necessary" (note the not-so-soft corncobs). The general store has been re-created, along with an excellent crafts shop, and the **Virginia Wine Museum** is on the premises. Behind the store is a grist mill that has operated continuously since 1797.

Dining: Unless you're picnicking at Monticello, plan your visit to Michie Tavern to coincide with lunchtime, for hot meals are still served to weary travelers for reasonable pence in the "Ordinary," a converted log cabin with original hand-hewn walls and beamed ceilings. An all-you-can-eat buffet of southern fare is priced at under $10 for adults and $5 for children 6 to 11 (under 6, free). You'll dine off pewter plates at rustic oak tavern tables, and in winter there's a blazing fire. The meal is served daily from 11:30am to 3pm.

✪ Ash Lawn-Highland

C.R. 795. ☎ **804/293-9539.** Admission $6 adults, $5.50 seniors, $3 children 6–11, under 6 free. Mar–Oct, daily 9am–6pm; Nov–Feb, daily 10am–5pm. Follow the directions to Monticello. Ash Lawn is 2¹/₂ miles past Monticello on James Monroe Parkway (C.R. 795).

Fifth president James Monroe fought in the Revolution, was wounded in Trenton, and went on to hold more public offices than any other president. Monroe's close friendship with Thomas Jefferson brought him to the Blue Ridge mountains of Charlottesville, where Jefferson wished to create "a society to our taste." In 1793, Monroe purchased 1,000 acres adjacent to Monticello and built an estate he called Highland (the name Ash Lawn dates to 1838). Before he could settle in, however, Washington named him minister to France and sent him to Paris for 3 years. During his absence, Jefferson sent gardeners over to start orchards, and the Madisons also made agricultural contributions. Nevertheless, by the time Monroe returned he was in financial difficulties, and his "cabin castle" developed along more modest lines than originally intended. When he retired from office in 1825, his debts totaled $75,000, and he was forced to sell the beloved farm where he had hoped to spend his last days. A later owner, John Massey, built a two-story addition to the main house in 1884.

Today Monroe's 535-acre estate is owned and maintained as a working farm by his alma mater, the College of William and Mary. Livestock, vegetable and herb gardens, and Colonial craft demonstrations recall the elements of daily life on the Monroes' plantation. Horses, sheep, and cattle graze in the fields while peacocks roam the boxwood gardens. Five of the original rooms remain, along with the basement kitchen, the overseer's cottage, restored slave quarters, and the old smokehouse. On a 40-minute **house tour,** you'll see some of the family's original furnishings and artifacts and learn a great deal about the fifth president.

Many special events take place at Ash Lawn-Highland: The outdoor **Summer Festival** features opera and contemporary music performances, and a major Colonial arts festival, **Plantation Days,** in July showcases dozens of 18th-century crafts, historic reenactments, period music performances, and dancing horses (dressage).

On the grounds are a gift shop and picnic tables.

MORE ATTRACTIONS IN TOWN

✪ University of Virginia

University Avenue. ☎ **804/924-7969.** 45-minute tours given daily at 10 and 11am and 2, 3, and 4pm. Self-guided walking tour brochures available. Closed 3 weeks around Christmas.

Jefferson's University of Virginia is graced with spacious lawns, serpentine-walled gardens, colonnaded pavilions, and a classical rotunda inspired by the Pantheon in Rome. Jefferson regarded its creation as one of his three greatest achievements—all the more remarkable since it was begun in his 73rd year. He was in every sense the university's father, since he conceived it, wrote its charter, raised money for its construction, drew the plans, selected the site, laid the cornerstone in 1817, supervised construction, served as the first rector, selected the faculty, and created the curriculum. His good friends Monroe and Madison sat with him on the first board, and Madison succeeded him as rector, serving for eight years.

Focal point of the university and starting point for **tours** is the Rotunda (at Rugby Road), today restored as Jefferson designed it. Some 600 feet of tree-dotted lawn extends from the south portico of the Rotunda to what is now Cabell Hall, designed at the turn of the 20th century by Stanford White. On either side of the lawn are pavilions still used for faculty housing, each of a different architectural style "to serve as specimens for the Architectural lecturer." Behind are large gardens (originally used by faculty members to grow vegetables and keep livestock) and the original student dormitories, used—and greatly coveted—by students today; though centrally heated, they still have working fireplaces. The room Edgar Allan Poe occupied when he was a student here is furnished as it would have been in 1826 and is open to visitors.

Paralleling the lawn are more rows of student rooms called the Ranges. Equally spaced within each of the Ranges are "hotels," originally used to accommodate student dining. Each hotel represented a different country, and the students would have to eat the food and speak the language of that country. Although a wonderful idea on Jefferson's part, it lasted only a short while since everyone wanted to eat French but not German.

Albemarle County Court House

501 E. Jefferson St., at 5th St. East. Free admission. Mon–Fri 9am–5pm.

The center of village activity in Colonial days, today the Court House in the historic downtown area has a facade and portico dating from the Civil War. There's no tour here, but you can take a glance at Jefferson's will in the County Office Building. It's easy to imagine Jefferson, Madison, and Monroe talking politics under the lawn's huge shade trees.

The Downtown Mall

Main St. between 2nd Street West and 6th Street East. ☎ **804/296-8548** for mall events.

You can stroll into the 20th century along a charming pedestrian brick mall extending for about eight blocks on downtown Main Street. You can park free for two hours with merchant validation in the lot at 505 E. Market St. or on any of the lots along Water Street. In addition to shops and restaurants, the mall has a six-screen movie theater and ice skating rink on its west end. It's all enhanced by fountains, benches under shade trees, and big pots of flowers.

McGuffey Art Center

201 Second St. NW, between Market and Jefferson streets. ☎ **804/295-7973**. Free admission. Tues–Sat 10am–5pm, Sun 1–5pm.

At the center, located just a block off the Mall, local artists and craftspeople have studio exhibits and sell their creations. The **Second Street Gallery,** showing contemporary art from all over the United States, is also located here.

Virginia Discovery Museum

East End of Downtown Mall. ☎ **804/977-1025**. Admission $4 adults, $3 seniors and children 1–13. Tues–Sat 10am–5pm, Sun 1–5pm.

The Virginia Discovery Museum is a place of enchantment offering numerous hands-on exhibits and programs for young people. Here kids can dress up as firefighters, soldiers, police, and other grownups. The Colonial Log House, an authentic structure that once stood on a site in New Bedford, Virginia, is outfitted with the simple furnishings appropriate to an early-19th-century life-style. A series of fascinating exhibits deals with the senses, and the Fun and Games exhibit has a wonderful array of games, including bowling and giant checkers. An arts and crafts studio, an active beehive, and a changing series of traveling and made-on-site exhibits round out the fun.

MONTPELIER & OTHER NEARBY ATTRACTIONS

Montpelier

Va. 20, Montpelier Station. ☎ **703/672-2728** or 672-2206. Admission (including 10-minute slide show, bus tour of grounds, and house tour) $6 adults, $5 seniors, $1 children 6–11, under 6 free. Mar 16–Dec 31, daily 10am–4pm; Jan 2–Mar 15, Fri–Sat 10am–4pm. Closed New Year's Day, Thanksgiving, and Christmas. Montpelier is 25 miles northeast of Charlottesville. Take U.S. 29N to U.S. 33E at Ruckersville. At Barboursville, turn left onto Va. 20N.

This 2,700-acre estate looking upon the Blue Ridge Mountains was home to three generations of the Madison family from 1723 to 1844. James Madison was just 26 when he ensured that the 1776 Constitutional Convention in Williamsburg would include religious freedom in the Virginia Declaration of Rights. As a member of the federal Constitutional Convention in 1787, he worked for passage of the Bill of Rights and for the creation of the executive departments, efforts that earned him the title "Father of the Constitution." After four terms in Congress (1789–97), Madison retired to his father's modest two-story redbrick Georgian residence, and with advice from his good friend Jefferson, expanded its proportions. In 1801, Madison became secretary of state under Jefferson and in 1809 succeeded Jefferson as president, leading the fledgling nation during the War of 1812.

The estate changed hands many times between 1844 and 1901, when it was purchased by William du Pont Sr. He enlarged the mansion and added barns, staff houses, a saw mill, a blacksmith shop, a train station, a dairy, and greenhouses. His wife created a 2¹/₂-acre formal garden. And when daughter Marion du Pont Scott inherited the property, she had a steeplechase course built on it and initiated the **Montpelier Hunt Races,** which are still held here every November. The National Trust acquired the property following her death in 1984 and opened it to the public in 1987. Restoration efforts are still in progress, with attention focused on making the property an interpretive monument to Madison's life, ideas, and contributions, especially as they relate to the Constitution and Bill of Rights.

Oakencroft Vineyard

Barracks Road. ☎ **804/296-4188.** Free admission. Apr–Dec, daily 11am–5pm; Jan–Mar, Sat–Sun 11am–5pm. Drive 3¹/₂ miles west of U.S. 29 on Barracks Road.

There have been vineyards in the Piedmont since the 18th century, and Jefferson hoped to someday produce quality wines in Virginia. Today his dream is a reality, and many area wineries offer tours and tastings. A case in point is Oakencroft Vineyard, set on 17 acres of rolling farmland with a lake and Blue Ridge Mountain views. Hand-hewn beams adorn the tasting room, where visitors can sample 10 different varieties for free, and there are trestle tables for al fresco lunching (bring your own picnic). A tour takes about 20 minutes.

For a list of other Charlottesville-area wineries, pick up a brochure at the visitors center.

Walton's Mountain Museum

Schyler. ☎ **804/831-2000.** Admission $4 adults, $3 seniors and children 13–18, children under 13 free. Mar–Nov daily 10am–4pm. Closed Easter Sunday, second Sat in Oct, Thanksgiving. From I-64 take U.S. 29 south 18 miles. Turn left on Va. 6, go east 6 miles to C.R. 800, turn right and go south 2 miles to Schyler and follow signs.

There is no real "Walton's Mountain," but Hollywood screenwriter Earl Hamner Jr. based characters of the popular TV series *The Waltons* on real folks he knew growing up during the Depression in the picturesque hamlet of Schyler (pronounced *SKY-lar).* Hamner worked closely with hometown residents to create this charming museum in the old elementary school across the street from his boyhood home. Photos of the real characters are displayed beside those of the actors who played them on television, and fans of the warm-hearted series will get a kick out of seeing the set of John-Boy's bedroom. All profits are plowed back into the community, including a computer learning center in the old school.

ACCOMMODATIONS

In addition to the establishments recommended below, Charlottesville has several national chain hotels and motels. The sleek, high-rise Omni Charlottesville Hotel is on Main Street at the west end of the Downtown Mall. Others are the Sheraton Inn Charlottesville, Best Western Mount Vernon, Comfort Inn, Hampton Inn, Days Inn, Econo Lodge South, and Econo Lodge North.

Bed-and-breakfast accommodations in elegant homes and private estate cottages are handled by Guesthouses Reservation Service, Inc., P.O. Box 5737, Charlottesville, VA 22905 (☎ 804/979-7264, fax 804/293-7791). You can write or fax for a brochure, but reservations must be made by phone. Rates range from $56 and up for singles or $60 and up for doubles. Credit cards can be used only for deposits. The office is open Monday through Friday from noon to 5pm.

EXPENSIVE

✪ Boar's Head Inn & Sports Club

200 Ednam Dr., Charlottesville, VA 22903. ☎ **804/296-2181** or 800/476-1988. Fax 804/971-5733. 175 rms and suites. A/C TV TEL. $115–$180 single or double; $250–$275 suite. Extra person $10. Weekend and other packages available. AE, CB, DC, MC, V. Free parking. Drive about 2 miles west of downtown Charlottesville on U.S. 250.

Named for the traditional symbol of hospitality in Shakespeare's England, the Boar's Head is a combination of rural charm and sophisticated facilities. The focal point is a reconstructed historic grist mill that was dismantled and brought here in the early 1960s. It houses the Tavern, the Garden Room, the Old Mill dining room, and some guest rooms. Adjoining low-rise wings are more modern, though furnishings throughout are Colonial reproductions. Some rooms offer lake views; some have working fireplaces. Each suite has one bedroom and one sitting room, with either a kitchenette or a wet bar.

The Boar's Head is one of the best places in the region to take off on a hot-air balloon ride.

Dining/Entertainment: Open for all three meals, the Old Mill Room offers candlelit dining in a historic setting of beamed ceilings, multipaned windows, and random-width plank floors. Among its offerings are Virginia-accented dishes such as hunter's chili with beef and venison. The adjacent Terrace Lounge offers indoor and outdoor seating, an appetizer menu, and Wednesday-to-Saturday piano music. Racquets Restaurant and Lounge provides healthy salads, sandwiches, and daily specials.

Services: Room service, concierge, nightly turndown, complimentary morning newspaper, in-room coffee/tea service, free airport shuttle. Concierge section has bathrobe, hairdryer, computer hookup, complimentary morning newspaper.

Facilities: Indoor and outdoor tennis, squash, platform tennis, fishing, jogging trail, bicycles, health club, three pools (including an Olympic-size model), adjacent 18-hole golf course, gift shop, massages, facials.

MODERATE

✪ Courtyard by Marriott

638 Hillsdale Dr., Charlottesville, VA 22901. ☎ **804/973-7100** or 800/321-2211. Fax 804/973-7128. 150 rms, 12 suites. A/C TV TEL. Sun–Thurs, $69 double; Fri–Sat, $75 double. Extra person $10. Children under 18 stay free in parents' room. AE, CB, DC, DISC, MC, V. Free parking. From the U.S. 250 Bypass, take U.S. 29 north 1½ miles to sign on right. Hotel abuts Fashion Square mall.

This member of the fine chain designed for business travelers (but equally comfortable for any traveler) is set on a hill well off the highway. Its beige-colored 2½-story building houses nicely decorated rooms with little extras, like piping-hot water taps for instant coffee and tea, which are provided. Every bedroom has a walk-in closet, working desk, and couch (some are convertible). Interior rooms open onto the court-yard—a spacious grass-and-stone patio area with lounge chairs, umbrella tables, and a white-latticed gazebo.

Moderately priced breakfasts are served in the marble-floored lounge, which has a working fireplace and a bar open daily from 5 to 10pm. Facilities include a pool, exercise room, Jacuzzi, and coin-op laundry.

English Inn of Charlottesville

2000 Morton Dr., Charlottesville, VA 22901. ☎ **804/971-9900** or 800/786-5400. Fax 804/977-8008. 88 rms. A/C TV TEL. $60–$89 double. Rates include continental breakfast. Extra person $7. Children under 12 stay free in parents' room. AE, CB, DC, MC, V. Free parking. Follow U.S. 29 north to just south of the U.S. 250 Bypass.

A traditionally English Tudor–style building is the setting for this hospitable inn. You'll feel as though you're in the staid precincts of an English club when you enter the comfortable wood-paneled lobby, its floors strewn with Oriental rugs. Step down into the Conservatory, where cozy seating areas with wing chairs and small tables in front of an oversize fireplace make a perfect setting for the continental break-fast served daily. Rooms are variously decorated, many in Queen Anne–style repro-duction pieces; others are more contemporary looking. Each room has a desk. The hotel has no food service other than breakfast. Facilities include a pool, exercise room, and sauna.

INEXPENSIVE

Holiday Inn Monticello

1200 Fifth St., Charlottesville, VA 22902. ☎ **804/977-5100** or 800/HOLIDAY. Fax 804/293-5228. 131 rms. A/C TV TEL. $75 double. Extra person $8. Children under 18 stay free in parents' room. AE, CB, DC, DISC, MC, V. Free parking. Take Exit 120 from I-64 and drive north (you will be on Fifth Street) over the highway; the hotel is on the right.

This pleasant Holiday Inn offers an easy-going atmosphere, a hospitable staff, and spacious accommodations. A sixth-floor suite has a full kitchen and separate bedroom and living room. A large outdoor pool is open seasonally. The on-premises restau-rant serves a complimentary continental breakfast and has full-service dining nightly.

NEARBY ACCOMMODATIONS

✪ Keswick Hall

701 Country Club Dr. (P.O. Box 68), Keswick, VA 22947. ☎ **804/979-3440** or 800/274-5391. Fax 804/979-3457. 48 rms and suites. $160–$645. Rates include full breakfast. AE, DC, CB, MC, V. Free parking. From Charlottesville take I-64 east to Shadwell (Exit 124), then Va. 22 east to estate.

Thomas Jefferson might explode with anger were he to see the grand lounge of this super-luxury estate, for hanging there is an original oil painting of Augusta, Princess of Wales—mother of the mad King George III against whom Jefferson and his pals rebelled in 1776. It's all part of Sir Bernard Ashley's highly successful effort to cre-ate an authentic English-style country inn smack in the middle of "Mr. Jefferson's Country." Sir Bernard—"B.A." to both friends and staff—restored and expanded the 1912-vintage Italianate Crawford Villa to house 48 rooms and suites, all furnished with his own extensive collection of antiques and his late wife Laura Ashley's prints on wallpaper, upholstery, and curtains. Many of the units have fireplaces, claw-footed tubs, and views over a golf course redesigned by Arnold Palmer, but don't expect to find these in the 14 least expensive "house rooms." All guests can roam around the vast public rooms on the main level, including a main lounge with fireplace and terrace with golf course view.

Dining/Entertainment: Dining here is gourmet, with such offerings as a saddle and leg of local rabbit with morel flan, potato fondant, and a white bean tomato ragout (you get the picture). Dinners are fixed price at $57, while lunches cost $25. English afternoon tea is free to guests, who can dine at the adjoining Keswick Club's bistro.

Services: Twice daily maid service, social director, masseur, babysitting.

Facilities: Guests have complimentary use of the private Keswick Club's golf course, tennis courts, fitness center, and indoor-outdoor heated pool.

○ The Inn At Monticello

Va. 20 (Rte. 19, Box 112), Charlottesville, VA 22902. ☎ **804/979-3593.** Fax 804/296-1344. 5 rms, including 2 suites. A/C. $110–$140 double. Rates include full breakfast. MC, V. Free parking. From I-64, take Va. 20S and continue past the visitor center for about ¹/₃ mile. The inn is on your right.

This beautiful two-story white-clapboard country house sits well back from the road on a manicured lawn ornamented in spring with blooming dogwood trees and azaleas. Boxwoods, tall shade and evergreen trees, shrubs, and a bubbling brook make an exceptionally lovely setting. Guests enter via the front porch into a double sitting room, dramatically furnished with crimson walls, two fireplaces, and a handsome collection of antiques. Guest rooms are individually decorated and have such special features as a working fireplace, a private porch, or a four-poster canopy bed. Guests can relax outdoors on a hammock or on the front verandah lined with wicker rockers. There's a croquet course on the sweeping lawn.

○ Silver Thatch Inn

3001 Hollymead Dr., Charlottesville, VA 22911. ☎ **804/978-4686.** Fax 804/979-6156. 7 rms. A/C. $110–$150 double. Rates include continental breakfast. Extra person $25. AE, CB, DC, MC, V. Free parking. Hollymead Drive is just off U.S. 29 (right turn), about 8 miles north of town.

Occupying a rambling white-clapboard house, a section of which dates back to Revolutionary days, this charming hostelry is located on a quiet road and set on nicely landscaped grounds. Attractively decorated with authentic 18th-century pieces, the original part of the building now serves as a cozy common room, where guests are invited for afternoon refreshments. The 1812 center part of the house is now one of the dining rooms. Guest rooms are lovely, with down comforters on four-poster canopied beds, antique pine dressers, carved walnut-and-mahogany armoires, and exquisite quilts. Several rooms have working fireplaces. Hosts Vince and Rita Scoffone are on hand to help make arrangements for nearby activities—trail rides, jogging, tennis, swimming, golf, fishing, and biking. Telephones and TVs are available in the common areas.

Dinner is served in candlelit rooms open to the public (inn guests must reserve a table in advance, since this is one of the area's most popular dining venues). Nightly specials might include grilled breast of duck basted with a beer barbecue sauce or sautéed Texas antelope. The list of Virginian and Californian wines has been cited for excellence.

A MOUNTAIN GETAWAY

Wintergreen Resort

Wintergreen, VA 22958. ☎ **804/325-2200** or 800/325-2200. Fax 804/325-8003. 1,300 units. A/C TV TEL. $110–$150 nightly, $75–$98 per night for a week stay, studio, double occupancy.

Packages available. AE, MC, V. Take I-64 west to Exit 107 and follow U.S. 250 west; turn left onto C.R. 151 south, then right on C.R. 644 for 4¹/₂ miles to resort. It's about 43 miles from Charlottesville.

With 6,700 of its 11,000 acres dedicated to the remaining undisturbed forestland, Wintergreen offers year-round vacation activities in a magnificent Blue Ridge Mountain setting. While skiing, golf, horseback riding, mountain biking, swimming in a lake, and canoeing are the big draws here, Wintergreen also has a Nature Foundation which offers guided hikes, seminars, and camps for children.

The resort's focal point is the tastefully lodgelike Inn, which has a huge grist-mill wheel occupying the two-story registration area. Most accommodations are in small enclaves scattered throughout the property, but there are also two- to seven-bedroom homes, one- to four-bedroom condos, and studios and lodge rooms. Since the homes and condos are privately owned, furnishings are highly individual, ranging from country quaint to sleek and sophisticated settings of cutting-edge design. Each condo is appointed with a modern kitchen, a living area, a bathroom for each bedroom, and a balcony or patio (the mountain views are superb); most have working fireplaces.

Dining/Entertainment: Wintergreen has several full-service restaurants. The Copper Mine Restaurant and Lounge, at the Inn, offers noteworthy American cuisine in a relaxed casual setting. The Garden Terrace Restaurant in the sports center offers healthy cuisine in a smoke-free environment. Cooper's Vantage is a casual spot for family dining and features live entertainment. The Rodes Farm Inn has family-style country meals. The Verandah specializes in Virginia regional items, and the Trillium House offers fine dining in a charming country inn.

Facilities: Skiing (17 slopes and trails), 36 holes of championship golf, hiking, nature programs, horseback riding, mountain biking, spa, massage, tennis, indoor and outdoor pools, lake swimming and canoeing, fishing, children's center, health club, hair salon, shops, grocery store.

DINING

In addition to the establishments below, the Old Mill Room in the Boar's Head Inn, Keswick Hall, and the Silver Thatch Inn offer exceptional dining (see "Accommodations," above).

EXPENSIVE

✪ C&O Restaurant

515 E. Water St. ☎ **804/971-7044.** Reservations required upstairs, not accepted downstairs. Main courses $18–$27. MC, V. Downstairs, Mon–Fri 11:30am–3pm; daily 5:30–10:30pm. Upstairs, seatings Mon–Sat at 6:30 and 9:30pm. FRENCH.

The unprepossessing brick front, complete with a faded Pepsi sign, might make you think twice, but don't be deterred. Located a block off the Mall, this establishment has a fine upstairs restaurant and a lively downstairs bistro. The elegant dining quarters upstairs have received kudos from major critics. Raved a *Food & Wine* reviewer: "I can assure you that not since Jefferson was serving imported vegetables and the first ice cream at Monticello has there been more innovative cooking in these parts." And should you need further reassurance, the entrance, warmed by a wood-burning fireplace, is most welcoming. Upstairs menus change daily, with fine French cuisine always offered.

While men must wear jackets upstairs, the lively downstairs bistro is much less formal. Entrees like crabcakes and spicy ribeye steak are dinnertime favorites down there. The setting is a mix of exposed brick and rough-hewn barnwood, subdued lighting, and walls hung with an array of prints and photos. A bit of charm is added by white-clothed tables adorned with attractive flower arrangements. Premium wines by the glass are available upstairs or down.

MODERATE

Eastern Standard Restaurant and ESCAFE

Downtown Mall, west end. ☎ **804/295-8668.** Reservations accepted in restaurant. Main courses $7–$17. AE, DC, DISC, MC, V. Restaurant, Tue–Thurs 5–10pm; Fri–Sat 5–11pm; cafe, Tues–Sat 5pm–midnight. AMERICAN/MEDITERRANEAN/ASIAN.

This upstairs-downstairs operation paradoxically is the last building on the western end of the Downtown Mall. Its airy contemporary decor is lovely. The downstairs cafe has sage green walls hung with a collection of memorabilia, black-leather booths, and a cream-colored pressed-tin ceiling. The upstairs restaurant sports oak floors with antique carpets, potted birds of paradise, gold walls, and big arched windows overlooking the Mall. Warm-weather seating is available on the mall or out back.

Menus change frequently, but appetizers might include pesto sun-dried tomato polenta wrapped with roasted eggplant, or perhaps Jeanne Moreau's spicy sesame noodles. There are usually 10 or so entree choices, such as New York strip au poivre or a stuffed chicken breast with raspberry Dijon sauce. Desserts, made on the premises, include such delectables as Belgian chocolate truffles. Dinner downstairs features similar selections, with additional lower-priced options like scallops and angel hair pasta tossed with scallions, diced tomatoes, and a Dijon cream sauce.

INEXPENSIVE

The Hardware Store

316 E. Main St. (Downtown Mall). ☎ **804/977-1518.** Sandwiches, salads, soups, main courses, soda fountain $1.75–$11.95. DC, MC, V. Mon 11am–5pm, Tues–Thurs 11am–9pm, Fri–Sat 11am–10pm. AMERICAN.

Old rolling ladders; stacks of oak drawers that once held screws, nuts, and bolts; and vintage advertising signs—all display the old-time origins of this high-energy spot popular with the college crowd. A long, narrow space with an upstairs gallery, it provides comfortable seating in spacious leather-upholstered booths. Specialties include quiches and crêpes, crabcakes, salads, an enormous variety of hamburgers, sandwiches, baked potatoes with great toppings, platters of fried fish, and barbecued ribs. There are soda-fountain treats, and pastries and cakes run the gamut from dense double-chocolate truffle cake to southern pecan pie. The Hardware Store has a fully stocked bar.

Miller's

109 W. Main St. ☎ **804/971-8511.** Main courses $5.50–$9.50; sandwiches $3.50–$4.95. AE, MC, V. Mon–Sat 11:30am–1:30am (lunch Mon–Fri 11:30am–2pm; light fare daily 2–5:30pm and 10:30pm–midnight). AMERICAN.

Miller's is a converted old-time pharmacy with the original white-tile floor, pressed-tin ceiling, mahogany soda fountain as a back bar, and cherry woodwork and shelving. Walls display historic photos of old Charlottesville drugstores. Out front on the Mall, tree-shaded tables are enclosed by planters with flowers. Roast beef and turkey, roasted and carved on the premises and served on homemade French bread, are available at lunch and dinner. Dinner entrees might include fresh seafood, chicken, vegetable stir-fry, and fettuccine marinara. Desserts are homemade. Wine, beer, and mixed drinks are served until 2am. There's nighttime entertainment—jazz or blues—and there's a nominal cover charge after 9:30pm.

The Virginian
1521 W. Main St. ☎ **804/984-4667**. Sandwiches and burgers $5–$6; main courses $7–$12. AE, MC, V. Mon–Fri 9am–2am, Sat–Sun 10am–2am. AMERICAN.

Dating from 1921, Charlottesville's oldest restaurant is the best of the student hangouts lining Main Street in The Corner neighborhood opposite the university. This simpatico spot has roomy oak booths and an always well-populated bar. Good jazz or rock is played at a low-decibel level, and shaded wall sconces provide subdued lighting. All the fare is homemade, including yummy fresh-baked breads. At lunch or dinner you can't go wrong with a heaping bowl of pasta, whose proportions will stuff a voracious student. Oven-fresh desserts change daily; the chocolate pecan pie is scrumptious.

BREAKFAST & LIGHT FARE

The Coffee Exchange
120 E. Main St. ☎ **804/295-0975.** Soups, salads, and sandwiches $2–$6.50. Mon–Sat 8am–5pm, Sun 9am–5pm. AMERICAN.

This small eatery on the Mall is a pristinely charming setting in which to enjoy fresh-roasted coffee and fresh-from-the-oven croissants. They come in many varieties—plain, almond-strawberry, raspberry-cheese, cinnamon, blueberry, and chocolate—and there are also scones, cookies, muffins, and sticky buns. Later in the day, try the Exchange for sandwiches (like chicken salad, turkey and Swiss, and roast beef—all made from meats cooked on the premises), a cold pasta-primavera salad, or a stuffed baked potato. The bakery goodies are excellent, and the aroma of fresh-baked breads and roasted coffee is ambrosial. With its bright atmosphere, this is a popular place for hearty breakfasts Monday to Friday until 11:30am, Saturday and Sunday until 3pm, and for afternoon tea.

2 Lynchburg

66 miles S of Charlottesville; 112 miles W of Richmond, 52 miles E of Roanoke

A large white-granite rock on the riverbank at Ninth Street in Lynchburg marks where John Lynch, Quaker son of an Irish immigrant, began operating a ferry across the river in 1757. The town that grew up near the spot became a rich and important shipping point in the late 18th and 19th centuries, as nearby farmers brought their tons of tobacco here to be hauled downstream by shallow-draft "bateaux" to Richmond's cigarette factories and deepwater port.

Today the Lynchburg area offers visitors a look at Jefferson's country home, Poplar Forest, and Red Hill, the plantation where Patrick Henry spent his last years. For Civil War buffs, the principal attraction is nearby Appomattox Court House, where Lee surrendered to Grant, thus ending the nation's bloodiest conflict.

ESSENTIALS

VISITOR INFORMATION   The **Lynchburg Visitors Information Center,** 216 12th St., at the corner of Church Street (P.O. Box 2027), Lynchburg, VA 24505 (☎ 804/847-1811, or 800/532-7821), is open daily from 9am to 5pm and provides maps, brochures, and self-guided walking tours of historic districts. From the U.S. 29 Expressway, take Exit 1A, follow Main Street west to 12th Street, and turn left.

GETTING THERE   By Plane   The Lynchburg Regional Airport, U.S. 29, 8 miles south of downtown (☎ 804/847-1632), has service via USAir, Delta, United, and ASA.

Lynchburg

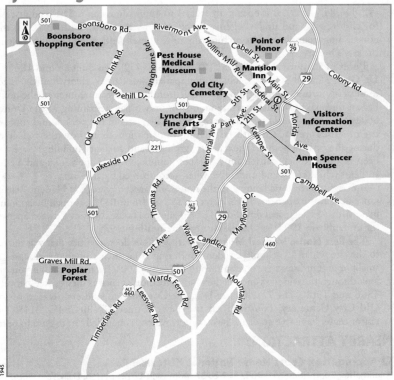

By Train   At the Amtrak station, Kemper Street and Park Avenue (☎ 800/872-7245), there is daily "Crescent" service to New York City and New Orleans.

By Bus   Frequent bus service is available at the Greyhound/Trailways Terminal, Wildflower Drive at Odd Fellows Drive (☎ 804/846-6614, or 800/231-2222).

By Car   From Charlottesville and I-64, the shortest route is U.S. 29 south. From Richmond, follow U.S. 360 west to U.S. 460, which goes directly to Lynchburg. From Roanoke, take U.S. 460 east. U.S. 29 and U.S. 501 together form the Lynchburg Expressway, a freeway that crosses the James River and almost forms a beltway around the city.

AREA CODE   The telephone area code for Lynchburg is 804, although 540 begins a few miles west of the city.

ATTRACTIONS IN TOWN

Start your sojourn in Lynchburg at the visitor center (see above), where you can get free walking tour guides to the Court House Hill historic district downtown and to other distinctive Federal- and Victorian-period residential neighbors.

Downtown, begin at **Monument Terrace,** on Court Street between 9th and 10th streets. This imposing 139-step staircase was built as a memorial to soldiers of all America's wars. At the base of the staircase on Church Street stands a statue of a World War I doughboy. From there you can see the imposing Greek Revival facade of the **Old Court House,** on Court Street between 8th Street and 10th Street

(☎ 804/847-1459). It is open daily from 1 to 4pm; admission is $1 for adults, free for children 12 and under when accompanied by an adult. Built in 1855, this outstanding example of civic architecture now houses artifacts and displays tracing the city's history.

Point of Honor, 112 Cabell St. (☎ 804/847-1459), was built around 1815 for Dr. George Cabell Sr., whose most famous patient was Patrick Henry but who made most of his fortune shipping tobacco. Aside from its architectural interest (the house has an unusual octagonal bay facade, one of only a pair remaining in the United States), Point of Honor is a showcase of decorative arts of the period, and tours of the premises are packed with fascinating information about how the rich lived during the Federal period. The gardens, grounds, and auxiliary buildings have also been restored. Open daily from 1 to 4pm; admission is $3 for adults and $1 for students (children 12 and under free when accompanied by an adult).

A designated historic landmark, the home and garden cottage of Harlem Renaissance poet **Anne Spencer,** 1313 Pierce St. (☎ 804/846-0517), is open by appointment with a $2 suggested donation. The red-shingled house, built by Edward Spencer for his family in 1903, was her home until her death in 1975.

The **Pest House Medical Museum** is a tiny 1840s doctors office that was moved to the site where Lynchburg residents suffering from such contagious diseases as smallpox and measles were quarantined in the early 1800s. It's not open, but you can look through the windows and see the tools of medical science as they existed between 1860 and 1900. The Pest House is in the Confederate soldiers' section of the **Old City Cemetery,** Fourth Street and Taylor Street (☎ 804/847-1811). The visitor center has a free guide to the cemetery, which is open daily from 8am to 6pm.

NEARBY ATTRACTIONS

✪ Appomattox Court House National Historical Park

Appomattox Court House. ☎ **804/352-8987.** Admission $2 per person. Daily 9am–5pm. The park is on Va. 24, about 3 miles north of U.S. 460 and about 22 miles east of Lynchburg.

Here, in the parlor of Wilmer McLean's home, Robert E. Lee surrendered the Army of Northern Virginia to Ulysses S. Grant on April 9, 1865, thus ending the bitter Civil War. Today the 20 or so houses, stores, courthouse, and tavern that comprised the little village called Appomattox Court House have been restored, and visitors can walk the country lanes in the rural stillness where these events took place. At the visitors center, pick up a map of the park. Upstairs, slide presentations and museum exhibits include fascinating excerpts from the diaries and letters of Civil War soldiers.

Buildings open to the public include McLean's house, Clover Hill Tavern, Meeks' Store, the Woodson Law Office, the courthouse (totally reconstructed), jail, and Kelly House. Surrender Triangle, where the Confederates lay down their arms and rolled up their battle flags, is outside Kelly House.

There are picnic tables at the Appomattox Wayside. No cars are allowed in the village.

Thomas Jefferson's Poplar Forest

Forest, Va. ☎ **804/525-1806.** Admission $5 adults, $1 children. Apr–Nov, Wed–Sun 10am–4pm (last tour begins at 3:45pm). Closed Dec–Mar. The main entrance is on C.R. 661, 1 mile from U.S. 221 via C.R. 811 and about 6 miles southwest of town.

At Thomas Jefferson's retreat home, you can see the restoration of a National Historic Landmark in progress. Opened to the public in 1985, octagonal Poplar Forest is now undergoing archaeological research and architectural restoration, and visitors are able to see relics from the buildings and grounds as they are brought to light and exhibited. At one time the seat of a 4,819-acre plantation and the source of much of Jefferson's income, Poplar Forest was designed by him to utilize light and air flow to the maximum in as economical a space as possible. In 1806, while he was president, Jefferson himself assisted the masons in laying the foundation for the dwelling. It was his final private architectural masterpiece.

Red Hill, Patrick Henry National Memorial

Brookneal. ☎ **804/376-2044.** Admission $3 adults, $2 seniors over 65, $1 students. Apr–Oct, daily 9am–5pm; Nov–Mar, daily 9am–4pm. Closed New Year's Day, Thanksgiving, and Christmas. Red Hill is 35 miles from Lynchburg. Take U.S. 501 south to Brookneal, then Va. 40 east and follow the brown signs.

The fiery orator's last home, Red Hill is a modest frame farmhouse with several dependencies, including the overseer's cottage Patrick Henry used as a law office. Henry retired to Red Hill in 1794 after serving five terms as governor of Virginia. Failing health forced him to refuse numerous posts, including chief justice of the United States, secretary of state, and minister to Spain and France. He died here on June 6, 1799, and is buried in the family graveyard.

Begin your tour at the visitors center, where you can see an enlightening 15-minute video about Henry's years here and visit the museum with the world's largest assemblage of Henry memorabilia. Centerpiece is Peter Rothermel's famous painting *Patrick Henry before the Virginia House of Burgesses,* depicting his "If this be treason, make the most of it" speech against the Stamp Act in 1765. The site contains a reconstruction of his 18th-century plantation, which consists of his actual law office, the main house reconstructed on the original foundation, the carriage house, and other small buildings. You can't miss the most striking feature of the landscape: Standing 64 feet high and spanning 96 feet, the Osage Orange Tree is listed in the American Forestry Hall of Fame.

Booker T. Washington National Monument

Hardy. ☎ **540/721-2094.** Free admission. Daily 9am–4:30pm. From Lynchburg, take U.S. 460 west to Va. 122 south.

At this memorial to one of America's great African-American leaders, visitors can conjure up the setting of Booker T. Washington's childhood in reconstructed farm buildings and demonstrations of farm life and slavery in Civil War–era Virginia. Although Washington called his boyhood home a plantation, the Burroughs farm was small, with just 207 acres and never more than 11 slaves. His mother was the cook, and the cabin where he was born was also the kitchen. His family left the farm in 1865, when he was 9. He determinedly sought an education and actually walked most of the 500 miles from his new home in West Virginia to Hampton Institute. He worked his way through school and achieved national prominence as an educator, founder of Tuskegee Institute in Alabama, author, and advisor to presidents. In 1956, a century after he was born, this national monument was established to honor his life and work.

Begin at the visitors center, which offers a slide show and a map with a self-guided plantation tour and nature walks that wind through the original Burroughs property.

ACCOMMODATIONS

In addition to the two downtown establishments described below, several chain motels sit in the suburbs near the U.S. 29 expressway. At the Chandler's Mountain Road exit are the **Lynchburg Hilton, Hampton Inn,** and **Days Inn.** At Odd Fellows Road are **Comfort Inn** and **Holiday Inn Lynchburg.**

Holiday Inn Select

601 Main St., Lynchburg, VA 24504. ☎ **804/528-2500** or 800/465-4329. Fax 804/528-0062. 238 rms. A/C TV. $79–$85 double. AE, DC, CB, DISC, MC, V. Free parking. From U.S. 29, take Main Street (Exit 1-A) west.

Although primarily a business hotel, this eight-story brick building is just five blocks from Court House Square and the downtown sights. An impressive, colonial-style lobby with fountain leads to Jefferson's Restaurant, which offers all three meals at reasonable prices. The medium-size rooms have wing chairs, dark wood desks and armoires, and baths equipped with hairdryers and coffeemakers. Upper level rooms have great views over the town. On the second floor, a weight room opens to an outdoor pool.

Lynchburg Mansion Inn Bed & Breakfast

405 Madison St., Lynchburg, VA 24504. ☎ **804/528-5400** or 800/352-1199. 5 rms. A/C TV TEL. $89–$119 double. Rates include full breakfast. AE, DC, MC, V. Free parking. From U.S. 29 take Main Street (Exit 1-A) west. Turn left on 5th Street and right on Madison Street.

This two-story Spanish Georgian mansion, set behind a cast-iron fence in downtown Lynchburg between Fourth and Fifth streets, fits right in with the other Victorian mansions on Quality Row in the Garland Hill Historic District. A massive two-story six-columned portico heralds the entrance, and guests drive up past the carriage house to the porte-cochere side entrance. The front door opens to a 50-foot great hall, with soaring ceilings and polished cherrywood columns and wainscoting. With remote-control color TVs, clock radios, and private baths, guest rooms are extremely spacious and beautifully furnished in a variety of stunning decors— Victorian, French country, and nautical. You'll find a morning newspaper at your door, and a fresh-brewed pot of coffee and pitcher of juice is set out to tide over early risers until the full, silver-service breakfast. There's a hot tub on the back porch.

DINING

✪ Café France

Forest Plaza West Shopping Center, 3225 Old Forest Rd. ☎ **804/385-8989.** Reservations suggested. Main courses $10–$20. AE, DC, MC, V. Tue–Sat 11:30am–3pm and 5:30–10pm. From downtown, take the Lynchburg Expressway (U.S. 29/U.S. 501) to Old Forest Road. The shopping center is half a mile north on the right. INTERNATIONAL.

Entry to this casual, very popular storefront eatery is through a deli with an immense selection of imported wines and beers, all available for table service. The very modern dining room, with unusual V-shaped mirrors along one wall, has table, booth, and even some counter seating. Despite the name, locals flock here for an interesting variety of well-prepared cuisines, from Caribbean chicken in a mango salsa sauce to Chesapeake crab cakes sautéed in wine and butter. The changing menu is bound to offer something to pique your palate.

Crown Sterling

6120 Fort Ave., at U.S. 501. ☎ **804/239-7744.** Reservations recommended on weekends. Main courses $11.50–$20. AE, DC, DISC, MC, V. Mon–Sat 5:30–10pm. From downtown, go south on the Lynchburg Expressway (U.S. 29); stay on it when it become U.S. 501. Exit north on Fort Avenue. The restaurant is at the exit on the right. STEAKS.

Dark wood paneling, fireplaces, crisp table linens, and formally attired veteran waiters lend elegance to this steakhouse, famous since 1969 for its tender, perfectly char-broiled beef. The "house dinner" is an 8-ounce ribeye accompanied by salad bar, potato or rice, a glass of wine, and a wonderful parfait of homemade red wine sauce over chocolate chip ice cream—all for $15. If cholesterol is a concern, the coals do a wonderful job on chicken and swordfish, the latter spiced with special seasonings. Despite the Crown Sterling's elegance, men may wear dress shorts (no hats, ragged jeans, or T-shirts, please).

✪ Emil's Café & Rotisserie

Boonsboro Shopping Center, Boonsboro Rd. (U.S. 501 Business). ☎ **804/384-3311.** Reservations recommended for the Rotisserie. Cafe, main courses $5.75–$14.50. Rotisserie, main courses $11.95–$18.50. AE, DC, DISC, MC, V. Mon–Sat 10am–10pm. From downtown, go west on Main Street, which becomes first Rivermont Avenue and then Boonsboro Road. Boonsboro Shopping Center is on the left 3 miles west of downtown. CONTINENTAL.

Run with loving care by the Gabathuler family (husband Urs is the chef), this unpretentious cafe and elegant Rotisserie have a common foyer and offer excellent preparations. The more casual cafe has a greenhouse look with many hanging plants. Salads, sandwiches, and hot entrees are available for lunch (try crabmeat imperial on an English muffin or seafood au gratin). For dinner, a homemade lentil soup might presage the likes of Wiener schnitzel or shrimp kebabs béarnaise. Desserts such as *zuppa inglese* are extraordinary for such an inexpensive place.

In contrast, the Rotisserie is a formal dining room with Victorian etched-glass dividers, brass chandeliers, and seating in comfortable armchairs. Appetizers like angel-hair pasta with crème fraîche and shrimp, baked Brie, and oysters stuffed with crabmeat are followed by entrees like oven-baked quail stuffed with apple and served with grapes and zinfandel sauce or beef Stroganoff in sour-cream-and-burgundy sauce, served with tiny dumplings. Bananas Foster and cherries jubilee are among the rich desserts.

The Farm Basket

2008 Langhorne Rd. ☎ **804/528-1107.** Box lunch $6.50; sandwiches $3.50–$5. MC, V. Lunch counter, Mon–Sat 10am–3pm; shops, Mon–Sat 10am–5pm. AMERICAN.

A charming little complex of shops backing onto a creek, the Farm Basket specializes in freshly made box lunches you can carry out or eat in the shop or on the back deck overlooking the stream. The menu changes daily, but the box lunch always includes a choice of sandwich, salad, dessert, and drink—for example, sandwich choices of chicken-salad roll, ham hoecake, and beef biscuit; salads like tomato aspic or three bean; and, for dessert, lemon bread with cream cheese or apple-dapple cake. Fresh fruit and yogurt, barbecued sandwiches with coleslaw, and smoked turkey croissant are à la carte options.

PICNIC FARE

When you set out from Lynchburg to see area sights, it's a good idea to take along a picnic lunch. In addition to the box lunches prepared by the **Farm Basket** (see above), you can shop for picnic fare in the **Lynchburg Community Market,** at Bateau Landing, Main Street and 12th Street (☎ 804/847-1499), open Monday through Friday from 8am to 2pm and Saturday from 6am to 2pm.

8

The Shenandoah Valley

Native Americans called the 200-mile-long valley in northwestern Virginia "Shenandoah," meaning Daughter of the Stars. Today the Shenandoah National Park provides spectacular landscapes and a plethora of hiking and riding trails, and protects the beauty and peace of the Blue Ridge Mountains along the eastern boundary of the valley. Along the Blue Ridge crest, the 105-mile-long Skyline Drive—one of America's great scenic drives—runs the full length of the park and connects directly with the Blue Ridge Parkway, which continues south into North Carolina.

Down on the rolling valley floor lie picturesque small towns steeped in American history dating to the early 1700s, when pioneers moved west from the Tidewater. Scottish-Irish and German emigrants from Pennsylvania later settled this rich farming country and built their farmhouses of stone. Lord Fairfax sent George Washington west to survey the valley, and there are reminders of his visit in Natural Bridge, where he carved his initials. Winchester has preserved the office he occupied during the French and Indian Wars.

The Shenandoah Valley played a major role in the Civil War. Stonewall Jackson left his home and work at Lexington's Virginia Military Institute to become one of the leading figures of the Confederacy. Major valley engagements included the legendary battle at New Market, when the entire VMI Corps of Cadets fought heroically. After the war, Robert E. Lee settled in Lexington as president of what is now Washington and Lee University, and both he and Jackson are buried there.

Woodrow Wilson was born in Staunton in 1856, and a museum adjoining his restored birthplace pays tribute to his peace-loving ideals.

Visit the Shenandoah Valley to discover its picturesque and historic towns; to hike the Appalachian Trail and other tracks that criss-cross the mountains; to enjoy the sights, colors, and aromas of the changing seasons; to marvel at the subterranean landscapes of stalagmites and stalactites in one of its many caverns; to rough it at a mountain camp or enjoy the luxury of a great resort; to raft, canoe, kayak, or just lazily float down the river in an inner tube; or to shop for antiques at some of Virginia's largest and best shops.

Shenandoah Valley

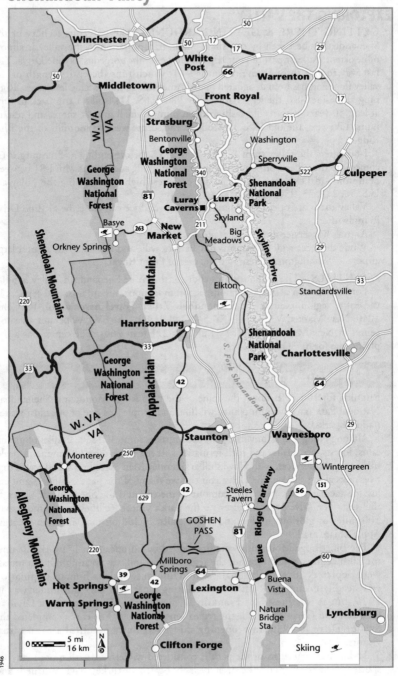

Winchester

White Post

50
50
17
17
17

66

Warrenton

29

Middletown

W. VA
VA

Strasburg

Bentonville

Front Royal

211

Washington

Sperryville

522

Culpeper

George
Washington
National
Forest

George
Washington
National
Forest

81

340

Luray
Caverns

Luray

211

Skyland

Shenandoah
National
Park

Basye

263

New
Market

Orkney Springs

220

Shenedoah Mountains

Mountains

Big
Meadows

Skyline Drive

29

Elkton

Standardsville

33

Harrisonburg

33

33

George
Washington
National
Forest

42

Appalachian

S. Fork Shenandoah R.

Shenandoah
National
Park

Charlottesville

64

W. VA
VA

Monterey

250

Staunton

Waynesboro

29

Wintergreen

George
Washington
National
Forest

629

42

Steeles
Tavern

56

151

Allegheny Mountains

220

GOSHEN
PASS

Blue Ridge Parkway

81

Millboro
Springs

60

39

42

64

Hot Springs

Warm Springs

Lexington

Buena
Vista

George
Washington
National
Forest

Natural
Bridge
Sta.

Lynchburg

0   5 mi
         16 km

N

Clifton Forge

Skiing

1946

EXPLORING THE VALLEY

GETTING THERE & GETTING AROUND The gorgeous scenery of the Shenandoah is best seen by car, since public transportation in the valley is almost nonexistent. At least part of your trip should be on the gorgeous Skyline Drive. The fast way to and through the region is I-81, which runs the entire length of the valley floor and has been designated one of America's 10 most scenic interstates. Running alongside I-81, the legendary Valley Pike (U.S. 11) is like a trip back in time at least 50 years, with its old-fashioned gas pumps, small motels, shops, and restaurants. Likewise, the old U.S. 340 follows the scenic western foothills of the Blue Ridge.

I-66 enters the valley from Washington, D.C., before ending at Strasburg. I-64 comes into the valley from both east and west, running contiguous with I-81 between Staunton and Lexington. Other major east-west highways crossing the valley are U.S. 50, 211, 33, 250, and 60.

Valley roads are open year round, but snow and ice can close the Skyline Drive in midwinter.

Amtrak has service directly to Staunton.

While there are regional airports in Charlottesville and Roanoke, the nearest large airport is Washington Dulles, 50 miles east of Front Royal.

ESSENTIALS The telephone area code for the entire Shenandoah Valley is **540.**

For information about attractions, accommodations, restaurants, and services in the entire region, contact the **Shenandoah Valley Travel Association,** P.O. Box 1040, New Market, VA 22844 (☎ 540/740-3132). The SVTA operates a visitors center in New Market, just off I-81 at U.S. 211 (exit 264). The center has a free phone line for hotel reservations.

1 Shenandoah National Park & the Skyline Drive

Running for 105 miles down the spine of the Blue Ridge Mountains, Shenandoah National Park is a haven for plants, wildlife, and people (it's one of our most visited national parks).

Although long and skinny, the park encompasses some 300 square miles of mountains, forests, waterfalls, and rock formations. It has more than 60 mountain peaks higher than 2,000 feet, with Hawksbill and Stoney Man exceeding 4,000 feet. From overlooks along the Skyline Drive you can see many of the park's wonders and enjoy spectacular views over the Piedmont to the east and the Shenandoah Valley to the west. The drive provides access to the park's visitor facilities and to more than 500 miles of glorious hiking and horse trails, including the Maine-to-Georgia Appalachian Trail.

The Blue Ridge Mountains were first settled by Europeans in 1716. By the time the 20th century rolled around, the region's thin soil was wearing out, its forests were depleted, its game animals were dying out, and its human population was steadily declining. Plans for establishing a national park got under way in 1926, but it was President Franklin D. Roosevelt's Depression-era Civilian Conservation Corps that built the recreational facilities. The corps completed the Skyline Drive in 1939, thus opening this marvelously beautiful area to casual visitors.

Today over two-fifths of the park is considered wilderness, with more than 100 species of trees. Animals like deer, bear, bobcat, and turkey have returned, and sightings of deer and smaller animals are frequent.

JUST THE FACTS

ACCESS POINTS AND ORIENTATION   The park and its Skyline Drive have four entrances. Most used is the northernmost **Front Royal** entry on U.S. 340 near the junction of I-81 and I-66, about 1 mile south of Front Royal and 90 miles west of Washington, D.C.

The two middle entrances are at **Thornton Gap,** 33 miles south of Front Royal on U.S. 211 between Sperryville and Luray; and at **Swift Run Gap,** 68 miles south of Front Royal on U.S. 33 between Standardsville and Elkton.

The southern gate is at **Rockfish Gap,** 105 miles south of Front Royal at I-64 and U.S. 250, some 21 miles west of Charlottesville and 18 miles east of Staunton.

MILE POSTS   The Skyline Drive is marked with Mile Posts, starting at zero at the Front Royal entrance and increasing as you go south, with Rockfish Gap on the southern end at Mile 105.

DISTRICTS   The access roads divide the park into three areas: Northern District between Front Royal and U.S. 211 at Thornton Gap (Mile 0 to Mile 31.5); Central District between Thornton Gap and U.S. 33 at Swift Run Gap (Mile 31.5 to Mile 65.7); and Southern District between Swift Run Gap and I-64 at Rockfish Gap (Mile 65.7 to Mile 105).

INFORMATION   For free information, call or write Superintendent, Shenandoah National Park, Route 4, Box 348, Luray, VA 22835 (☎ 540/999-3500). Ask specifically for a copy of *Shenandoah Overlook,* a tabloid newspaper that gives seasonal ranger programs and other more detailed information than is contained in the park's general brochure. Also request maps to specific trails, which are not shown on the excellent road map contained in the general brochure. The headquarters is four miles west of Thornton Gap and five miles east of Luray on U.S. 211.

The best source from which to purchase information is the **Shenandoah Natural History Association,** also at Route 4, Box 348, Luray, VA 22835 (☎ 540/999-3582). The association has a bookstore behind the park headquarters, but it also sells its publications at the park's visitor centers (see below). We highly recommend the enormously informative *Guide to Shenandoah National Park and Skyline Drive* by the late Henry Heatwole, which the association keeps updating and sells for $6.50. This book is an indispensable aid for anyone who wants to thoroughly explore the park, as it gives a mile-by-mile description of what you will (or can) see, including all 112 hiking trails.

For guidebooks and detailed topographic maps of the park's three districts, write or call the **Potomac Appalachian Trail Club,** 118 Park St., Vienna, VA 22180 (☎ 703/242-0315, or 703/242-0965 for a tape of the club's activities). The PATC helps build and maintain the park's portion of the Appalachian Trail, including trail cabins (see "Hiking & Other Sports," below). The PATC is part of the **Appalachian Trail Conference,** P.O. Box 807, Harpers Ferry, WV 25425-0807 (☎ 304/535-6331), which covers the entire trail from Maine to Georgia.

FEES, REGULATIONS & BACK COUNTRY PERMITS   Entrance permits good for seven consecutive days are $5 per car, $3 for each pedestrian or biker. A Shenandoah Passport ($15) is good for one year, as is the National Park Service's Golden Eagle Passport ($25). Park entrance is free to holders of Golden Access (for disabled U.S. citizens) and Golden Age (U.S. citizens 62 or older) passports. The former is free; the latter is available at the entrance gates for $10.

Speed limit on the Skyline Drive is a strictly enforced 35 m.p.h. Plants and animals are protected, so all hunting is prohibited. Pets must be kept on a leash at all times and are not allowed on some trails. Wood fires are permitted only in fireplaces in developed areas. The Skyline Drive is a great bike route, but neither bicycles nor motor vehicles of any sort are allowed on the trails.

Most of the park is open to backcountry camping. Permits are required; get them free at the entrance gates, visitor centers, or by mail from park headquarters (see "Information," above). Campers are required to leave no trace of their presence. No permits are required for backcountry hiking, but the same "no-trace" rule applies.

VISITOR CENTERS   There are two park visitor centers. The **Dickey Ridge Visitor Center,** at Mile 4.6, is open April to November. **Byrd Visitor Center,** at Mile 51 in Big Meadows, is open daily from early April through December and on an intermittent schedule in January, February, and March. They provide information, maps of nearby hiking trails, interpretive exhibits, films, slide shows, and nature walks. There is a small information center at Loft Mountain (Mile 79.5). In addition, the privately run **Rockfish Gap Information Center,** on U.S. 211 outside the park's southern gate, has information about the park and the surrounding area.

SEASONS   The park is most popular between October 10 and 25, when the gorgeous fall foliage peaks and weekend traffic on the Skyline Drive reaches bumper-to-bumper proportions. Fall also tends to have more clear days than summer, when lingering haze can obscure the views. In spring, the green of leafing trees moves up the ridge at the rate of about 100 feet a day. Wildflowers begin to bloom in April, and by late May the azaleas are brilliant and the dogwood is putting on a show. Nesting birds abound, and the normally modest waterfalls are at their highest during spring, when warm rains melt the highland snows. You'll find the clearest views across the distant mountains during winter, but many facilities are closed then, and snow and ice can shut down the Skyline Drive.

AVOIDING THE CROWDS   With its proximity to the sprawling Washington, D.C., metropolitan area, the park is at its busiest on summer and fall weekends and holidays. The fall foliage season in October is the busiest time, however, and reservations for October accommodations in or near the park should be made as much as a year in advance. The best time to visit, therefore, is during the spring and on weekdays from June through October. When the Central District around Big Meadows and Skyland is packed, there may be more space available in the Northern and Southern Districts.

RANGER PROGRAMS   The park has a wide variety of ranger-led activities—nature walks, interpretive programs, cultural and history lectures, campfire talks. Most are held at or near Dickey Ridge Visitor Center in the north; Byrd Visitor Center and the Big Meadows and Skyland lodges and campground in the center; and at Loft Mountain campground in the south. Schedules are published seasonally in the *Shenandoah Overlook,* available at the entrance gates, visitor centers, and from park headquarters.

SEEING THE HIGHLIGHTS

Unless you're caught in heavy traffic on fall foliage weekends, you can drive the entire length of the **Skyline Drive** in about three hours without stopping. But why rush? Give yourself at least a day for this drive, so lovely are the views from its 75 designated scenic overlooks. Stop for lunch at a wayside snack bar, a lodge, or one of seven official picnic grounds (for that matter, any of the overlooks will suffice for an impromptu picnic). Better yet, get out of your car and take at least a short hike down one of the hollows to a waterfall.

If you have only one day, head directly to the Central District between Thornton Gap and Swift Run Gap, the most developed but also the most interesting part of the park. It has the highest mountains, best views, nearly half of the park's 500 miles of hiking trails, and the park's only stables and overnight accommodations. Most visitors make Big Meadows or Skyland their base of operations for stays of more than a day, but if you plan to do this, *place your lodge reservations early* (see "Accommodations," below).

SCENIC OVERLOOKS   Among the more interesting of the 75 designated overlooks along the drive are the **Shenandoah Valley Overlook** (Mile 2.8), with views west to the Signal Knob of Massanutten Mountain across the south fork of the river; **Range View Overlook** (Mile 17.1; elev. 2,800 feet), providing fine views of the central section of the park, looking south; **Stony Man Overlook** (Mile 38.6), offering panoramas of Stony Man Cliffs, the valley, and the Alleghenies; **Thoroughfare Mountain Overlook** (Mile 40.5; elev. 3,595 feet), one of the highest overlooks, with views from Hogback Mountain south to cone-shaped Robertson Mountain and the rocky face of Old Rag Mountain; **Old Rag View Overlook** (Mile 46.5), dominated by Old Rag, sitting all by itself in an eastern extremity of the park; and **Franklin Cliffs Overlook** (Mile 49), offering a view of the cliffs and the Shenandoah Valley and Massanutten Mountain beyond.

WATERFALLS   Only one waterfall is visible from the Skyline Drive, at Mile Post 1.4, and it is dry part of the year. On the other hand, 15 other falls are accessible via hiking trails (see "Hiking," below).

HIKING & OTHER SPORTS

HIKING   The number one outdoor activity here is hiking; the park's 112 hiking trails total more than 500 miles, varying in length from short walks to a 95-mile segment of the Appalachian Trail running the entire length of the park. Access to the trails is marked along the Skyline Drive. There are parking lots at the major trailheads, but these quickly fill on weekends.

We strongly recommend that you obtain maps and trail descriptions before setting out—even before leaving home if possible. Free maps of each trail are available at the visitor centers, which also sell the topographic maps published by the Potomac Appalachian Trail Conference as well as a one-sheet map of all the park's walks published by Trails Illustrated ($8). Also, the Shenandoah Natural History Association's *Guide to Shenandoah National Park and Skyline Drive* has detailed descriptions of all the major hikes. See "Information," above, for addresses and phone numbers.

At the minimum, take one of the short hikes on nature trails at Dickey Ridge Visitor Center, Byrd Visitor Center/Big Meadows, and Lewis Mountain. There's also an excellent 1.6-mile nature hike at Stoney Man (Mile 41.7).

Here are a few of the more popular trails:

White Oak Canyon: Beginning at Mile 42.6 just south of Skyland, this steep gorge has been described as the park's "scenic gem." The five-mile trail goes through an area of wild beauty, passing no less than six waterfalls and cascades. The upper reaches to the first falls are relatively easy, but farther down the track can be rough and rocky. Total climb is about 1,000 feet, so allow 4¹/₂ hours.

Cedar Run Falls: Several trails begin at Hawksbill Gap (Mile 45.6). One is a moderately difficult 3¹/₂-mile round-trip down to Cedar Falls and back; give yourself four hours. A short but steep trail leads 1.7 miles round-trip to the summit of Hawksbill Mountain, the park's highest at 4,050 feet. Some parts are moderately rough, and the total climb is 1,557 feet, so allow four hours for the round-trip. You can also connect from Cedar Run to White Oak Canyon, a 7.3-mile loop that will take all day.

Dark Hollow Falls: One of the park's most popular hikes is the one-mile walk to Dark Hollow Falls, the closest cascade to the Skyline Drive. The trail begins at Mile 50.7 near the Byrd Visitor Center. Allow 1 1/2 hours for the round-trip. Another trail from the parking area goes half a mile to Big Meadows Swamp, a great place for wildflowers.

Camp Hoover/Mill Prong: Starting at the Milan Gap parking area (Mile 52.8), this four-mile round-trip drops down the Mill Prong to the Rapidan River, where President Herbert Hoover, an avid fisherman, had a camp during his administration (it was sort of the Camp David of his day). The total climb is 850 feet; allow four hours.

South River Falls: Third highest in the park, South River Falls drop a total of 83 feet in two stages. From the parking lot at South River Overlook (Mile 62.7), the trail is a moderately easy 2.6 miles round-trip, with a total climb of about 850 feet. Allow 2 1/2 hours.

Doyles River Falls: Starting at a large parking lot at Mile 81.1, a trail drops to a small waterfall in a natural amphitheater surrounded by large trees. The hike is 2.7 miles round-trip, with a few steep sections in its 850-foot climb; allow three hours.

Appalachian Trail: Access points to the Appalachian Trail are well marked at overlooks along the Skyline Drive. Along the trail, five backcountry shelters for day use each offer only a table, fireplace, pit toilet, and water. The **Potomac Appalachian Trail Club,** 118 Park St. SE, Vienna, VA 22180 (☎ 703/242-0693), maintains seven huts and six fully enclosed cabins that can accommodate up to 12 people. The fee for the huts is $1 per night. Cabins cost $4 per person on weekdays, $14 on weekends. Both huts and cabins must be reserved in advance with the PATC.

FISHING The park's streams are short, with limited fishing. Only native brook trout may be taken, and some streams are "catch-and-release," meaning you must release your catch back into the water. Only artificial lures are allowed, and you must get a Virginia fishing license (five-day licenses are available at the entry gates, visitor centers, wayside facilities, and camp stores inside the park, or at sporting goods stores outside).

The park publishes a free recreational fishing brochure and an annual list of streams open for fishing; both are available from park headquarters or at the visitor centers.

HORSEBACK RIDING Horses are allowed only on trails marked with yellow, and even then only via guided expeditions with **Skyland Stables** (☎ 540/999-2210), on the Skyland Lodge grounds (Mile 41.8). Rides cost $10 per hour. Pony rides for children are $5 per 30 minutes. Children must be 58 inches tall to ride the horses. The stables operate from April to November, depending on the spring and fall weather.

CAMPING

The park has three campgrounds with tent and trailer sites: **Big Meadows** (Mile 51.2); **Lewis Mountain** (Mile 57.5); and **Loft Mountain** (Mile 79.5). The Lewis Mountain and Loft Mountain campgrounds offer overnight sites on a first-come, first-served basis at $12 per site per night. They are open from mid-May to late October. Big Meadows is open from early April to the end of October, and reservations can be made up to eight weeks in advance by writing or calling MISTIX, P.O. Box 85705, San Diego, CA 92138 (☎ 800/365-CAMP). If you phone your reservation, use SHEN as the four-letter designator when asked. Big Meadows charges $14 per night.

The **Shenandoah Valley Travel Association,** P.O. Box 1040, New Market, VA 22844 (☎ 540/740-3132), publishes a list of private campgrounds outside the park.

ACCOMMODATIONS

The park concessionaire is **Aramark Virginia Sky-Line Co.,** P.O. Box 727, Luray, VA 22835 (☎ 540/743-5108, or 800/999-4714), which operates food, lodging, and other services for park visitors. Reservations, especially for the peak fall season, should be made well in advance.

In addition to the two lodges mentioned below, housekeeping cottages are available at Lewis Mountain. Contact the Aramark Virginia Sky-Line Co. for information.

See the sections that follow in this chapter for accommodations in nearby towns.

Big Meadows Lodge

Mile 51.2. ☎ **540/999-2211** or 800/999-4714. 92 rms. $76–$90 main lodge, $67–$76 motel; $110–$120 suite; $67–$76 cabin rms. Extra person $5. MC, V. Closed Nov to early May.

Accommodations at Big Meadows comprise rooms in the main lodge and in rustic cabins, and multiunit lodges with modern suites.

Big Meadows is a major recreational center; many hiking trails start here, and this is also the site of the Byrd Visitor Center. The resort is built near a large grassy meadow where families of deer often come to graze at dawn and dusk. A grocery store is nearby.

The dining room features traditional regional dishes like fried chicken, mountain trout, and country ham. Blackberry–ice cream pie with blackberry syrup is a dessert specialty. Wine, beer, and cocktails are available. During the season live entertainment keeps the Taproom busy.

Skyland Lodge

Mile 41.8. ☎ **540/999-2211** or 800/999-4714. 177 rms, including 20 cabins and 6 suites. Doubles $76–$96 in lodge, $47–$86 in cabins, $109–$151 in suites. Highest rates charged in Oct. Weekday packages available. AE, DC, DISC, MC, V.

Skyland was built by naturalist George Freeman Pollock in 1894 as a summer retreat atop the highest point on the drive. Encompassing 52 acres, the resort offers rustic wood-paneled cabins as well as modern motel-type accommodations with wonderful views. Some of the buildings are dark-brown clapboard, others fieldstone, and all nestle among the trees. The central building has a lobby with a huge stone fireplace, TV (also in some, but not all, rooms), and comfortable seating areas.

Complete breakfast, lunch, and dinner menus are offered at reasonable prices. Dinner entrees include vegetarian lasagna, steak, roast turkey, and pan-fried rainbow trout. There's a fully stocked taproom.

DINING

In addition to the lodges, there are daytime restaurants and snack bars at Elkwallow Wayside (Mile 24.1), Panorama-Thornton Gap (Mile 31.5), and Loft Mountain (Mile 79.5).

Picnic areas with tables, fireplaces, water fountains, and restrooms are at Dickey Ridge (Mile 4.6), Elkwallow (Mile 24.1), Pinnacles (Mile 36.7), Big Meadows (Mile 51), Lewis Mountain (Mile 57.5), South River (Mile 62.8), and Loft Mountain (Mile 79.5).

2 Winchester

76 miles W of Washington, D.C.; 189 miles NW of Richmond

Virginia's present-day Apple Capital, Winchester was the site of a Shawnee Indian campground before it was settled by Pennsylvania Quakers in 1732. Thanks to its strategic site at the northern end of the Shenandoah Valley, it changed hands no fewer than 72 times during the Civil War. In more recent years, Winchester was the birthplace of novelist Willa Cather and the hometown of country music great Patsy Cline. It's also famous for the Shenandoah Apple Blossom Festival in May, one of the region's most popular events.

ESSENTIALS

VISITOR INFORMATION The **Winchester/Frederick County Visitors Center,** 1360 S. Pleasant Valley Rd., Winchester, VA 22601 (☎ 540/662-4135, or 800/662-1360), is open daily from 9am to 5pm; closed major holidays. Take Exit 313 off I-81, go west on U.S. 50, and follow the signs. Another source of information is the **Kurtz Cultural Center** (☎ 540/722-6367), at Cameron and Boscawen Streets in the heart of Winchester's historic district. It's open Monday to Saturday from 10am to 5pm, Sunday from noon to 5pm. Both centers distribute free maps and walking tour brochures to the Old Town historic district. The Kurtz Cultural Center also has a section devoted to the Civil War and sells books about the valley's role in that conflict.

GETTING THERE Winchester is on I-81, U.S. 11, U.S. 522, U.S. 50, and Va. 7.

EXPLORING THE TOWN

Begin your tour at the Winchester/Frederick County Visitors Center (see above), where you can see an 18-minute film about Winchester and Frederick County. The center's "Patsy Cline Corner" includes her very own jukebox. The staff will point the way to Cline's home, Gant's Drug Store (where she worked), GNM Music (where she cut her first record), and her grave in Shenandoah Memorial Park, three miles south of town on U.S. 522.

Both the visitor center and the Kurtz Cultural Center sell discounted **block tickets** to the town's three major museums. Price of the ticket is $7.50 for adults, $6.50 for seniors, and $4 for children 6 to 12 (under 6 free).

Abram's Delight

1340 S. Pleasant Valley Rd. ☎ **540/662-7384.** Admission (without block ticket) $3.50 adults, $3 seniors, $1.75 children. Mon–Sat 10am–4pm, Sun noon–4pm. Closed Nov–Mar.

Adjoining the visitors center is this native-limestone residence built in 1754 by Quaker Isaac Hollingsworth on a pretty site beside a lake. The house is fully restored and furnished with simple 18th-century pieces appropriate to Isaac's time.

Stonewall Jackson's Headquarters

415 N. Braddock St. (between Peyton Street and North Avenue). ☎ **540/667-3242.** Admission (without block ticket) $3.50 adults, $3 seniors, $1.75 children. Mon–Sat 10am–4pm, Sun noon–4pm. Closed Nov–Mar.

This Victorian cottage, used by Stonewall Jackson in the winter of 1861–62, is filled with maps, photos, and memorabilia, making it a must for Civil War buffs.

Washington's Office Museum

32 W. Cork St. (at Braddock Street). ☎ **540/662-4412.** Admission (without block ticket) $3.50 adults, $3 seniors, $1.75 children. Mon–Sat 10am–4pm, Sun noon–4pm. Closed Nov–Mar.

On the short seven-block walk here, you can't miss the elaborately designed Handley Library, at the corner of Braddock Street and Piccadilly Street, adorned with a full panoply of Classic Revival statues and columns, topped off with a dome. Across the street from the library is the white-columned Elks building; in 1864–65 it was the headquarters of Union Gen. Philip Sheridan (see "Middletown and Strasberg," below). Washington's office is a very small log cabin museum with relics of the French and Indian and later wars.

I Fall to Pieces

Early life wasn't particularly easy for a Winchester native named Virginia Hensley. Her family was poor, and she had to quit high school and take a job in a drugstore. But Virginia had a great voice—a voice that would someday propel her into the Country Music Hall of Fame.

Only die-hard country music fans know her by her real name, of course, for at age 21 she married a man named Gerald Cline. It was under the name Patsy Cline that Virginia Hensley sang "Walkin' After Midnight" on the nationally televised "Arthur Godfrey's Talent Scouts." The record of that song sold a million copies in 1955.

Difficult times set in again, however, and Patsy disappeared from the charts. Her marriage to Gerald Cline failed, she remarried, and took two years off to have a baby. But then in 1960, she won a spot on the Grand Ole Opry and recorded one of country music's classics, "I Fall to Pieces."

Her career took off, and songs like "Crazy," "Leavin' on Your Mind," and "Imagine That" will forever be linked to Patsy Cline.

It all came to an abrupt end in March 1963 when she, Hawkshaw Hawkins, and the Cowboy Copas were killed in a plane crash on their way back to Nashville. Winchester's own Patsy Cline was brought home and buried in Shenandoah Memorial Park.

WHERE TO STAY

The interchange of I-81 and U.S. 50 (Exit 313) has Winchester's major shopping mall, several national restaurants, and chain motels including **Hampton Inn, Best Western Lee-Jackson Motor Inn, Quality Inn East, Travelodge of Winchester,** and **Super 8.**

✪ L'Auberge Provençale

U.S. 340, White Post, VA 22663. ☎ **540/837-1375** or 800/638-1702. Fax 504/837-2004. 9 rms, 1 suite. A/C. $145–$195 double. Rates include full breakfast. AE, CB, DC, MC, V. From I-81, take U.S. 50 east seven miles and turn right on U.S. 340; the inn is a mile on the right.

Master chef Alain Borel and his vivacious wife Celeste have managed to re-create the look, feel, and cuisine of Provence in a 1750s fieldstone farmhouse romantically set in the eastern foothills of the Blue Ridge. In the original main house are three intimate dining rooms and a comfortable parlor to which guests are invited for predinner drinks in front of the fireplace. Three of the 10 guest rooms are in this building; antiques and beautiful fabrics complement the Colonial farmhouse's fine features. The remaining cozy accommodations, in an adjoining gray-clapboard addition, are individually decorated with Victorian and European pieces and lovely French provincial print fabrics. A hospitable plate of inn-baked buttery cookies and fresh fruit is set out in each room. Exceptional works of fine art—including prints by renowned artists and a unique selection of carved wooden animals and small handcrafted bird sculptures—adorn the guest rooms.

Dining/Entertainment: Chef Borel uses the finest-quality ingredients, many from his own garden or local farmers, to create his superb provençal cuisine. The five-course prix-fixe dinner ($55 per person) might begin with savory smoked rabbit with fresh local morels and crème fraîche served over pasta, followed by an artichoke stuffed with duck confit. After a refreshing sorbet, diners are offered such main courses as Moroccan-spiced Canadian salmon with couscous and charred tomato compote with curry oil. The elaborate desserts might include a delicate orange waffle with sundried-cherry ice cream and berry compote. Even breakfast is a splendid repast at L'Auberge Provençale, and Alain will provide a gourmet picnic lunch on request.

WHERE TO DINE

Cork Street Tavern

8 W. Cork St. (at South Loudon St.). ☎ **540/667-3777.** Reservations accepted. Main courses $7.50–$14. AE, DC, DISC, MC, V. Mon–Sat 11am–midnight, Sun noon–10pm. AMERICAN.

Just around the corner from South Loudon Street—a pedestrian mall at the heart of Winchester—this ancient pub with small, dark rooms, fireplace, trophies, and photos of modern movie stars makes a fine place for lunch or a snack while touring the downtown sites. The house specialty is barbecued ribs, but the menu offers a wide range of other main courses, sandwiches, burgers, and salads.

Old Post Office Restaurant

200 N. Braddock St. (at Piccadilly St.). ☎ **540/722-9881.** Reservations accepted. Main courses $13–$22.50. AE, DC, DISC, MC, V. Mon–Fri 11:30am–2:30pm; Mon–Thurs 5–9pm; Fri–Sat 5–10pm. AMERICAN.

Entry to this upscale eatery is on the former loading docks of the Old Post Office, where mail went in and out of this classic brick building from 1909 until 1976. The former mail handling room is now richly paneled and carpeted. Tall windows let plenty of light onto widely spaced tables at lunch, when a variety of soups, salads, sandwiches, and light entrees draw the local business crowd. Seasonal dinner menus feature such nicely prepared offerings as salmon baked in papillote with almonds and ginger.

3 Middletown & Strasburg

Middletown: 13 miles S of Winchester, 174 miles NW of Richmond, 76 miles W of Washington, D.C.; Strasberg: 6 miles S of Middletown

Middletown's historic sights will interest history and architecture buffs, while its Wayside Theatre will entertain theater enthusiasts. An extraordinary collection of shops makes Strasburg seem like heaven to antiques shoppers. Both hamlets have exceptional country inns offering antique-filled accommodations and fine dining.

It was to Strasburg that Gen. Stonewall Jackson brought the railroad locomotives he stole from the Union during his daring Great Train Raid on Martinsburg, West Virginia. He rolled the iron beasts down the Valley Pike to the existing station at Strasburg, which is now a local museum.

ESSENTIALS

VISITOR INFORMATION   The **Winchester/Frederick County Visitors Center** (see Section 2 of this chapter) has in-depth information about Middletown. For Strasburg, contact the **Chamber of Commerce,** P.O. Box 42, Strasburg, VA 22657 (☎ 540/465-9197). The chamber has an information booth in the Strasberg Emporium (see "Antiquing," below).

GETTING THERE   From I-81, take Exit 302 west to U.S. 11 into Middletown. Take Exits 298 or 300 into Strasburg.

A PLANTATION HOME

✪ Belle Grove Plantation
U.S. 11 South, Middletown. ☎ **540/869-2028.** Admission $5 adults, $4.50 seniors, $2.50 students 12–17; children under 12 free. Mon–Sat 10am–4pm (last tour at 3:15pm), Sun 1–5pm (last tour at 4:15pm). Closed mid-Nov to mid-Mar except candlelight tours at Christmas. From Winchester, take I-81 south to exit 302 at Middletown, then U.S. 11 south 1 mile.

One of the finest homes in the Shenandoah Valley, this beautiful stone mansion was built in the late 1700s by Maj. Isaac Hite, whose grandfather, Joist Hite, first settled in the valley in 1732. At the request of James Madison, brother-in-law of Isaac Hite, Thomas Jefferson was actively involved in Belle Grove's design. The Palladian-style front windows and columns are just two examples of Jefferson's influence.

The house suffered considerable damage in 1864 during the Battle of Cedar Creek. Now owned by the National Trust, Belle Grove is at once a working farm, a restored 18th-century plantation house, and a center for the study and sale of traditional rural crafts. The interior is furnished with period antiques. Below the front portico is the entrance to the crafts center and gift shop, featuring an outstanding selection of locally made quilts, pillows, small rugs, and other handworked items.

ANTIQUING

After perusing the shops along U.S. 11 at Middletown, antiques lovers will want to continue their hunt in nearby Strasberg, which has a bevy of fine outlets at the intersection of U.S. 11 and Va. 55. The ✪ **Strasburg Emporium,** 110 N. Massanutten St. (☎ 540/465-3711), is one of the state's largest shops, an enormous warehouse that's open daily from 10am to 5pm.

You can't buy them, but there are plenty of antiques to inspect across Va. 55 at the **Strasburg Museum** (☎ 540/465-3175), in the old train station where Stonewall Jackson brought his stolen locomotives. Admission is $2 for adults, $1 for teenagers, 50¢ for children under 12. The museum is open from May to October daily from 10am to 4pm.

WHERE TO STAY & DINE

Hotel Strasburg
201 Holliday St., Strasburg, VA 22657. ☎ **540/465-9191** or 800/348-8327. Fax 540/465-4788. 19 rms, 6 suites. A/C TV TEL. $75–$87 double; $99–$199 Jacuzzi suite. Weekend and other packages available. AE, CB, DC, MC, V. Parking on street. From I-81, take Exit 298 and go south on U.S. 11 1¹/₂ miles to the first traffic light; turn right one block, left at the light (Holliday Street).

Strasberg likes to call itself the Antiques Capital of Virginia, and this restored Victorian hotel, built at a hospital in 1895, is furnished with an impressive collection of period pieces. Most are supplied by the Strasburg Emporium (see "Antiquing," above) and are for sale. Hence, the decor changes constantly. Some rooms have Jacuzzis.

Dining/Entertainment: Known for its Russian sauerkraut soup, the dining room is open for all three meals. Dinner entrees might include shrimp-and-scallop cassoulet; chicken breast with walnuts and bacon in cream sauce; or Bavarian pork chops with onions, apples, and sauerkraut. A first-floor pub offers friendly conversation and libation.

Wayside Inn
7783 Main St., Middletown, VA 22645. ☎ **540/869-1797.** Fax 540/869-6038. 24 rms and suites. A/C TV TEL. $75–$125 double. Weekend and other packages available. AE, DC, MC, V. From I-81, take Exit 302 to U.S. 11 (Main Street).

This rambling white roadside inn first offered bed and board to Shenandoah Valley travelers in 1797. It became a stagecoach stop some 20 years later when the Valley Pike was hacked out of the wilderness, and it has continued to be an inn ever since. In the 1960s, a Washington financier and antiques collector restored it, and today rooms are beautifully decorated with an assortment of 18th- and 19th-century pieces. Each room's decor reflects a period style, from Colonial to elaborate Victorian Renaissance Revival. Expect to find canopied beds, armoires, highboys, writing desks, antique clocks, and stenciled or papered walls adorned with fine prints and oil paintings.

Dining/Entertainment: Regional American cuisine is served in seven antiques-filled dining rooms. Dinner entrees include whole stuffed valley trout, roast duckling, and smothered chicken in white wine. Breakfast and lunch are also available; cocktails are served in the Coachyard Lounge.

MIDDLETOWN AFTER DARK

Wayside Theatre
Main Street (U.S. 11), Middletown. ☎ **540/869-1776.** Admission for single show: $15 Wed and Sat matinee; $17 Wed, Thurs, and Sun night; $20 Fri and Sat night. Senior and student discounts available.

Since 1961, the Wayside (which stands near the Wayside Inn) has staged fine productions by contemporary dramatists, including Peter Shaffer, Neil Simon, Wendy Wasserstein, Garson Kanin, and Alan Ayckbourn. Peter Boyle, Susan Sarandon, Jill Eikenberry, and Donna McKechnie began their careers here. The season runs from the end of May to mid-October, and a Christmas show is staged in December. The Curtain Call Café offers posttheater light fare and a chance for audience members to mingle with the performers.

4 Front Royal

20 miles SE of Strasburg; 174 miles NW of Richmond; 70 miles W of Washington, D.C.

At the northern end of the Skyline Drive, the Front Royal area offers easy access to the Shenandoah National Park and its many outdoor activities. During the summer months, it also is a hotbed for canoeing, rafting, kayaking, and inner tubing on the sometimes lazy, sometimes rapid South Fork of the Shenandoah River. As a base of operations to explore the region, it provides some fine accommodations and dining choices, especially at a nationally famous, five-star inn and restaurant in nearby "Little" Washington.

ESSENTIALS

VISITOR INFORMATION   Contact the **Front Royal/Warren County Chamber of Commerce Visitors Center,** 414 E. Main St. (P.O. Box 568), Front Royal, VA 22630 (☎ 540/635-3185, or 800/338-2576). Open daily from 9am to 5pm. From I-66, follow U.S. 340 into town and turn left on Main Street at the Warren County Courthouse.

GETTING THERE   From I-66, take Exit 6, U.S. 340/U.S. 522 south; it's five minutes to town. Front Royal is also easily reached from I-81 by taking I-66 east to Exit 6.

EXPLORING THE TOWN & TOURING THE SKYLINE CAVERNS

Begin your tour at the Front Royal/Warren County Visitors Center, in the old yellow train station at 414 E. Main St., which provides free walking and driving tour brochures. Highlights in the historic downtown are both on Chester Street a block north of the visitor center: the **Warren Rifles Confederate Museum** (☎ 540/ 636-6982), which has a collection of Civil War firearms, battleflags, and uniforms, and the adjacent **Belle Boyd Cottage** (☎ 540/636-1446), where infamous Confederate spy Belle Boyd pillow-talked with her unsuspecting Union lovers.

Skyline Caverns

U.S. 340, 1 mile south of Shenandoah National Park entrance. ☎ **540/635-4545** or 800/ 296-4545. Admission $10 adults, $9 seniors, $5 children 7–13, children under 13 free. June 15– Labor Day daily 9am–6:30pm; Mar 15–June 14 and Labor Day–Nov 14 Mon–Fri 9am–5pm, Sat–Sun 9am–6pm; Nov 15–Mar 14 daily 9am–4pm.

There are many caverns beneath the Blue Ridge Mountains, but the first one you'll encounter coming from the north is Skyline Caverns, which boasts unique rock formations called anthodites—delicate white spikes that spread in all directions from their position on the cave ceiling. Their growth rate is only about 1 inch every 7,000 years. A sophisticated lighting system dramatically enhances such formations as the Capitol Dome, Rainbow Trail, and Painted Desert. A miniature train covering about half a mile is a popular attraction for kids. The temperature in the caverns is a cool 54°F year-round, so take a sweater even in summer.

SPORTS & OUTDOOR ACTIVITIES

HORSEBACK RIDING The 4,200-acre **Marriott Ranch,** Route 1, Hume, VA 22639 (☎ 540/364-2627), offers 1¹/₂-hour guided trail rides, buggy rides, summer sunset rides, and Saturday-night "Steak Bakes." Whether you plan to ride or just want to see the ranch, it's an interesting excursion. You can also rent horses and take lessons at **Massanutten Trail Rides, Inc.,** on C.R. 619 south of Front Royal (☎ 540/636-6061).

GOLF Duffers are welcome at **Shenandoah Valley Golf Club** (☎ 540/635-3588) and **Bowling Green Country Club** (☎ 540/635-2095). Call for directions and starting times.

WHERE TO STAY

Front Royal has several motels, two of them with national chain affiliation: **Quality Inn Skyline Drive** and **Super 8.**

River Rafting & Canoeing

The streams flowing west down from Shenandoah National Park wind up in the South Fork of the Shenandoah River, which winds its way through a narrow valley between the Blue Ridge and Massanutten Mountain, another long ridge cutting this part of the Shenandoah Valley in two.

The switchbacks of the South Fork are the region's main center for river rafting, canoeing, and kayaking from mid-March to mid-November. The amount of recent rain will determine whether you go white water rafting, canoeing, kayaking, or just lazily floating downstream in an inner tube.

Outfitters providing equipment and guides include **Front Royal Canoe Co.,** P.O. Box 473, Front Royal, VA 22630 (☎ 540/635-5440); **Downriver Canoe Company,** P.O. Box 10, Bentonville, VA 22610 (☎ 540/635-5526); and **River Rental Outfitters,** P.O. Box 145, Bentonville, VA 22610 (☎ 540/635-5050, or 800/RAPIDS-1). Bentonville is a small village on U.S. 340 about eight miles south of Front Royal.

Call or write for reservations and prices.

⑤ Caledonia Farm-1812

47 Dearing Rd., Flint Hill, VA 22627. ☎ **540/675-3693** or 800/262-1812. Manual-start fax on both numbers. 2 rms, 2 suites. A/C. $80 double with shared bath; $140 suite. Rates include full breakfast. DISC, MC, V. From Front Royal, take U.S. 522 south 12 miles to Flint Hill and turn right onto C.R. 641, to C.R. 606 to C.R. 628; look for a sign indicating a right turn to the farm about a mile past the last intersection.

This 1812 Federal-style stone farmhouse, a short drive from Front Royal in the beautiful foothills of the Blue Ridge, comprises not only a delightful B&B but a 52-acre working cattle farm. Scenic old barns, livestock and domestic animals, and open pastureland make for a pastoral setting. The common rooms are furnished with country charm. A breezeway connects the main house with the romantically private 2¹/₂-room guesthouse. All accommodations offer lovely views of the Blue Ridge, as well as working fireplaces. TVs and VCRs are available on request.

Chester House Inn

43 Chester St., Front Royal, VA 22630. ☎ **540/635-3937** or 800/621-0441. Fax 540/635-3937. 6 rms and suites (5 with bath). A/C. $65–$110 double. Rates include continental breakfast. AE, MC, V.

A stately 1905 Georgian Revival mansion set on two pretty acres of gardens, Bill and Ann Wilson's B&B is a friendly place, attractively furnished with a mix of antiques and reproductions. The premier accommodation is the Royal Oak Suite, a spacious high-ceilinged bedroom with a fireplace, separate sitting room, and private bath; it overlooks formal boxwood gardens. Another charmer is the Blue Ridge Room, which has a wrought iron king bed and an old coal stove. There's a dining room, game room, and TV parlor, as well as terraced gardens adorned with a fountain, statuary, and brick walls.

A NATIONALLY RENOWNED INN & RESTAURANT

✪ Inn at Little Washington

Middle and Main streets (P.O. Box 300), Washington, VA 22747. ☎ **540/675-3800.** Fax 540/675-3100. 9 rms, 3 suites. A/C TEL. $240–$450 double; $480–$590 suite. Rates include continental breakfast. MC, V. From Front Royal, take U.S. 522 south 16 miles, then west on U.S. 211 to Washington.

As glowing notices in the *New York Times, Washington Post,* and *San Francisco Chronicle* attest, the Inn at Little Washington is simply one of America's finest restaurants and country inns. Located in the sleepy village of Washington, Virginia (population about 160), it was opened as a restaurant in 1978 by owners Patrick O'Connell, who is the chef, and Reinhardt Lynch, who serves as maître d'hôtel.

Rooms are magnificently furnished according to the design of an English decorator; her original sketches are framed and hang in the inn's upstairs hallways. The two bilevel suites have loft bedrooms, balconies overlooking the courtyard garden, and bathrooms with Jacuzzi tubs. You'll find terry robes, thick towels, hairdryers, and elegant toiletries in the sumptuous bathrooms. No detail has been overlooked—antiques, Oriental rugs, extravagantly canopied beds, hand-painted ceiling borders, and faux woodwork adorn the rooms.

Dining/Entertainment: The 65-seat restaurant pays homage to French cuisine but relies on regional products—trout, Chesapeake Bay seafood, cheese from nearby dairies, wild ducks—for culinary inspiration. Patrick O'Connell changes the menu constantly for his fabulous fixed-price dinners ($78 Sunday to Thursday, $88 Friday, $98 Saturday). They might begin with a timbale of Virginia lump crabmeat and spinach mousse before continuing with an entree such as veal Shenandoah with local cider, apples, and apple brandy; or barbecued grilled boneless rack of lamb in pecan crust with shoestring sweet potatoes. Desserts include warm custard bread pudding with Jack Daniels sauce and swans of white-chocolate mousse in passion-fruit purée. Make your dinner reservations well in advance.

WHERE TO DINE

Feed Mill Restaurant

500 E. Main St. (next to visitor center). ☎ **540/636-3123.** Reservations not necessary. Sandwiches $3–$4.75; main courses $10–$17. AE, MC, V. Daily 11am–3pm, Sun–Thurs 4–9pm, Fri–Sat 4–10pm. Bar open to midnight. AMERICAN.

Occupying a picturesque 1922 mill building, this pub-like establishment has massive supporting columns and ceiling beams of chestnut. The distinctive trompe l'oeil murals representing Front Royal's pioneer and 19th-century eras were executed by artist Patricia Windrow, who also painted the unusual "Not So National Zoo" mural on the side of her gallery, nearby at 401 E. Main St. Lunch fare includes soups, spicy chili, salads, and overstuffed deli sandwiches. Main courses, served with salad, vegetables, potato, and homemade breads, range from vegetarian lasagna to chicken baked with apples, walnuts, and mushrooms in a wine sauce. In the "2 Left" Lounge adjoining the restaurant there's entertainment on weekends.

5 Luray

6 miles W of Shenandoah National Park; 91 miles SW of Washington, D.C.; 135 miles NW of Richmond

The most visited caverns in the East draw thousands of tourists to Luray, seat of Page County. Lush farmland surrounds the town, which also serves as the main gateway to the Shenandoah National Park's popular Central District. The park headquarters and Thornton Gap entry are just a few miles up U.S. 211.

ESSENTIALS

VISITOR INFORMATION   The **Page County Chamber of Commerce,** 46 E. Main St., Luray, VA 22835 (☎ 540/743-3915), will supply information in advance and make same-day hotel reservations at its visitor center, which is open daily 9am to 7pm from Memorial Day through October, daily 9am to 5pm the rest of the year.

GETTING THERE   From Shenandoah National Park, take U.S. 211 west. From I-81, follow U.S. 211 east. U.S. 340 is also a major north-south thoroughfare.

EXPLORING THE CAVERNS

In addition to monumental columns in rooms more than 140 feet high, this labyrinth of underground chambers is noted for the beautiful cascades of natural colors found on interior walls. A U.S. Registered Natural Landmark, ✪ **Luray Caverns** (on U.S. 211) also combines the works of man and nature into an unusual organ with a sound system directly connected to stalactites. Music is produced when the stalactites are electronically tapped by rubber-tipped plungers controlled by an organist.

For additional information, call **540/743-6551.** Admission is $11 for adults, $9 seniors, $5 children 7–13, under 7 free. From June 15 to Labor Day, hours are daily from 9am to 7pm; March 15 to June 14 and the day after Labor Day to November 14, daily 9am–6pm; and from November 15 to March 14, Monday to Friday 9am to 4pm, Saturday and Sunday 9am to 5pm. Conducted tours follow a system of brick and concrete walkways and take about an hour.

Admission to the caverns includes the **Historic Car and Carriage Caravan,** a collection of antique carriages, coaches, and cars—including actor Rudolph Valentino's

1925 Rolls Royce. The complex also includes a snack bar, gift shop, and fudge kitchen.

WHERE TO STAY

Luray has one national chain motel: **Ramada Inn,** which is on the U.S. 211 Bypass northeast of town. Just as bed-and-breakfasts proliferated during the 1980s and early 1990s, mountain cabins are the latest trend here. Most require at least a week's rental. The visitor center (see above) will provide a list of cabins.

The Cabins at Brookside

U.S. 211 East, Luray, VA 22835. ☎ **540/743-5698** or 800/299-2655. 8 cabins. A/C. $70–$180 double. AE, DC, DISC, MC, V. From Luray, go east 4¹/₂ miles on U.S. 211. From Shenandoah National Park Headquarters, go west half a mile on U.S. 211.

Owners Bob and Cece Castle remodeled this 1940s roadside service station/motel into a collection of log-look cabins with comfortable Williamsburg-style furnishings throughout. Although they lie along busy U.S. 211, the rear of the cabins open to decks or sunrooms overlooking a bubbling brook, and road noise dies down after dark. Three units have Jacuzzis, four have fireplaces, and one has a kitchen (the others, refrigerators). The rustic Brookside Restaurant on the premises serves inexpensive home cooking. This is the closest accommodation to Shenandoah National Park.

Luray Caverns Motel West

U.S. 211 Bypass West, Luray, VA 22835. ☎ **540/743-4536.** 19 rms, 1 apt. A/C TEL TV. $54–$66 double, $104 apt. AE, DISC, MC, V.

Operated and spotlessly maintained by Luray Caverns, this older one-story motel with a plantation facade sits just across the road from the caverns entrance. Although dated, the spacious rooms all have pleasant views across pastureland to the Blue Ridge Mountains.

A related establishment, the less appealing but equally clean **Luray Caverns Motel East** (☎ 540/743-4531), is a short distance away on U.S. 211.

WHERE TO DINE

Parkhurst Restaurant

U.S. 211, 2¹/₂ miles west of Luray Caverns. ☎ **540/743-6009.** Reservations recommended. Main courses $9–$21. AE, DISC, MC, V. Sun–Thurs 4–10pm, Fri–Sat 4–11pm. AMERICAN/ ITALIAN.

An inn-like ambiance pervades this cozy establishment, built in 1938 as a country motel but operated as a restaurant since 1978. A small central dining room has knotty pine paneling, but the choice tables here are in an enclosed verandah with views across the parking lot to the mountains. Lots of plants and quiet music create a romantic atmosphere in which to enjoy a mix of cuisine ranging from southern fried chicken to veal Oscar (with king crab). Colonial steak is a house variation on prime rib: partially roasted, then finished on the grill with seasoned butter.

6 New Market: A Civil War Battlefield & the Endless Caverns

16 miles W of Luray; 110 miles SW of Washington, D.C.

Even if your knowledge of the Civil War doesn't extend much beyond distinguishing the troops in gray from the troops in blue, you'll be fascinated by the exposition of the Civil War in the Hall of Valor Museum in **New Market Battlefield Historical**

Impressions

Gentlemen . . . I trust you will do your duty.
—General Breckinridge, Battle of New Market, May 15, 1864

I look back upon that orchard as the most awful spot on the battlefield.
—Cadet John C. Howard, Battle of New Market, May 15, 1864

Park, New Market (☎ 540/740-3101). To reach the museum from I-81, Exit 264, take U.S. 211W, then an immediate right onto C.R. 305 (George Collins Parkway); the battlefield park is 1³/4 miles away, at the end of the road. From Luray, follow U.S. 211W, as above.

The park commemorates 257 Virginia Military Institute teenagers, whom Gen. John Breckinridge ordered to New Market in a desperate move to halt advancing Union troops. The boys marched in the rain for four days to reach the front line. They charged the enemy on May 15, 1864, won the day, and returned home victorious, with only 10 cadets killed and 47 wounded. Hearing of the battle, Grant exclaimed, "The South is robbing the cradle and the grave." At the visitors center you can see two films, one about the battle, the other about Stonewall Jackson's Shenandoah campaign. The final Confederate assault on the Union line is covered in a self-guided one-mile walking tour of the grassy field. In the center of the line of battle was the Bushong farmhouse, today a museum of 19th-century valley life.

The park is open daily from 9am to 5pm; admission is $5 for adults, $2 for children 7 to 15 (under 7 free) and includes the battlefield, Hall of Valor Museum, and Bushong Farm.

Three miles south of New Market Battlefield on U.S. 11 is **Endless Caverns** (☎ 540/740-3993). Its natural beauty is enhanced by the dramatic use of lighting to display spectacular rooms, each boasting a variety of stalactites, stalagmites, giant columns, and limestone pendants orchestrated into brilliant displays of nature's work. Endless Caverns maintains a year-round temperature of 56°F. **Tours** are given March 15 to June 14, daily from 9am to 5pm; June 15 to Labor Day, daily from 9am to 7pm; the day after Labor Day to November 14, daily from 9am to 5pm; and November 15 to March 14, daily from 9am to 4pm. Admission is $10 for adults, $5 for children ages 3 to 12, under 3 free.

7 Staunton

42 miles S of New Market; 142 miles SW of Washington, D.C.; 92 miles NW of Richmond

Settled well before the Revolution, Staunton (pronounced "*Stan*-ton") was a major stop for pioneers on the way west. It was Virginia's capital for 17 days during June 1781, when then-governor Thomas Jefferson fled Richmond in the face of advancing British troops. When the Central Virginia Railroad arrived in 1854, Staunton became a booming regional center.

Today the town is noted as the birthplace of Woodrow Wilson, our 28th president. Along with Wilson's first home, many of Staunton's 19th-century downtown buildings have been refurbished and restored, including the train station and its adjacent Wharf District (now a shopping and dining complex). The town also is home to a fascinating museum that explains the origins of the unique Shenandoah Valley farming culture. And country music lovers will find another shrine here in the hometown of the Statler Brothers.

ESSENTIALS

VISITOR INFORMATION Contact the **Staunton–Augusta County Travel Information Center,** 1303 Richmond Ave., Staunton, VA 24404 (☎ 540/332-3972, or 800/332-5219). The center is at Exit 222 of I-81; go west on U.S. 250 and follow the signs. It's open daily from 9am to 5pm. The **Staunton Welcome Center** is on the grounds of Woodrow Wilson Birthplace, 24 N. Coalter St. (☎ 540/332-3971). Both centers provide free walking tour maps to Staunton's historic downtown.

GETTING THERE Staunton is at the junctions of I-64 and I-81 and U.S. 11 and U.S. 250.

Amtrak trains serve Staunton's station at 1 Middlebrook Ave. (☎ 800/872-7245). The nearest regional airport is in Charlottesville (see Chapter 7).

SEEING THE SIGHTS

Museum of American Frontier Culture

U.S. 250, half a mile west of I-81. ☎ **540/332-7850.** Admission $7 adults, $6.50 seniors, $3 children 6–12, under 6 free. Mid-Mar to Nov daily 9am–5pm; Dec to mid-March daily 10am–4pm.

In light of its history as a major stopping point for pioneers, Staunton is a logical location for this museum, which consists of 17th-, 18th-, and 19th-century working farmsteads representing the origins of the Shenandoah's early settlers—Northern Irish, English, and German—and explaining how aspects of each were blended into a fourth farm, the typical Colonial American homestead. Staff members in period costumes plant fields, tend livestock, and do domestic chores.

Statler Brothers Complex

501 Thornrose Ave. (near Norfolk Avenue). ☎ **540/885-7927.** Free admission. Tours Mon–Fri 2pm. Souvenir shop Mon–Fri 10:30am–3:30pm.

The singing Statler Brothers grew up in Staunton, and after they made it big in Nashville, they bought the old neighborhood elementary school and turned it into their office complex. One tour a day takes visitors through the building and lets them see the brothers' awards and a mass of memorabilia sent to them by adoring fans.

✪ Woodrow Wilson Birthplace

24 N. Coalter St. ☎ **540/885-0897.** Admission $6 adults, $5.50 seniors, $2 children 6–12, under 6 free. Mar–Dec daily 9am–5pm. Call for winter hours.

This handsome Greek Revival building, built in 1846 by a Presbyterian congregation as a manse for their ministers, stands next to an excellent museum detailing Wilson's life. As a minister, Wilson's father had to move often, and so the family left here when the future president was only 2. The house is furnished with many family items, including the crib Wilson slept in and the chair in which his mother rocked him. The galleries of the museum next door trace Wilson's Scottish-Irish roots, his academic career as a professor and president at Princeton University, and, of course, his eight presidential years (1913–21). America's entry into World War I and Wilson's unsuccessful efforts to convince the U.S. Senate to participate in the League of Nations are also explored. Don't overlook the beautiful garden or the carriage house that shelters Wilson's presidential limousine, a shiny Pierce-Arrow.

WHERE TO STAY

Staunton has several national chain motels near I-81. Those near Exit 222 (U.S. 260) include **Comfort Inn, Econo Lodge,** and **Super 8.** Near Exit 225 (Woodrow

Wilson Parkway), the **Holiday Inn Golf & Conference Center** is adjacent to the Country Club of Staunton, where guests can play. There also are several bed-and-breakfast homes in the area; ask the visitor center for a list.

✪ Belle Grae Inn

515 W. Frederick St., Staunton, VA 24401. ☎ **540/886-5151.** 18 rms, including suites and small cottage. A/C. $69–$110 double; $99–$139 suite. Rates include full breakfast. Packages available. AE, MC, V. From I-81, take Exit 222 west and follow signs to Wilson Birthplace; once there, turn left on Frederick Street to inn.

This beautifully restored 1873 Victorian house, with white gingerbread trim and an Italianate wraparound front porch, sits well back from the street atop a sloping lawn. It houses eight guest rooms, which are the least expensive here. The property now occupies an entire city block, and most accommodations are in adjoining 19th-century houses, all of them beautifully restored. Rooms throughout are furnished in period antiques and reproductions, with wicker pieces, Oriental rugs, and canopied four-poster, sleigh, and brass beds. Some rooms have fireplaces, and most have phones and TVs. There are also TVs in the Garden Room and the main-house sitting room.

   Dining/Entertainment: Staunton's finest cuisine is served in the Garden Room or an adjoining dining room in the main house. "You can eat fried chicken at home," says proprietor Michael Organ, "here you can have quail." There's also a light-fare menu available.

WHERE TO DINE

⑤ The Beverly Restaurant

12 E. Beverly St. (between Augusta and New streets). ☎ **540/886-4317.** Reservations accepted. Sandwiches $2.50–$4; main courses $3.50–$6.50. MC, V. Mon–Fri 6:30am–7pm, Sat 6:30am–4pm. AMERICAN.

Family owned and operated since 1961, this storefront eatery in the heart of the business district harkens back to that nearly bygone era when even hash-house cooks made everything from scratch. You won't find pre-packaged mashed potatoes among the home cooking here. Says co-owner Paul Thomas: "We've got a potato peeler back there that came over on the *Mayflower.*" The fresh fare is typically small-town southern: rib-eye steaks, fried shrimp or fish, veal cutlets, roast beef. The Beverly is famous hereabouts for high English tea at 3pm Wednesday and Friday.

The Depot Grille

In Staunton Station, 42 Middlebrook Ave. (at South Augusta Street). ☎ **540/885-7332.** Reservations not necessary. Main courses $7–$14.50. AE, DISC, MC, V. Daily 11am–midnight. AMERICAN.

In the Wharf District's restored train station, this popular steak-and-seafood house has a festive atmosphere, highlighted by a long Victorian bar and railroad memorabilia. Seating is in spacious wood-paneled booths or Windsor chairs at small wooden tables. A seasoned crabcake sandwich, with french fries or coleslaw, is $7; a grilled chicken-breast sandwich, $5. Black Angus sirloin for two makes a hearty dinner and comes with salad, fresh bread, potato, and vegetable. A children's menu offers a choice of four entrees, each just $2.

   Also in Staunton Station, **The Pullman Restaurant,** 36 Millbrook Ave. (☎ 540/885-6612), is a similar establishment. Nearby in the Wharf District, **J. Ruggles Warehouse** (☎ 540/886-4399) is a lively restaurant-bar fronting a municipal parking lot on Johnson Street at Central Avenue. Locals describe a visit to these three institutions as pub crawling.

A PICNIC STOP

A good place to stop for a picnic lunch midway between Staunton and Lexington is the picturesque **Cyrus McCormick Farm** (☎ 540/377-2255). From I-81, Exit 205 is well marked to the village of Steele's Tavern and the McCormick birthplace, but the scenic way to get there from Staunton is via U.S. 11 South. In a lovely rural setting, it contains a small blacksmith shop and other log cabins in which exhibits include a model of McCormick's invention, the first reaper. Open daily from 8am to 5pm; no admission fee.

A SIDE TRIP TO VIRGINIA'S SWITZERLAND

Because of its rugged beauty, mountainous Highland County west of Staunton is known as "Virginia's Switzerland." In fact, the 50-mile drive on U.S. 250 from Staunton to the little town of **Monterey** is one of the state's most scenic excursions. The road climbs over first Shenandoah Mountain (3,760 feet) and then Bull Pasture Mountain (3,240 feet) before descending into Monterey, whose white churches conjure up images of New England hamlets.

Monterey is home to the popular Highlands Maple Festival in March, and to **Highland Adventures,** P.O. Box 151, Monterey, VA 24465 (☎ 540/468-2722), a company specializing in caving, rock climbing, mountain biking, and other outdoor adventures in the Allegheny Highlands of Virginia and West Virginia. For more information, write the **Highland County Chamber of Commerce,** P.O. Box 223, Monterey, VA 24465.

From Monterey, you can take U.S. 220 south along the Jackson River to Warm Springs and Hot Springs (see below), and from there to Lexington via Va. 39 and the dramatic Goshen Pass.

8 Warm Springs & Hot Springs

Hot Springs: 220 miles SW of Washington, D.C., 160 miles W of Richmond; Warm Springs: 5 miles N of Hot Springs

At temperatures ranging from 94° F to 104°F, thermal springs rise throughout the mountains and valleys of Bath County, which have made this highlands region a retreat since the 18th century. (The Homestead, one of the nation's premier spas at Hot Springs, has been operating since 1776.)

ESSENTIALS

VISITOR INFORMATION Contact the **Bath County Chamber of Commerce,** Hot Springs, VA 24445 (☎ 540/839-5409, or 800/628-8092). The office and visitor center is on U.S. 220 near the junction with Main Street. Open Monday to Friday from 9am to 5pm.

GETTING THERE U.S. 220 runs north and south through Hot Springs and Warm Springs, with easy access to I-64 at Covington, 20 miles south of Hot Springs. The scenic way to get there is via Va. 39 from Lexington, a 42-mile drive that follows the Maury River through Goshen Pass. You can also make the scenic loop through "Virginia's Switzerland," described in the Staunton section, above.

The nearest place with regular air service is Roanoke Regional Airport; Woodrum Livery Service (☎ 540/345-7710) offers connecting transportation. The nearest Amtrak station is in Clifton Forge, VA (☎ 800/872-7245).

TAKING THE WATERS & ENJOYING AN ACCLAIMED SUMMER MUSIC FESTIVAL

Most famous of the thermal springs are five miles up the road at the **Warm Springs,** opened in 1761 and still utilizing its 19th-century white clapboard bathhouses. The crystal-clear waters of these natural rock pools circulate gently and offer a wonderfully relaxing experience. Open mid-April through October daily from 10am to 6pm; closed November to mid-April. The charge is $7 per one-hour session.

There's music in the mountain air on summer weekends at the **Garth Newel Chamber Music Center,** P.O. Box 240, Warm Springs, VA 24484 (☎ 540/839-5018), on U.S. 220 between the villages of Warm Springs and Hot Springs. This annual summer chamber music festival has been drawing critical acclaim since the early 1970s. Garth Newel also sponsors a series of unique Music Holiday Weekend Retreats in spring, fall, and winter, including Christmas and New Years. Accommodations and dining at the on-site Manor House are part of the package. Call or write for details.

WHERE TO STAY & DINE
IN HOT SPRINGS

This tiny village spreads out from The Homestead resort along Main Street, where you'll find a country grocery store, an interesting crafts outlet called the Bacova Guild Showroom (☎ 540/839-2105), and The Homestead-owned Sam Snead's Tavern (see below).

✪ The Homestead

Off U.S. 220, Hot Springs, VA 24445. ☎ **540/839-1776** or 800/838-1766. Fax 540/839-7670. 440 rms, 81 suites. A/C MINIBAR TV TEL. $190–$270 double for standard room; higher rates for superior and deluxe rooms and suites. Add $47 per person per day for optional breakfast and dinner. Children 12 and under stay free in parents' room; children 13 and over pay $35 per day. Weekend and other packages available. AE, DC, DISC, MC, V.

With a prodigious reputation dating back to 1766, this famous spa and golf resort has been host to Presidents Jefferson, Wilson, Hoover, F.D.R., Truman, Eisenhower, Carter, and Reagan, plus social elites like the Henry Fords, John D. Rockefeller, the Vanderbilts, and Lord and Lady Astor.

A clock tower tops the hotel's main building of red Kentucky brick with white-limestone trim. Guests enter via the magnificent Great Hall, lined with 16 Corinthian columns and a 211-foot floral carpet. Two fireplaces, wing chairs, Chippendale-reproduction tables with reading lamps, and deep sofas create a warm atmosphere. Afternoon tea is served here daily to the light classical background music of the piano.

Guests have a variety of accommodations in rooms and suites with a Virginia country manor ambiance and custom designed mahogany furniture. Most units offer spectacular mountain views, and the 81 suites in the South Wing have working fireplaces, private bars, sun porches, two remote-control TVs, and two phones.

Dining/Entertainment: Renovations have turned The Homestead's historic Dining Room into a lush palm court, in which an orchestra performs every evening during six-course dinners. The adjoining Commonwealth Room is adorned with murals of such Virginia landmarks as Mount Vernon and Monticello. Tables throughout are elegantly appointed. Under the supervision of European-trained chefs, the cuisine features regional favorites like fresh rainbow trout, grilled lamb chops, and roast beef with Armagnac sauce. Cocktails, hors d'oeuvres, and after-dinner espresso are served in the View Lounge. Other options include The Grille, and casual dining in the Casino and in Café Albert. Across Main Street from the hotel, Sam Snead's Tavern is a lively pub serving traditional American fare (open Wednesday to Monday from 5 to 10pm). Evening entertainment includes live music, dancing, and free movies.

Services: Room service, concierge, travel agency, children's programs.

Facilities: Three outstanding golf courses (Lanny Wadkins is the resident PGA pro), spa with full health club facilities, indoor and outdoor pools, 12 tennis courts, bowling, fishing, hiking trails, horseback and carriage rides, ice skating on an Olympic-size rink, lawn bowling and croquet, billiards, sporting clays and skeet trap, downhill and cross-country skiing mid-December to March, warm springs pools, horseshoes, volleyball, video game room, board games, 21 boutique and specialty shops, beauty salon. *Note:* Nonguests can pay to use all of The Homestead's facilities except the indoor pool.

⑤ Roseloe Motel

U.S. 220 North (Route 2, Box 590), Hot Springs, VA 24445. ☎ 540/839-5373. 14 rms. A/C TV TEL. $44–$50 double. AE, DC, DISC, MC, V. From Hot Springs, go north three miles on U.S. 220.

At the opposite extreme from The Homestead, this brick-fronted, family-owned motel offers inexpensive, well-maintained, and clean rooms virtually across the highway from the Garth Newel Chamber Music Center. Six units have full kitchens, while two have kitchenettes. The others have refrigerators.

IN WARM SPRINGS

A charming little community with many historic homes, Warm Springs centers around its thermal pools, described above. There's an unstaffed visitor center kiosk, on U.S. 220 just south of the Va. 39 junction, which usually has copies of a walking tour brochure to the little village (if it doesn't, the Bath County Chamber of Commerce in Hot Springs does).

Anderson Cottage Bed & Breakfast

Old Germantown Road, Warm Springs, VA 24484. ☎ 540/839-2975. 2 rms (1 with shared bath), 2 suites, separate guest cottage. $60–$110 double. Rates include full breakfast. No credit cards. From Va. 39, turn left onto Germantown Road (C.R. 692), to fourth house on left.

One of Bath County's oldest buildings, this log-and-white-clapboard cottage has been in owner Jean Randolph Bruns's family since the 1870s. The setting is an expansive lawn with a warm stream flowing through the property in the heart of the picturesque village. The house has appealing country charm, with many family heirloom pieces and photos, wide-board floors, Oriental rugs, working fireplaces, and lots of loaded bookcases. Accommodations are individually decorated and exceptionally spacious. Originally an 1820s brick kitchen, the Guest Cottage is ideal for families, with two bedrooms, two baths, a full kitchen/dining/sitting room with fireplace, and a living room.

Inn at Gristmill Square

C.R. 645, Warm Springs, VA 24484. ☎ 540/839-2231. Fax 540/839-5770. 16 rms, 1 suite. A/C TV TEL. $85–$95 double. Rates include continental breakfast. MAP (including five-course dinner and gratuities) $155–$165 double. DISC, MC, V. From U.S. 220N, turn left onto C.R. 619 and right onto C.R. 645.

Five restored 19th-century buildings, including an old mill, comprise this unique hostelry. It includes the Blacksmith Shop, which houses a country store; the Hardware Store, with seven guest units; the Steel House, with four accommodations; and the Miller's House, with four rooms. Furnishings are charming period pieces, with comfortable upholstered chairs, brass chandeliers, quilts on four-poster beds, marble-top side tables, and working fireplaces. Breakfast is served in your room in a picnic basket. Other facilities include an outdoor pool, three tennis courts, and a sauna.

Dining/Entertainment: The rustic Waterwheel Restaurant and Simon Kenton Pub are cozy spots in the old mill building. The restaurant features notably good American cuisine, with entrees like grilled trout, pork Calvados, and filet of salmon with béarnaise sauce. Wines are displayed among the gears of the waterwheel. The restaurant also serves Sunday brunch.

A NEARBY COUNTRY INN

✪ Fort Lewis Lodge

HCR 3, Box 21A, Millboro, VA 24460. ☎ **540/925-2314.** Fax 540/925-2352. 13 rms, 2 cabins. $130–$150 double. MC, V. From Warm Springs, go 13 miles east on Va. 39, turn left on Indian Draft Road (C.R. 678) and drive north 10.8 miles, then turn left on Indian Road (C.R. 625) to entrance.

Owners John and Caryl Cowden have one of Virginia's most unusual country inns on their farm beside the Cowpasture River, which cuts a north-south valley over the mountain from Warm Springs. Fort Lewis Lodge is very popular with families getting away from Washington, D.C., and other nearby cities, so book early.

The rooms here are in a reconstructed barn; in fact, an outside spiral staircase leads to three rooms inside the attached silo. One end of the rough-look barn now is a comfortable lounge with stone fireplace and large windows looking out to a Jacuzzi-equipped deck and the farmland and mountains beyond. Other guests stay in hand-hewn log cabins, each with a fireplace.

The Cowdens' summertime garden supplies flowers and vegetables for excellent meals served in the old Lewis Mill, whose upstairs has been turned into a games room. A screened porch to one side shelters Buck's Bar, serving beer and wine. Activities include biking, hiking, and swimming and fishing for trout in the Cowpasture River.

9 Lexington: A College Town with a Slice of American History

36 miles S of Staunton; 180 miles SW of Washington, D.C.; 138 miles W of Richmond

A lively atmosphere prevails in Lexington, which consistently ranks as one of America's best small towns. Fine old homes line tree-shaded streets, among them the house where Stonewall Jackson lived when he taught at the Virginia Military Institute. A beautifully restored downtown looks so much like it did in the 1800s that scenes for the recent movie *Sommersby* ware filmed on Main Street (Richard Gere was "hanged" behind the Jackson House while Jodie Foster looked on). After the Civil War, Robert E. Lee came here to serve as president of what was then Washington College; he and his horse Traveller are buried here. And General George C. Marshall, winner of the Nobel Peace Prize for his post–World War II plan to rebuild Europe, graduated from VMI, which has built a fine museum to his memory.

Washington and Lee University has one of the oldest and most beautiful campuses in the country. Built in 1824, Washington Hall is topped by a replica of a master-piece of American folk art, an 1840 carved-wood statue of George Washington. The massive trees dotting the campus are believed to have been planted by Lee.

Sometimes called the West Point of the South, VMI opened in 1839 on the site of a state arsenal, abutting the Washington and Lee campus (one school has brick walkways; the other, concrete). The most dramatic episode in VMI's history took place during the Civil War at the Battle of New Market on May 15, 1864, when the corps of cadets helped turn back a larger Union army (see the New Market section, above). A month later, Union Gen. David Hunter got even, bombarding Lexington and burning down VMI.

If you have time to stop in only one Shenandoah Valley town, make it Lexington.

ESSENTIALS

VISITOR INFORMATION   The **Visitor Center,** 106 E. Washington St., Lexington, VA 24450 (☎ 540/463-3777), is a block from Main Street. This excellent source is the place to begin your tour of Lexington, for it has museumlike displays about the town's history, distributes free walking tour brochures and other information, and will make same-day hotel reservations. Be sure to see the engrossing slide show about Lexington history. The center is open daily from 8:30am to 6pm June, July, and August, from 9am to 5pm the rest of the year.

GETTING THERE   Lexington is on both I-81 and I-64, and U.S. 60 and U.S. 11 go directly into town.

EXPLORING THE TOWN

Seeing the downtown sights is easy and enjoyable via **Lexington Carriage Company** (☎ 540/463-3777), whose horse-drawn carriages depart the Visitor Center for 45-minute narrated tours daily from 9:30am to 4:30pm during the summer, from 9am to 5pm during April, May, September, and October. Fares are $9 for ages 15 to 60, $8 for seniors, $6 for children 7 to 14, and $2 for kids under 7.

✪ Lee Chapel and Museum

Washington and Lee University. ☎ **540/463-8768.** Free admission. Mid-Oct to mid-Apr, Mon–Sat 9am–4pm; mid-Apr to mid-Oct, Mon–Sat 9am–5pm, Sun 2–5pm. Washington and Lee University borders Washington Street, Jefferson Street, and Letcher Avenue; the chapel is closest to Letcher Avenue.

This magnificent Victorian-Gothic chapel of brick and native limestone, today used for concerts and other events, was built in 1867 at the request of General Lee. A white-marble sculpture of Lee by Edward Valentine portrays the general recumbent. Lee's remains are in a crypt below the chapel. His office was in the lower level of the building, and it is now part of the chapel museum, preserved just as he left it on September 28, 1870. His beloved horse, Traveller, is buried in a plot outside the office.

Among the museum's most important possessions are Charles Willson Peale's portrait of George Washington wearing the uniform of a colonel in the British Army and the painting of General Lee in Confederate uniform by Theodore Pine. The two portraits hang in the chapel auditorium.

✪ Virginia Military Institute Museum

Jackson Memorial Hall, VMI Campus. ☎ **540/464-7232.** Free admission. Mon–Sat 9am–5pm, Sun 2–5pm.

The VMI Museum displays uniforms, weapons, and memorabilia from cadets who attended the college and fought in numerous wars. Of special note: the world-famous H. M. Steward Antique Firearm Collection; the VMI coatee (or tunic) that belonged to Gen. George S. Patton Jr., VMI 1907; Stonewall Jackson's uniform coat worn at VMI and the bullet-pierced raincoat he was wearing when accidentally shot by his own men at Chancellorsville; and (thanks to taxidermy) Jackson's war horse, Little Sorrel.

✪ George C. Marshall Museum

VMI Campus. ☎ **540/463-7103.** Free admission. Mar–Oct daily 9am–5pm; Nov–Feb daily 9am–4pm.

Impressions

Let us cross the river and rest under the shade of the trees.
—Stonewall Jackson's last words, May 10, 1863

This impressive white building houses the archives and research library of General of the Army George C. Marshall. A 1901 graduate of VMI, Marshall had an illustrious career including service in France in 1917, when he was aide-de-camp to General Pershing. In World War II he was army chief of staff, then secretary of state and secretary of defense under President Truman. He is best remembered for his Marshall Plan, which fostered the economic recovery of Europe after the war. For his role in promoting peace, he became the first career soldier to be awarded the Nobel Peace Prize.

○ Stonewall Jackson House

8 E. Washington St. ☎ **540/463-2552.** Admission $5 adults, $2.50 children ages 6–12, under 6 free. Mon–Sat 9am–5pm, Sun 1–5pm; open until 6pm in summer. Guided tours begin on the hour and half hour (last tour at 4:30pm). Closed New Years Day, Easter, Thanksgiving, Christmas.

Maj. Thomas Jonathan Jackson came to Lexington in 1851 to take a post as teacher of natural philosophy (physics) and artillery tactics at VMI. Jackson lived here with his wife, Mary Anna Morrison, from early 1859 until he answered General Lee's summons to Richmond in 1861; it was the only house he ever owned. Photographs, text, and a slide show tell the story of the Jacksons' stay here. Upstairs, much of their furniture is placed as it was. Appropriate period furnishings duplicate the items on the inventory of Jackson's estate made shortly after he died near Chancellorsville in 1863. His body was returned to Lexington and was buried in Stonewall Jackson Memorial Cemetery on South Main Street.

Virginia Horse Center

Va. 39, north of I-64. ☎ **540/463-7060.** Admission varies by event; most are free. Open year-round. From downtown, take U.S. 11 north, turn left on Va. 39 a tenth of a mile north of I-64. The center is a mile on the left.

Sprawling across nearly 400 acres, the Virginia Horse Center offers horse shows, educational seminars, and sales of fine horses. Annual events include draft pulls, rodeos, various competitions, and competitive breed shows. In April, the center holds a Horse Festival showcasing the entire Virginia industry. For a full program of events, contact the center at P.O. Box 1051, Lexington, VA 24450.

THE NATURAL BRIDGE

Thomas Jefferson called this hugely impressive limestone formation "the most sublime of nature's works . . . so beautiful an arch, so elevated, so light and springing, as it were, up to heaven." The bridge was part of a 157-acre estate Jefferson acquired in 1774 from George III. It was included in the survey of western Virginia carried out by George Washington, who carved his initials into the face of the stone. This geological oddity rises 215 feet above Cedar Creek; its span is 90 feet long and spreads at its widest to 150 feet. The Monocan Indian tribes worshipped it as "the bridge of God." Today it is also the bridge of man, as U.S. 11 passes over it.

The Natural Bridge is now a small tourist-industry enclave, with a department-store-size souvenir shop, restaurant, hotel, campground, wax museum, and zoo. During summer, a 45-minute sound-and-light show called *The Drama of Creation* is conducted nightly beneath the bridge.

For more information, call **540/291-2121** or 800/533-1410. Admission is $8 for adults, $4 for children. The bridge itself is open daily 8am to dusk, and is located 12 miles south of Lexington (from I-81, take Exit 175).

SHOPPING

Lexington's charming 19th-century downtown offers many interesting shops. **Artists in Cahoots,** in the Alexander-Witherow House, 1 Washington St. (☎ 540/464-1147), a cooperative venture run by local artists and craftspeople, features an outstanding selection of paintings, sculptures, wood and metal crafts, hand-painted silk scarves, hand-blown glass, Shaker-design furniture, and gold, silver, and porcelain jewelry. **Virginia Born & Bred,** 16 W. Washington St. (☎ 540/463-1832), has made-in-Virginia gifts.

Antique hunters will find fascinating browsing at the **Lexington Antique & Craft Mall** (☎ 540/463-9511), in which 250 dealers occupy 40,000 square feet of space. They offer country and formal furniture, glassware, books, quilts, folk art, and much more. It's in the Kroger Shopping Center on U.S. 11, about half a mile north of downtown. Open Monday to Thursday from 10am to 6pm, Friday and Saturday from 10am to 8pm, Sunday from 12:30 to 5pm; winter hours vary.

SPORTS & OUTDOOR ACTIVITIES

CANOEING, KAYAKING & RAFTING   The Maury River, which runs through Lexington, provides some of Virginia's best white-water rafting and kayaking, especially through the Goshen Pass, on Va. 39 northwest of town. The Visitor Center has information about numerous put-in spots, or you can rent equipment or go on expeditions on the Maury and James Rivers with **James River Basin Canoe Livery,** U.S. 60 East (Route 4, Box 125), Lexington, VA 24450 (☎ 540/261-7334). Call or write for schedules and reservations.

HIKING   Two linear parks connect to offer hikers and joggers nearly 10 miles of gorgeous trail between Lexington and Buena Vista, a railroad town seven miles to the southeast. The major link is the **Chessie Nature Trail,** which follows an old railroad bed along the Maury River between Lexington and Buena Vista. No vehicles (including bicycles) are allowed. The Chessie trail connects with a walking path in **Woods Creek Park,** which starts at the Waddell School on Jordan Street and runs down to the banks of the Maury. Both trails are open from dawn to dusk. The Visitor Center has maps and brochures.

WHERE TO STAY

Lexington offers several chain motels, especially at the intersection of I-64 and U.S. 11, 1¹/₂ miles north of downtown. These include **Holiday Inn, Comfort Inn, Econo Lodge,** and **Super 8.**

HISTORIC COUNTRY INNS

Historic Country Inns, 11 N. Main St., Lexington, VA 24450 (☎ 540/463-2044, fax 540/463-2044), owns the three hostelries described below. Reservations should be made through Historic Country Inns.

Alexander-Witherow House and McCampbell Inn

Entered from Washington Street off North Main Street. ☎ **540/463-2044.** 14 rms, 8 suites. A/C TV TEL. $95–$140 double. Rates include continental breakfast. MC, V. Parking lot behind the McCampbell Inn.

The Alexander-Witherow House is a lovely late Georgian town house built in 1789 as a family residence over a store. The ground floor is occupied by Artists in Cahoots (see "Shopping," above). Accommodations include homey suites with separate living rooms and small kitchens. Furnishings offer traditional comfort, with wing chairs, four-poster beds, and hooked rugs on wide-board floors.

The McCampbell Inn, across the street, houses the main office for Historic Country Inns; guests at both hostelries eat breakfast here. Begun in 1809, with later additions in 1816 and 1857, it occupies a rambling building, with rooms facing both Main Street and the quieter back courtyard. Furnishings are a pleasant mix of antiques and reproductions.

✪ Maple Hall

On U.S. 11. ☎ 540/463-6693. 21 rms and suites. A/C TV. $95–$165 double; $135 guest house. Rates include breakfast. MC, V. Take U.S. 11 seven miles north of town near Exit 195 of I-81.

This handsome redbrick white-columned 1850 plantation house offers a restful country setting. Old boxwood surrounds the inn, which consists of a main house, a restored Guest House, and a Pond House. Rooms are individually furnished, many with antiques, Oriental rugs, and massive Victorian pieces; 10 rooms have working fireplaces. The Guest House has a living room, kitchen, and three bedrooms with baths. The Pond House, added in 1990, contains four suites and two minisuites. Guests relax on the shaded patio, on porches with rocking chairs, and on back verandas overlooking the fishing pond and nearby hills. A pool, tennis court, and three-mile hiking trail are on site.

Dining/Entertainment: Elegant dining in pretty gardenlike surroundings attracts a good following to the Maple Hall restaurant, open daily for dinner. Specialties are the likes of grilled quail, chicken breast sauté provençal, and filet mignon wrapped in bacon and served with béarnaise sauce.

BED & BREAKFASTS

Llewellyn Lodge

603 S. Main St., Lexington, VA 24450. ☎ **540/463-3235** or 800/882-1145. 6 rms. A/C. $65–$90 double. Rates include full breakfast. AE, MC, V.

A 55-year-old brick Colonial-style house, the Llewellyn Lodge is within easy walking distance of all of Lexington's historic sites. On the first floor are a cozy sitting room with working fireplace and a TV room. Guest rooms are decorated in exceptionally pretty color schemes. All rooms have ceiling fans. Co-host John Robinson has hiked just about every trail and fished every stream in the Blue Ridge Mountains; he is a font of information about what to do outdoors.

Seven Hills Inn

408 S. Main St., Lexington, VA 24450. ☎ **540/463-4715**. Fax 540/463-6526. 7 rms. A/C. $75–$124 double. Rates include full breakfast. MC, V.

Built in 1928 as a fraternity house, this three-story brick Colonial was later a boys home, then a girls home, and since 1990 has been a luxury bed-and-breakfast. All rooms are spacious, with antique reproductions, four-poster beds, and large baths (one has a Jacuzzi tub). A plethora of English and Japanese antiques graces the public rooms on the first floor. The basement has a large paneled TV lounge, where smoking is permitted. A professional innkeeper provides gourmet breakfasts featuring such goodies as Virginia ham biscuits and deep-dish Swedish pancakes.

WHERE TO DINE

While you're walking around town, stop in at Lexington's famous **Sweet Things,** 106 W. Washington St. (☎ 540/463-6055), for a cone or cup of "designer" ice cream or frozen yogurt. Television weatherman Willard Scott raves about the fresh pastries at **Country Kitchen Bakery,** 8 N. Main St. (☎ 540/463-5691). It's open Tuesday to Friday from 7am to 5pm, Saturday from 7am to 2pm, and is a great place for breakfast.

Harbs'

19 W. Washington St. ☎ **540/464-1900.** Sandwiches $3–$6; main courses $8–$11. MC, V. Mon 8am–8pm, Tues–Thurs 8am–10pm, Fri–Sat 8am–11pm, Sun 9am–3pm. AMERICAN.

A favorite of university students and townsfolk, Harbs' has a French bistro look, with black-and-white-tile floors, small cafe tables, walls hung with work by local artists, and, in fine weather, al fresco dining on the back patio. Good mornings begin at Harbs' with oversize muffins, bagels, or Belgian waffles with a steaming cup of coffee. Lunch and dinner feature an array of sandwiches—hero-size or on whole-wheat, Branola, or rye bread or a pita or kaiser roll. Pitas are stuffed with tangy hummus or tabbouleh and vegetables. A chicken taco salad is also a good lunchtime choice. The dinner menu changes often and might include blackened tuna with pink and green peppercorns. At night, Harbs' often features entertainment such as classical or bluegrass music or a poetry reading.

The Palms

101 W. Nelson St. ☎ **540/463-7911.** Main courses $7.25–$13.50. MC, V. Mon–Fri 11:30am–1am, Sat–Sun 10am–11pm. AMERICAN.

With neon palms in its storefront window, this plant-filled eatery offers a congenial faux-tropical setting for hearty meals. Deli sandwiches run the gamut from roast beef to smoked turkey. Mexican specialties like tacos and burritos spice up the proceedings. Dinner entrees, served with salad, vegetable, and bread, include choices like fettuccine Alfredo, shish kebab, lamb chops, and mahi mahi. At lunch or dinner, the hearty burgers will not disappoint. The Palms has a full bar and serves Sunday brunch.

✪ Willson-Walker House Restaurant

30 N. Main St. ☎ **540/463-3020.** Reservations required at dinner. Main courses $10–$19; sunset special $10. AE, MC, V. Tues–Sat 11:30am–2:30pm and 5:30–9pm. AMERICAN.

Occupying the first floor of an 1820 Greek Revival home, this distinctive restaurant, furnished in period antiques, offers first-rate regional cuisine. In good weather, the most popular tables are on first- and second-floor verandas behind massive two-story white columns. At lunch, the $5 chef's special includes choice of soup or salad, entree, homemade muffins and rolls, and beverage. Changing monthly, the menu offers such tempting starters as crepes filled with Scottish smoked salmon, dill cream cheese, capers, and red onions. Main courses might include lobster medallions with papaya crème Anglaise, sautéed sea scallops with pink grapefruit buerre blanc, or roast pork loin with Granny Smith apples and fresh ginger cream.

LEXINGTON AFTER DARK

The ruins of an old limestone kiln provide the backdrop for the open-air **Theater at Lime Kiln,** Borden Road off U.S. 60W (☎ 540/463-3074), which presents musicals, plays, and concerts from Memorial Day to Labor Day at 8pm. Typical productions have ranged from a Civil War epic called *Stonewall Country,* based on Jackson's life, to Shakespeare, Appalachian folktales, and even water puppeteers from Vietnam. Tickets to plays and musicals are $5 to $20, and concerts run $6 to $20; seniors and students pay $2 less. To reach the theater from downtown Lexington, take U.S. 11 south and turn right onto U.S. 60 west.

The Southwest Highlands

You soon notice after leaving the city of Roanoke that I-81 begins to climb as it heads into Virginia's Southwest Highlands, the state's increasingly narrow "tail" hemmed in by West Virginia, Kentucky, Tennessee, and North Carolina. Down the center of the Highlands runs the rolling Great Valley of Virginia, whose floor averages 2,000 feet in altitude. Just as they delineate the Shenandoah Valley, the Blue Ridge Mountains form the eastern boundary of the Southwest Highlands, but here they are dwarfed by the ridges to the west. While peaks above 4,000 feet are rare up in the Shenandoah, here they regularly exceed that altitude, with Mount Rogers reaching 5,729 feet, the highest point in Virginia.

Thousands of acres of this beautiful country are preserved in the Jefferson National Forest and in Mount Rogers National Recreation Area, which rivals the Shenandoah National Park with 300 miles of hiking and riding trails, including its own stretch of the Appalachian Trail. Two other major walks lure hikers to follow old railroad beds along river banks: the Virginia Creeper and New River Trails.

The Highlanders are justly proud of their history, which includes Daniel Boone's blazing the Wilderness Road through these mountains, plateaus, and hollows to Cumberland Gap and on into Kentucky. Gorgeous Abingdon and other small towns still have log cabins from those frontier days.

The Highlanders also have preserved their ancient arts, crafts, and their renowned mountain music. Abingdon hosts both Virginia's official state theater and its Highlands Festival, one of America's top annual arts and crafts shows. The coal mining town of Big Stone Gap has its own drama about mountain life. The famous Carter family makes mountain music at tiny Maces Spring, and fiddlers from around the world gather every August for their old-time convention at Galax.

EXPLORING THE SOUTHWEST HIGHLANDS

GETTING THERE & GETTING AROUND   Given the distances, the lack of public transportation, and the need to be able to explore the area's spectacular scenery at leisure, traveling by car is the only way to go. I-81 runs the entire length of the highlands and is its major thoroughfare. U.S. 11 follows I-81, and the Blue Ridge Parkway parallels it to the east. I-77 cuts north-south through the center of the region (the section from Wytheville north to Bluefield, W. Va., is one of America's most dramatically scenic interstates). Otherwise, byways in the region are mountain roads: narrow, winding, and sometimes steep, so give yourself ample time to get to your destination.

The area's only air gateway is Roanoke Regional Airport (☎ 540/362-1999), served by USAir, Delta, American, and United Airlines. The nearest Amtrak train station is in Clifton Forge, 45 miles northwest of Roanoke on I-64. Amtrak has a Thruway bus connection from Clifton Forge to Roanoke. For information call ☎ 800/872-7245.

ESSENTIALS   The telephone area code for the entire Southwest Highlands is 540. The one-stop source for regional information is **The Highlands Gateway Visitor Center,** Drawer B-12, Max Meadows, VA 24360 (☎ 540/637-6766 or 800/446-9670). Funded by the National Forest Service, this state-of-the-art center is in the Factory Merchants Outlet Mall at Exit 80 off the joint I-81/I-77 near Fort Chiswell. It has brochures from all towns in the region, a touch-screen computer, and a small theater showing a video about Mount Rogers National Recreation Area. It sells National Forest topographical maps, Appalachian Trail maps and guide books— even mountain music tapes and Smokey the Bear dolls. Open Monday to Saturday from 9am to 5pm, Sunday from noon to 5pm.

1 The Blue Ridge Parkway

Maintained by the National Park Service, the 470-mile Blue Ridge Parkway links the Shenandoah National Park in Virginia to the Great Smokey Mountains National Park in North Carolina. It begins at the southern terminus of the Skyline Drive and winds through the Blue Ridge Mountains. Magnificent vistas and the natural beauty of the forests, wildlife, and wildflowers combine with pioneer history to make this a fascinating route for at least part of your journey.

Consider driving between Lexington and Roanoke via the northern section. Beyond Roanoke, the parkway runs through lower country, with more meadows and less mountain scenery. On the other hand, the 62-mile stretch from Otter Creek south to Roanoke Mountain crosses the James River Gorge; climbs Apple Orchard Mountain, the highest parkway point in Virginia (3,950 feet); and has the most spectacular overlooks and the best selection of visitor activities. At times the road here follows the ridgeline, rendering spectacular views down both sides of the mountains at once. It also has the Peaks of Otter Lodge, the only place actually on the parkway where you can spend the night (see "Accommodations," below).

There are also many **hiking trails,** including the Appalachian Trail, which follows the parkway from Mile 0 to about Mile 103. Most trails are at or near the visitor centers (see below), which distribute free trail maps.

JUST THE FACTS

ACCESS POINTS AND ORIENTATION   The northern parkway entrance is at the southern end of the Skyline Drive, in Rockfish Gap on U.S. 250 at Exit 99 off I-64. The major access points in Virginia are U.S. 60 east of Buena Vista; U.S. 501 between Buena Vista and Lynchburg (Otter Creek and the James River Gorge); U.S. 460, Va. 24, and U.S. 220 near Roanoke; U.S. 58 at Meadows of Dan; and I-77 at Fancy Gap.

Unlike the Skyline Drive, which is surrounded by a national park, the parkway for most of its route runs through mountain meadows, private farmland, and forests (some but not all of them national forests). Nature hikes, camping, and other

The Southwest Highlands

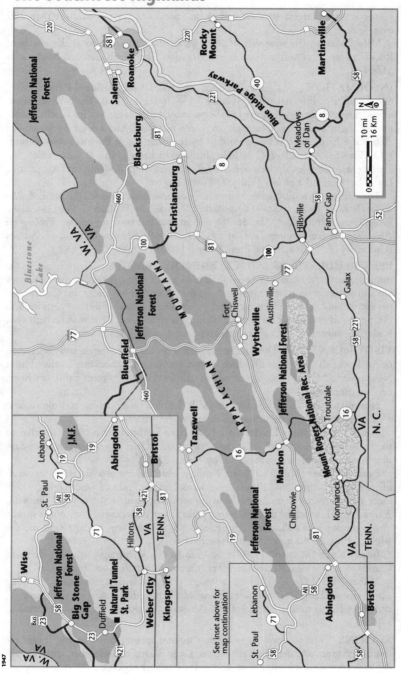

1947

visitor activities largely are confined to the visitor centers and to more than 200 overlooks.

Mile Posts on the west side of the parkway begin with zero at the northern Rockfish Gap entry and increase as you go south. The North Carolina border is at Mile 218.

INFORMATION   For general information, contact the **National Park Service,** 400 BB&T Building, Asheville, NC 28801 (☎ 704/298-0298). The NPS sends out a brochure with an excellent map of the parkway, but you can ask for specific information about hiking trails, campgrounds, and bicycling. Also ask for a copy of *The Blue Ridge Parkway Directory,* published by the **Blue Ridge Parkway Association,** P.O. Box 453, Asheville, NC 28802. This booklet has a wealth of information, including maps and descriptions of nearby attractions, shops, lodging, and restaurants. It also has a calendar of when the wildflowers bloom.

The directory is available free at the visitor centers, which also sell the detailed *Blue Ridge Parkway: Rockfish Gap to Grandfather Mountain* by William G. Ford (Menasha Ridge Press, Birmingham, Ala., $6.95), and an excellent book for hikers, *Walking the Blue Ridge: A Guide to the Trails of the Blue Ridge Parkway* by Leonard M. Adkins (University of North Carolina Press, Chapel Hill, $12.95).

FEES, REGULATIONS & BACKCOUNTRY PERMITS   There is no fee for using the parkway. Maximum speed limit is 45 m.p.h. along the entire route. Bicycles are allowed only on paved roads and parking areas, not on the trails. Camping is permitted only in designated areas (see "Camping," below). Fires are permitted in campgrounds and picnic areas only. Hunting is prohibited. Pets must be kept on a leash. No swimming is allowed in parkway ponds and lakes.

VISITOR CENTERS   There are several visitor centers along the parkway, including one at **Rockfish Gap** (Mile 0), which is open year-round. Others may be closed from November to March. Since the centers are the focal points of most visitor activities, here's a rundown:

Humpback Rocks Visitor Center (Mile 5.8) has picnic tables, rest rooms, and a self-guiding trail to a reconstructed mountain homestead.

James River Visitors Center (Mile 63.6) has a footbridge that crosses the river to the restored canal locks, exhibits, and a nature trail. Otter Creek wayside has a daytime restaurant and campground just up the road.

Peaks of Otter (Mile 85.9) has a 2-mile hike to the site of a historic farm, wildlife and Native American exhibits, rest rooms, and the Peaks of Otter Lodge, which looks across a picturesque little lake to appropriately named Sharp Top Mountain. A trail leads to the top of this 3,875-foot peak, or you can take the campstore's shuttle bus to the top and walk down. Bus fares are $1.50 one-way, $2.50 round-trip for adults, $1 and $1.50 for children, respectively.

Rocky Knob (Mile 167.1) has some 15 miles of hiking trails (including the Rock Castle Gorge National Recreational Trail), a comfort station, and picnic area.

Mabry Mill (Mile 176) has a picturesque grist mill with a giant wheel spanning a little stream. Displays of pioneer life, including crafts demonstrations, are featured, and the restored mill still grinds flour. A restaurant, open May through October, adjoins.

SEASONS   The parkway is at its best during spring, when young leaves are multihued green and the wildflowers bloom, and during mid-October, when changing leaves are at their blazing best (and traffic is at its heaviest).

CAMPING

Campgrounds are at **Otter Creek,** Mile 60.8; **Peaks of Otter,** Mile 86; **Roanoke Mountain,** Mile 120.4; and **Rocky Knob,** Mile 174.1. Campgrounds are open from about May 1 to early November, depending on weather conditions. Drinking water and rest rooms are provided, shower and laundry facilities are not. There are tent and trailer sites, but none has utility connections. Charge per night for each site is $9 for 2 adults, $2 each extra adult, free for children under 18. Golden Age and Golden Access Passport holders are entitled to a 50% discount. Daily permits are valid only at the campground where purchased.

Housekeeping cabins are available at Rocky Knob; to make reservations, write Rocky Knob Cabins, Meadows of Dan, VA 24120 (☎ 540/593-3503).

ACCOMMODATIONS

Peaks of Otter Lodge

Milepost 86 (P.O. Box 489), Bedford, VA 24523. ☎ **540/586-1081** or 800/542-5927 in Virginia and North Carolina. 60 rms, 3 suites. A/C. $67 double; $80–$90 suite. Extra person $5. Children under 16 stay free in parents' room. MC, V. Free parking.

At Peaks of Otter, everything is in harmony with nature—from the lakeside mountain setting to the rustic room decor of natural rough-grained wood with slate-top furnishings. The main lodge building has a restaurant, a crafts and gift shop, and a games and TV room with a view of the lake. Accommodations are in motel-like attached units on a grassy slope overlooking the lake. Each room has a private balcony or terrace to maximize the splendid view, but only suites have TVs and phones. Reservations are accepted beginning October 1 for the *following* year's fall foliage season. Winter and early spring are not overly crowded, but reservations should be made 4 to 6 weeks ahead for all good-weather months.

The lodge's dining room is low key and pleasant, with a cathedral ceiling, hanging plants, and windows on the lake. Reasonably priced American fare is served at all three meals. There is a full bar.

2 Roanoke

189 miles SW of Richmond; 232 miles SW of Washington, D.C.

Virginia's largest metropolitan area west of Richmond, Roanoke likes to call itself the capital of the Blue Ridge. It's also known as "Star City," for the huge lighted star overlooking the city from Mill Mountain.

There was no star on the mountain when Colonial explorers discovered the Roanoke Valley in the 17th century. They established several small settlements here, including one named Big Lick. When the Norfolk and Western Railroad arrived in the 1880s and laid out a town for future development, it decided that Roanoke—a Native American word for shell money—was a much more prosperous-sounding name for its new city than Big Lick. Roanoke boomed until its economy was shaken by the railroad's decline in the mid-20th century. Milestones in its recovery have been construction of the Civic Center, a convention and cultural complex, and the restoration of Market Square around the Historic City Market.

With its zoo and hands-on educational museums, Roanoke has special appeal to children. Families can easily spend a full day and more exploring its sights.

ESSENTIALS

VISITOR INFORMATION Contact the **Roanoke Convention and Visitors Bureau,** 114 Market St., Roanoke, VA 24011 (☎ 540/342-6025, or 800/635-5535). Just a few doors north of Market Square, the chamber's Visitor Center is the best place to pick up maps and walking tour brochures before starting your tour of Roanoke. It's open daily from 9am to 5pm.

GETTING THERE **By Car** From I-81, take I-581 into the heart of Roanoke. When I-581 stops, U.S. 220 picks up to form a freeway all the way through town.

By Plane The **Roanoke Regional Airport** (☎ 540/362-1999) is 5¹/₂ miles northwest of downtown off I-581.

GETTING AROUND Area bus service is provided by **Valley Metro** Monday to Saturday from 5:45am to 8:45pm. The downtown transfer point is Campbell Court, 17 W. Campbell Ave. Call 540/982-2222 for schedules and fares. The visitor center distributes free Ride Guide route maps.

SEEING DOWNTOWN

❂ **Market Square** is the center of downtown Roanoke at Market Street and Campbell Avenue. As they have for more than a century, stands and shops at the **Historic City Market** display plants, flowers, fresh fruits and vegetables, dairy and eggs, and farm-cured meats. Nearby restored Victorian-era storefronts house trendy restaurants, gift shops, art galleries, clothiers, a book-and-music emporium, plus two spiffed-up relics from the past: Agnew Seed Store, which still uses its old-fashioned oak drawers; and Wertz's Country Store, carrying a gourmet selection of local produce. The landmark **Market Building** houses a food court offering the downtown lunch crowd an international menu, from Chinese egg rolls to North Carolina–style barbecue. The market and food court are open Monday to Saturday.

Next-door, a five-story converted warehouse known as **Center in the Square** houses three museums and a theater:

Science Museum of Western Virginia and Hopkins Planetarium (☎ 540/342-5710) will fascinate children with hands-on high-tech exhibits. Open Monday through Saturday from 10am to 5pm and Sunday from 1 to 5pm; admission is $5 for adults, $4 for seniors, $3 for students 3 to 12, free for children under 3.

Roanoke Valley History Museum (☎ 540/342-5770) houses documents, tools, costumes, and weapons that tell the story of Roanoke from pioneer days to the 1990s. Open Tuesday to Saturday from 10am to 4pm, and Sunday from 1 to 5pm; admission is $2 for adults, $1 for seniors and children 6 to 12, free for children under 6.

Art Museum of Western Virginia (☎ 540/342-5760) displays ancient and contemporary works, from tribal African to contemporary American. Open Tuesday through Saturday from 10am to 5pm and Sunday from 1 to 5pm. Admission is free.

Mill Mountain Theater (☎ 540/342-5740, or 800/317-6455) offers children's productions, lunchtime readings, and year-round matinee and evening performances on two stages. Productions range from Shakespeare to minstrels. A recent season featured *The King and I, Romeo and Juliet, Forever Plaid*, and *Joseph and the Amazing Technicolor Dream Coat.* Tickets are $10 to $13 for the intimate Theater B, $14 and $23 for the Main Stage. Seniors, students, and children receive discounts.

Five blocks west of Market Square in a restored freight depot, the **Virginia Museum of Transportation,** 303 Norfolk Ave. at Third St. (☎ 540/342-5670), gives kids a chance to climb aboard a caboose, stroll through a railway post office car, and see the classic steam giants up close. Open March to December on Monday through Saturday from 10am to 5pm and on Sunday from noon to 5pm; closed Mondays in January and February. Admission is $5 for adults, $4 for seniors, $3 for students 13 to 18, free for children under 13.

ATTRACTIONS AT MILL MOUNTAIN

Sitting between the city and the Blue Ridge Parkway, Mill Mountain offers both a landmark and panoramic views over Roanoke Valley. The two main attractions are on Mill Mountain Spur Road, which leaves the parkway at Mile 120 and enters the city south of downtown as Walnut Avenue.

Roanoke citizens know they're home when they can see the white neon **Star on the Mountain.** Erected in 1949 as a civic pride project, it stands 88$^1/_2$ feet tall, uses 2,000 feet of neon tubing, and is visible from most parts of the city. There's an excellent viewpoint at the base.

Nearby, kids will enjoy **Mill Mountain Zoological Park** (☎ 540/343-3241), a 3-acre home to 40 animal species, including monkeys, prairie dogs, hawks, and a tiger. Open daily from 10am to 4:30pm (until 7pm Friday in summer). Admission is $4 for adults, $3.60 for seniors, $2.75 for children 2 to 11, free for children under 2.

It's a scenic 7-mile drive from Mill Mountain to ❂ **Virginia's Explore Park** (☎ 540/427-1800), a 1,300-acre reserve in the Roanoke River gorge. This new park sports a reconstructed 18th-century settlement and 8 miles of nature trails. More than 1,000 acres of its hills and wetlands are set aside as a natural area where humans are limited to hiking, wildlife viewing, and environmental research. The village has a blacksmith and wheelwright shop, the Brugh Tavern (appropriately pronounced "Brew"), a German-style "bank" barn, a school, a mountain church, and several houses, all of them moved to the site from elsewhere. There's also a working farm. The park is open April to October on Monday, Saturday, and Sunday from 9am to 5pm. Admission is $4 for adults, $2.50 for students, free for children under 6. The road to the park leaves the Blue Ridge Parkway at Mile 115. Follow the signs.

WHERE TO STAY

Roanoke and its sister city of Salem have a number of chain motels, most on I-81 and I-581. Closest to downtown Roanoke are **Holiday Inn Civic Center** and **Days Inn,** both on Orange Avenue near Exit 4 off I-581. Near the airport, Exit 3 off I-581 (Herschberger Road) has a **Sheraton Inn, Best Western,** and **Comfort Inn.** Farther out, I-581's Exit 2 (Peters Creek Road) has a **Hampton Inn, Super 8,** and another **Holiday Inn.**

❂ Hotel Roanoke & Conference Center

110 Shenandoah Ave., Roanoke, VA 24016. ☎ **540/985-5900** or 800/222-TREE. Fax 540/853-8264. 332 rms and suites. A/C TV TEL. $79–$149 double, $99–$450 suites. Packages available. AE, CB, DC, DISC, MC, V. Parking $3. From I-581 south, take Exit 5, cross Wells Avenue into parking lot.

The Norfolk and Western Railroad built this grand Tudor-style hotel in a wheat field in 1882, even before it changed the name of Big Lick to Roanoke. Heated by steam from the railroad's maintenance shops and cooled by America's first hotel air-conditioning system (circulating ice water), it became a resort as well as a stop-over. Some 26 passenger trains a day rolled into the station at the foot of the hill, and virtually every celebrity passing though Roanoke stayed here, among them William Jennings Bryan, Amelia Earhart, Joe DiMaggio, Jack Dempsey, Elvis Presley, and Presidents Eisenhower, Nixon, Ford, Reagan, and Bush. For the locals, it was *the* place for wedding receptions, reunions, beauty pageants, and other special events.

In 1989, the Norfolk and Western's successor corporation closed the hotel and gave it to Virginia Polytechnic Institute (VPI), the state's land-grant university at Blacksburg. With massive help from Roanokers, VPI raised and spent $42 million restoring the public areas, rebuilding the rooms and suites, and adding a 63,000-square-foot conference center and an enclosed, climate-controlled pedestrian walkway across the railroad tracks to Market Square. With much fanfare, the hotel reopened in 1995 under management of Doubletree Hotels.

Even if you don't stay here, it's worth a walk uphill just to see the rich, black walnut–paneled lobby with its Oriental rugs and leather lounge furniture; the oval-shaped Palm Court lounge with its pineapple central fountain and four lovingly restored murals of Colonial and Victorian Virginians dancing the reel, waltz, minuet, and quadrille; and the elegant Regency Room, where waiters in starched tunics deliver the hotel's signature peanut soup.

The building was gutted and rebuilt above the public areas, so all the rooms and suites are completely modern. Given the odd shape of the building, there now are 92 room configurations, with many sloping ceilings and gable windows.

Dining/Entertainment: In addition to peanut soup, the Regency Room serves venison, quail, pink speckled trout, sweet potato chips, and other historic dishes, all at moderate prices. Pub fare is available in the knotty Pine Room, which has a large bar, sports TV, and billiard table.

Services: Room service, laundry, concierge, nightly turndown, free newspaper.

Facilities: Fitness center, outdoor pool.

Roanoke Airport Marriott

2801 Hershberger Rd. NW, Roanoke, VA 24017. ☎ **540/563-9300** or 800/228-9290. 320 rms. A/C TV TEL. $79–$129 double. Extra person $10. Children under 18 stay free in parents' room. Weekend packages available. AE, CB, DC, DISC, MC, V. Free parking. From I-581 south, take Exit 3W, Hershberger Road; make a right U-turn at the first light; the hotel is on the left.

Seeming more Californian than Virginian, this eight-story Marriott is built like a Mediterranean villa, utilizing decorative objects from Italy, France, and Spain in the spacious lobby, where brick walls, Oriental rugs, and a huge fireplace provide a warm atmosphere. A concierge level offers upgraded amenities and a private lounge. Rooms are conventionally decorated with brass-trimmed dark-wood traditional pieces.

Dining/Entertainment: Remington's is the Marriott's fine-dining spot, with beamed ceilings, stucco walls, and French provincial armchairs. An inviting room with skylights and high ceilings, Lily's is open for all meals. There is also a lobby bar and an entertainment lounge.

Services: 24-hour room service, courtesy airport shuttle, free newspaper.

Facilities: Indoor and outdoor pools, fitness center, sauna, whirlpool, two lighted tennis courts, gift shop.

WHERE TO DINE

✪ Buck Mountain Grille

5002 Franklin Rd. (U.S. 220), at Blue Ridge Parkway. ☎ **540/776-1830.** Reservations accepted. Main courses $8–$18. AE, DC, DISC, MC, V. Daily 11am–3pm, Tues–Thurs and Sun 5–9pm, Fri–Sat 5–10pm. From downtown, take Franklin Road (U.S. 220) south 7 miles. From Blue Ridge Parkway, exit U.S. 220 east, make a U-turn to restaurant. INTERNATIONAL.

This roadside, peaked-roof establishment is a fine place for lunch while driving the Blue Ridge Parkway or for dinner while overnighting in Roanoke. There's some counter and booth seating here, but most tables with glass over linen are in a pleasant dining room whose white walls sport for-sale works by local artists. The menu offers a mix of cuisine, with innovative new American and Mediterranean dishes predominating. Nightly specials feature Roanoke's freshest seafood. We enjoyed perfectly charbroiled salmon with a maple glaze. Vegetarians can choose from several offerings, and there's a children's menu.

Macado's

120 Church St. ☎ **540/342-7231.** Sandwiches $2.95–$4.95; main courses $4.95–$6.95. AE, MC, V. Daily 11:30am–1am. AMERICAN.

The whole family will enjoy this lively spot, part of a successful Virginia chain. The decor is eclectic—old Coke ads, beer signs, an elk head, and other odds and ends on the walls; a small airplane is suspended in midair, and there are many hanging plants. Seating, on several levels, is divided by brass rails into intimate areas. The menu offers sandwiches, salads, soups, and hot entrees. Pita pizzas and baked potatoes topped with cheese sauces are other options. Ice-cream sodas, sundaes, apple cobbler, and pecan pie are among the desserts. There's a full bar.

⑤ The Roanoker Restaurant

2522 Colonial Ave., south of Wonju St. ☎ **540/344-7746.** Reservations not accepted. Main courses $7–$9. MC, V. Mon–Thurs 7am–9pm, Fri–Sat 7am–10pm, Sun and holidays 8am–9pm. From downtown, go south on Franklin Road, turn right on Brandon Avenue, left on Colonial Avenue. From I-581, go south to Wonju Street exit, turn right, then left on Colonial Ave. SOUTHERN.

A very popular local restaurant since 1941, The Roanoker occupies a Colonial-style building surrounded by much-needed parking lots. Several dining rooms have booth seating arranged to provide privacy. Antique signs from Roanoke businesses adorn the walls. Every Roanoker with a car seems to have breakfast here, so fluffy are the homemade biscuits served with spicy sausage gravy. The lunch and dinner menus change daily, depending on available produce. Fresh vegetables may include skillet-fried yellow squash, a mouth-watering southern favorite.

A NEARBY MOUNTAIN RESORT

Mountain Lake

Mountain Lake, VA 24136. ☎ **540/626-7121** or 800/346-3334. Fax 540/626-7172. 100 rms, including 16 cabins. TEL. Main hotel, $165 double; Chestnut Lodge $195 double. Rates include breakfast and dinner. Children 12 and older in parents' room are charged $25 per day; ages 5–12, $15; 4 and under, free. AE, DC, DISC, MC, V. Closed Nov–Apr. From I-81 south, take Exit 37, U.S. 460 west; turn right onto C.R. 700 and it's 7 miles to Mountain Lake.

If you saw the movie *Dirty Dancing*, you're already familiar with this rustic mountaintop resort. Surrounded by a 2,600-acre wildlife conservancy, it consists of a main building (a stately, rough-cut-stone lodge) with clusters of small white-clapboard summer cottages nearby. The lobby has thick rugs over a terra-cotta-tile floor and comfortable seating in front of a massive fireplace. Complimentary tea and coffee are always kept hot on the sideboard. A stone archway separates the lobby from the adjoining bar and lounge.

The popular parlor suites have Jacuzzis and fireplaces, and some rooms offer full lake views. Decor has a warm, traditional look, with dark-wood Chippendale-reproduction furnishings. Cottages are more simply furnished, although guests here have porches with rockers. Chestnut Lodge, a recent addition, is a three-story gray-clapboard building set on the side of a hill. Rooms here are decorated in country style, with fireplaces and private balconies.

Dining/Entertainment: The spacious, romantic stone-walled dining room has windows providing panoramic lake views and serves sophisticated cuisine. There's also a snack bar in the Recreation Barn.

Facilities: Health club with sauna and weight room; clothing/souvenir/sporting goods shops; summer program for children; Recreation Barn for Ping-Pong, billiards, and evening entertainment; hiking trails; tennis; boathouse with canoes and rowboats; fishing.

3 Wytheville

74 miles SW of Roanoke; 49 miles NE of Abingdon; 306 miles SW of Washington, D.C.; 247 miles SW of Richmond.

Sitting on a relatively flat plateau, Wytheville's strategic position in the center of the Highlands has made it a major crossroads since trappers and hunters came into the region in the early 1700s. After a treaty with hostile Native Americans opened Kentucky for settlement in 1775, Daniel Boone built the Wilderness Road through the Highlands to Cumberland Gap. Monroe Street in downtown Wytheville was part of that route, and log cabins left over from those days still stand on Main Street.

The Wilderness Road is long gone, but I-81 and I-77 meet here today, giving Wytheville a motel room for every family in town, plus a host of places to dine. Since accommodations are relatively scarce in this sparsely populated region, these facilities make Wytheville a well-equipped base from which to explore Mount Rogers National Recreation Area (see the next section) and other sights in the central portion of the Highlands.

ESSENTIALS

VISITOR INFORMATION   The **Wytheville-Bland Chamber of Commerce,** P.O. Box 533, Wytheville, VA 24382 (☎ 540/223-3355), supplies information about the town, including a walking tour brochure to the historic district. It has a visitor center in the Municipal Building, Monroe Street and 1st Street. There also are roadside tourist information kiosks at all interstate exits leading into town.

GETTING THERE   I-81 and I-77 meet on the outskirts of Wytheville. To get into town, take Exit 67, 70, or 73 off I-81. U.S. 11 and U.S. 21 meet in downtown.

WHAT TO SEE & DO
ATTRACTIONS IN TOWN

An 1830s mayor decided Wytheville needed wide streets to keep fires from spreading, so even though the town dates to 1757, the broad avenues he built deprive it of the beauty of quaint old towns like Lexington and Abingdon. With the South's only salt mine and an important lead mine nearby, Union troops attacked the crossroads village and burned many historic homes and businesses during the Civil War. One area remained untouched, however, and you will want to examine the **Old Log Houses,** on Main Street (U.S. 11) between 5th and 7th streets. Some of them have been turned into shops and a restaurant (see "Where to Dine" below).

Another house that escaped Civil War destruction—but not bullet holes—was the **Rock House Museum,** at Monroe and Tazewell streets (no phone). A national and state historic landmark, this Pennsylvania-style stone structure was built in 1820. The museum has a collection of historic artifacts from the region. Admission is free, but it's open only Sundays from 2 to 4:30pm.

In the present-day business district at Main and Tazewell streets, **Skeeter's** is an old-fashioned shop famous for its Southern-style hot dogs (steamed roll, chili, onions, mustard, and relish). Although it's not open to the public, upstairs in the building next door was the **Birthplace of Edith Bolling Wilson,** wife of Staunton-born President Woodrow Wilson.

OUTDOOR ACTIVITIES

Wytheville is near the headquarters and central entry to the ✪ **New River Trail State Park,** an exceptional hiking, biking, and horse path running 57 miles from Galax to Pulaski. The trail follows an old railroad bed beside the picturesque New River, which despite its name is in geologic terms one of the oldest rivers in the United States (it predates the Appalachian Mountains).

The Wytheville entry is 17 miles south of town at **Shot Tower Historical State Park,** on U.S. 52 near Exit 5 off I-77. Overlooking the New River, the park features a stone shot tower built about 1807. Molten lead poured from the top of the tower fell 150 feet into a kettle, thus cooling and turning into round shot. The led was mined at nearby Austinville, birthplace of Stephen Austin, the "Father of Texas." Admission to the park and trail is free, but there's a $1-per-car parking fee. The visitor center, which also is headquarters for New River Trail State Park, is open Monday to Thursday from 8am to 4pm. Rangers conduct tours of the tower from Memorial Day to Labor Day on Saturday, Sunday, and holidays from 10am to 6pm.

Other entries to the New River Trail are at Draper, near Exit 92 off I-81; Allisonia and Hiwassee, both on C.R. 693; Barren Springs, on Va. 100; Austinville, on Va. 69; Ivanhoe, on Va. 94; Byllesby Dam, on C.R. 602; and at Galax, on U.S. 58. There's also a branch trail to Fries, on Va. 94.

Horse trailer parking is permitted only at Shot Tower State Park, Draper, and the Cliffview Ranger Station near Galax. Bike rentals are available at **New River Bicycles** in Draper (☎ 540/980-1741), which also runs a shuttle along the trail. **Allisonia Trading Post** (☎ 540/980-2051) also runs a shuttle and rents horses, bikes, canoes, and inner tubes. **Cliffview Trading Post** (☎ 540/238-1530), at the Cliffview Ranger Station near Galax, rents horses.

For more information, write or call New River Trail State Park, Route 1, Box 81X, Austinville, VA 24312 (☎ 540/699-6778).

SHOPPING

Three log cabins in **Old Town Square,** Main Street at 7th Street, have been turned into boutiques, among them the **Wilderness Road Trading Post,** purveyor of Appalachian crafts, pottery, and toys.

Wytheville's most famous shops are near each other on the service road between Exits 77 and 80 off I-81: **Snooper's Antique & Craft Mall** (☎ 540/637-6441) and **Old Fort Emporium Antique Mall** (☎ 540/228-GIFT). Both are cooperatives, with vendors selling a wide range of antiques, collectibles, and gifts. Both are open from Memorial Day to Labor daily from 10am to 8pm, to 7pm in spring and fall, to 6pm in winter.

WHERE TO STAY

Wytheville has more than 1,200 motel rooms, most in national chain establishments along I-81. Exit 73 has the largest concentration: **Days Inn, Econo Lodge, HoJo Inn, Holiday Inn,** and **Motel 6.** Exit 72 is next, with **Best Western, Ramada Inn,** and **Super 8.** There's also a **Comfort Inn** at Exit 70.

WHERE TO DINE

✪ The Log House 1776 Restaurant

520 E. Main St. (U.S. 11), at 7th St. ☎ **540/228-4139.** Reservations recommended. Main courses $10–$15. AE, MC, V. Mon–Sat 11am–3pm and 4–10pm. From I-81, take Exit 67 or 73 and follow U.S. 11 to the restaurant. AMERICAN.

Although clapboard additions were added to this historic building in 1804 and 1898, the main dining room here is in a log house built in 1776. Modern gas logs now burn in the dining room fireplaces, but antiques augment the Colonial charm of the square. Among the offerings are such Virginia fare as peanut soup; Confederate beef stew, a very sweet concoction of beef, vegetables, and apples, which General Lee fed his troops; and Thomas Jefferson's favorite chicken marengo, which he brought home from his stint as ambassador to France.

Scrooge's Restaurant

At Comfort Inn, Halston Rd at 4th Ave. ☎ **540/228-6622.** Reservations not accepted. Main courses $7–$14. AE, DC, MC, V. Sun–Thurs 5–10pm, Fri–Sat 5–11pm. From downtown, take 4th Avenue north across I-81, turn right on Halston Road. From I-81, take Exit 70, follow signs to Comfort Inn. INTERNATIONAL.

Cartoons of Dickens' Ebeneezer Scrooge make this English-style establishment a fun place, especially those on the sports-bar walls showing him scowling his way through such modern activities as tennis and golf. The house specialty is "pig and pepper soup," a spicy mixture of smoked sausage, potatoes, and pepper corns that will warm the innards after a cold day on the New River Trail. The menu also features the likes of charbroiled steaks and chicken in a Dijon mustard sauce and seafood like scallops parmesan over fettucine. There's a "Tiny Tim" menu for kids.

4 Mount Rogers National Recreation Area

Noted for its 300 miles of hiking, mountain biking, cross country skiing, and horse trails, Mount Rogers National Recreation Area includes 117,000 forested acres running some 60 miles from the New River southwest to the Tennessee line. Included is its namesake, Virginia's highest peak at 5,729 feet. Nearby White Top is the state's second highest point at 5,520 feet. Most of the land, however, flanks Iron Mountain, a long ridge running the area's length. Wild ponies range the extensive upland meadows, introduced to keep them mowed.

Not all of this remote expanse is pristine, for as part of the Jefferson National Forest, it's subject to multiple uses such as hunting and logging. Nevertheless, there are three preserved wilderness areas and plenty of other backcountry to explore, and the mountain scenery is among the best in Virginia. Among its many trails is the Virginia Creeper Trail, the Virginia Highlands Horse Trail, and a stretch of the Appalachian Trail. A spur off the Appalachian Trail goes to the summit of Mount Rogers.

JUST THE FACTS

ACCESS POINTS AND ORIENTATION   Access roads from I-81 are U.S. 21 from Wytheville; Va. 16 from Marion; C.R. 600 from Chilihowie; Va. 91 from Glades Spring; and U.S. 58 from Damascus and Abingdon. C.R. 603 runs 13 miles lengthwise through beautiful highland meadows from Troutdale (on Va. 16) to Konnarock (on U.S. 58).

INFORMATION   Since the area is vast and most facilities widespread, it's a good idea to get as much information in advance as possible. Contact the **Mount Rogers National Recreation Area,** Route 1, Box 303, Marion, VA 24254 (☎ 540/783-5196). If you're driving from the north on I-81, stop at the **Highlands Gateway Visitor Center,** Drawer B-12, Max Meadows, VA 24360 (☎ 540/637-6766, or 800/446-9670), in the Factory Merchants Outlet Mall at Exit 80 near Fort Chiswell. Like the recreation area itself, both visitors centers are operated by the National Forest Service. They have free brochures describing the trails, campgrounds, and wilderness areas, and they sell a one-sheet topographic map of the area for $3. The topographic map does not show the trails, so if writing or calling, specifically request trail, campground, horseback riding, and recreation area brochures.

FEES, REGULATIONS & BACKCOUNTRY PERMITS   There is no charge to drive through the area, but day use fees from $1 to $3 per vehicle apply to specific recreational areas, payable on the honor system. Except for the Appalachian Trail and some others reserved for hikers, mountain bikes are allowed but must give way to horses. Bikers and horseback riders must walk across all bridges and trestles. Hikers must not spook the horses. Fishing requires a Virginia license. The "No Trace Ethic" applies: Leave nothing behind, and take away only photographs and memories.

VISITOR CENTER   The visitor center is 6 miles south of Marion on Va. 16 (take Exit 45 off I-81 and go south). Exhibits and a 10-minute video explain the area. It is open from Memorial Day to October, Monday to Thursday from 8am to 5:30pm, Saturday from 9am to 5pm, and Sunday from 8am to 4:30pm. Off-season, it's open Monday to Friday from 8am to 4:30pm.

SEASONS   The area is most crowded on summer and fall weekends and holidays. Spring is punctuated by wildflowers in bloom (the calendars published by the Blue Ridge Parkway are generally applicable here), while fall foliage is at its brilliant best in mid-October. Cross-country skiers use the trails during winter. Summer thunderstorms, winter blizzards, and fog anytime of the year can pose threats in the high country, so caution is advised.

SEEING THE HIGHLIGHTS

If you don't have time to camp and hike, you can enjoy the lovely scenery from your car. From Marion on I-81, take Va. 16 south 16 miles to the country store at Troutdale. Turn right there on C.R. 603 and drive 13 miles southwest to U.S. 58. Turn right there and drive 20 miles down Straight Branch—a misnomer if there ever was one—to I-81 at Abingdon.

OUTDOOR ACTIVITIES

HIGH COUNTRY HIKING   Almost two-thirds of the area's 300 miles of trails are on four routes: the local stretch of the **Appalachian Trail** (64 miles), the **Virginia Highlands Horse Trail** (66 miles), and the **Iron Mountain Trail** (51 miles). Many of the other 67 trails connect to these main routes, and many can be linked into circuit hikes.

You can walk for days on the white-blaze Appalachian Trail without crossing a paved road, especially on the central stretch up and down the flanks of Mount Rogers between C.R. 603 and C.R. 600. A spur goes to the top of the mountain. A very popular alternate route, the blue-blaze **Mount Rogers Trail** leaves C.R. 603 near Grindstone Campground; a spur from that track goes down into the pristine Lewis Fork Wilderness before rejoining the Appalachian Trail.

Running across the southern end of the area, the ✪ **Virginia Creeper Trail** offers a much easier but no less beautiful hike. This 34-mile route follows an old railroad bed from Abingdon to White Top Station, at the North Carolina line on the southern flank of White Top Mountain. It starts at 2,065 feet altitude in Abingdon, drops to 2,000 feet at the town of Damascus (11 miles east on U.S. 58), then climbs to 3,675 feet. Now on display at the Abingdon trailhead (see below), an early steam engine had such a tough time with this grade that it became facetiously known as the "Virginia Creeper."

The eastern 16 miles run through Mount Rogers National Recreation Area. Beginning 2 miles east of Damascus, the stretch between Green Cove Station and Iron Bridge crosses High Trestle (about 100 feet high) and has swimming holes in the adjacent stream. Green Cove is a seasonal Forest Service information post with portable toilets.

Hikers, bikers, and horseback riders all are allowed on the Virginia Creeper Trail, which is free.

Blue Blaze Bike & Shuttle Service in Damascus (☎ 540/475-5095 or 800/475-5905) provides bike rentals and operates a daily shuttle along the trail during the summer months, on Saturday and Sunday during spring and fall. Fares are $10 from Abingdon to the top, $8 from Damascus. Bike rentals are $25 for all day, $15 half a day, $5 if you take the shuttle.

HORSEBACK RIDING Riders can use 150 miles of the area's trails, including Iron Mountain, New River, and the Virginia Highlands Horse Trail, which connects Elk Garden to Va. 94. Horse camps are at Fox Creek, on Va. 603; Hussy Mountain, near Speedwell; and Raven Cliff, about 4 miles east of Cripple Creek. They have toilets and drinking water for horses (but no water for humans).

Mount Rogers High Country Outdoor Center, on C.R. 603 near Troutdale (☎ 540/677-3900), has day rides and overnight pack trips by horse, pack mule, or covered wagon. Reservations are required, so phone for information and current prices.

CAMPING

In addition to the horse camps mentioned above, the recreation area has several other campgrounds, all open from mid-March through December. On C.R. 603, **Grind-stone** is the base camp for hikers heading up Mount Rogers. It has a 1/2-mile nature trail and weekend ranger programs. On U.S. 58 near C.R. 603, **Beartree** is a popular recreation site, since it has a sand beach on a 12-acre lake stocked with trout for fishing. Both Grindstone and Beartree have flush toilets and warm showers but no trailer hookups. Fees are $10 per site from May through September; $4 during March, April, October, and November.

WHERE TO STAY

There are no hotels, motels, or inns within Mount Rogers National Recreation Area. The nearest motels are in Wytheville (see above), Abingdon (see below), and Marion (a Holiday Inn). The nearest accommodations are at:

Fox Hill Inn

Route 2 (Va. 16), Troutdale, VA 24378. ☎ **540/677-3313** or 800/874-3313. 6 rms, 1 suite. $75 double. Rates include full breakfast. Children stay free in parents' room. DISC, MC, V. From I-81, take Exit 45 at Marion, then Va. 16 south 20 miles. Inn is on left, 2 miles south of the country store at Troutdale.

On a secluded hilltop surrounded on three sides by gorgeous mountain views, this comfortable country home offers a big living room with a fireplace, a dining room and terrace with great mountain views, and a roomy country kitchen. A basement game room has Ping-Pong and board games. Very spacious guest rooms are furnished in simple country style. This is also a working farm, where cattle and sheep graze the meadows, and children can get a real feel for farm life. Canoe trips on the New River, horseback riding, mountain biking, and camping trips can be arranged.

5 Abingdon

49 miles SW of Wytheville; 133 miles SW of Roanoke; 437 miles SW of Washington, D.C.;
315 miles SW of Richmond

While on his first expedition to Kentucky in 1760, Daniel Boone camped at the base of a hill near a small Halston Valley settlement known as Black's Fort. When wolves came out of a cave and attacked his dogs, Boone named the place Wolf Hill. Boone and other pioneers opened the area for settlement, and by 1778, a thriving community named Abingdon had grown up around Black's Fort and Wolf Hill. The fort has been replaced by the Washington County Court House, but Boone's cave is still behind one of the historic homes which line tree-shaded Main Street. Indeed, Abingdon today looks much as it did in those early years, making it one of Virginia's best small towns to visit.

Abingdon's beauty and historic charm have attracted more than its share of actors, artists, craftspeople, and even a few writers. People drive hundreds of miles to attend shows at The Barter, Virginia's official State Theater, and the town is crowded the first two weeks of August for the popular Virginia Highlands Festival, a display of the region's best arts and crafts.

Abingdon also is a convenient base for a scenic driving tour westward to Big Stone Gap in the Appalachian coal fields (and yet another fine theater), and for an evening drive to the little community of Maces Spring, where the famous Carter family makes mountain music every Saturday night.

ESSENTIALS

VISITOR INFORMATION Contact the **Abingdon Convention & Visitors Bureau,** Cummings Street, Abingdon, VA 24210 (☎ 540/676-2282 or 800/435-3440). In a Victorian house on a large lot, the visitor center is on the left as you drive into town on U.S. 58. Open daily from 9am to 5pm.

GETTING THERE From I-81, take Exit 17 and follow U.S. 58 East directly into town. U.S. 11 runs east-west along Main Street.

WHAT TO SEE & DO

In addition to attending the Barter Theatre (see below), it's worth a stop in Abingdon just to stroll down lovely **Main Street,** where 30 homes and buildings—with birthdates ranging from 1779 to 1925—wait to be observed. Stop at the visitors bureau (see above) for a free copy of their self-guided walking tour and start strolling.

OUTDOOR ACTIVITIES Take Pecan Street south off Main Street to the western head of the **Virginia Creeper Trail,** where sits the creeping old steam engine that gave the trail its name. Bike rentals are available at the trailhead from April to October from **Highlands Bike Rentals** (☎ 540/628-9672). Open Saturday from 9am to 6pm, Sunday from 10am to 6pm. During the week you can rent from **Highlands Ski & Outdoor Center,** on West Main Street near I-81 (☎ 540/682-1329). Rates at both are $25 per day, $15 per half day, and $7 per hour. **Blue Blaze Bike & Shuttle Service** in Damascus (☎ 540/475-5095, or 800/475-5905) provides bike rentals and operates a daily shuttle along the trail. For details, see "Outdoor Activities" in the Mount Rogers National Recreation Area section, above.

SHOPPING Mountain arts and crafts are for sale in the **Cave House Crafts Shop,** 279 E. Main St. (☎ 540/628-7721), a 140-member cooperative housed in an 1858

Victorian home built in front of the cave from whence came the wolves who attacked Daniel Boone's dogs in 1760.

Original artworks are on display and for sale in the **Arts Depot,** located in the old freight station on Depot Square (☎ 540/628-9091); visitors are welcome to watch artists at work in their studios Thursday, Friday, and Saturday from 11am to 3pm.

Main Street has no less than 10 **antique shops,** which you will pass during your walking tour.

Dixie Pottery, 5 miles south of Abingdon on U.S. 11 ($^1/_2$ mile south of Exit 13 off I-81), is a huge supermarket-style store selling decorative objects and housewares from around the world—everything from birdhouses handcrafted in North Carolina to papier-mâché fruits and vegetables from Mexico.

WHERE TO STAY

I-81 has three chain motels: **Comfort Inn** at Exit 14, **Super 8** at Exit 17, and **Holiday Inn Express** at Exit 19.

⑤ Alpine Motel

822 E. Main St. (P.O. Box 615), Abingdon, VA 24212. ☎ **540/628-3178.** Fax 540/628-4217. 19 rms. A/C TEL TV. $45 double. AE, DISC, MC, V.

Located just off Exit 19 of I-81 near several restaurants, this older but extraordinarily well maintained 1960s-vintage motel has mountain views from 15 of its 19 rooms. Owners Jim and Gloria Stroup keep their very spacious units spotlessly clean, and they have equipped them with 25-inch cable TVs. Their rates are somewhat higher during the Highlands Festival.

✪ Camberley's Martha Washington Inn

150 W. Main St., Abingdon, VA 24210. ☎ **540/628-3161** or 800/555-8000. Fax 540/628-8885. 61 rms and suites. A/C TV TEL. $100–$150 double; $175–$325 suite. Children under 12 staying in parents' room $10. Free parking.

In the heart of the historic district, the stately Greek Revival portico of the Martha Washington Inn creates a formal facade for this $2^1/_2$-story redbrick hotel, the center portion of which was built as a private residence in 1832. White-wicker rocking chairs give the front porch the look of an old-time resort. The lobby and adjoining parlor—setting for daily afternoon tea—are elegantly decorated, with original marble fireplaces and crystal chandeliers. There are regular and deluxe rooms, the latter more lavishly appointed, with rich fabrics and fine antiques. Suites have museum-quality furnishings. One, decorated in red silk with lavish gold-leaf trim, has a working fireplace. Two executive level suites have fireplaces, Jacuzzis, and steam showers.

Dining/Entertainment: First Lady's Table is open for breakfast, lunch, and dinner and serves traditional southern fare. The small, elegant Epicurean Room offers fine, fixed-price dinners (coat and ties required). The Pub is a cozy cocktail spot, and there's a lounge for entertainment and dancing.

Services: Room service (7am to 10pm), nightly turndown, shoeshine, concierge.

Summerfield Inn

101 W. Valley St., Abingdon, VA 24210. ☎ **540/628-5905.** 7 rms. A/C TEL. $70–$125 double. Rates include breakfast. AE, MC, V. On-site parking lot. Closed Jan–Feb.

One block from Main Street and the Barter Theatre, this gracious 1920s Colonial Revival residence is set back from the quiet street on an expansive lawn. Bright with flower boxes, the inviting verandah is lined with wicker rockers. A spacious foyer leads to a cozy library where guests can relax and watch TV. The dining room, with a handsome sideboard gleaming with a silver tea set, features a magnificent long oval table and period chairs. Adjacent is a cheerful sun room. A portrait of hosts Don and

Champe Hyatt's children graces one wall of the living room, furnished with a piano, Queen Anne–period wing chair, and plush Regency-style sofas flanking the fireplace. The guest rooms offer both the ambiance of a private home and the luxurious comfort of a fine hotel. Each is decorated in pastel colors and elegantly furnished with antique pieces and reproductions. Beside the main house, the "Cottage" houses three deluxe rooms, including a honeymoon suite with TV and Jacuzzi. Breakfast is served at guests' convenience from 7 to 9am.

WHERE TO DINE

✪ The Tavern
222 E. Main St. ☎ **540/628-1118.** Reservations advised. Main courses $11–$18. All year, Mon–Sat 11am–10pm, Apr–Sept, Sun noon–8pm. GERMAN/AMERICAN.

The oldest building in Abingdon, the Tavern was built in 1779 as an overnight inn for stagecoach travelers. Exposed brick and stone walls, log beams, and hand-forged locks and hinges make for an appropriately rustic setting. Downstairs has an antique bar and a cozy waiting lounge with fireplace. Upstairs are three dining rooms and a porch overlooking a brick terrace under huge shade trees. The menu reflects the present owners' German and American backgrounds. Lunch has bratwurst with green peppers and onions, as well as Reubens and smoked turkey club sandwiches. At dinner, you can choose from Wiener schnitzel, *kassler ripchen* (German smoked pork loin), shrimp provençal, veal or shrimp picatta, or southern fried chicken.

✪ Starving Artist Cafe
134 Wall St., Depot Square. ☎ **540/628-8445.** Reservations not accepted. Main courses $13–$17. AE, MC, V. Mon 11am–2pm, Tues–Sat 11am–3pm and 5–9pm. AMERICAN.

Despite its unpretentious location at Depot Square, this charming cafe lacks nothing in the way of culinary sophistication. The food is both innovative and delicious and is prepared using only the freshest of ingredients. The setting is low-key: Seating is at silver-painted ice-cream parlor chairs and tables, and walls are adorned with a changing display of local artists' work. In summer there's outdoor dining on the patio. The cafe does not lack for customers either, and the small dining room is usually full; arrive off-hours or prepare for a wait—it's worth it. Smoked salmon with Dijon-horseradish sauce and garlic bread, and French onion soup are among the appetizer choices. The chef makes superb pan-blackened prime rib with Cajun spices (Friday and Saturday nights only), and sautéed yellowfin tuna garnished with shiitake mushrooms and snow peas. All entrees are served with a choice of wild rice, rosemary potatoes, twice-baked potato, or home or Cajun fries; hot bread; and a salad. Freshly baked desserts are excellent. At lunch, the menu bestows artists' names on the sandwiches: The Andy Warhol is the POP-est burger in town, and the Leonardo da Vinci features spicy Italian meatballs on a hoagie with fresh tomato-basil sauce and melted provolone.

Hardware Company Restaurant
260 W. Main St. ☎ **540/628-1111.** Reservations not necessary. Main courses $11–$17. AE, MC, V. Daily 11am–midnight. AMERICAN.

An appropriate name, for this building housed a hardware store from 1885 until 1983. Many of the old features remain: pressed tin ceiling, rolling ladder, brick walls, and the old oak counter, now a long and friendly bar. The walls are hung with old-fashioned hardware-store memorabilia. Patrons sit at wooden booths upholstered in black leather, oak tables, and Windsor chairs. A balcony overlooking the main dining area and bar provides extra space. This is probably the most popular restaurant in town, offering homemade American fare, albeit with a Mexican twist such as a

---

Hams for *Hamlet*

The career of an aspiring Virginia-born actor named Robert Porterfield came to a screeching halt during the Great Depression. Giving up on Broadway, he and 22 other unemployed actors came to Abingdon during the summer of 1932 and began putting on plays and shows.

Their first production was John Golden's *After Tomorrow,* for which they charged an admission of 40¢ or the equivalent in farm produce. Thus did their little operation become known as the Barter Theatre.

Playwrights who contributed—among them Noël Coward, Thornton Wilder, Robert Sherwood, Maxwell Anderson, and George Bernard Shaw—were paid with a token Virginia ham. A vegetarian, Shaw returned the smoked delicacy and requested spinach instead. Porterfield and his crew obliged.

The first season wound up with a profit of $4.30, two barrels of jelly, and a collective weight gain of 300 pounds!

---

burger with salsa, guacamole, sour cream, and jalapeños. Dinner entrees include quesadillas, char-broiled chicken, and prime rib. Desserts (even the ice cream) are homemade: A dark chocolate coated cheesecake with layers of chocolate, praline, and almonds is outstanding.

At the rear of the building, the Main Street Yacht Club Lounge has a round fireplace, sports TVs, and food service after 4:30pm.

EVENING ENTERTAINMENT

✪ Barter Theatre

At the corner of West Main and College streets. ☎ **540/628-3991** or 800/368-3240. Sat evening $17; Fri evening and Sat matinee $15; Wed and Thurs evenings and Sun, Wed, and Thurs matinees $13.

The official policy still permits barter for admission (with prior notice), but theatergoers now pay cash to attend the State Theater of Virginia, America's longest-running professional repertory theater. The building itself was built around 1832 as a Presbyterian church and later served as a meeting hall for the Sons of Temperance. It was the town hall and opera house when Robert Porterfield brought his unemployed actors here in 1932 (see box). Now performed by an Actor's Equity company, recent productions have included *The Miracle Worker, Lend Me a Tenor, Other People's Money,* and *Kuru.* The theater's impressive alumni include Hume Cronyn, Patricia Neal, Fritz Weaver, Ernest Borgnine, Gregory Peck, and Ned Beatty. The season runs from April through December.

✪ Carter Family Fold Music Shows

C.R. 614, Maces Spring. ☎ **540/386-9480.** Music show tickets $3.50 adults, $1 children 6–12, under 6 free. From Abingdon, take I-81 south 17 miles to Bristol, U.S. 58 west 19 miles to Hiltons, C.R. 614 east 3 miles to auditorium.

Mountain music fans think the 78-mile round-trip from Abingdon to the Carter Family Music Center is well worth it, for here they can see and hear the best regional artists every Saturday night. This is as pure as it gets, for the descendants of country music legends A. P. Carter, wife Sara, and sister-in-law Maybelle won't allow electronic equipment in their unpretentious auditorium, which occupies a huge shed. Local residents are adept at traditional styles like buck dancing and clogging on a small dance floor in front of the stage. An annual festival the first weekend in August (same time as the Virginia Highlands Festival in Abingdon) draws many well-known singers and music groups, clog-dance performers, and local artisans who sell crafts. A family museum in A. P. Carter's country store is open on Saturday from 5 to 7pm, before the show.

AN EASY EXCURSION TO BIG STONE GAP

The mountains get steeper and the valleys narrower as you head west from Abingdon into Virginia's share of the Appalachian coal fields. Following I-81 south, U.S. 58 west, U.S. 23 north, and Alternate U.S. 58 east, you can make a scenic loop through these hollows.

From Abingdon, take I-81 south 17 miles to Bristol, then follow the winding U.S. 58 west across the mountains 40 miles to **National Tunnel State Park,** where you can take a cable car ride down a 400-feet-deep gorge to railroad tracks emerging from the mouth of an 850-feet-long tunnel cut by an underground river. The park has nature trails, interpretive programs, campground, swimming pool, and a small but very good museum explaining the tunnel's geological formation. Admission to the park is free; cable car rides cost $2 round-trip. The park is open daily from 8am to dusk; the cable car, daily from 10am to 5pm. For information, contact the park at Route 3, Box 250, Duffield, VA 24244 (☎ 540/940-2674).

From Duffield, you can make a sidetrip west, 55 miles in each direction on U.S. 58, to **Cumberland Gap National Historical Park**, at the confluence of Virginia, Kentucky, and Tennessee. During the 1780s, more than 300,000 settlers followed Daniel Boone to Kentucky through the gap, at that time the only way to get wagons through the otherwise unbroken Allegheny Front. It still is a major local thoroughfare, with a four-lane highway through the gap.

After Duffield, U.S. 23 climbs north through Jefferson National Forest into the mining town of **Big Stone Gap.** Take the first U.S. 23 Business exit and follow it to the **Regional Tourist and Information Center,** where you can get a walking tour brochure. The center is housed in Interstate Railroad Private Car Number 101, built in 1870. Visitors are welcome to poke through its staterooms and dining room. The center and car are open from Memorial Day to Labor Day, Monday to Wednesday from 10am to 5pm, Thursday to Saturday from 10am to 8pm, and Sunday from noon to 4pm; the rest of the year, Monday to Friday from 9am to 5pm. For information in advance, contact the center at P.O. Box 236, Big Stone Gap, VA 24219 (☎ 540/523-2060).

Big Stone Gap was the hometown of John Fox Jr., author of *Trail of the Lonesome Pine*. His sentimental drama—a coal field lass falls for a Yankee mining engineer and becomes a worldly woman—is reenacted in the outdoor **June Tolliver Playhouse,** on Clinton Avenue near East 4th Street (☎ 540/523-1235). Shows are July and August on Thursday, Friday, and Saturday nights. Tickets are $8 for adults, $6 for seniors, and $5 for children. The playhouse is adjacent to the **June Tolliver House & Craft Shop** (☎ 540/523-4707), home of the heroine's real-life role model.

The **John Fox, Jr., Museum** (☎ 540/523-2747, or 540/523-4707), in his charming 1888 house on Shawnee Avenue between East 2nd and East 3rd streets, is filled with family furnishings and mementos. It is open from Memorial Day to Labor Day Tuesday and Wednesday from 2 to 5pm and Thursday to Sunday from 2 to 6pm; admission is $3 for adults and $1 for students.

The **Southwest Virginia Museum,** West 1st Street and Wood Avenue (☎ 540/523-1322), is housed in a renovated 1888 residence and displays artifacts of the history and culture of the area. The **Harry W. Meador, Jr., Coal Museum,** Shawnee

Avenue at East 3rd Street (☎ 540/523-4950), explains the industry that has been the backbone of the local economy for more than a century.

From Big Stone Gap, take U.S. 23 north, then Alternate U.S. 58 east back to Abingdon. The rest of the trip is easy, since both highways are four lanes.

AN EASY EXCURSION TO CRAB ORCHARD

About one hour north of Abingdon on U.S. 19/460 just west of Tazewell, the **Crab Orchard Museum and Pioneer Park of Southwestern Virginia** (☎ 540/988-6755) is an exceptionally interesting museum with exhibits devoted to prehistoric times, Native Americans, the Revolutionary War, the Civil War, and the domestic life and home industries of the area. Outdoors are original farm dwellings, shops, and barns outfitted in typical pioneer fashion. Admission is $5 for adults, $4 for seniors, and $2 for children 13 to 18. The museum is open April to October, Monday to Saturday from 9am to 5pm, Sunday from 1 to 5pm; November to March, Monday to Saturday from 9am to 5pm.

Richmond 10

Richmond supplanted the more militarily vulnerable Williamsburg as Virginia's capital in 1780, and it has been the scene of much of the state's history ever since. It was in St. John's Church that Patrick Henry concluded his address to the second Virginia Convention with the stirring words "Give me liberty or give me death." The traitorous Benedict Arnold led British troops down what is now Main Street in 1781 and set fire to many buildings, including tobacco warehouses—in those days the equivalent of banks. Cornwallis briefly occupied the town; Lafayette came to the rescue.

It was during the Civil War, however, that Richmond made its mark on American history. Here Jefferson Davis presided over the Confederate Congress, and Robert E. Lee accepted command of Virginia's armed forces. For four years the Union army tried to capture it. Battling troops often surrounded the city, overflowing its tobacco warehouses with prisoners of war, its hospitals with the wounded, its cemeteries with the dead.

The city has a host of monuments, battlefields, and museums that recall its role during the Civil War, and just 30 minutes south on I-95 sits Petersburg, where the war's last great battle sealed Richmond's fate. But there also are more modern attractions to keep visitors busy, including an excellent fine arts museum, a hands-on science museum with a state-of-the-art planetarium, and a lovely botanical garden. And a short drive north of the city is that most modern of all attractions, Paramount's King's Dominion theme park.

1 Orientation

ARRIVING

BY PLANE **Richmond International Airport,** Airport Drive off I-64, I-295, and Williamsburg Road (U.S. 60) (☎ 804/226-3052), locally known as Byrd Field, is about 15 minutes east of downtown. The major airlines serving the airport are American, Continental, Delta, Northwest, United, and USAir.

There's no public bus service from the airport into Richmond. **Groome Transportation** (☎ 804/222-7222, or 800/552-7911 in Virginia) offers 24-hour service to downtown; the cost is $13 for one person, $17.25 for two people, $20.75 for three people, and $6.25 each for four or more. You can hire an entire car for $26.

> ### ❓ Did You Know?
>
> - The Houdon statue of George Washington in the Rotunda of the State Capitol is the only one ever made of the first president from life.
> - Richmond is the only major metropolitan area in the country that has white-water rafting trips in the heart of the city.
> - Swollen with the rainstorms of Hurricane Agnes in 1972, the James River rushed down the streets of Shockoe Bottom, causing damage in excess of $350 million. Now this area is behind a flood wall.
> - The oldest lawmaking body in the western hemisphere, the General Assembly of Virginia, has convened in Richmond since 1788.

By Car   Two major interstate highways intersect in Richmond—**I-64,** traveling east-west, and **I-95,** traveling north-south. **I-295** bypasses the city. **U.S. 60** (east-west) and **U.S. 1** and **U.S. 301** (north-south) are other major arteries.

Approximate driving distances in miles to Richmond: from Atlanta, 511; from Boston, 535; from Columbus, Ohio, 440; from Miami, 950; from New York, 340; from Philadelphia, 235; from Washington, D.C., 100.

By Train   Several daily **Amtrak** trains pull into the station at 7519 Staples Mill Rd., north of Exit 185 off I-64 (☎ 804/264-9194 or 800/872-7245). Bus Route 27 connects the station to downtown (see "Getting Around," below).

By Bus   Greyhound/Trailways offers regularly scheduled service to Richmond; the terminal is at 2910 N. Boulevard (☎ 804/353-8903 or 800/231-2222), at Exit 78 of I-95, near the Metro Richmond Visitors Center.

VISITOR INFORMATION

The **Metro Richmond Convention and Visitors Bureau,** 550 E. Marshall St. (Box C-250), Richmond, VA 23219 (☎ 804/782-2777 or 800/365-7272), provides information in advance and operates 4 visitor information centers. One is in the bureau's offices on the second floor of Sixth Street Marketplace, on Marshall Street at 6th Street. The bureau is open Monday to Friday from 8:30am to 5pm.

Drivers approaching via I-95/I-64 can take Exit 78 to the **Metro Richmond Visitors Center,** 1710 Robin Hood Rd. near the Boulevard (☎ 804/358-5511), opposite The Diamond baseball park. The center occupies an old railroad station, and it has a huge steam locomotive, a red caboose, and several other cars on display in a small park with picnic area. Open September through May, daily from 9am to 5pm; June through August, until 7pm.

A third is in the **Bell Tower** (☎ 804/648-3146), on the Capitol grounds near 9th Street and Marshall Avenue. It's open Monday to Saturday from 9am to 5pm, Sunday from noon to 5pm.

Lastly, the **Richmond International Airport Visitors Center** (☎ 804/236-3260) is open Monday to Saturday from 9am to 5pm, Sunday from noon to 5pm, with additional hours to accommodate incoming flights.

The Metro Richmond Visitors Center and the airport office will make same-day hotel reservations, often at discount rates.

CITY LAYOUT

Richmond is located at the fall line of the James River. Although the city has spread southward, all the hotels, restaurants, and historic sites of interest to visitors are north

Impressions

Broad-streeted Richmond . . . The trees in the streets are old trees used to living with people.
Family trees that remember your grandfather's name.
— Stephen Vincent Benet, *John Brown's Body*

of the river. A series of bridges connects the city, and there is also access to two islands, Brown's Island and Belle Isle. **Brown's Island** is separated from the mainland by the old **Kanawha Canal,** on which 19th-century barges carried cargo around the rapids, and is accessible by a footbridge from South 7th and Tredegar streets. It is rather flat and traversed by train tracks on its river side. **Belle Isle,** once the site of an infamous Civil War prison, is a more scenic spot, located in the middle of the James River. It is accessible via a footbridge under the Lee Bridge; there are signs on Third and Fifth at Byrd Street, directing visitors to Tredegar Street and thence to the bridge.

   Foushee Street divides street numbers east and west, while **Main Street** divides them north and south. **Broad Street** is the major east-west thoroughfare, and it's one of the few downtown streets with two-way traffic.

NEIGHBORHOODS IN BRIEF

Metropolitan Richmond grew from east to west, along the banks of the James River. As you explore the neighborhoods described below (moving roughly from east to west), you'll get a good sense of Richmond's history.

Church Hill   This east Richmond neighborhood is largely residential, with an abundance of 19th-century Greek Revival residences. St. John's Church is the outstanding landmark of the area. Bordering Church Hill is:

Tobacco Row   Paralleling the James River for about 15 city blocks between 20th and Pear streets, this is Richmond's latest urban redevelopment area; handsome old redbrick warehouses are being converted into apartment houses here.

Shockoe Bottom   Shockoe Bottom is roughly bounded by Dock and Broad streets and 15th and 20th streets, with the heart at the 17th Street Farmer's Market between East Main and East Franklin streets. Richmond's first real business district, it once encompassed tobacco factories, produce markets, slave auction houses, warehouses, and shops, and it retains much of its original character. Today old-fashioned groceries with signs in their windows for fresh chitterlings stand alongside trendy shops and restaurants-bars, which make this Richmond's prime nightlife district. Shockoe Bottom also is home to the Edgar Allan Poe House and the old train station, whose spectacular clock tower is visible to travelers on I-95.

Shockoe Slip   This warehouse and commercial area was reduced to rubble in 1865 and rebuilt as a manufacturing center after the war. Although it has lost some of its luster to Shockoe Bottom, Shockoe Slip today is a tourist mecca, its quaint cobblestone streets, old-fashioned street lamps, and renovated warehouses and residences housing lively restaurants, art galleries, nightspots, and fashionable shops. The Slip adjoins downtown on the east, roughly between 10th and 14th streets and Main and Canal streets.

Downtown   West and north of Shockoe Slip, downtown includes the old and new city halls, the state capitol, and other government buildings of Capitol Square; and the historic homes and museums of the Court End area, notably the Valentine Museum, Museum and White House of the Confederacy, and John Marshall House. The

---

Of Swords and Tennis Racquets

Richmond has changed in many ways since it fell to Grant's army in 1865, not the least of which is in its demographics. Most descendants of the defeated Confederate soldiers have fled to Richmond's sprawling suburbs, while descendants of the slaves those soldiers fought so hard to keep in bondage now control the city council. This new majority set the city's remaining old-line residents on ear recently by voting to place the statue of an African-American among those of the Civil War heroes lining Monument Avenue. The issue wasn't settled as we went to press, but by the time you visit Richmond, this hallowed avenue may sport the likeness of the late Arthur Ashe—Richmond's most famous modern son—holding not a sword but a tennis racquet.

---

financial and business center of Richmond, downtown also encompasses the Coliseum, the Carpenter Center for the Performing Arts, and the Sixth Street Marketplace.

Jackson Ward   Jackson Ward, north of Broad Street, is a downtown National Historic District and home to many famous African-Americans, including the first woman bank president in the United States, Maggie Walker, and legendary tap dancer Bill "Bojangles" Robinson, who donated a stoplight for the safety of children crossing the intersection of Leigh Street and Chamberlayne Avenue (where a monument to him stands today). Notable, too, is the fine ornamental ironwork gracing the facades of many Jackson Ward residences.

The Fan   Just west of downtown, the Fan is named for the shape of the streets, which "fan" out from downtown. Bordered by West Broad and Boulevard and West Main and Belvidere, it includes Virginia Commonwealth University and many turn-of-the-century town houses, now occupied by homes, apartments, restaurants, and galleries. Monument Avenue's most scenic blocks, with the famous Civil War statues down its median strip, are in the Fan.

Carytown   Just west of the Boulevard, Carytown has been called Richmond's answer to Georgetown. Cafes, restaurants, boutiques, and the restored Byrd Theatre, an old movie palace, bring Saturday-afternoon crowds to stroll West Cary Street.

2 Getting Around

BY PUBLIC TRANSPORTATION

The Greater Richmond Transit Company (☎ 804/358-GRTC) operates the **public bus** system. Base fare is $1.25. Service on most routes begins at 5am and ends at midnight. GRTC has an information booth in Sixth Street Marketplace, Marshall Avenue and 6th Street, where you can get a route map.

BY TAXI

Call **Yellow Cab Service Inc.** (☎ 804/222-7300) or **Veterans Cab Assn.** (☎ 804/329-1414). Fares are approximately $1.50 per mile.

BY CAR

Richmond is fairly easy to navigate by car, although all but a few streets are one-way. Left turns from a one-way street onto another one-way street may be made at red lights after a full stop.

Metropolitan Richmond

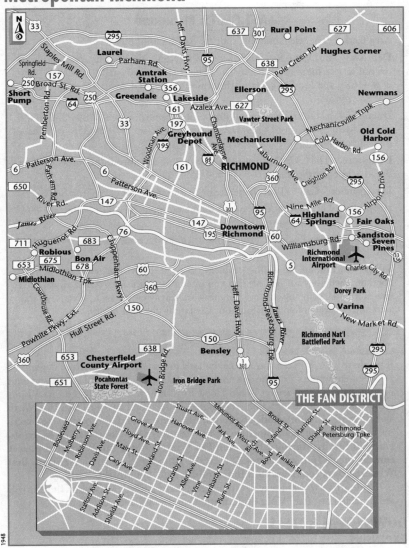

Car Rentals   Major car rental companies at the airport are **Thrifty** (☎ 804/222-7022 or 800/367-2277), **Avis** (☎ 804/222-7416 or 800/331-1212), and **Hertz** (☎ 804/222-7228 or 800/654-3131).

BY BICYCLE

Bikes can be rented at **Two Wheel Travel,** 2934 W. Cary St. (☎ 804/359-2453), in Carytown 2 blocks west of Boulevard.

FAST FACTS: Richmond

Area Code   The telephone area code for Richmond is 804.

Dentists   The Dental Referral Service (☎ 804/649-0283) operates a professional referral service for general dental care. The Richmond Dental Society (☎ 804/276-4168), the local chapter of the American Dental Association, also has a referral service.

Doctors   The Greater Richmond Physician Referral Service (☎ 804/330-4000) and the Medical College of Virginia Associated Physicians (☎ 804/358-6100) have trained personnel to help choose a physician.

Drugstore   The CVS Pharmacy chain has a 24-hour store at the corner of West Broad Street and the Boulevard (☎ 804/359-2497).

Emergencies   Call 911 for the police or an ambulance or to report a fire.

Hospitals   The Medical College of Virginia Hospital, 401 N. 12th St. (☎ 804/786-9000), is in downtown Richmond.

Luggage Storage/Lockers   You'll find them at the train station, 7519 Staples Mill Rd.

Safety   Richmond has a drug problem, so ask at the visitor centers or at your hotel desk whether a neighborhood you intend to visit is safe. Avoid all deserted streets after dark. In any city, even in the most heavily visited areas, it's wise to stay alert and be aware of your surroundings, whatever the time of day.

3 Accommodations

If you have a car, you can stay at a chain hotel or motel a few miles from downtown at less expensive rates than the downtown establishments mentioned below, and with no parking fees. Two are on Robin Hood Road near the Metro Richmond Visitor Center and The Diamond, home of baseball's Richmond Braves: **Days Inn North** and **Howard Johnson's Lodge & Suites.** Also convenient to downtown, the Executive Center area on West Broad Street has **Comfort Inn, Courtyard by Marriott, Fairfield Inn by Marriott, Hampton Inn West, Holiday Inn West, Red Carpet Inn, Shoney's Inn,** and **Super 8.** Near the airport in Sandston are **Hilton, Best Western, Days Inn, Hampton Inn, Holiday Inn,** and **Motel 6.**

If you arrive without a reservation, the Metro Richmond Visitor Bureau will assist making one (see "Visitor Information" under "Orientation," above).

DOWNTOWN HOTELS
EXPENSIVE

Berkeley Hotel

1200 E. Cary St., Richmond, VA 23219. ☎ **804/780-1300.** Fax 804/343-1885. 55 rms. A/C TV TEL. $115–$149 double. Extra person $10. Weekend and other packages available. AE, CB, DC, DISC, MC, V. Complimentary valet parking.

A handsome redbrick facade provides access to the old-world interior of this elegant little Shockoe Slip hostelry. Although it was opened in 1988, the hotel creates the illusion that it was built hundreds of years ago. Rooms are very residential in feel, luxuriously appointed, with fine period-reproduction furnishings, floral-print bedspreads and draperies, and walls hung with botanical prints; some have Jacuzzis.

Dining/Entertainment: Every chef in town says that the Berkeley has Richmond's finest dining, with such dinnertime offerings as a barbecued breast of duck with quinoa and honey roasted onions, Moroccan spiced Atlantic salmon with papaya salsa, and grilled beef tenderloin with braised portobello mushrooms and creamed spinach. Nightingale's Lounge adjoins.

Services: Concierge.

Facilities: Pool and health club nearby.

○ Jefferson Hotel

Franklin and Adams streets, Richmond, VA 23220. ☎ **804/788-8000** or 800/484-8014. Fax 804/225-0334. 274 rms. A/C MINIBAR TV TEL. $165–$205 double. Extra person $10. Children under 17 stay free in parents' room. Weekend and other packages available. AE, CB, DC, MC, V. Parking available.

A stunning beaux arts sightseeing attraction in its own right, the Jefferson was opened in 1895 by Maj. Lewis Ginter, who wanted his city to have one of the finest hotels in America. He hired the architectural firm of Carrère & Hastings, which had designed the monumental New York Public Library. The magnificent limestone-and-brick facade here is adorned with Renaissance-style balconies, arched porticos, and an Italian clock tower. Two-story faux-marble columns, embellished with gold leaf, encircle the Rotunda, or lower lobby. Acres of Oriental area rugs define the central seating area, furnished with elegant tufted-leather sofas amid potted palms. The marble Grand Staircase, magnificently wide and red-carpeted, leads to the Palm Court upper lobby under a stained-glass domed skylight; 9 of its 12 panes are original Tiffany glass.

Furnished with custom-made 18th-century-reproduction pieces, the rooms have hosted hundreds of notables, including Charles Lindbergh, Henry Ford, Charlie Chaplin, even Elvis Presley, and Presidents Harrison, McKinley, Wilson, Coolidge, and both Roosevelts. F. Scott and Zelda Fitzgerald held glamorous parties here.

Dining/Entertainment: Sunday brunch in the Rotunda is a bountiful all-you-can-eat feast in opulent surroundings. T.J.'s (as in Thomas Jefferson) is a restaurant, bar, and oyster bar just off the Rotunda. Off the Palm Court there's elegant dining at Lemaire's (named for the real T.J.'s maître d'), a warren of seven handsome rooms, one featuring a library. Dinners here feature regional entrees such as roast pheasant stuffed with fresh oysters and Virginia ham in wine sauce.

Services: 24-hour room service, concierge, nightly turndown, babysitting, complimentary newspaper, same-day valet/laundry service; shuttle to theaters and Shockoe Slip can be arranged.

Facilities: Gift shop, health club.

Omni Richmond Hotel

100 S. 12th St., Richmond, VA 23219. ☎ **804/344-7000** or 800/THE-OMNI. Fax 804/648-6704. 303 rms, 6 suites. A/C MINIBAR TV TEL. $89–$159 double. Extra person $15. Children under 12 stay free in parents' room. Weekend and other packages available. AE, CB, DC, DISC, MC, V. Parking $10 Mon–Fri, $2.50 Sat–Sun.

In the James Center office towers, the Omni is across the street from Shockoe Slip's boutiques, restaurants, and clubs. It boasts a handsome pink-marble lobby, with green-velvet-upholstered chairs and sofas around a working fireplace. Rooms are decorated in soft pastels, and some have spectacular views of the nearby James River. Club-floor rooms offer access to a private lounge, where a complimentary continental breakfast and afternoon refreshments are served weekdays.

Dining/Entertainment: The upscale Gallego Restaurant and Winebar features classic American fare. Café Gallego is a more casual venue opening to the office tower's atrium. The Market, a gourmet take-out deli, has breakfast pastries and other bakery treats, sandwiches, and pizzas.

Services: Room service (7am to midnight), concierge.

Facilities: Indoor/outdoor pool with sun deck, squash and racquetball courts, and Nautilus equipment are on the premises, available to Omni guests for $10 per day. James Center shops adjoin the hotel lobby.

Richmond Marriott

500 E. Broad St., Richmond, VA 23219. ☎ **804/643-3400** or 800/228-3400. Fax 804/788-1230. 401 rms, 10 suites. A/C TV TEL. $116 double; $200–$500 suite. Weekend and other packages available. AE, CB, DC, DISC, MC, V. Self-parking $5; valet parking $7. Bus: 1, 2, or 3.

Ideally located for convention goers at the Sixth Street Marketplace shops, the Marriott is connected via a skywalk to the Richmond Convention Center. Many of the exceptionally spacious and handsomely furnished accommodations offer panoramic city views.

Dining/Entertainment: J.W.'s Steakhouse serves breakfast, lunch, and dinner in a cheerful atmosphere. Sporting events are aired on the big TV in Triplett's, the lobby lounge and cocktail bar.

Services: Concierge, free newspaper.

Facilities: Health club, game room, indoor pool, gift shop.

MODERATE

✪ Linden Row Inn

100 E. Franklin St., Richmond, VA 23219. ☎ **804/783-7000** or 800/348-7424. Fax 804/648-7504. 70 rms, 7 suites. A/C TV TEL. $84–$144 single or double; $114–$144 suite. Rates include continental breakfast. Extra person $5. Children under 18 stay free in parents' room. AE, CB, DC, MC, V. Valet parking $3.

One of the best-run hotels we've ever encountered, this row of seven 140-year-old Greek Revival town houses and their garden dependencies is within walking distance of Shockoe Slip, Capitol Square, and the financial center. Not only the facades have remained intact; original interior features such as fireplaces, marble mantels, and crystal chandeliers still grace the inn.

Rooms in the main houses, all with windows nearly reaching 12-foot ceilings, have a harmonious mix of late Empire and early-Victorian pieces, with beautiful wallpapers, damask draperies, flower-patterned carpets, and marble-top dressers. Back rooms overlook a brick-walled garden and patio, and the garden dependencies (small, separate buildings) of the original town houses have been restored and offer accommodations with private entrances, pine furniture, and handmade quilts.

Dining/Entertainment: The inn's dining room is a cozy, low-ceilinged precinct with whitewashed-brick walls; Continental cuisine with a southern accent is offered in the evening. An inviting selection of cheese, crackers, and drinks in the early evening and hot beverages after dinner are laid out buffet style in two handsomely furnished parlors, with leather couches and working fireplaces.

Services: Concierge; free daily newspaper; limo service; room service (7 to 9am and 5:30 to 10pm).

Facilities: Use of YMCA Fitness Center free to guests.

Radisson Hotel Richmond

555 E. Canal St., Richmond, VA 23219. ☎ **804/788-0900** or 800/333-3333. Fax 804/788-0791. 300 rms. AC TV TEL. $69–$109 double. Extra person $10. AE, DC, DISC, MC, V. Parking $5.

You can't mistake the Radisson for any other building in town—it's a starkly modern, triangular 16-story high-rise with reflecting glass windows. Mirrored sliding closet doors reflect the clean, simple look of the rooms, which boast such nice touches as Edward Hopper prints on the walls. Most rooms offer stunning city views.

Downtown Richmond Accommodations & Dining

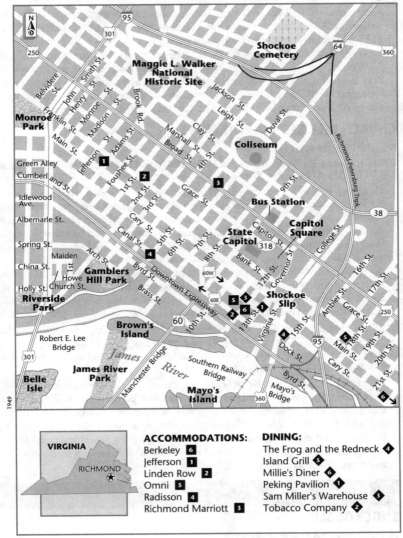

ACCOMMODATIONS:
Berkeley **6**
Jefferson **1**
Linden Row **2**
Omni **5**
Radisson **4**
Richmond Marriott **3**

DINING:
The Frog and the Redneck ◆**4**
Island Grill ◆**5**
Millie's Diner ◆**6**
Peking Pavilion ◆**1**
Sam Miller's Warehouse ◆**3**
Tobacco Company ◆**2**

Dining/Entertainment: The 555 Canal Club is a pleasant lounge. The Pavilion, a casual eatery, serves a buffet breakfast daily from 6:30am; it's also open for lunch and dinner.

Services: Room service (6:30am to 11pm).

Facilities: Indoor pool, health club, sauna, Jacuzzi, Nautilus equipment, gift shop.

DOWNTOWN BED & BREAKFASTS

Carefully chosen bed-and-breakfast accommodations are offered by **Bensonhouse of Richmond,** 2036 Monument Ave., Richmond, VA 23220 (☎ 804/353-6900).

Administrator Lyn Benson has ten listings, all within 5 to 15 minutes of major attractions. All her hosts are knowledgeable about the city. Rates range from $89 to $135 for a double, continental breakfast included. Many hosts even prepare a full breakfast. Ms. Benson's own B&B, **Emmanuel Hutzler House** (address above; ☎ 804/355-4885), is an Italian Renaissance–style inn, built in the 1900s with beautiful mahogany paneling, leaded-glass windows, and a coffered-beam ceiling, all lovingly restored. Her spacious guest rooms are handsomely furnished with antiques and boast TVs, private baths (some with Jacuzzis), and in-room telephones.

CHURCH HILL BED & BREAKFASTS

Mr. Patrick Henry's Inn

2300-02 E. Broad St., Richmond, VA 23223. ☎ **804/644-1322** or 800/932-2654. 4 suites. A/C TV TEL. $95–$125 double. Rates include full breakfast for two. AE, DC, DISC, MC, V.

One block west of historic St. John's Church, these two Greek Revival town houses are in Richmond's oldest neighborhood. Innkeepers James and Lynn News have turned their first two floors over to a tavern and colonial-style restaurant, where James's cooking has received critical acclaim. The tavern on the basement level has low beamed ceilings and whitewashed-brick walls; it serves up light fare. The outdoor garden patio offers al fresco dining in good weather. All accommodations have working fireplaces and kitchenettes, and one has a private balcony overlooking the garden. Furnishings are a mix of antiques and reproductions, featuring four-poster beds, wing chairs, and pretty ruffled curtains. St. John's landmark church is just a block away, and the Richmond battlefield headquarters are close by.

William Catlin House Bed & Breakfast Inn

2304 E. Broad St., Richmond, VA 23223. ☎ **804/780-3746.** 5 rms (3 with bath). A/C. $75 double with shared bath, $95 double with private bath; $150–$160 suite. Rates include breakfast and taxes. DISC, MC, V. Parking on street.

Occupying an 1845 Greek-Revival residence, this inn offers a comfortable home away from home. Sliding doors separate a plush first-floor parlor from the dining room, where breakfast is served. Guest accommodations are in the basement and on the second and third floors. They're tastefully furnished with period pieces, lace curtains, fireplaces, and charming decorative pieces like spinning wheels or dried-flower arrangements. Hosts Robert and Josephine Martin provide evening snacks of sherry and mints as well as a delicious full breakfast.

4 Dining

SHOCKOE SLIP

✪ The Frog and the Redneck

1423 E. Cary St., between 14th and 15th Sts. ☎ **804/648-3764.** Reservations recommended. Main courses $14–$20. AE, DC, DISC, MC, V. Mon–Fri 5:30–10pm, Sat 5–10:30pm. FRENCH/AMERICAN.

This facetious name derives from co-owner and chef Jimmy Sneed, who grew up in the South and then worked as an under-chef at Jean-Louis Paladin's renowned French restaurant in Washington, D.C. Jimmy excellently blends the "Frog" style of cooking he learned there with local "Redneck" ingredients. For example, instead of Bayonne ham and melon, Jimmy offers Virginia ham and local cantaloupe as an appetizer. Some of the largest lumps of backfin Chesapeake crab meat we've ever seen floated in his delicious pimento-accented sweet red pepper soup. As his signature dish, Jimmy packs those giant lumps into the best sautéed crabcakes we've ever tasted. Jimmy changes his menu daily to incorporate the freshest local produce. A suggestion: Try his five-course sampler menu, a deal at $35 a person. Meanwhile, co-owner Adam Steely presides over a spacious bistro-style dining room with mirrors on the posts supporting the upper floors of a converted warehouse. As would be expected, the wine list carries a good selection of French and Virginian vintages.

Peking Pavilion

1302 E. Cary St., at 13th St. ☎ **804/649-8888.** Reservations recommended. Main courses $8.75–$22.50. AE, MC, V. Sun–Thurs 11:30am–9:30pm, Fri 11:30am–10:45pm, Sat 5–10:30pm. CHINESE.

The exquisite wood carvings and tapestries on the walls and the dragon-motif-backed chairs of this plush choice are from mainland China. Yet, for all its elegance, Peking Pavilion offers surprisingly inexpensive combination lunch platters—entree with soup, spring roll, and fried rice for $5.25 to $7. House special entrees lead off with Peking duck with crispy skin and tender meat, Chinese pancakes, spring onions, and plum sauce. Or you might try Seafood Delight, a combination of shrimp, scallops, lobster, and chicken sautéed in a rich, spicy sauce.

Sam Miller's Warehouse

1210 E. Cary St., between 12th and 13 Sts. ☎ **804/643-1301.** Reservations suggested, especially for dinner on weekends. Main courses $13–$22. AE, DC, MC, V. Daily 11am–11pm; Sun brunch 10am–5pm; Fri–Sat entertainment until 2am. AMERICAN.

A popular pub since the Slip's revival, Sam Miller's seating is in cozy booths, and small dark-green tole lamps on the tables keep lighting romantically low. At lunch, terrific sandwiches include beef barbecue with coleslaw, crabcakes, and a juicy 5-ounce hamburger. Chesapeake Bay seafood and prime rib are dinner-menu highlights. Among the seafood entrees, all served with vegetable du jour and wild rice or baked potato, are fresh broiled or blackened bluefish; shrimp stuffed with crab imperial; and an enormous seafood platter piled high with scallops, oysters, clams, shrimp, fresh fish, and crab cake.

The Tobacco Company

1201 E. Cary St., at 12th St. ☎ **804/782-9431.** Reservations recommended. Main courses $14–$22. AE, DC, MC, V. Mon–Sat 11:30am–2:30pm, Sun 10:30am–2:30pm; Mon–Fri 5:30–10:30pm, Sat 5–11pm, Sun 5:30–10pm. AMERICAN.

Appropriately, this dining-entertainment complex is housed in a former tobacco warehouse converted to a sunny, plant-filled three-story atrium. An exposed antique elevator carries guests from the first-floor cocktail lounge to the two dining floors above. Nostalgic touches abound—brass chandeliers, a cigar-store Indian, even an old ticket booth that is now the hostess desk. Tiffany-style lamps cast a glow on the various seating areas, which are handsomely sectioned off by white porch-style banisters. Exposed-brick walls are festooned with antique collector's items.

Contemporary American cuisine is featured. Lunch specialties could be as light as a vegetarian stir-fry, as hearty as chicken chimichangas. Also on tap are omelets, salads, sandwiches, and burgers. At dinner, you might begin with shrimp and Virginia ham with papaya or an innovative pairing of mushrooms and escargots, then move on to the house special: slow roasted prime rib with seconds on the house. There's live music in the Club downstairs Tuesday to Saturday nights, with dancing Thursday to Saturday.

SHOCKOE BOTTOM

Island Grill

14 N. 18th St., between Franklin and Main streets. ☎ **804/643-2222.** Reservations recommended, especially for dinner. Main courses $12–$25. AE, DC, DISC, MC, V. Mon–Fri 11:30am–2:30pm; Mon–Thurs 5:30–10:30pm, Fri–Sat 5:30pm–midnight. AMERICAN/CARIBBEAN.

This tropical-themed spot has two dining rooms whose chic decor is highlighted by black-and-teal floral-print banquettes and comfortable chairs. Silver wall sconces light the room at night, and expansive windows give plenty of light by day. Start here with hearty deep-fried clam fritters or tasty plantains stuffed with spiced shredded beef. Entrees may include Jamaican roast pork, marinated and roasted with a guava glaze and served with tropical-fruit chutney. Entrees come with beans and rice, fried sweet plantains, and a vegetable. You can opt for a light dessert like the island parfait (layers of pineapple-papaya ice cream, strawberry-mango sorbet, and fresh whipped cream). To end dinner in good style, Island Grill offers espresso, flavored cappuccino, or such exotic concoctions as café Antigua—coconut rum, mocha liqueur, and whipped cream.

CHURCH HILL

✪ Millie's Diner

2603 E. Main St., at 26th St. ☎ **804/643-5512.** Reservations not accepted. Main courses $14.50–$22. AE, DC, DISC, MC, V. Tues–Thurs 11am–2pm and 5:30–10:30pm, Fri 11am–2pm and 5:30–10:30pm, Sat 10am–3pm and 5:30–10:30pm, Sun 9am–3pm and 5:30–9:30pm. ECLECTIC.

Once Millie's really was a diner, and the counter, booths, and open kitchen from those days are still here. It's not a diner anymore, however, for now a talented young chef works the gas stove, turning out a brilliant variety of dishes. His spicy Thai shrimp with asparagus, red cabbage, shiitake mushrooms, cilantro, lime, peanuts, and hot chilis over fettucine is always on the blackboard menu, which otherwise changes every two weeks. Sometimes he features southern-influence cooking, sometimes dishes from the Pacific Rim countries. Whatever, he prepares everything from scratch—as you watch, if you grab a counter seat. Excellent fare, an entertaining wait staff, and hearty portions make this noisy eatery highly popular among Richmond's young professionals.

THE FAN

Strawberry Street Café

421 N. Strawberry St., between Park and Stuart avenues. ☎ **804/353-6860.** Reservations needed only for large groups. Main courses $6–$13; weekend brunch buffet $8. AE, MC, V. Mon–Fri 11:30am–2:30pm, Sat 11am–5pm, Sun 10am–5pm; Mon–Thurs and Sun 5–10:30pm, Fri–Sat 5pm–midnight. AMERICAN.

The Strawberry Café is decorated in turn-of-the-century style, with a beautiful oak bar, *Casablanca*-inspired fan chandeliers, and a plant-filled cafe-curtained window. Flower-bedecked tables (candlelit at night) add a cheerful note. At lunch or dinner, you can help yourself to unlimited offerings from a bountiful salad bar. At lunch, you might get a broccoli-and-Cheddar quiche or a 6-ounce burger. At dinner, entrees like broiled Maryland lump crabcakes include fresh vegetable and potato du jour. There's luscious chocolate cake for dessert. The weekend unlimited brunch bar lets you create a memorable meal from an assortment of fresh fruits, yogurt, baked ham, pastries, hot entree, salads, homemade muffins, and beverage.

Grace Place

826 W. Grace St., between Schaeffer and Laurel streets. ☎ **804/353-3680.** Main courses $5.50–$9.50. MC, V. Mon–Fri 11am–9pm, Sat 11am–9:30pm. VEGETARIAN.

A relic from The Fan's hippie days, this delightful vegetarian restaurant occupies the second floor of a classic Victorian home. It has pine plank floors, white and unpainted brick walls hung with paintings by local artists, a fireplace, pots of geraniums in lace-curtained windows, and flower-bedecked oak tables. Low-key, low-decibel recorded classical or folk music helps set the tone; occasionally there's even a guitarist on hand. In good weather, all dining is al fresco on the outdoor patio under shade trees. Throughout the day you can order big salads and sandwiches, such as falafel, avocado melt, and pizza in a pita. Evening specials include pastas, burritos, and other substantial items. Wine, beer, and coffee are available. Purists have a wide selection of herbal teas and specialty drinks like organic carrot juice and smoothies—icy fruit-and-yogurt shakes. Homemade desserts range from sugarless (apple crisp) to sinful (cheesecake).

⑤ Joe's Inn

205 N. Shields Ave., between Grove and Hanover streets. ☎ **804/355-2282.** Reservations not accepted. Main courses $6–$9.50. AE, MC, V. Mon–Thurs 9am–midnight, Fri–Sat 8am–2am, Sun 8am–midnight. ITALIAN.

This very popular neighborhood hangout has been serving terrific Greek-accented Italian fare since 1952, including veal parmigiana, seafood, pizzas, and pasta. The house specialty is gargantuan portions of spaghetti. Two can easily share an order of spaghetti à la Joe, which arrives steaming hot en casserole, bubbling with a layer of baked provolone between the pasta and heaps of rich meat sauce. Soups, salads, omelets, and sandwiches are also options. Stop by for a mouth-watering stack of hotcakes or French toast at breakfast. Joe's occupies two storefronts: a dining room side and a bar side with sleek mahogany booths and ornate brass-trimmed ceiling fans.

⑤ Texas-Wisconsin Border Café

1501 W. Main St., at Plum St. ☎ **804/355-2907.** Main courses $4.50–$6.50. MC, V. Daily 11am–2am, brunch Sat–Sun 11am–3pm. AMERICAN.

The Texas-Wisconsin Border Café is exactly what its name evokes: a lively rustic/western/hip eatery offering the kind of cookoff-winning chili and chili-parlor ambiance seldom found outside the Lone Star State. The setting: a longhorn steer horn over the door, fans suspended from a dark-green pressed-tin ceiling, pine-wainscoted cream walls hung with boar and elk heads, photos of everyone from Pancho Villa to LBJ, and works of local artists. The music is mellow rock, blues, or country. Sporting events are aired on the TV over the bar serving more than a dozen brands of bottled beers plus four on tap. The food is all fresh and homemade. From Texas comes "widow-maker" chili and "oil field" beans, plus other Tex-Mex offerings. From Wisconsin there's bratwurst stew, kielbasa, and potato pancakes. Homemade desserts like cheesecake and rich chocolate cake round things (and people) out.

CARYTOWN

✪ Ristorante Amici

3343 W. Cary St., between Freeman Rd. and S. Dooley St. ☎ **804/353-4700.** Reservations recommended. Main courses $13–23. AE, MC, V. Sun–Thurs 5:30–10pm, Fri–Sat 5:30–11pm. NORTHERN ITALIAN.

This delightful establishment seats diners upstairs in a brilliantly white-stucco room graced with hand-stenciled vine leaves over the windows and door. On the street floor is a small bar and seating at several additional tables for dinner, and during good weather, patrons are served at umbrella tables on a sidewalk patio. The owners of Amici (which means "friends" in Italian) hail from Cervinia, a small resort in the Italian Alps, where they perfected their craft—and perfection in the culinary arts is what they have achieved here. You might begin with grilled portobello mushrooms with garlic, basil, and olive oil; and thin slices of veal loin with delicate tuna sauce. Among the entree highlights we enjoyed on a recent visit were a superb sausage-stuffed roast quail with herb sauce; sautéed breast of chicken with eggplant, mozzarella, and tomato sauce; and baked filet of salmon with baby shrimp, fresh tomatoes, and cream sauce. Stunning desserts include a wicked tiramisù made with ladyfingers soaked in espresso and Kahlúa, topped with a layer of mascarpone cheese, and covered with shaved chocolate. The wine list is surprisingly affordable, with both international and domestic selections.

PICNIC FARE

One of the best places to get picnic supplies is at **Padow's Hams & Deli,** 1110 E. Main St., between 11th and 12th streets (☎ 804/648-4267), in the heart of downtown Richmond. The Padow family has been purveying fine Virginia hams since 1936, but that's not all you'll find in their deli, where downtown Richmonders flock at lunch to eat in or take out breakfast and lunch fare (open Monday to Friday from 7am to 5pm). There are about 50 sandwich combinations ranging from $3 to $8.50—from Smithfield ham biscuits to bagel, lox, and cream cheese. Box lunches, for $2.50 above the price of the sandwich, include a canned drink, small salad or chips, and dessert of the day. Fresh and hot chili or Brunswick stew are other possibilities. This is the place for visitors to pick up such gourmet gift items as a Smithfield ham, slab bacon, Virginia peanuts, Padow's own bottled preserves, or a gift pack of selected items (Padow's will handle shipping).

In Carytown, **Coppola's Delicatessen,** 2900 W. Cary St. at S. Colonial Ave. (☎ 804/359-NYNY) evokes New York's Little Italy with an aromatic clutter of cheeses, sausages, olives, pickles, and things marinated. Behind-the-counter temptations include pasta salads, antipasti, cannolis, specialty sandwiches, and pasta dinners. Coppola's is so New York that it "imports" Thuman's low-fat, low-salt deli meats from New Jersey. Prices are low; this is a down-to-earth deli, not a pretentious gourmet emporium, though the fare is as good as any the latter offer. There are some tables inside and a few out on the street.

5 Attractions

For a free overall view of the city, start at the observation deck of the **New City Hall,** 900 Broad St. at 9th Street, for a magnificent panorama of Richmond and the James River. You'll also get a fine bird's-eye view of the 1894 **Old City Hall,** diagonally across Broad Street between 9th and 10th streets, a dramatic Victorian Gothic with gray-stone walls three feet thick. Now a private office building, it has an interior courtyard that's a three-story marvel of painted cast iron. Visitors are welcome to enter the first floor during business hours. It's well worth the stop.

Several of Richmond's attractions are nearby, and you can buy a **Court End block ticket** to them for $14 for adults, $12 for seniors, $7 for children 7 to 12, under 7 free; the block ticket covers the Museum and White House of the Confederacy, Valentine Museum, John Marshall House, and St. John's Church.

THE TOP ATTRACTIONS

✪ Virginia State Capitol

Ninth and Grace streets. ☎ **804/786-4344.** Free admission. Tours given Apr–Nov, daily 9am–5pm; Dec–Mar, Mon–Sat 9am–5pm, Sun 1–5pm.

Thomas Jefferson was minister to France when he was commissioned to work on a capitol building for Virginia. He closely patterend the Classical Revival building on the Maison Carrée, a Roman temple built in Nîmes during the 1st century A.D., which he greatly admired. The colonnaded wings on either side were added between 1904 and 1906. Today the building is the second-oldest working capitol in the United States, in continuous use since 1788.

The central portion is the magnificent Rotunda, its domed skylight ceiling ornamented in Renaissance style. The room's dramatic focal point is Houdon's life-size statue of George Washington, said to be a perfect likeness. "That is the man, himself," said Lafayette. "I can almost realize he is going to move." A Carrara-marble bust of Lafayette by Houdon also graces the Rotunda, as do busts of the seven other Virginia-born presidents.

Resembling an open courtyard, the old Hall of the House of Delegates, where the Virginia House of Delegates met from 1788 to 1906, is now a museum. Here, in 1807, Washington Irving took notes while John Marshall tried and acquitted Aaron Burr of treason. The room was also a meeting place of the Confederate Congress. In the former Senate chamber, now used for occasional committee meetings, Stonewall Jackson's body lay in state after his death in 1863.

Free 30-minute **tours** are given throughout the day. After the tour, explore the **Capitol grounds.** To the east is the **Executive Mansion,** official residence of governors of Virginia since 1813. Another historic building is the old **Bell Tower,** built in 1824, often the scene of lunch-hour entertainment in summer. The Bell Tower houses a visitor center, where you can obtain information about Richmond and other Virginia destinations.

✪ Museum of the Confederacy

1201 E. Clay St. ☎ **804/649-1861.** Museum $5 adults, $4 senior citizens, $3 students and children 7–12, children under 7 free. Combination ticket (White House and museum) $8 adults, $7 seniors, $5 students. White House and museum, Mon–Sat 10am–5pm, Sun noon–5pm.

This fine museum houses the largest Confederate collection in the country, much of it contributed by veterans and their descendants. All the war's major events and campaigns are documented, and exhibits include period clothing and uniforms, a replica of Lee's headquarters, the role of African-Americans in the Civil War, Confederate memorabilia, weapons, and art.

Next door is the **White House of the Confederacy.** When the capital of the Confederacy moved to Richmond, the city government leased this 1818 mansion as a temporary home for President Jefferson Davis. It was the center of wartime social and political activity in Richmond. In 1891, a group of civic-minded Richmond women acquired the property and began a long restoration of the White House.

Visitors begin a **tour** in the lower-level exhibit area, where there's a history of the museum. Upstairs, the entrance hall is notable for its bronzed classical Comedy and Tragedy figures holding exquisite gas lamps. Formal dinners, luncheons, and occasional cabinet meetings were held in the dining room, a Victorian chamber with ornate ceiling decoration; some of the furniture in this room is original to the Davis family. Guests were received in the center parlor, interesting now for its knickknacks produced by captured Confederate soldiers and for an 1863 portrait of Davis. Upstairs are the bedrooms and the Oval Office in which Davis conducted the business of war.

Valentine Museum

1015 E. Clay St. ☎ **804/649-0711.** Admission $5 adults, $4 seniors, $3 children 7–12, under 7 free. Mon–Sat 10am–5pm, Sun noon–5pm. Free parking on premises.

Named for Mann S. Valentine II, a 19th-century businessman and patron of the arts whose fortune was based on a patent medicine called Valentine's Meat Juice, this museum documents the history of Richmond from the 17th through the 20th centuries. It includes the elegant Federal-style Wickham House, built in 1812 by attorney John Wickham, Richmond's wealthiest citizen who had helped defend Aaron Burr in 1807. Wickham assembled the finest talents of his day to design and decorate his mansion and entertained Richmond's social elite here, along with such visiting notables as Daniel Webster, Zachary Taylor, John Calhoun, Henry Clay, and William Thackeray.

Highlights include spectacular decorative wall paintings, perhaps the rarest and most complete set in the nation; the Oval Parlor, designated as "one of the hundred most beautiful rooms in America"; and the circular Palette Staircase. Slave and servant quarters have been restored to reveal the lives of the residents who supported the Wickhams' lavish life-style. Guided house **tours,** included in the price of admission to the museum, are given hourly.

Valentine purchased the house in 1882, converted it into a private museum, and left it to the public when he died. Exhibits cover social and urban history, decorative and fine arts, textiles, architecture, and more. An ongoing display, "Shared Spaces, Separate Lives," utilizes touch-screen audiovisual elements and surround-sound special effects to explore the history of Richmond's complex race relationships. Lunch in Wickham's Garden Café is offered weekdays.

John Marshall House

818 E. Marshall St., at Ninth Street. ☎ **804/648-7998.** Admission $3, $2.50 seniors, $1.25 ages 7–12, under 7 free. Apr–Sept, Tues–Sat 10am–5pm; Oct–Dec, Tues–Sat 10am–4:30pm.

This historic property is the restored home of John Marshall, a giant in American judicial history. As its chief justice from 1801 to 1835, Marshall essentially established the power of the United States Supreme Court through his doctrine of judicial review, under which federal courts can overturn acts of Congress. Earlier, Marshall served in the Revolutionary army, argued cases for George Washington (his close personal friend), served as ambassador to France under John Adams, and had a brief term as secretary of state. He was a political foe of his cousin, Thomas Jefferson.

Largely intact, the house Marshall built between 1788 and 1790 is remarkable for many original architectural features—exterior brick lintels, interior wide-plank pine floors, wainscoting, and paneling. Marshall's own furnishings and personal artifacts have been supplemented by period antiques and reproductions. A guided **tour** of the house takes about 20 minutes.

St. John's Church

2401 E. Broad St. ☎ **804/648-5015.** Admission $2 adults, $1 children 7–18, under 7 free. Tours given Mon–Sat 10am–3:30pm, Sun 1–3:30pm; services Sun at 8:30 and 11am.

Originally known simply as the "church on Richmond Hill," St. John's dates to 1741, but its congregation was established in 1611. Alexander Whitaker, the first rector, instructed Pocahontas in Christianity, baptized her, and married her to John Rolfe. The church building is best known as the 1775 meeting place of the second Virginia Convention. Attending were Thomas Jefferson, George Wythe, George Mason, Benjamin Harrison, George Washington, Richard Henry Lee, and many other major historic

Downtown Richmond Attractions

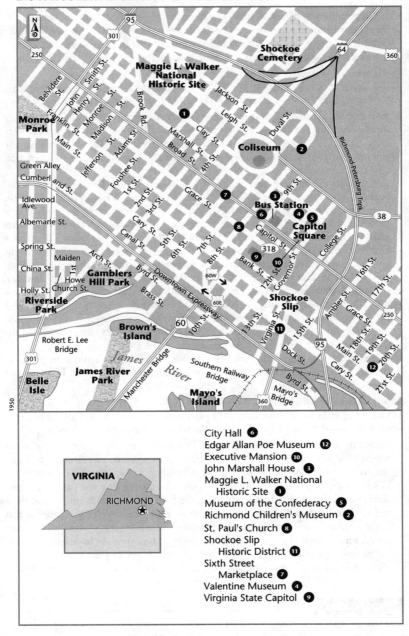

City Hall **6**
Edgar Allan Poe Museum **12**
Executive Mansion **10**
John Marshall House **3**
Maggie L. Walker National
Historic Site **1**
Museum of the Confederacy **5**
Richmond Children's Museum **2**
St. Paul's Church **8**
Shockoe Slip
Historic District **11**
Sixth Street
Marketplace **7**
Valentine Museum **4**
Virginia State Capitol **9**

personages. In support of a bill to assemble and train a militia to oppose Great Britain, Patrick Henry stood up and delivered his incendiary speech: "Is life so dear, or peace so sweet, as to be purchased at the price of chains or slavery? Forbid it, Almighty God! I know not what course others may take, but as for me, give me liberty or give me death."

On the 20-minute guided **tour,** you'll see the original 1741 entrance and pulpit, the exquisite stained-glass windows, and the pew where Patrick Henry sat during the convention. From the last Sunday in May through the first Sunday in September, there's a living-history program at 2pm re-creating the second Virginia Convention.

◉ Richmond National Battlefield Park

Headquarters, 3215 E. Broad St., at 33rd St. ☎ **804/226-1981.** Free admission. Chimborazo Visitor Center, daily 9am–5pm. Closed New Year's Day, Thanksgiving, and Christmas.

As the political, medical, and manufacturing center of the South and the primary supply depot for Lee's Army of Northern Virginia, Richmond was a prime military target throughout the Civil War. Seven major drives were launched against the city between 1861 and 1865. The bloody battlefields ring Richmond's eastern side, now mostly suburbs.

A 60-mile driving tour begins at the **Chimborazo Visitor Center** on East Broad Street at 33rd Street, at the site of one of the Confederacy's largest hospitals (about 76,000 patients were treated here). A 12-minute slide show about the Civil War is shown throughout the day, and you can rent a 3-hour auto-tape tour with cassette player that covers the Seven Days Campaign of 1862. You can also view a 25-minute film here called *Richmond Remembers;* it documents the socioeconomic impact of the Civil War on the Confederate capital. Park rangers are on hand to answer all questions.

There are smaller visitor centers at **Fort Harrison,** about 8 miles southeast, and at **Cold Harbor,** about 10 miles northeast, both open daily during summer (check with Chimborazo for hours). The latter was the scene of a particularly bloody 1864 encounter during which 7,000 of Grant's men were killed or injured in just 30 minutes. Programs with costumed Union and Confederate soldiers reenacting life in the Civil War era take place during the summer.

It's convenient to combine a battlefield tour with visits to the James River plantions (see the Williamsburg, Jamestown, and Yorktown chapter), since Fort Harrison and some other sites are near Va. 5, the plantations route.

Edgar Allan Poe Museum

1914-1916 E. Main St. ☎ **804/648-5523.** Admission $5 adults, $4 seniors, $3 students, under 6 free. Sun–Mon 1–3:30pm, Tues–Sat 10am–4pm. Free parking on premises.

Enclosing an "Enchanted Garden," the Poe Museum consists of four buildings wherein the poet's rather sad life and career are documented. The museum complex centers on the Old Stone House, the oldest building in Richmond, dating to about 1736. He did not live in this house, but the 15-year-old Poe was part of a junior honor guard that escorted Lafayette when the famous general was entertained there in 1824. Today the Old Stone House contains a shop and a video presentation that initiates guided tours of the museum. The other three buildings were added to house the growing collection of Poe artifacts and publications, now the largest in existence.

Poe was orphaned at age two and taken into the home of John and Frances Valentine Allan, from whom came his middle name. As a young man, Poe worked as

Impressions

As the sun rose on Richmond, such a spectacle was presented as can never be forgotten by those who witnessed it. . . . All of the horrors of the final conflagration, when the earth shall be wrapped in flames and melt with fervent heat, were, it seemed to us, prefigured in our capital.

—An Observer, April 3, 1865

an editor, a critic, and a writer for the *Southern Literary Messenger*. The desk and chair he used at the *Messenger* are among the photographs, portraits, documents, and other memorabilia on display. Most fascinating is the Raven Room displaying artist James Carling's evocative illustrations of *The Raven*. Tours of the museum are given throughout the day.

Maggie L. Walker National Historic Site

110 ¹/₂ E. Leigh St., between First and Second streets. ☎ **804/780-1380**. Free admission. Wed–Sun 9am–5pm. Closed New Year's Day, Thanksgiving, and Christmas.

Daughter of a former slave, Maggie Mitchell Walker was an unusually gifted woman who achieved success in the world of finance and business and rose to become the first woman bank president in the country. Originally a teacher, Walker, after her marriage in 1886, became involved in the affairs of a black fraternal organization, the Independent Order of St. Luke, which grew under her guidance into an insurance company, and then into a full-fledged bank, the St. Luke Penny Savings Bank. The bank continues today as the Consolidated Bank and Trust, the oldest surviving African-American-operated bank in the United States. Walker also became editor of a newspaper and created and developed a department store. Her residence from 1904 until her death in 1934, this house remained in her family until 1979. It has been restored to its 1930 appearance.

○ Virginia Museum of Fine Arts

The Boulevard and Grove Avenue. ☎ **804/367-0844**. Admission by suggested donation $4. Tues–Sun 11am–5pm, Thurs to 8pm. Free parking.

Any city would be proud of this museum, noted for the largest public Fabergé collection outside Russia—more than 300 objets d'art created at the turn of the century for Tsars Alexander III and Nicholas II. The Imperial jewel-encrusted Easter eggs evoke what art historian Parker Lesley calls the "dazzling, idolatrous realm of the last czars."

Highlights include the Goya portrait *General Nicholas Guye*, a rare life-size marble statue of Roman emperor Caligula, Monet's *Iris by the Pond*, and six magnificent Gobelins *Don Quixote* tapestries. And that's not to mention works of de Kooning, Gauguin, van Gogh, Delacroix, Matisse, Degas, Picasso, Gainsborough, and others; antiquities from China, Japan, Egypt, Greece, Byzantium, Africa, and South America; art from India, Nepal, and Tibet; and an impressive collection of contemporary American art.

The museum also contains the 500-seat **TheatreVirginia** (see "Richmond After Dark," below) and a low-priced cafeteria overlooking a waterfall cascading into a pool with a Maillol sculpture.

Science Museum of Virginia/Ethyl Universe Theater

2500 W. Broad St., three blocks east of the Boulevard. ☎ **804/367-1080** or 800/659-1727 for show times and ticket prices. Admission $7.50 adults, $7 seniors and children 4–12. Exhibits, summer, Mon–Thurs 9:30am–5pm, Fri–Sat 9:30am–5pm, Sun noon–5pm; winter, Mon–Sat 9:30am–5pm, Sun noon–5pm. Theater, Mon–Thurs 11am–5pm, Sun 1–5pm. Free parking.

There are few DO NOT TOUCH signs in the galleries here, for hands-on exhibits are the norm in this science museum with state-of-the-art planetarium, making it ideal for youngsters. For example, in "Computer Works," visitors create programs, discuss their problems with a computer shrink, and play "assistant" for a computer magician. One wing features exhibits on aerospace, energy and electricity, chemistry, and physics. Elsewhere, you'll learn about optical illusions inside a giant kaleidoscope, try to get your bearings in a full-size distorted room, and crawl into a space capsule.

Not to be missed are the shows at the 275-seat Ethyl UNIVERSE Planetarium/Space Theater, which shows spectacular Omnimax films as well as the most sophisticated special-effect multimedia planetarium shows. And the building itself merits attention; it's the beaux arts former Broad Street Station, designed in 1919 by John Russell Pope (architect of the Jefferson Memorial, the National Archives, and the National Gallery of Art in Washington). With a soaring rotunda, classical columns, vaults, and arches, Pope created it to evoke a sense of wonder—very fitting for a museum of science.

Lewis Ginter Botanical Garden At Bloemendaal

1800 Lakeside Ave. ☎ **804/262-9887.** Admission $3 adults, $2 seniors, $1 children 2–12, under 2 free. Daily 9:30am–4:30pm. Take I-95N to Exit 80 (Brook Road) and turn left at Hilliard Road to Lakeside.

In the 1880s, self-made Richmond millionaire, philanthropist, and amateur horticulturist Lewis Ginter (a founder of the American Tobacco Company) built the Lakeside Wheel Club as a summer playground for the city's elite. The resort boasted a lake, a nine-hole golf course, cycling paths, and a zoo. At Ginter's death in 1897, part of his vast fortune went to his niece, Grace Arents, who converted the property to a hospice for sick children and named it Bloemendaal for Ginter's ancestral village in the Netherlands. An ardent horticulturist, she imported rare trees and shrubs and constructed greenhouses. A white gazebo and trellised seating areas were covered in rambling roses and clematis. Large beds on the front lawn were planted with shrubs and flowers. Grace died in 1926, leaving her estate to the city of Richmond to be maintained as a botanical garden and public park. An admissions brochure suggests routes through the gardens and highlights significant aspects of the collection. There's a delightful Tea House on premises for lunch.

Maymont House and Park

Just north of the James River between Va. 161 and Meadow St. ☎ **804/358-7166.** Free admission (donations suggested). Apr–Oct, daily 10am–7pm; Nov–Mar, daily 10am–5pm. Go south 2 miles to the end of Boulevard; follow signs to the parking area. Bus: 3.

In 1886, Maj. James Henry Dooley, another of Richmond's self-made millionaires, purchased a 100-acre dairy farm on which to build a 33-room mansion surrounded by beautifully landscaped grounds. The mansion is in the Romanesque Revival style, with colonnaded sandstone facade, turrets, and towers. The architectural details of the formal rooms reflect various periods, most notably 18th-century French. The dining room has a stunning coffered oak ceiling; the library, a stenciled strapwork ceiling. A grand stairway leads to a landing from which rise two-story-high stained-glass windows. And the house is elaborately furnished with pieces from many periods chosen by the Dooleys—Oriental carpets, an art nouveau swan-shaped bed, marble and bronze sculpture, porcelains, tapestries, and Tiffany vases.

The Dooleys lavished the same care on the grounds. They placed gazebos wherever the views were best, laid out Italian and Japanese gardens, and planted horticultural specimens and exotic trees culled from the world over. The hay barn today is the **Mary Parsons Nature Center.** There are outdoor animal habitats for birds, bison, beaver, deer, elk, and bear. At the **Children's Farm,** youngsters can feed chickens, piglets, goats, peacocks, cows, donkeys, and sheep. A collection of late-19th- and early-20th-century horse-drawn carriages—surreys, phaetons, hunting vehicles—is on display at the **Carriage House.** Carriage rides are a weekend afternoon option April through mid-December.

Guided **tours** of the house are given continuously between noon and 4:30pm Tuesday through Sunday. For information on tram rides through the park, call 804/358-7167. There's a parking lot off Spottswood Road near the Children's Farm, and another at Hampton Street and Pennsylvania Avenue near the house and gardens.

Hollywood Cemetery

412 S. Cherry, at Albemarle Street. ☎ **804/648-8501.** Free admission. Daily 8am–5pm.

Perched on the bluffs overlooking the James River not far from Maymont, Hollywood Cemetery is the serenely beautiful resting place of 18,000 Confederate soldiers, two American presidents (Monroe and Tyler), six Virginia governors, Confederate President Jefferson Davis, and Confederate Gen. J. E. B. Stuart; the latter, one of 22 Confederate generals interred here. Designed in 1847, it was conceived as a place where nature would remain undisturbed. Its winding scenic roads, flowering trees, stone-bridged creeks, and ponds are largely intact today. The section in which the Confederates are buried is marked by a 90-foot granite pyramid, a monument constructed in 1869.

Agecroft Hall

4305 Sulgrave Rd. ☎ **804/353-4241.** Admission $4.50 adults; $4 senior citizens, $2.50 students, $2.50 gardens only. Tues–Sat 10am–4pm, Sun 12:30–5pm.

Agecroft Hall is an authentic late-15th-century Tudor manor house built in Lancashire, England. When it was threatened with destruction in the 1920s, Mr. and Mrs. T. C. Williams Jr. bought it and had it carefully taken down and shipped to Richmond for reconstruction in an elegant neighborhood overlooking the James. Today Agecroft serves as a museum portraying the social history and material culture of an English gentry family of the late Tudor and early Stuart eras. Typical of its period, the house has ornate plaster ceilings, massive fireplaces, rich oak paneling, leaded- and stained-glass windows, and a two-story Great Hall with a mullioned window 25 feet long. Furnishings authentically represent the period. Adjoining the mansion are a formal sunken garden, resembling one at Hampton Court Palace, and a formal flower garden, Elizabethan knot garden, and herb garden. Visitors see a 12-minute slide show about the estate followed by a half-hour house **tour.** Plan time to explore the gardens as well.

Wilton House

S. Wilton Rd. ☎ **804/282-5936.** Admission $4 adults, $3 students, children under 6 free. Mar–Jan, Tues–Sat 10am–4:30pm, Sun 1:30–4:30pm; Feb by appointment only. Closed National holidays. Take Va. 147 (Cary Street Road) west and turn south on Wilton Road.

Originally built on the James River about 14 miles below Richmond in 1753 by William Randolph III, this stately Georgian mansion was painstakingly dismantled and reconstructed on this bluff overlooking the river in 1933. Most of the original brick, flooring, and paneling were saved. Wilton's design has been attributed to a leading Williamsburg architect, Richard Taliaferro. It was part of a 2,000-acre plantation where the Randolphs entertained many of the leading figures of the day, including George Washington, Thomas Jefferson, and Lafayette.

The house has a fine collection of period furnishings throughout. All rooms feature handsome pine paneling, some with fluted pilasters and denticulated cornices.

ORGANIZED TOURS

The **Historic Richmond Foundation Tours,** 707-A E. Franklin St. (☎ 804/780-0107), offers a variety of well-planned guided tours daily, some in comfortable, air-conditioned 24-passenger vans, others on foot. Their "Old Richmond Today," a 2½-hour tour of the historic neighborhoods plus the State Capitol, is offered daily in the morning; the cost is $16 for adults, $13 for children 6 to 12. A 1½-hour "Richmond Highlights" tour takes place Monday to Saturday afternoons. A tour of the Civil War battlefields is on the second, third, and fourth Sundays of April through October.

A Riverboat Cruise Modern technology's answer to an 1850s riverboat, the paddle-wheeler *Annabel Lee* (☎ 804/664-5700 or 800/752-7093) makes a variety of lunch, dinner, and sightseeing cruises down the James River, some as far as the famous plantations. She operates from April to mid-October. Call for all prices and departure times. Reservations are a must, especially on weekends.

NEARBY ATTRACTIONS

About 14 miles north of Richmond on I-95 is the small community of Ashland in Hanover County, which has deep historical roots. Patrick Henry once tended bar at Hanover Tavern, built in 1723 and now home of the Barksdale Dinner Theatre (see "Richmond After Dark," below), which is opposite the 1735 Hanover County Courthouse.

✪ Scotchtown

Rte. 2, Beaverdam, VA. ☎ **804/227-3500.** Admission $5 adults, $4 seniors, $2 children 6–12, under 6 free. Apr, Sat 10am–4:30pm, Sun 1:30–4:30pm; May–Oct, Tues–Sat 10am–4:30pm, Sun 1:30–4:30pm. Nov–Mar open by appointment only. From Ashland, follow Va. 54 west, then the signs for Scotchtown at C.R. 685 north.

One of Virginia's oldest plantation houses, Scotchtown is a charming one-story white-clapboard home, in a parklike setting of small dependencies and gardens. The house was built by Charles Chiswell of Williamsburg, probably around 1719. Patrick Henry bought the house in 1770, and from 1771 to 1778 he lived here with his wife, Sarah, and their six children. Sadly, Sarah was mentally ill during much of the time and was eventually confined to a room in the basement. The manor house has been beautifully restored and furnished with 18th-century antiques, some associated with the Henry family. In the study, Henry's mahogany desk-table still bears the ink stains made by him, and bookshelves still contain his law books. A walnut cradle used by several of his children is now in the guest bedroom. Scotchtown also has associations with another historical figure—Dolley Madison. Her mother was a first cousin to Patrick Henry, and Dolley and her mother lived here while their family was moving back to this area from North Carolina.

✪ Paramount's King's Dominion

Doswell, VA. ☎ **804/876-5000.** Admission $27.95 adults and children 7 and above; $19.95 children 3–6; $22.95 seniors age 55 and over. Consecutive two-day passes and season passes good for unlimited use at any Paramount park in the United States also available. Hours may vary a bit from year to year, but generally the park is open Memorial Day–Labor Day, daily 9:30am–8 or 10pm; April–May and Labor Day–early October, Sat–Sun 9:30am–8 or 10pm. Take Va. 30 (Exit 98) off I-95.

One of the most popular theme parks in the East, this 400-acre family-oriented fanciful facility has a variety of rides and shows, many of them with themes from Paramount movies and TV shows. A ride simulator combines moving seats, a giant-screen image, digital audio technology, and other special effects with actual film footage from the movie *Days of Thunder,* its name. Another ride is a totally enclosed, multiple inversion launch coaster named "Outer Limits: Flight of Fear," after the popular TV series "Outer Limits."

And that's just the beginning, for the park has an ice-skating show featuring music from Paramount movies; a walk-of-fame salute to Paramount's movie history; several new walk-around characters, including Klingons, Vulcans, and Romulans from *Star Trek;* and an outdoor laser-and-fireworks show portraying adventure scenes from such Paramount movies and TV programs as *Mission: Impossible, Top Gun,* and

Beverly Hills Cop. There's even an area called *Wayne's World,* featuring the aptly named "Hurler" roller coaster, and a children's fantasy area called Hanna-Barbera Land.

White Water Canyon is a wet-and-wild ride simulating white-water rafting. There's more watery fun in Hurricane Reef, with 15 water slides; a refreshing raft ride; and Splash Island, designed for younger children with a wading pool and pint-sized slides.

6 Sports & Outdoor Activities

SPECTATOR SPORTS

AUTO RACING   The place to go in Virginia is **Richmond International Raceway,** located at the Virginia State Fairgrounds, between Laburnum Avenue and the Henrico Turnpike/Meadowbridge Road (☎ 804/329-6796). Major annual races include the Pontiac Excitement 400 and Hardee's Frisco 200 NASCAR races in March, plus the NASCAR Winston Cup Miller Genuine Draft 400 and the Grand National Autolite Platinum 250 in September. The Raceway is Virginia's largest sports facility, attracting crowds of 70,000 or more annually.

BASEBALL   The **Richmond Braves,** the top minor-league club in the Atlanta Braves' organization since 1966, compete in the 10-team International League from April through mid-September. All home games are played at The Diamond, a 12,500-seat modern baseball stadium located at 3001 N. Boulevard (Exit 78 off the I-64/I-95 junction). Call 804/359-4444 for tickets or information.

COLLEGE SPORTS   The **University of Richmond** basketball team competes in the Colonial Athletic Association from November through the beginning of March at the Robins Center, College Road between Boatwright and River roads (☎ 804/289-8388). The football team, the Spiders, plays from mid-September to mid-November at the UR stadium, McCloy and Freeman streets (☎ 804/289-8388).

Virginia Commonwealth University fields a basketball team, the Rams, that plays from November to mid-March at the Coliseum (☎ 804/282-7267).

ICE HOCKEY   Richmond's pro hockey team, the **Renegades,** belongs to the East Coast Hockey League and plays home games from October through March at the Coliseum, 601 E. Leigh St. at 7th Street (☎ 804/643-7825).

SOCCER   The **Richmond Kickers** play professional soccer games at the University of Richmond Soccer Complex (☎ 804/282-6776).

OUTDOOR ACTIVITIES

GOLF   Golf courses abound in the Richmond area. Among them are the **Belmont Park Recreation Center,** 1800 Hilliard Rd. (☎ 804/266-4929), with greens fees of $11 weekdays, $13 on weekends and holidays, when reservations are a good idea; and **Glenwood Golf Club,** Creighton Road (☎ 804/226-1793), with greens fees of $13 weekdays, $18 weekends and holidays.

WHITE-WATER RAFTING   You don't have to go to the remote mountains to ride the rapids, for **Richmond Raft Company,** 4400 E. Main St. at Water Street (☎ 804/222-7238), has trips on the James through the heart of Richmond. Water levels aren't always predictable, but the James usually is high and fast enough from March to November, with spring best for fast water.

7 Shopping

Richmond's neighborhoods have a number of specialty shops, which we survey below. For distinctive souvenirs, don't forget museum gift shops, especially those at the Science Museum, Art Museum, Museum and White House of the Confederacy, Valentine Museum, and Children's Museum.

Sixth Street Marketplace This glass-enclosed downtown pedestrian mall occupies 3 blocks of 6th Street between East Grace Street and the Richmond Coliseum. It has about 35 retail stores, restaurants, and the unique **Arts on the Square,** a gallery where more than a dozen artists work in open studios and exhibit their works ranging from painting, sculpture, and hand-painted textiles to jewelry and pottery. A glass-enclosed pedestrian walkway spanning Broad Street leads to numerous fast-food counters and the Metro Richmond Convention and Visitors Bureau. There's a "Friday Cheers" street party with live bands and refreshments every Friday from May to October between 5 and 9pm in Festival Park, at the north end of the marketplace next to the coliseum. The shops are open Monday to Friday from 10am to 6pm, Sunday from 12:30 to 5:30pm.

Shockoe Slip On East Cary Street, from 12th to 14th streets, the converted warehouse district has a profusion of trendy clothing stores, restaurants, art galleries, and entertainment venues along its cobblestone streets. Among the special shops here are Toymaker of Williamsburg and Beecroft & Bull, a fine men's clothier.

✪ Carytown The best place in town for a shopping stroll, the 7 blocks of West Cary Street between The Boulevard and Nasemond Street—known collectively as Carytown—are lined with a mix of small stores and interesting cafes. The old **First Baptist Church,** 3325 W. Cary St., has been transformed into an inviting retail complex, with the high-fashion Annette Dean's, Karina beauty salon, and Simon's Café (which has outdoor tables). Antique hunting is good here, especially at **The Antiques Gallery,** 3140 W. Cary St. (☎ 840/358-0500), and at **Martha's Mixture Antiques,** 3445 W. Cary St. (☎ 804/358-5827). Another interesting shop is **Z Rosa,** 3113 W. Cary St. (☎ 804/355-8755), which has one-of-a-kind, museum-quality tribal art, tapestries, African art, and gold and silver jewelry. You'll also find gourmet food shops, ethnic restaurants, secondhand clothing stores, and the landmark **Byrd Theater,** which now shows second-run films at discount prices.

West End The fashionable West End neighborhood features **The Shops at Libbie and Grove,** at the intersection of the 5700 block of Grove and the 400 block of Libbie, an enclave of distinctive women's fashions and specialty shops. It's especially worth browsing here for decorative items—anything from needlepoint pillows to an abstract wallhanging. Low-scale buildings and a relaxed atmosphere give this area its casual charm.

A short drive north, **West End Antiques Mall,** 6504 Horsepen Rd. (☎ 804/285-1916, or 800/280-1916), has more than 85 dealers offering a wide range of antiques and collectibles. From Libbie and Grove avenues, drive north on Libbie, turn left on Broad Street, then left on Horsepen Road. The mall is on the right.

Mechanicsville Four miles north of I-295 and 7 miles from downtown, this small town turned suburb is known for the Civil War battles which raged nearby. Among antique hunters, however, Mechanicsville is famous for Antique Village, on U.S. 301 (☎ 804/746-8914), where some 16 dealers purvey a treasure trove of relics.

8 Richmond After Dark

Richmond is no New York or London, so you won't be attending internationally recognized theaters and music halls here. Nevertheless, you might be able to catch visiting productions and artists at several large venues. The city also has its own ballet company and theater groups, and live music usually rocks Shockoe Bottom after dark.

Current entertainment schedules can be found in the Thursday "Weekend" section of the *Richmond Times-Dispatch,* the city's daily newspaper. The tabloid newspaper *Style Weekly* provides details on theater, concerts, dance performances, and other happenings. Another tabloid, the *Richmond Music Journal,* contains a rundown on what's going on in the city's music scene. The latter two publications are free and widely available at the visitor centers and in hotel lobbies.

Tickets can be reserved through **Ticketmaster** (☎ 800/736-2000).

MAJOR CONCERT HALLS & ALL-PURPOSE AUDITORIUMS

Carpenter Center for the Performing Arts
600 E. Grace St., at Sixth Street Marketplace. ☎ **804/782-3900.**

Built in 1928 by John Eberson, this former Loew's Theater was restored in 1983 to its Moorish splendor, complete with twinkling stars and clouds painted on the ceiling overhead. The center hosts national touring companies for dance, orchestral, and theatrical performances, including Broadway road shows. The **Richmond Ballet** (see "The Performing Arts," below), the **Virginia Opera** (☎ 804/643-6004), and the **Richmond Symphony** (☎ 804/788-1212) perform here as well.

Dogwood Dell
Byrd Park, Boulevard and Idlewild Avenue. ☎ **804/780-8683.**

In the summer months, Richmond goes outdoors to Byrd Park for free Festival of Arts music and drama performances under the stars in this tiered grassy amphitheater. Bring the family, spread a blanket, and have a picnic.

The Mosque
Main and Laurel streets. ☎ **804/780-4213.**

Adjacent to the bustling campus of Virginia Commonwealth University, this recently renovated, 3,500-seat hall is decorated with exotic mosaics and pointed-arch doorways. Offerings range from stage productions to nationally known musicians. The Mosque also is venue to the **Richmond Forum** (☎ 804/330-3993), which presents stimulating discussions of current topics by figures such as Gen. Norman Schwarzkopf, H. Ross Perot, and talk-show host Larry King.

Richmond Coliseum
601 E. Leigh St. ☎ **804/780-4970.**

The Coliseum hosts everything from the Ringling Bros. and Barnum & Bailey circus to rock concerts. It's the largest indoor entertainment facility in Virginia and can seat about 12,000. Major sporting events—wrestling, ice hockey, basketball— are also scheduled here.

THE PERFORMING ARTS

Theater If there's no touring company in town, you can catch family plays and musicals at **Theatre IV,** 114 W. Broad St. (☎ **804/344-8040**), which performs in the Empire Theater, at Broad Street and Jefferson Street. The 535-seat **TheatreVirginia,**

in the Virginia Museum of Fine Arts, 2800 Grove Ave. (☎ 804/367-0831), offers a good variety of mostly tried-and-true theater such as *The Pirates of Penzance, Driving Miss Daisy,* and *South Pacific.* The season runs from October to the end of April.

Dinner Theater   Two nearby dinner theaters also offer popular musicals and dramas. About 13 miles north of downtown, the **Barksdale Theatre,** on U.S. 301 opposite Hanover Courthouse (☎ 804/730-4860), is the nation's oldest dinner theater, occupying historic Hanover Tavern (where Patrick Henry once tended bar). Dinner and shows are Wednesday through Saturday evenings and Sunday matinees year-round. About 11 miles south of downtown in Colonial Heights, the **Swift Creek Mill Playhouse,** on U.S. 1 (☎ 804/748-5203), is housed in a 300-year-old grist mill along Swift Creek. Performances are Wednesday through Saturday nights.

Dance   The **Richmond Ballet** (☎ 804/359-0906) performs from mid-October through April at both the Carpenter Center for the Performing Arts and at TheatreVirginia. Their productions run the gamut from classical to modern, from *Swan Lake* to Balachine's *Apollo.*

THE CLUB & MUSIC SCENE

No establishment in Virginia can sell alcoholic beverages by the drink without also serving food, and they must bring in at least as much money from the sale of vittles as from booze. Accordingly, the club and music scene is found at Richmond's many restaurant-bars.

This is especially true in **Shockoe Bottom,** the city's funky nightlife district. Shockoe Bottom essentially occupies the square block beginning with the 17th Street Farmers Market and going east along East Main and East Franklin streets to 18th Street. Its pubs go up and down in popularity, so the joints we visited recently may not be in vogue when you get there. If you can find a parking space, you can easily see for yourself what's going on by bar-hopping around Shockoe Bottom's busy developed block (but *do not* wander off into deserted streets).

The **Flood Zone,** 18th and Main Sts. (☎ 804/643-6006), is Shockoe Bottom's large concert hall, with anything from reggae to rock to country. **Sunset Bar & Grille,** 1814 E. Main St. (☎ 804/643-2926), brings in new recording artists. **Memphis Bar & Grill,** 119 N. 18th St. (☎ 804/783-2608), carries an Elvis Presley theme (the menu offers bleu suede chicken), but the music varies across the spectrum from jazz to rockabilly. Country and western and bluegrass usually take center stage at **Moondance Saloon and Restaurant,** 9 N. 17th St. (☎ 804/788-6666).

For seeing and being seen, the **1708 Social Club,** 1708 E. Main St. (☎ 804/783-1798), actually is an upscale private club (if there's space, visitors pay $4 for a temporary membership). The hottest conversation pub in town during our recent visit was **Havana '59,** 16 N. 17th St. (☎ 804/649-2822), home of fresh juices, Cuban fare, and trendy cigar smoke.

Note: Many Shockoe Bottom establishments are closed Sunday and Monday, and they may extract a cover charge depending on who's making the music.

Up Cary Street in Shockoe Slip, **The Tobacco Company,** 1201 E. Cary St. (☎ 804/782-9555), has acoustic jazz upstairs Tuesday through Saturday and dancing downstairs Thursday through Saturday from 9:45pm to 1am. No cover first floor, $3 cover downstairs.

9 An Easy Excursion to Petersburg

In the 1860s, Petersburg was a vital rail junction which Grant recognized as the key to his quest to take Richmond. When every effort to capture the Confederate capital failed, Grant in an inspired move crossed the James River south of Richmond and advanced on Petersburg. Lee's forces weren't cooperative, however, and a tragic 10-month siege ensued. Finally, on April 2, Grant's all-out assault smashed through Lee's right flank, and that night Lee retreated west. A week later came the surrender at Appomattox Court House.

Today Petersburg is a quiet southern town on the banks of the Appomattox River 23 miles south of Richmond on I-95. When there, take Washington Street (Exit 52) west and follow the Petersburg Tour signs to the **Visitors Center,** 425 Cockade Alley (P.O. Box 2107), Petersburg, VA 23804 (☎ 804/733-2400, or 800/368-3595), where you can obtain a complimentary parking permit (valid for 1 day), maps, and literature. The center is open daily from 9am to 5pm.

OLD TOWN ATTRACTIONS

The visitor center is in Petersburg's historic **Old Town,** which was severely damaged by a tornado in 1993 (hence, the vacant lots). There's still a flea market in the refurbished old South Side railroad station on River Street, across from the visitors center, and the downtown attractions mentioned below have reopened. The **Appomattox Iron Works Industrial Heritage Park,** a fine example of an Industrial Revolution factory, wasn't so fortunate; it was still closed for repairs during our recent visit. Call 804/733-7300 to find out whether it has reopened.

Tours of three Old Town attractions begin at the **Siege Museum,** 15 W. Bank St. (☎ 804/733-2400), which tells the story of everyday life in Petersburg up to and during the siege in displays and an exceptionally interesting film narrated by actor Joseph Cotten, whose family lived in Petersburg during the Civil War. The museum is in the old Merchant Exchange, a magnificent Greek Revival temple-fronted building. Open daily from 10am to 5pm.

The **Trapezium House,** at Market and High streets (☎ 804/733-2400), is an amusing curiosity built without any right angles, supposedly because its owner was frightened by tales of ghosts who lurked in them. Open March to October, daily from 10am to 5pm.

Centre Hill Mansion, 1 Centre Hill Circle (☎ 804/733-2400), between Adams and Tabb streets, is a nicely restored 1823 mansion furnished with Victorian pieces. Open daily from 10am to 5pm.

Admission to each of these downtown attractions is the same: $3 for adults, $2 seniors and children 7 to 12.

FORT LEE AREA

The army's **Quartermaster Museum** (☎ 804/734-4203) is at Fort Lee, on East Washington Street (Va. 36) 3 miles east of Old Town. It has uniforms and equipment from all of America's wars, including a Jeep with a luxurious Mercedes car seat specially installed for Gen. George S. Patton during World War II. The Quartermaster Museum is open Tuesday to Friday from 10am to 5pm and Saturday, Sunday, and federal holidays from 11am to 5pm; admission is free. From the Petersburg Battlefield, go east on Va. 36, take the first right into Fort Lee (no pass required), then the first left to the museum.

✪ Petersburg National Battlefield

E. Washington St. (Va. 36), 2^1/$_2$ miles east of downtown. ☎ **804/732-3531.** Admission $4 per car, $2 per biker or pedestrian. Visitor center, daily 8am–5pm; battlefield, daily 8am–dusk.

At the visitor center, a multimedia presentation elucidates the story of the 10-month siege that lasted from mid-June 1864 to early April 1865. The battlefield encompasses some 2,646 acres. The 4-mile battlefield driving tour has wayside exhibits and audio stations; some stops have short walking trails. Most fascinating is the site of the Crater, literally a huge depression blown into the ground when a group of Pennsylvania volunteer infantry, including many miners, dug a passage beneath Confederate lines and exploded 4 tons of powder, creating the 170-by 60-foot crater. The carnage was sickening; thousands of men on both sides were killed or wounded during the ensuing battle. An extended 16-mile driving tour follows the entire siege line.

CRATER ROAD AREA

Old Blandford Church

319 S. Crater Rd. (U.S. 301), at Rochelle Lane. ☎ **804/733-2400.** Admission $3. Mar–Oct, Mon–Sat 9am–5pm, Sun 12:30–5pm; Nov–Feb, Mon–Sat 10am–5pm, Sun 12:30–4pm. Take Bank Street east and turn right on Crater Road; it's about 2 miles south of downtown Petersburg.

In addition to boasting one of the largest collections of Tiffany-glass windows in existence, Old Blandford Church is noted for the first observance of Memorial Day. The church was built in 1735 but was abandoned in the early 1800s when a new Episcopalian church was built closer to the town center. During the Civil War, the building became a hospital for troops wounded in nearby battlefields, and many of them were later buried in the church graveyard. After the war, a group of Petersburg schoolgirls and their teacher came here to decorate the soldiers' graves. The ceremony was witnessed by a visitor, Mary Logan, wife of Union Gen. John A. Logan, who was head of the Grand Army of the Republic, the major organization of Union army veterans. Under the Logans' initiative, the G.A.R. sponsored the idea of a national day of memorial, which was first observed nationwide in 1868. The Tiffany windows were designed as a memorial to the Confederate dead. The 13 Confederate states each sponsored one window. The 14th was commissioned by the local Ladies Memorial Association. The artist himself, Louis Comfort Tiffany, gave the church the 15th window, a magnificent "Cross of Jewels" that is thrillingly illuminated at sunset. This gift from a talented Northerner is a prized symbol of the postwar reconciliation of North and South.

WHERE TO STAY

National chain motels near I-95 and Washington Street (Exit 52) include **Best Western, Holiday Inn, Howard Johnson, Ramada Inn,** and **Super 8.**

Mayfield Inn

3348 W. Washington St. (P.O. Box 2265), Petersburg, VA 23804. ☎ **804/861-6775.** 2 rms, 2 suites. A/C. $69–$95 double. Rates include full breakfast. MC, V. From Richmond, take I-95 south to Exit 52 onto Washington Street (U.S. 1) west. The inn is about 3 miles from the exit.

Built as a plantation around 1750 by a member of the House of Burgesses, this stately brick inn was moved to its present site on a 4-acre plot of land in 1969. General Lee is thought to have spent the night here before going on to Appomattox. The present owners, Jamie and Dot Caudle, acquired it in 1979 and spent five years restoring it and furnishing it with antiques and period reproductions. Much of the interior is original, including seven working fireplaces. Rooms are large and luxurious. The largest bedroom has a four-poster canopied bed, dormer windows, a love seat, and a small table with a pewter tea service cozily set in front of the fireplace. Hearty country breakfasts are served downstairs in a formal dining room. Guests can stroll in a lovely colonial herb garden or lounge at the pool or in the gazebo.

WHERE TO DINE

✪ King's Barbeque

3221 West Washington St. (U.S. 1 South). ☎ **804/732-5861.** Main courses $4–$9. MC, V. Daily 7am–9pm. Follow U.S. 1 south 3 miles from downtown. AMERICAN.

Open since 1946, this Petersburg institution supplies some of the best barbecue in the entire South. The setting is a vast room with Colonial-style Formica-top tables and Windsor chairs. Notice the shelves over the lunch counter; they are lined with an extraordinary collection of pig dolls and figurines, including a Miss Piggy bank. Pork, beef, ribs, and chicken constantly smoke in an open pit right in the dining room. Unlike most other barbecue emporia, the pork and beef are served just as they come from the pit. Aficionados can enjoy the smoked flavor au natural, or apply sauce from squeeze bottles. The menu also offers such southern standbys as crispy fried chicken, ham steak, and seafood items like salmon cakes and fried oysters. Side orders of barbecued beans, yam puffs, and fried potato cakes are highly recommended. Fluffy homemade biscuits and hot apple pie are house specialties.

If you're going to Old Blandford Church, **King's Barbecue No. 2**, 2910 S. Crater Rd. (☎ 804/732-0975), has the same menu and is equally as good.

The French Betsy's Orleans House

21 W. Old St., in Old Town. ☎ **804/732-8888.** Reservations not necessary. Main courses $9–$12; Sun buffet brunch $12. AE, MC, V. Mon–Wed 11:30am–10pm, Thurs–Sat 11:30am–midnight, Sun 10:30am–9pm. CAJUN/CREOLE.

The French Betsy's Orleans House takes its name from Betsy Allerque, identified in old documents as a "French Colored Woman" who emigrated to Petersburg from Haiti after the revolution against France in 1798 and operated a tavern near this site until 1815. The present building was constructed after the 1993 tornado destroyed much of Old Town, including the restaurant's historic quarters. The seven dining rooms in the new digs each has its variation on a New Orleans Bourbon Street theme. Shrimp Creole, soft-shell crab étoufée, and other offerings also harken to Louisiana. There are live bands here on Thursday nights, some Fridays and Saturdays, and always during a scrumptious Sunday brunch, which features a carvery buffet. Dining and weekend music move outside to the patio during warm weather.

11 Williamsburg, Jamestown & Yorktown

The narrow peninsula between the James and York rivers saw the very beginnings of Colonial America and the rebellion that eventually created the United States. Visitors today can virtually relive that early history in the beautifully restored 18th-century town of Colonial Williamsburg, see the earliest permanent English settlement in North America at Jamestown, and walk the ramparts where Washington decisively defeated Cornwallis, thus turning the colonists' dream of a new nation into a reality. And along the James River they can tour the tobacco plantations that created Virginia's first great wealth.

The area today is one of America's family vacation meccas, and not only for its historic sights. The multimillion-dollar theme park Busch Gardens Williamsburg brims with entertainment and thrilling rides, and Water Country USA offers summertime fun with watery rides and attractions. And there's also world-class shopping in the numerous factory outlet stores near Williamsburg. With so much to see and do—for all ages—you'll find this "Historic Triangle" a wonderful place to explore.

1 Williamsburg

150 miles S of Washington, D.C.; 50 miles E of Richmond

"I know of no way of judging the future," said Patrick Henry, "but by the past." That particular quotation couldn't be more apt as an introduction to Williamsburg. For one thing, Patrick Henry played a very important role here when, as a 29-year-old backcountry lawyer, he spoke out against the Stamp Act in the House of Burgesses in 1765. Many considered him an upstart and called the speech traitorous; others were inspired to revolution.

Another reason the quote is so apt: If you can judge the future by the past, you'll never have a better opportunity of doing so. Williamsburg is unique even in history-revering Virginia. It's gone beyond restoring and re-creating important colonial sites. Most of the year (except May 15 to July 4), a British flag flies over the Capitol. Here women wear long dresses and ruffled caps, men don powdered wigs, colonial fare is served in restaurants, blacksmiths' and harnessmakers' shops line cobblestone streets, and the local militia drills on Market Square. He may be a modern actor, but your casual conversation with "Thomas Jefferson" about the rights of man will seem almost real.

ESSENTIALS

VISITOR INFORMATION   In addition to the Colonial Williamsburg Visitor Center, mentioned below, visitor information and one of the best maps of the area is available from the **Williamsburg Area Convention & Visitor Bureau,** 201 Penniman Rd., Williamsburg, VA 23187 (☎ 804/253-0192 or 800/368-6511).

GETTING THERE   By Plane   Newport News/Williamsburg Airport (☎ 804/877-0221) is 14 miles east of Williamsburg, but most flights to the area come into Norfolk International Airport (☎ 804/857-3351) or Richmond International Airport (☎ 804/226-3052), both of which are about 45 miles from town via I-64.

By Car   I-64 passes Williamsburg on its way between Richmond and Norfolk. From Washington, D.C., follow I-95 south to I-295 south to I-64 east. For the historic area, take Exit 238 (Va. 143) off I-64 and follow the signs south to Va. 132 and Colonial Williamsburg. U.S. 60 is the old highway paralleling I-64; it's known as Richmond Road west of Williamsburg. The scenic Va. 5 runs between Richmond and Williamsburg, passing the James River plantations. The freeway-grade Va. 199 forms a beltway around the southern side of the city; it joins I-64 at Exits 234 and 242.

By Train   Amtrak has service directly to Williamsburg. The train station, at Boundary and Lafayette streets (☎ 804/229-8750 or 800/872-7245), is within walking distance of the historic area.

By Bus   There is bus service via **Greyhound/Trailways** (☎ 800/231-2222). The bus depot (☎ 804/229-1460) is at the train station, Boundary and Lafayette streets.

AREA CODE   The telephone area code is 804.

ORIENTATION & GETTING AROUND

ARRIVING   Since cars are not allowed—except in a limited way—into the Historic Area between 8am and 10pm daily, drivers must park at the Colonial Williamsburg Visitor Center (see below) and take a shuttle bus (see "Getting Around," below, for details) to 10 stops at historic sites.

VISITOR INFORMATION   The entire operation is overseen by the Colonial Williamsburg Foundation, a nonprofit educational organization whose activities include an ongoing restoration. To serve the annual one million visitors (many of whom come back three and four times), they've created the Colonial Williamsburg Visitor Center off U.S. 60 Bypass, just east of Va. 132 (P.O. Box 1776), Williamsburg, VA 23187 (☎ 804/220-7645 or 800/HISTORY). You can't miss it; bright-green signs point the way from all access roads to Williamsburg.

Open 365 days a year from 9am to 5pm January to March, till 8pm from Memorial Day to Labor Day, the center offers maps and guidebooks, tours, and information on lodgings, dining, and evening activities. The center shows a 35-minute orientation film, *Williamsburg—the Story of a Patriot,* continuously throughout the day. Be sure to pick up a copy of *Colonial Williamsburg Visitors Companion,* a tabloid newspaper telling exactly what's going on during your stay, including special evening programs.

The center also has two **reservations services** for Colonial Williamsburg Foundation operations: one for the foundation's **hotels** (☎ 804/220-7645 or 800/HISTORY), the other for its four colonial **taverns** (☎ 804/229-2141 or 800/TAVERNS). In summer it's essential to make these reservations well ahead of time.

Most important, the center is where you buy your **tickets** for the dozens of attractions that make up Colonial Williamsburg (see "What to See & Do," below).

Note: Historic Area attractions are open daily from 9am to 5 or 6pm, year-round.

CITY LAYOUT The 99-foot-wide **Duke of Gloucester Street** is the principal east-west artery of the Historic Area. The Capitol building sits at the eastern end of the street, and the Wren building of the College of William and Mary is at the western end. The other two major streets are **Francis Street** and **Nicholson Street.** Merchant Square shops and services are between the Historic Area and the college, on the western end of Duke of Gloucester Street. The visitor center is north of the Historic Area.

GETTING AROUND Bus service from the visitor center begins at 8:50am and serves the Historic Area with frequent departures until 10pm. There's also a footpath from the visitor center to the Historic Area.

HISTORY & BACKGROUND

To understand how Williamsburg all came about, we must travel back almost 300 years to 1699. In that year, following the destruction of the State House by fire (the third to burn down) and following nearly a century of famine, fevers, and battles with neighboring tribes, the beleaguered Virginia Colony abandoned the mosquito-infested swamp at Jamestown for a planned Colonial city 6 miles inland. They named it Williamsburg for the reigning British monarch, William of Orange.

Royal Gov. Francis Nicholson laid out the new capital with public greens and a half-acre of land for every house on the main street. People used their lots to grow vegetables and raise livestock. Most houses were whitewashed wood frame (trees being more abundant than brick), and kitchens were in separate structures to keep the houses from burning down. A "palace" for the royal governor was completed in 1720.

The town prospered and soon became the major cultural and political center of Virginia. The government met here four times a year during "Publick Times," when rich planters and politicos (one and the same in most cases) converged on Williamsburg and the population, normally about 1,800, doubled. Shops displayed their finest imported wares, and there were balls, horse races, fairs, and auctions.

Until the government was moved to Richmond in 1780 to be safer from British attack, Williamsburg played a major role as a seat of royal government and later as a hotbed of revolution. Here occurred many of the seminal events leading up to the Declaration of Independence. Thomas Jefferson and James Monroe studied at the College of William and Mary. Jefferson was also the second state governor and last occupant of the Governor's Palace before the capital moved to Richmond (Patrick Henry was the first). During the Revolution, Williamsburg served as the wartime capital for four years and was variously the headquarters of Generals Washington (he planned the siege of Yorktown in George Wythe's house), Rochambeau, and Cornwallis.

A Reverend & a Rockefeller Williamsburg ceased to be an important political center after 1780, but it remained a quaintly charming Virginia town for another 150 years or so, unique only in that it changed so little. As late as 1926, the Colonial town plan was virtually intact, including numerous original 18th-century buildings. Then the Reverend W. A. R. Goodwin, rector of Bruton Parish Church, envisioned restoring the entire town to its Colonial appearance as a tangible symbol of our early history. He inspired John D. Rockefeller Jr., who during his lifetime contributed some $68 million to the project and set up an endowment to help provide for permanent restoration and educational programs. Today, gifts and bequests by thousands of Americans sustain the project Goodwin and Rockefeller began.

Williamsburg Reborn Today the Historic Area covers 173 acres of the original 220-acre town. A mile long, it encompasses 88 preserved and restored houses, shops,

Williamsburg

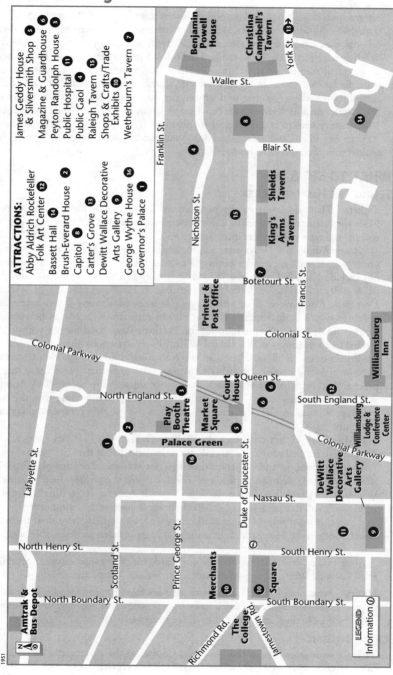

ATTRACTIONS:

Abby Aldrich Rockefeller Folk Art Center ⑫
Bassett Hall ⑭
Brush-Everard House ②
Capitol ⑧
Carter's Grove ⑬
Dewitt Wallace Decorative Arts Gallery ⑨
George Wythe House ⑯
Governor's Palace ①

James Geddy House & Silversmith Shop ⑤
Magazine & Guardhouse ⑥
Peyton Randolph House ③
Public Hospital ⑪
Public Gaol ④
Raleigh Tavern ⑮
Shops & Crafts/Trade Exhibits ⑩
Wetherburn's Tavern ⑦

taverns, public buildings, and outbuildings that survived to the 20th century. More than 500 additional buildings and smaller structures have been rebuilt on their original sites after extensive archaeological, architectural, and historical research. Williamsburg set a very high standard for other Virginia restorations. Researchers investigated international archives, libraries, and museums and sought out old wills, diaries, court records, inventories, letters, and other documents. The architects carefully studied every aspect of 18th-century buildings, from paint chemistry to brickwork. And archaeologists recovered millions of artifacts while excavating 18th-century sites to reveal original foundations. The Historic Area also includes 90 acres of gardens and greens, and 3,000 surrounding acres serve as a "greenbelt" against commercial encroachment.

WHAT TO SEE & DO
SEEING THE HISTORIC AREA

Tickets   There are two types of general admission tickets available. Both entitle you to see the orientation film at the visitor center, use the Historic Area transportation system, and take a 30-minute introductory tour.

A **Basic Admission Ticket** costs $25 for adults, $15 for children 6 to 12 (children under 6 enter free). It provides admission to most Historic Area attractions but does not include Carter's Grove, the Winthrop Rockefeller Archaeology Museum, the Abby Aldrich Rockefeller Folk Art Center, Bassett Hall, and the DeWitt Wallace Decorative Arts Gallery, all of which require separate admissions. If you have a day or less to visit, a Basic Admission Ticket may be sufficient. Our advice, however, is to shell out $30 ($18 for children) for the **Patriot's Pass,** good for one year of unlimited free admissions at all Colonial Williamsburg attractions plus special-interest guided tours and exhibits. There's so much to see and do that you don't want to have to pick and choose, probably omitting attractions that interest you in the process. And many of the attractions that charge supplements to the Basic Admission Ticket are must-sees, which means you will end up paying more than the cost of a Basic Admission Ticket. Patriot's Pass holders also get 50% off special programs and tours.

A **Museums Ticket** combines the Wallace Gallery, the Folk Art Center, and Bassett Hall for $10 adults, $6.50 children. It includes use of the bus system.

There may also be special **promotional passes** available. For example, Colonial Williamsburg, Jamestown Settlement, Yorktown Victory Center, Busch Gardens Williamsburg, and Water Country USA recently teamed up to offer a five-day admission to all five for $90 adults, $70 children. Inquire at the visitor center.

If you find your way to the Historic Area without stopping here first, there's a **ticket booth** at the Merchants Square shops, on Henry Street at Duke of Gloucester Street.

American Express, Diners' Club, MasterCard, and Visa credit cards are accepted at all Colonial Williamsburg ticket outlets, attractions, hotels, and taverns.

Hours   Attractions in the Historic Area are open from April to October daily from 9am to 6pm, November to March daily from 9:30am to 4:30pm. The taverns are open during evenings, and you can stroll the streets anytime.

✪ The Capitol

Virginia legislators met in the H-shaped Capitol at the eastern end of Duke of Gloucester Street from 1704 to 1780. America's first representative assembly, it had an upper house, His Majesty's Council of State, of 12 members appointed by the king for life. The lower body, the House of Burgesses, was elected by the freeholders of each county (there were 128 burgesses by 1776). They initiated legislation, then sent it to the Council for approval or rejection. The House of Burgesses became a training ground for patriots and future governors such as George Washington, Thomas Jefferson, Richard Henry Lee, and Patrick Henry. As 1776 approached, the burgesses passed increasing petitions and resolutions against acts of Parliament, especially the Stamp Act and the levy on tea—in Henry's words, "taxation without representation," a phrase that became a motto of the Revolution.

All civil and criminal cases (the latter punishable by mutilation or death) were tried in the General Court. Since juries were sent to deliberate in a third-floor room without heat, light, or food, there were very few hung juries. Thirteen of Blackbeard's pirate crew were tried here and sentenced to hang.

The original Capitol burned down in 1747, was rebuilt in 1753, and succumbed to fire again in 1832. The reconstruction is of the 1704 building, complete with Queen Anne's coat-of-arms adorning the tower and the Great Union flag flying overhead. **Tours** (about 25 minutes) are given throughout the day.

✪ The Governor's Palace

This meticulous reconstruction is of the Georgian mansion that was the residence and official headquarters of royal governors from 1714 until Lord Dunmore fled before dawn in the face of armed resistance in 1775, thus ending British rule in Virginia. As at other Williamsburg sites, where authentic period pieces were not available, reproductions have been crafted to exacting standards by artisans thoroughly schooled in 18th-century methods. The final five years of British rule is the period portrayed. Though the sumptuous surroundings, nobly proportioned halls and rooms, 10 acres of formal gardens and greens, and vast wine cellars all evoke splendor, the king's representative was by that time little more than a functionary of great prestige but limited power. He was more apt to behave like a diplomat in a foreign land than an autocratic colonial ruler.

Tours, given continuously throughout the day, wind up in the gardens, where you can explore at your leisure the elaborate geometric parterres, topiary work, bowling green, pleached allées, and a holly maze patterned after the one at Hampton Court. Plan at least 30 minutes to wander these stunning grounds and visit the kitchen and stable yards.

The Raleigh Tavern

This most famous of Williamsburg taverns was named for Sir Walter Raleigh, who personally launched the "Lost Colony," which disappeared in North Carolina some 20 years before Jamestown was settled. After the Governor's Palace, it was the social and political hub of the town, especially during crowded Publick Times. Regular clients included George Washington and Thomas Jefferson, who met here in 1774 with Patrick Henry, Richard Henry Lee, and Francis Lightfoot Lee to discuss revolution. Patrick Henry's troops gave their commander a farewell dinner at the Raleigh in 1776.

The original tavern was destroyed by fire in 1859. The present building was reconstructed on the original site in 1932. Its facilities include two dining rooms; the famed Apollo ballroom, scene of elegant soirees; a club room that could be rented for private meetings; and a bar where ale and hot rum punch were the favored drinks. In the tavern bakery you can buy 18th-century confections like gingerbread and Shrewsbury cake as well as cider to wash them down.

Wetherburn's Tavern

Though less important than the Raleigh, Wetherburn's also played an important role in Colonial Williamsburg. George Washington occasionally favored the tavern with

Strange Bedfellows

Williamsburg's taverns were crowded establishments during the busy Publick Times, when they offered accommodations, food, and libation to the wealthy planters and others who thronged the town. Thomas Jefferson wrote of the Raleigh Tavern: "Last night, as merry as agreeable company and dancing with Belinda in the Apollo [the Raleigh's ballroom] could make me, I never could have thought the succeeding Sun would have seen me so wretched."

Today's visitors may enjoy similar evenings at the local taverns today, but the degree of comfort found at Williamsburg's hosteleries has changed immeasurably since Jefferson's time. In those days, the taverns' upstairs bedrooms offered nothing in the way of privacy. Often five or more grown men would share a bed, sleeping cross-ways in a half-sitting position. A smelly pig farmer might sleep next to a wealthy planter, thus giving rise to the expression, "Politics makes strange bedfellows."

his patronage. And, like the Raleigh, it was mobbed during Publick Times and frequently served as a center of sedition and a rendezvous of Revolutionary patriots. The yellow-pine floors are original, so you can actually walk in Washington's footsteps; windows, trim, and weatherboarding are a mixture of old and new; and the outbuildings, except for the dairy, are reconstructions. Twenty-five-minute **tours** are given throughout the day.

The George Wythe House

On the west side of the Palace Green is the elegant restored brick home of George Wythe (pronounced "With")—foremost classics scholar in 18th-century Virginia, noted lawyer and teacher (Thomas Jefferson, Henry Clay, and John Marshall were his students), and member of the House of Burgesses. A close friend of Royal Governors Fauquier and Botetourt, Wythe nevertheless was the first Virginia signer of the Declaration of Independence. On principle, Wythe did not sign the Constitution, however, because it did not contain the Bill of Rights or antislavery provisions. The house, in which he lived with his second wife, Elizabeth Taliaferro (pronounced "Tolliver"), was Washington's headquarters prior to the siege of Yorktown and Rochambeau's after the surrender of Cornwallis. Open-hearth cooking is demonstrated in the outbuilding.

SHOPS, CRAFTS & TRADE EXHIBITS

Numerous 18th-century crafts demonstrations are on view throughout the Historic Area. Such goings-on were a facet of everyday life in this preindustrial era. Several dozen crafts are practiced in cluttered shops by more than 100 master craftspeople. They're an extremely skilled group, many having served up to seven-year apprenticeships both here and abroad. The program is part of Williamsburg's efforts to present an accurate picture of Colonial society, portraying the average man and woman as well as more illustrious citizens. Crafts displays are open five to seven days a week, with evening tours of candlelit shops available (visitors carry lanterns).

Here you can see at work a cabinetmaker, a wig maker, a silversmith, a printer and bookbinder, a maker of saddles and harnesses, a blacksmith, a shoemaker, a gunsmith, a milliner, a wheelwright, housewrights, and a candlemaker, all carrying on—and explaining—their trades in the 18th-century fashion.

Interesting in a morbid way is the apothecary shop, where sore feet were treated with leeches between the toes, a headache with leeches across the forehead, and a sore throat with leeches on the neck.

The Public Gaol

They didn't coddle criminals in the 18th century, for punishments included not only public ridicule (stocks and pillories) but also whipping, branding, mutilation, and hanging, the latter invoked not only for murder and treason but for burglary, forgery, and horse stealing. Imprisonment was not the usual punishment for crime in Colonial times, but persons awaiting trial (at the Capitol in Williamsburg) and runaway slaves sometimes spent months in the Public Gaol. In winter, the dreary cells were bitterly cold; in summer, they were stifling. Beds were rudimentary piles of straw; leg irons, shackles, and chains were used frequently; and the daily diet consisted of "salt beef damaged, and Indian meal." In its early days, the gaol doubled as a madhouse, and during the Revolution redcoats, spies, traitors, and deserters swelled its population.

The gaol opened in 1704. Debtors' cells were added in 1711 (though the imprisoning of debtors was virtually eliminated after a 1772 law made creditors responsible for their upkeep), and keepers' quarters were built in 1722. The thick-walled redbrick building served as the Williamsburg city jail through 1910. The building today is restored to its 1720s appearance.

The Peyton Randolph House

The Randolphs were one of the most prominent—and wealthy—families in Colonial Virginia. Sir John Randolph was a highly respected lawyer, Speaker of the House of Burgesses, and Virginia's representative to London, where he was the only Colonial-born Virginian ever to be knighted. When he died he left his library to 16-year-old Peyton, "hoping he will betake himself to the study of law." When Peyton Randolph died in 1775, his cousin, Thomas Jefferson, purchased his books at auction; they eventually became the nucleus of the Library of Congress. Peyton Randolph did follow in his father's footsteps, studying law in London after attending the College of William and Mary. He served in the House of Burgesses from 1744 to 1775, the last 9 years as Speaker of the House. Known as the great mediator, he was unanimously elected president of 1774's First Continental Congress in Philadelphia, and though he was a believer in nonviolence who hoped the colonies could amicably settle their differences with England, he was a firm patriot.

The house (actually, two connected homes) dates to 1715. It is today restored to reflect the period around 1770. Robertson's Windmill, in back of the house, is a post mill of a type popular in the early 18th century. The house is open to the public for self-guided tours with period-costumed interpreters in selected rooms.

The Brush-Everard House

One of the oldest buildings in Williamsburg, the Brush-Everard House was occupied without interruption from 1717—when Public Armorer and master gunsmith John Brush built it as a residence-cum-shop—through 1946. Charged not only with maintaining and repairing weaponry, Brush also had to take part in various ceremonies requiring gun salutes, such as royal birthdays. At one of these he wounded himself slightly and applied—without success—to the House of Burgesses for damages. Little else is known about him. He died in 1726. The most distinguished owner was Thomas Everard, clerk of York County from 1745 to 1771 and two-time mayor of Williamsburg. Though not as wealthy as Wythe and Randolph, he was in their elite circle. He enlarged the house, adding the two wings that give it a U shape. Today the home is restored and furnished to its Everard-era appearance. The smokehouse and kitchen out back are original. Special programs here focus on African-American life in the 18th century.

The James Geddy House & Silversmith Shop

This two-story L-shaped 1762 home (with attached shops) is an original building. Here visitors can see how a comfortably situated middle-class family lived in the 18th century. Unlike the fancier abodes you'll visit, the Geddy House has no wallpaper or oil paintings; a mirror and spinet from England, however, indicate relative affluence.

The Geddy dynasty begins with James Sr., an accomplished gunsmith and brass founder who advertised in the *Virginia Gazette* of July 8, 1737, that he had "a great Choice of Guns and Fowling Pieces, of several Sorts and Sizes, true bored, which he will warrant to be good; and will sell them as cheap as they are usually sold in England." He died in 1744, leaving his widow with eight children. His enterprising oldest sons, David and William, took over, offering their services as "Gunsmiths, Cutlers, and Founders," and on the side they did a little blacksmithing and engraving and sold cures for "all Diseases incident to Horses." A younger son, James Jr., became the town's foremost silversmith; he imported and sold jewelry and was a member of the city's Common Council involved in furthering the patriot cause. At a foundry on the premises, craftsmen cast silver, pewter, bronze, and brass items at a forge.

The Magazine & Guardhouse

The magazine is a sturdy octagonal brick building constructed in 1715 to house ammunition and arms for the defense of the British colony. It has survived intact to the present day. In colonial Williamsburg every able-bodied freeman belonged to the militia from the ages of 16 to 60 and did his part in protecting hearth and home from attack by local tribes, riots, slave uprisings, and pirate raids. The high wall and guardhouse were built during the French and Indian War to protect the magazine's 60,000 pounds of gunpowder. Today the building is stocked with 18th-century equipment—British-made flintlock muskets, cannons and cannonballs, barrels of powder, bayonets, and drums, the latter for communication purposes.

A 15-minute **horse-drawn carriage ride** around the Historic Area departs from a horse post in front of the magazine; cost is $7 per person.

The Courthouse

An intriguing window on Colonial life, criminal justice division, is offered in the courthouse, which dominates Market Square. An original building, the courthouse was the scene of widely varying proceedings, ranging from dramatic criminal trials to the prosaic issuance of licenses. Wife beating, pig stealing, and debtor and creditor disputes were among the cases tried in this restored building. Visitors can participate in the administration of Colonial justice at the courthouse by sitting on a jury or acting as a defendant. In Colonial times convicted offenders were usually punished immediately after the verdict. Punishments included public flogging at the whipping post (conveniently located just outside the courthouse) or being locked in the stocks or pillory, where they were subjected to public ridicule. Jail sentences were very unusual—punishment was swift and drastic, and the offenders then returned to the community, often bearing lifelong evidence of their conviction.

Bassett Hall

Though Colonial in origin (built between 1753 and 1766 by Col. Philip Johnson), Bassett Hall was the mid-1930s residence of Mr. and Mrs. John D. Rockefeller Jr., and it is restored and furnished to reflect their era. The mansion's name, however, derives from the ownership of Burwell Bassett, a nephew of Martha Washington who lived here from 1800 to 1839. The Rockefellers purchased the 585-acre property in the late 1920s and moved into the restored two-story dwelling in 1936. In spite of changes they made, much of the interior is original, including woodwork, paneling, mantels, and yellow-pine flooring. Much of the furniture is 18th- and 19th-century American in the Chippendale, Federal, and Empire styles. There are beautifully executed needlework rugs made by Mrs. Rockefeller herself, and six early-19th-century prayer rugs adorn the morning room. Hundreds of examples of ceramics and china are on display, as are collections of 18th- and 19th-century American and English glass, Canton enamelware, and folk art.

Reservations are required; make them at the Special Programs desk at the visitor center.

The Abby Aldrich Rockefeller Folk Art Center

The works of folk art displayed at Bassett Hall (above) are just a small sampling of enthusiast Abby Aldrich Rockefeller's extensive collection. This delightful museum contains more than 2,600 folk-art paintings, sculptures, and art objects. Mrs. Rockefeller was a pioneer in this branch of collecting in the 1920s and 1930s. Folk art is of interest not only aesthetically but as visual history; since Colonial times, untutored artists have creatively recorded everyday life.

The Folk Art Center collection includes household ornaments and useful wares (hand-stenciled bed covers, butter molds, pottery, utensils, painted furniture, boxes), mourning pictures (embroideries honoring departed relatives and national heroes), family and individual portraits, shop signs, carvings, whittled toys, calligraphic drawings, weavings, quilts, and paintings of scenes from daily life.

The Public Hospital

Opened in 1773, the "Public Hospital for Persons of Insane and Disordered Minds" was America's first lunatic asylum. Before its advent, the mentally ill were often thrown in jail or confined to the poorhouse. From 1773 to about 1820, "treatment" involved solitary confinement and a grisly course of action designed to "encourage" patients to "choose" rational behavior (it was assumed that patients willfully and mistakenly chose a life of insanity). So-called therapeutic techniques included the use of powerful drugs, submersion in cold water for extended periods, bleeding, blistering salves, and an array of restraining devices. On a self-guided tour, you'll see a 1773 cell with a filthy straw-filled mattress on the floor, ragged blanket, and manacles.

During what is called the Moral Management Period (1820–65), patients were seen to have an emotional disorder and were treated with kindness. The high point of the Moral Management Period was the administration of John Minson Galt II, from mid-1841 to his death in 1862. Galt created a carpentry shop, a shoemaking shop, a games room, and sewing, spinning, and weaving rooms. He conducted reading and music classes and organized evening lectures, concerts, and social gatherings. For all his good intentions, however, Galt admitted that "practice invariably falls short of theory." His rate of cure was not notable.

After Galt's death, the hospital was administered by nine different superintendents. Confidence in reform and government intervention on behalf of the unfortunate diminished in this age of Social Darwinism when the survival of the fittest was the new ethic. Though some of the improvements initiated during the Moral Management Period were extended, restraining devices once more came into vogue. This final period, when patients were essentially warehoused with little hope of cure, is known as the Custodial Care Period.

The self-guided tour sets one thinking about our often equally ineffective methods of treating the mentally ill today. The Public Hospital is open daily.

The DeWitt Wallace Decorative Arts Gallery

The Public Hospital serves as entrance to this 62,000-square-foot museum housing some 10,000 17th- to 19th-century English and American decorative art objects. In its galleries, you'll see period furnishings, ceramics, textiles, paintings, prints, silver, pewter, clocks, scientific instruments, mechanical devices, and weapons.

In the upstairs Masterworks Gallery, you will see a coronation portrait of George III of England and a Charles Willson Peale study of George Washington. Surrounding the atrium are some 150 objects representing the highest achievement of American and English artisans from the 1640s to 1800. At the east end of the museum, a 6,000-square-foot area with four galleries around a skylit courtyard is used for changing exhibits. On the first level, you'll see small exhibits of musical instruments, objects related to European conquest and expansion in the New World, and 18th-century dining items. A small cafe here offers light fare, beverages, and a limited luncheon menu.

The Lila Acheson Wallace Garden, on the upper level, centers around a pond with two fountains, a trellis-shaded seating area at one end, a 6-foot gilded bronze statue of *Diana* by Augustus Saint-Gaudens at the other. The garden is surrounded by a 19-foot-high, plum-colored brick wall embellished (in season) with flowering vines.

Admission for Patriot's Pass holders is $5. Single admission, which includes Basic Ticket holders, is $15.

Apart from the support of the Rockefellers, the $14 million for this project provided by *The Reader's Digest* owners DeWitt and Lila Acheson Wallace represents the largest gift in the history of Colonial Williamsburg.

✪ Carter's Grove

This magnificent plantation home has been continuously occupied since 1755 on a site that was settled over 3 1/2 centuries ago. Searching for traces of lost plantation outbuildings on the banks of the James, archaeologists have discovered here the "lost" 17th-century village of Wolstenholme Towne, site of a 20,000-acre tract settled in 1619 by 220 colonists who called themselves the Society of Martin's Hundred. The great Native American uprising of March 22, 1622, destroyed most of the settlement and left only about 60 living inhabitants, who fled to Jamestown.

Over a century later, Robert "King" Carter (Virginia's wealthiest planter) purchased the property for his daughter, Elizabeth. Between 1751 and 1754 Elizabeth's son, Carter Burwell, built the beautiful 2-story, 200-foot-long mansion that is considered "the final phase of the evolution of the Georgian mansion." The West Drawing Room—with its exquisite 1750 fireplace mantel and carved frieze panel—is often called the "Refusal Room"; legend has it that southern belle Mary Cary refused George Washington's proposal of marriage in this room and Rebecca Burwell said no to Thomas Jefferson here. In 1781, British cavalryman Banastre Tarleton headquartered at Carter's Grove and is said to have ascended the magnificent carved walnut stairway on his warhorse while hacking at the balustrade with his saber.

Despite Tarleton's abuse, Carter's Grove remains one of the best-preserved old houses in America.

Designed by famed architect Kevin Roche, the **Winthrop Rockefeller Archaeology Museum,** nestled into a hillside southeast of the mansion, identifies and interprets the Martin's Hundred clues and artifacts discovered on the site of the partially reconstructed Wolstenholme Towne. A permanent exhibit tells the story of the lost town's discovery through archaeological research. Two complete 17th-century helmets, the first intact close helmets found in North America, are displayed outside the small theater where a film recounts the story of their recovery and preservation. The museum also displays excavation photographs, audiovisual exhibits interpreting the weapons collection, agricultural tools, ceramics, and domestic artifacts. Museum hours are the same as those of Carter's Grove plantation (see below); admission is included in the Patriot's Pass; separate admission fee is $6.

A fascinating Carter's Grove site is the reconstruction of the slave quarters. Though wattled circular enclosures to house chickens and a cabin's stick-and-mud chimney reflect African traditions, by the 1770s (the period here portrayed) most slaves were at least second-generation Virginians. Some 24 slaves would have lived in these few pine-log cabins, sleeping on straw pallets placed on dirt floors. There are few possessions or furnishings, except in the foreman's (or senior slave's) house, wherein an actual bed, a chair and table, a mirror, and a piece of Delft china indicate favored status.

At the reception/orientation center, housed in a cedar building, visitors can view a 14-minute slide presentation on Carter's Grove, and an exhibit area displays historic photographs and documents. Allow at least 3 hours to see Carter's Grove. The house is open mid-March to late November and during Christmas season, Tuesday through Sunday from 9am to 4 or 5pm; the country road, which is one-way, is open from 9am to 5pm. Admission is free for Patriot's Pass holders; Basic Ticket holders pay $15 for adults and $9 for children.

The estate is reached via U.S. 60 East, 8 miles from the Colonial Williamsburg Historic Area. Visitors may return to the Historic Area via a stunningly scenic one-way country road traversing streams, meadows, woodlands, and ravines. A re-creation of a Colonial carriage pathway, the road is dotted with markers indicating old graveyards, Indian encampments, plantation sites, and other points of interest.

NEARBY ATTRACTIONS

✪ Busch Gardens Williamsburg

1 Busch Gardens Blvd., Williamsburg. ☎ **804/253-3350.** Admission $28.95 adults, $21.95 children 3–6 for unlimited rides, shows, and attractions (children 2 and under free). Nominal charge for headliner concert tickets. A three-day Busch Gardens/Water Country USA pass is available, as well as two-day and discount nighttime tickets. Late Mar to mid-May, Sat 10am–10pm, Sun 10am–7pm; mid-May to mid June, Sun–Fri 10am–7pm, Sat 10am–10pm; rest of June, daily 10am–10pm; July to late Aug, Sun–Fri 10am–10pm, Sat 10am–midnight; late Aug to Oct, Fri–Tues 10am–7pm. Also open Easter week, Sun–Fri 10am–7pm, Sat 10am–10pm. Parking is $4 in a 7,000-car lot. From Williamsburg, take U.S. 60E for about 3 miles.

At some point you'll need a break from early American history, especially if you have kids in tow. That's the time to head over to Busch Gardens Williamsburg, a 360-acre family entertainment park. True, it, too, is historically themed, with attractions in nine authentically detailed 17th-century European hamlets, but no mental effort is required to enjoy the rides, shows, and festivities.

One of the most popular rides is the terrifying Big Bad Wolf, a suspended roller coaster that culminates in an 80-foot plunge into the "Rhine River." Another "scream machine," the serpentine Loch Ness Monster with two interlocking 360-degree loops and a 130-foot drop, is one of the fastest coasters in America. "Escape from Pompeii" takes riders to the smoldering ruins of the ancient Italian city destroyed by a volcano.

Many rides and attractions—including an entire kiddie area called Land of the Dragons—are geared to younger visitors. Kids also love the Anheuser-Busch Clydesdale horses in Scotland, and crafts exhibits and medieval games at Threadneedle Faire.

Your one-price admission entitles you not only to unlimited rides but to top-quality musical entertainment, bird shows, ice-skating revues, and more. Get a show schedule when you come in.

Water Country USA

Va. 199. ☎ **804/229-9300.** Admission (including parking) $19.95 adults, $15.95 children 3–6, free for children 2 and under. May, Sat–Sun 10am–6pm; Memorial Day to mid-June, daily 10am–6pm; mid-June to mid-Aug, daily 10am–8pm; mid-Aug to Labor Day, daily 10am–7pm. Take Va. 199 to its intersection with I-64 and follow the signs.

Virginia's largest water-oriented amusement park features exciting water slides, rides, and entertainment set to a 1950s and '60s surf theme. The largest ride—Big Daddy Falls—takes the entire family on a colossal river rafting adventure. Or they twist and turn on giant inner tubes through flumes, tunnels, water "explosions," and down a waterfall to "splashdown." And there's much more, all of it wet and sometimes wild. It's a perfect place to chill out after a hot summer's day in the Historic Area.

ESPECIALLY FOR KIDS

In addition to the excitement at Busch Gardens Williamsburg and Water Country USA, families can enjoy many hands-on activities at the historic sites. At the **Powell House,** on Waller Street near Christiana Campbell's Tavern, families can participate in keeping a garden and managing a kitchen; here kids can dress up in 18th-century style. Another fun activity is at the **Governor's Palace,** where the dancing master gives lessons. During the summer kids can "enlist" in the militia and practice marching and drilling (we still have a snapshot of us holding a flint-lock back in the 1950s). Inquire at the visitor center for special themed tours in areas of your children's specific interest.

You don't have to be a guest of the Williamsburg Inn to take your kids to **Felicity's Tea,** a children's version of high English tea daily from 3:30 to 5pm in the inn's Regency Lounge.

Combining very modern technology with very old "guests," the **Prime Time History Hour** is a TV talk show featuring actors portraying Colonial characters, who tell their stories and answer questions. It takes place July and August on Wednesday, Friday, and Saturday from 4 to 5pm. The studio is in Hennage Auditorium, on South Henry Street at Ireland Street (☎ 804/220-7645). Admission is free. Reserve at the visitor center or ticket booth on Henry Street at Duke of Gloucester Street.

SHOPPING

IN THE HISTORIC AREA

Duke of Gloucester Street is the center for 18th-century wares created by craftspeople plying the trades of our forefathers. The goods offered include hand-wrought silver jewelry from the Sign of the Golden Ball, hats from the Mary Dickenson shop, pomanders to ward off the plague from McKenzie's Apothecary, hand-woven linens from Prentis Store, books bound in leather and hand-printed newspapers from the post office, gingerbread cakes from the Raleigh Tavern Bake Shop, and everything from foodstuffs to fishhooks from Greenhow and Tarpley's, a general store.

Not to be missed is **Craft House,** also run by the Colonial Williamsburg Foundation. There are two locations, one in Merchants Square, the other near the Abby Aldrich Rockefeller Folk Art Center. Featured at Craft House are exquisite works by master craftspeople and authentic reproductions of Colonial furnishings. There are also reproduction wallpapers, china, toys, games, maps, books, prints, and souvenirs aplenty.

Merchants Square "shoppes" at the west end of Duke of Gloucester Street offer a wide range of merchandise: antiquarian books and prints, 18th-century-style floral arrangements, candy, toys, handcrafted pewter and silver items, needlework supplies, and Oriental rugs. It's not all of the "ye olde" variety, however; you can also find a Baskin-Robbins ice-cream parlor, a drugstore that offers aspirin in lieu of leeches, a camera shop, and clothing stores. Merchants Square has free parking for its customers.

ON RICHMOND ROAD

Shopping in the Historic Area is fun, but the biggest merchandising draws are in Lightfoot, an area 5 to 7 miles west of town on Richmond Road (U.S. 60W).

Leading the list is the **Williamsburg Pottery Factory** (☎ 804/564-3326), a 200-acre shopping complex with more than 31 tin buildings selling merchandise from all over the world. It's all bought in large volume and sold at competitive prices. Shops on the premises sell Christmas decorations, garden furnishings, lamps, art prints, dried and silk flowers, luggage, linens, baskets, hardware, glassware, cookware, candles, wine, toys, crafts, clothing, food, jewelry, plants (there's a large greenhouse and nursery)—even pottery. There's plenty of quality and plenty of kitsch. It even has its own **Pottery Factory Outlets,** with discount offerings of 20 major manufacturers under one roof. They include Black & Decker, Van Heusen, Fieldcrest-Cannon, Manhattan, Izod, Oneida, Kid City, Pfaltzgraff, and Cabin Creek Furniture. Open daily from 8am to 7pm in summer, daily from 9am to 5pm the rest of the year.

Continue west 1¹/₂ miles on U.S. 60 and you'll come to the **Williamsburg Soap & Candle Company** (☎ 804/564-3354). Here you can see a narrated video presentation on candle making while watching the process through viewing windows that look out on the factory. There are interesting shops adjoining, and a cozy country-style restaurant is on the premises. It's open daily from 9am to 5pm, with extended hours in summer and fall.

Virtually next door is the **Williamsburg Doll Factory** (☎ 804/564-9703), with limited-edition porcelain collector's dolls. You can observe the dollmaking process and even buy parts to make your own. Other items sold here are stuffed animals, dollhouses and miniatures, clowns, and books on dolls. Open daily from 9am to 5pm.

Heading back to Williamsburg, you can peruse the discounted wares at more than 60 factory-owned stores and outlets under one roof at the **Williamsburg Outlet Mall** (☎ 804/565-3378), at the intersection of U.S. 60 and C.R. 646 (the latter leads to Exit 234 off I-64). Chocoholics beware: there's a branch of the gourmet Rocky Mountain Chocolate Factory here. Open Monday through Saturday from 9am to 9pm and Sunday from 9am to 6pm.

If you have any money left, there are 53 more shops in **Berkeley Commons Outlet Center,** on U.S. 60 between C.R. 646 and Airport Road (☎ 804/969-3767). Open April to December, Monday to Friday from 10am to 9pm; January to March, Sunday to Thursday from 10am to 6pm, Friday and Saturday from 10am to 9pm.

WHERE TO STAY

As one of the most popular and successful tourist attractions in the country, it's not surprising that Williamsburg has more than 9,000 hotel rooms. Most national chains are represented here, including **Best Western, Comfort Inn, Days Inn, Econo Lodge, Hampton Inn, Holiday Inn, Mariott, Quality Inn, Ramada Inn,** and **Travelodge.**

Colonial Williamsburg Foundation Hotels   Several accommodations choices within or adjacent to the Historic Area are operated by the Colonial Williamsburg

Foundation: the Williamsburg Inn (including the Colonial Houses and Taverns, and Providence Hall), the Williamsburg Lodge, Williamsburg Woodlands, and the nearby Governor's Inn. For reservations at any of these Colonial Williamsburg Foundation-owned properties, call the **visitor center reservations service** (☎ 800/HISTORY). Ask about special package deals.

VERY EXPENSIVE

✪ Williamsburg Inn

136 Francis St. (P.O. Box 1776), Williamsburg, VA 23187. ☎ **804/229-1000** or 800/HISTORY. Fax 804/220-7096. 102 rms. A/C TV TEL. $235–$300 single or double. AE, DC, DISC, MC, V. Free parking.

One of the nation's most distinguished hotels, this rambling white-brick Regency-style inn has played host to hundreds of VIPs, including heads of state from 17 countries and U.S. presidents Truman, Eisenhower, Nixon, Ford, and Reagan. It is considered one of the country's finest golf resorts, with three top-flight courses to play, including the noted Golden Horseshoe.

The lobby lounge is graced with Federal-style furnishings and two working fire-places. Complimentary tea is served every afternoon in the East Lounge. Rooms are exquisitely furnished in Regency reproductions, and guests are pampered with French-milled soap, hairdryers, and terry-cloth robes in the bath, plus fresh flowers. A special reduced-price ticket to the Historic Area is sold at the concierge desk daily. All guests staying in official Colonial Williamsburg hotels are invited to a special 2-hour guided walking tour of the Historic Area.

In addition to accommodations in the main inn building, there are some 84 rooms close by and within the Historic Area in the perfectly charming **Colonial Houses and Taverns**. Tastefully furnished with 18th-century antiques and reproductions, they are variously equipped with canopied beds, kitchens, living rooms, fireplaces, and/or siz-able gardens. The houses vary in size and can accommodate 2 to 12 comfortably. Rates range from $99 to $400.

Adjacent to the inn and golf course in a modern building called **Providence Hall,** rooms are furnished in a contemporary blend of 18th-century and Oriental style, with balconies or patios overlooking tennis courts and a beautiful wooded area. Complete ser-vices are provided by the inn. Rates, from $110 to $225, offer exceptionally good value.

Dining/Entertainment: The inn's Regency Lounge offers cocktails, light suppers, and entertainment nightly and hosts Felicity's Tea for children each afternoon. The Regency Dining Room features classic American cuisine at its finest. After 6pm, coats and ties required in the Regency Dining Room, jackets in the Regency Lounge. Regency Sunday brunch is served from noon to 2pm.

Services: Concierge, room service, babysitting.

Facilities: Croquet, Tazewell Club Fitness Center in the lodge available for inn guests, two 18-hole and one 9-hole golf courses, lawn bowling, 2 outdoor pools, 8 tennis courts, nature trail, croquet, family programs.

EXPENSIVE

Williamsburg Lodge

S. England St. (P.O. Box 1776), Williamsburg, VA 23187. ☎ **804/229-1000** or 800/HISTORY. Fax 804/220-7685. 315 rms. A/C TV TEL. $165–$183 single or double in Main and South wings; $200–$250 single or double in Tazewell and West wings. Extra person $12. Children under 18 stay free in parents' room. AE, DC, DISC, MC, V. Free parking.

The Williamsburg Lodge is located near the Williamsburg Inn and offers all the sports facilities of the inn and a pleasantly rustic interior. The flagstone-floored lobby is indeed lodgelike, with cypress paneling and a large working fireplace. And there's a covered verandah with rocking chairs overlooking two pools and a golf course. Accommodations are contemporary but warm and homey, with pretty print bedspreads, polished wood floors, and hand-crafted furniture. American folk art—decoys, samplers, and such—highlight the decor. West Wing rooms have window walls overlooking duck ponds or a wooded landscape. They're furnished in oak, cane, and bamboo, and 12 have working fireplaces. The Tazewell Wing is built around a central landscaped courtyard with informal lounge areas on all three floors. Guest rooms are attractively furnished with reproductions inspired by pieces in the Abby Aldrich Rockefeller Folk Art Center.

Dining/Entertainment: The attractive Bay Room overlooks a garden and fountain. On Friday and Saturday nights it features a Chesapeake Bay Feast, and on Sunday an omelet brunch buffet is the draw. The Garden Lounge has drinks and musical entertainment from early afternoon.

Facilities: All inn facilities are available to lodge guests. The Tazewell Club Fitness Center, with indoor lap pool, Keiser exercise machines, and aerobic classes, is in the lodge.

MODERATE/INEXPENSIVE

Governor's Inn

Va. 132 (Henry St.) (P.O. Box 1776), Williamsburg, VA 23187. ☎ **804/229-1000** or 800/ HISTORY. 200 rms. A/C TV TEL. $50–$90. AE, DC, DISC, MC, V. Free parking. Closed Jan–Feb.

Least expensive of the Colonial Williamsburg hotels, the Governor's Inn was recently taken over by the foundation and completely renovated and redecorated. Furnishings are clean and bright. A new wing was added as well as an outdoor swimming pool. It's near the visitors center on Va. 132, an extension of Henry Street.

Williamsburg Woodlands

Va. 132, off U.S. 60 Bypass (P.O. Box 1776), Williamsburg, VA 23187. ☎ **804/229-1000** or 800/HISTORY. Fax 804/220-7941. 315 rms. A/C TV TEL. $70–$115 single or double. Extra person $8. Children under 18 stay free in parents' room. AE, DC, DISC, MC, V. Free parking.

Set on 40 wooded acres with picnic tables under the pines, the Woodlands offers a lot for your money: You're right behind the visitor center; rooms are cheerful, attractive, and equipped with all the modern amenities; facilities include a jogging path, golf putting green, miniature golf course, shuffleboard, playground, horseshoes, volleyball, badminton, a nice-size swimming pool and sundeck, and a toddler's pool. And the Cascades restaurant and Woodlands Grill with cafeteria-style breakfast and lunch are steps away.

NEARBY ACCOMMODATIONS

To be sure of getting a room, you're well advised to reserve in advance. The **Williamsburg Hotel/Motel Association** (☎ 804/220-3330 or 800/446-9244) will make reservations for you in any price range. It's a free service. Their listings include most of the accommodations mentioned below.

EXPENSIVE

Kingsmill Resort

1010 Kingsmill Rd., Williamsburg, VA 23185. ☎ **804/253-1703** or 800/832-5665. Fax 804/ 253-3993. 352 units. A/C TV TEL. $120–$155 double room, $160–$530 suites. Packages available. AE, DC, DISC, MC, V. Free parking. From I-64, take Va. 199 (Exit 243) west to U.S. 60, go east to right turn at sign for Kingsmill on the James.

Nestled in a peaceful setting on beautifully landscaped grounds on the James River, the gray-clapboard Kingsmill resort complex is very much like a country club, with 2,900 acres of resort facilities, including the world-famous River Course, home of the Anheuser-Busch Golf Classic; the Plantation Course designed by Arnold Palmer; and the Bray Links Par Three (complimentary to guests). Kingsmill accommodations—guest rooms and one-, two-, and three-bedroom units—are in tastefully furnished villas overlooking the James River (most expensive), golf-course fairways, or tennis courts. They're in individually owned and furnished condos, so decors vary from handsome Colonial reproductions to sophisticated contemporary settings. Most suites have complete kitchens and living rooms with fireplaces. Daily housekeeping service, including fresh linens, is included.

Dining/Entertainment: All four dining rooms feature panoramic views of the James. In the Bray dining room, breakfast, lunch buffets, and à la carte evening meals are reasonably priced. More casual dining spots are Moody's Tavern, Peyton Grille, and Kingsmill Café in the golf clubhouse.

Services: Concierge, complimentary shuttle to Colonial Williamsburg and Busch Gardens Williamsburg, children's activity programs.

Facilities: Golf, 15 tennis courts, indoor and outdoor pools, racquetball courts, children's program, Nautilus exercise room, saunas, Jacuzzi, billiards, marina, gift shop, pro shop.

MODERATE

Courtyard by Marriott

470 McLaws Circle, Williamsburg, VA 23185. ☎ **804/221-0700** or 800/321-2211. Fax 804/221-0741. 142 rms, 9 suites. A/C TV TEL. $49–$109 double; $89–$169 suite. Children under 18 stay free in parents' room. AE, CB, DC, DISC, MC, V. Free parking. From Williamsburg, follow U.S. 60E for about 2 miles.

This four-story member of the fine chain designed by business travelers (and very comfortable for the rest of us) enjoys an attractively landscaped setting of trees and shrubs. A plant-filled lobby looks out to the courtyard and its good-size pool. Furnished with substantial oak pieces, the guest quarters feature large desks, separate seating areas, irons and boards, and piping-hot faucets for instant coffee or tea. Suites have full sofa-bedded living rooms with extra phones and TVs, plus wet bars with small refrigerators. The lobby restaurant offers a breakfast buffet. There's an exercise room with Jacuzzi.

Williamsburg Hospitality House

415 Richmond Rd., Williamsburg, VA 23185. ☎ **804/229-4020.** 297 rms, 9 suites. A/C TV TEL. $79–$150 single or double; $350 one-bedroom suite; $430 two-bedroom suite. AE, CB, DC, DISC, MC, V. Free parking.

Just two blocks from Colonial Williamsburg opposite William and Mary College, this four-story brick hotel is built around a central courtyard with flowering trees and plants and umbrella tables. Guest rooms and public areas are appointed with a gracious blend of 18th-century reproductions. The Colony dining room specializes in Colonial fare. Christopher's Tavern serves lunch, dinner, and light fare. Facilities include an outdoor pool and gift shop.

INEXPENSIVE

Carolynn Court

1446 Richmond Rd., Williamsburg, VA 23185. ☎ **804/229-6666** or 800/666-5880. Fax 804/220-9917. 65 rms. A/C TV TEL. $32–$52 double. Extra person $8. AE, CB, DC, DISC, MC, V.

This older, family-owned motel offers comfort at budget prices within 10 minutes of the Historic Area. The comfortable rooms are plainly furnished, clean, and inviting, with matching spreads and draperies and wood-paneled walls. All the rooms face the courtyard and outdoor pool. Free coffee is available, and there are picnic tables near the pool.

Motel 6

3030 Richmond Rd., Williamsburg, VA 23185. ☎ **804/565-3433.** 169 rms. A/C TV TEL. $30–$40 single; $6 each additional adult. Children under 18 stay free in parents' room. AE, DC, DISC, MC, V.

The only catch to snagging one of the low-priced rooms here is that you usually have to reserve far in advance, even though it is one of the largest members of this budget chain. A nice pool and sundeck are out back, and the woodsy location is a plus. There's an Outback Steakhouse in the parking lot, and the Holiday Inn next door has a coffee shop.

BED & BREAKFAST INNS

Liberty Rose

1022 Jamestown Rd., Williamsburg, VA 23185. ☎ **804/253-1260.** 4 rms. A/C TV. $110–$180 double. Rates include full breakfast. AE, MC, V. On-site parking.

Known as Williamsburg's most romantic B&B, this inn enjoys a premier location on a wooded hilltop just 1 mile from the Historic Area. Housed in a charming 70-year-old two-story white-clapboard residence with a dormered slate roof flanked by chimneys, Liberty Rose is furnished in delightful style; you'll find Victorian, French- and English-country, and 18th-century antiques and reproductions.

The elegant parlor, complete with grand piano that guests may play, has a working fireplace and comfortable chairs for relaxing. The accommodations are luxurious, each distinctively decorated. The Savannah Lace guest room has peach-colored wallpaper, an antique carved-mahogany queen-size bed with a pink goosedown duvet, a TV, bathrobes, and a bowl of chocolates; the bathroom, tucked into the side dormer room, has a claw-foot tub. A full breakfast is served on the morning porch; a typical menu might include fresh orange juice, eggs with bacon, French toast, and coffee or tea. An overall feeling of graciousness makes the Liberty Rose a real delight, a tranquil refuge from the rigors of sightseeing.

Williamsburg Manor Bed & Breakfast

600 Richmond Rd., Williamsburg, VA 23185. ☎ **804/220-8011** or 800/422-8011. 5 rms. A/C TV. $90 single or double. Rates include full breakfast. No credit cards. On-site parking.

Right in the heart of Williamsburg, two blocks from the Historic Area, this gracious 1928 Georgian Revival brick residence offers traditional comfort in nicely appointed rooms. Guests are invited to congregate in the living room, where there is a TV, magazines, and a great cookbook collection. In addition to the full breakfasts, host Laura Sisane offers, by prior reservation only, dinners for guests. Accommodations vary in size and furnishings, but you can expect to find four-poster beds, pretty wallpapers, white bedspreads, brass lamps, Oriental rugs, and wing chairs. The breakfast table, set with Villeroy & Boche china, might include fresh fruit, eggs in puff pastry with Surry bacon, homebaked breads or pastries, and coffee and tea.

WHERE TO DINE

Williamsburg abounds in restaurants catering to tourists. Most national chain fast food and family restaurants have outlets on Richmond Road (U.S. 60) on the west side of town. In addition to the restaurants in its accommodations (see

"Where to Stay," above), the Colonial Williamsburg Foundation runs four popular reconstructed Colonial taverns.

COLONIAL WILLIAMSBURG FOUNDATION TAVERNS

If you're planning on dinner at one of these restaurants, make your reservations first thing in the morning—if not a day or two before—by calling the Information Center (☎ 804/229-2141 or 800/TAVERNS). In the spring-to-fall season, it's a good idea to reserve even prior to arrival (you can do so up to 60 days in advance). Their business hours can vary slightly from those given below, especially in January and February when they can be closed for annual upkeep. All are reconstructed 18th-century "ordinaries" or taverns, and aim at authenticity in fare, ambiance, and costuming of the staff. All offer Colonial fare such as peanut soup, salad with chutney dressing, Brunswick stew, sautéed backfin crabmeat and ham topped with butter and laced with sherry, Sally Lund bread, and deep-dish Shenandoah apple pie, and they all have al fresco dining in good weather on brick patios under grape arbors. Low-priced children's menus are available. Their seasonal menus are posted at the ticket office on Henry Street at Duke of Gloucester Street.

Christina Campbell's Tavern

Waller St. ☎ **804/229-2141.** Reservations essential. Main Courses $17–$21. AE, DC, DISC, MC, V. Mon–Sat 5:30–9:30pm. COLONIAL.

Christina Campbell's Tavern, close to the Capitol, is "where all the best people resorted" circa 1765. George Washington was a regular (in 1772, he recorded in his diary that he dined here 10 times over a 22-month period). After the capital moved to Richmond, business declined and operations eventually ceased. In its heyday, however, the tavern was famous for seafood, and today that is once again the specialty. Campbell's is an authentic reproduction with 18th-century furnishings, blazing fireplaces, and flutists and balladeers to entertain diners.

Josiah Chowning's Tavern

Duke of Gloucester St. ☎ **804/229-2141.** Reservations suggested. Main courses $15–$20. AE, DC, DISC, MC, V. Daily 11:30am–3:30pm and 5–8:30pm; Gambols Pub, daily 9pm–midnight. COLONIAL.

In 1766, Josiah Chowning announced the opening of a tavern "where all who please to favour me with their custom may depend upon the best of entertainment for themselves, servants, and horses, and good pasturage." It's very charming, with low beamed ceilings, raw pine floors, and sturdy country-made furnishings. There are two working fireplaces, and at night one dines by candlelight.

Kings Arms Tavern

Duke of Gloucester St. ☎ **804/229-2141.** Reservations required. Main courses $17–$22. AE, DC, DISC, MC, V. Daily 11:30am–2:30pm; dinner, with three nightly seatings, 5:15–9:30pm. COLONIAL.

The Kings Arms Tavern, on the site of a 1772 establishment, is actually a re-creation of the tavern and an adjoining home. Outbuildings—including stables, a barbershop, laundry, smokehouse, and kitchen—have also been reconstructed. The original proprietress, Mrs. Jane Vobe, was famous for her fine cooking, and her establishment's proximity to the Capitol made it a natural meeting place during Publick Times. Today the 11 dining rooms (8 with fireplaces) are painted and furnished following authentic early Virginia precedent. The Queen Anne and Chippendale pieces are typical appointments of this class of tavern, and the prints, maps, engravings, aquatints, and mezzotints lining the walls are genuine examples of Colonial interior decorations. Balladeers wander the rooms during dinner and entertain.

Shields Tavern

Duke of Gloucester St. ☎ **804/229-2141.** Reservations essential. Main courses $16–$22. AE, DC, DISC, MC, V. Daily 8:30–10am and 11:30am–3:30pm and 5:30–9:30pm. COLONIAL.

With 11 dining rooms and a garden under a trumpet-vine-covered arbor that seats 200, Shields is the largest of the Historic Area's tavern/restaurants. It's named for James Shields who, with his wife, Anne, and family, ran a much-frequented hostelry on this site in the mid-1700s. Using a room-by-room inventory of Shields's personal effects—and as a result of detailed archaeological investigation—the tavern has been furnished with items similar to those used in the mid-18th century, and many of the rooms have working fireplaces. A specially designed rotisserie unit in the kitchen allows chefs here to approximate 18th-century roasting techniques. Shields is the only tavern open for breakfast. Strolling balladeers entertain at night.

OTHER HISTORIC AREA RESTAURANTS

A Good Place To Eat

410 Duke of Gloucester St., Merchants Square. ☎ **804/229-4370.** Breakfast $2.75–$4.50; lunch/dinner $2.50–$6.50. MC, V. Mid-march to Aug, daily 8am–10pm; Sept–Oct, daily 8am–8pm; Nov–Dec, daily 8am–7pm; Jan to mid-March, daily 8am–6pm. AMERICAN.

This is an especially good place for family meals. The food is high quality for a cafeteria operation—burger meat is prepared from the best cuts of chuck and round, breads and cakes are fresh baked, even the ice cream is homemade. And the setting is rather attractive. There's a big indoor dining room with terra-cotta-tile floors, imitation-oak Formica tables, and many hanging plants. Better yet is the outdoor seating at umbrella tables on a flower-bordered brick patio. Stop by for an inexpensive breakfast of scrambled eggs and ham with homemade biscuits, or a sweet-potato muffin and coffee. At lunch or dinner you can get a turkey sandwich, hamburger, or chef's salad. Leave room for a sundae with homemade ice cream and fresh whipped cream.

Berret's

199 S. Boundary St. ☎ **804/253-1847.** Reservations recommended for dinner. Main courses $14–$18. AE, MC, V. Mar–Dec, daily 11:30am–3pm and 5:30–10pm; Jan–Feb, Tues–Sun 11:30am–3pm and 5:30–10pm. SEAFOOD.

A congenial, casual place, Berret's has a popular raw bar that seems to be busy all day long, especially on weekends, when people stop in at all hours for half a dozen oysters or clams on the half shell. The adjoining restaurant is bright and airy, with several dining rooms. Seating is at booths upholstered in a nautical-blue leather and at light-wood tables covered with matching blue cloth. Canvas sail-cloth shades, blue-trimmed china, and marine artifacts on the walls make an appropriate backdrop for the excellent seafood specialties. A hearty portion of fresh New England mussels steamed with garlic and Chardonnay is a real bargain appetizer for $4.95. For your entree, try peanut-crusted softshell crabs served with peanut-bourbon butter. The menu features some incredible desserts, among them chocolate-marble cheesecake with raspberry filling and whipped cream. Berret's has an interesting selection of beers and specialty wines. For lunch there are bouillabaisse, always a vegetarian entree, and sandwiches and salads.

✪ Trellis Cafe, Restaurant & Grill

Duke of Gloucester St., Merchants Sq. ☎ 804/229-8610. Reservations suggested at dinner. Main courses $14–$23; fixed-price dinner $20. AE, MC, V. Mon–Sat 11:30am–9:30pm, Sun 11:30am–3pm and 5–9:30pm. AMERICAN.

Evocative of California's delightful wine-country restaurants in both decor and exciting, contemporary cuisine, it is entered via a grapevine-covered trellis. Inside, the Garden Room is the plushest setting, with apricot-velvet furnishings. The Trellis Room is country-contemporary in feel, with forest-green upholstered pine furnishings and walls minimally adorned with vineyard baskets full of dried flowers and antique French farm implements. In the Grill Room, you can watch food being prepared over an open hearth using Texas mesquite wood. Very cozy is the Vault Room, with tables under an arched ceiling of narrow heart-of-pine beams. In the Café Bar walls are hung with antique wine-motif prints. And if the weather is fine, you might dine al fresco on the planter-bordered brick terrace.

One of the co-owners, executive chef Marcel Desaulniers, has brought national recognition to the Trellis with his outstanding regional cuisine. He was the first chef from the South to be honored by the James Beard Foundation, whose awards are considered the Oscars of the culinary industry. Desaulniers was also named to *Food and Wine* magazine's honor roll of American chefs and to *Who's Who of Cooking in America*. He changes the menu every season to take advantage of seasonal specials and combines the best in foods from different regions of the United States, all imaginatively prepared. Desaulniers is the author of three best-selling cookbooks, *The Trellis Cookbook, The Burger Meisters,* and *Death by Chocolate.* Needless to say, his chocolate desserts are not to be missed.

NEARBY RESTAURANTS

⑤ Giuseppe's Italian Cafe

5601 Richmond Hwy. (U.S. 60), in Ewell Station Shopping Center. ☎ **804/565-1977.** Reservations not accepted. Main courses $4.50–$17. DISC, MC, V. Mon–Thurs 11:30am–2pm and 5–9pm, Fri 11:30am–2pm and 5–9:30pm, Sat 5–9:30pm. ITALIAN. From Historic District, go 4 miles west on U.S. 60 to shopping center on left.

This pleasant local favorite may be difficult to see from Richmond Highway (it's at the end of a strip mall with a Food Lion supermarket at its center), but it's a great place for a meal during or after a shopping expedition. Chef Dan Kennedy may have an Irish name, but he's adept at spinning out the likes of chicken Antonio in a subtly spicy pepper pesto sauce. He also offers heaping plates of spaghetti, a page full of vegetarian pastas, and single-size pizzas with some unusual toppings such as smoked oysters. All entrees come with a salad or a bowl of hearty lentil-and-andouille-sausage soup. There are two dining rooms here plus heated sidewalk seating.

Le Yaca

U.S. 60E, in the Village Shops at Kingsmill. ☎ **804/220-3616.** Reservations recommended. Fixed-price dinners $25–$39. AE, CB, DC, MC, V. Mon–Sat 11:30am–2pm and 6–9:30pm. FRENCH. From the Historic Area, go east on U.S. 60 to Va. 199; the shops are just east of the interchange.

Centered on a large open hearth, on which a leg of lamb is often roasting during cold weather, Le Yaca is charmingly provincial, with glossy oak floors, rough-hewn beams overhead, and romantic soft lighting from oil candles and shaded lamps. Pale-peach walls are hung with lovely prints of Paris scenes. At lunch a create-your-own-salad table has all you might desire of 15 scrumptious French salads including, perhaps, pasta salad, cucumber in fresh cream, potato salad with lamb, carrots rapé, seafood and rice, and tomato vinaigrette; fresh-baked bread and butter is included. A fixed-price dinner might begin with mountain-style onion soup, an entree of salmon in parchment, an array of fresh vegetables, salad, and then a *marquise au chocolat*—rich chocolate truffles afloat on crème anglaise.

✪ Old Chickahominy House

1211 Jamestown Rd., at Va. 199. ☎ **804/229-4689.** Breakfast $3.50–$6.50; lunch $4–$7.50.
V. Daily 8:30am–2 or 3pm. TRADITIONAL SOUTHERN.

The Old Chickahominy House is a reconstructed 18th-century house with mantels
from old Gloucester homes and wainscoting from Carter's Grove. Floors are bare oak,
and walls, painted in traditional Colonial colors, are hung with gilt-framed 17th- and
18th-century oil paintings. Three adjoining rooms house an antique/gift shop. The
entire effect is extremely cozy and charming, from the rocking chairs on the front
porch to the blazing fireplaces within. Authentic southern fare is featured at breakfast and lunch. The house specialty in the morning is the plantation breakfast—real
Virginia ham with two eggs, biscuits, cured country bacon and sausage, grits, and
coffee. At lunch, Miss Melinda's special is a cup of Brunswick stew with Virginia ham
on hot biscuits, fruit salad, homemade pie, and tea or coffee. After dining it's fun to
roam through the warren of antiques-filled rooms. Also check out the Shirley
Pewter Shop next door.

PICNIC FARE & WHERE TO EAT IT

There are benches throughout the restored area (lots of grass, too), and if you have
a car you can drive to nearby scenic picnic areas off Colonial Parkway. **The Cheese
Shop,** 424 Prince George St. in Merchants Square, between North Boundary and
North Henry streets (☎ 804/220-0298), is a good place to purchase take-out sandwiches and other fixings. Open Monday to Saturday from 10am to 6pm.

2 Jamestown

9 miles SW of Williamsburg

The story of Jamestown, the first permanent English settlement in the New World,
is documented here in museum exhibits and living-history interpretations. The
exploits of Capt. John Smith, leader of the colony; his legendary rescue from execution by the Native American princess Pocahontas; the arrival of the first African-
Americans; and a vivid picture of life in 17th-century Virginia are all part of the first
chapter of American history interpreted here at the site of the first colony. Archaeologists have excavated more than 100 building frames, evidence of manufacturing
ventures (pottery, winemaking, brickmaking, and glass blowing), early wells, and old
roads, as well as scores of artifacts of everyday life—tools, utensils, ceramic dishes,
armor, keys, and the like.

   Allow a full day for your visit and consider packing a lunch. Other than a cafe at
Jamestown Settlement, there are few restaurants, so you may want to take advantage
of the picnic areas at the National Park Service site.

ESSENTIALS

TOURIST INFORMATION   Two important Jamestown sites commemorate the
first permanent English settlement in the New World. Jointly administered by the
National Park Service and the Association for the Preservation of Virginia Antiquities, Jamestown Island is where the original colony was founded. For information
about **Jamestown Island,** contact the NPS, P.O. Box 210, Yorktown, VA 23690
(☎ 804/229-1733). At the adjoining Jamestown Settlement, under the jurisdiction
of the Commonwealth of Virginia, a living-history museum complex re-creates the
daily life of the settlers. For **Jamestown Settlement** information, write P.O. Box JF,
Williamsburg, VA 23187 (☎ 804/253-4838). See below for **combination ticket** information combining Settlement admission with Yorktown Victory Center admission.

GETTING THERE **By Car** From Williamsburg, follow the Jamestown Road, Va. 31S, or the Colonial Parkway.

WHAT TO SEE & DO

Jamestown Island

This historic site, separated by an isthmus from the mainland, is at the western terminus of the Colonial Parkway. At the Ranger Station entrance gate, you'll pay an $8 per car admission. The gate is open daily from 8:30am to 5:30pm in summer, 8:30am to 5pm in spring and fall, 8:30am to 4:30pm in winter. You can stay on the grounds until dusk.

Exploration of the site of the first permanent English settlement in North America begins at the **visitor center** (☎ 804/229-1773). Open daily from 9am to half an hour after the gate closes, it contains an information desk, an exhibit area, and a theater in which a 15-minute orientation film tells the story of Jamestown from its earliest days to 1698, when the capital of Virginia moved to Williamsburg and Jamestown became a sleepy little village. Be sure to inquire at the reception desk about special programs offered on-site that day; events might include a ranger-led walking tour, a costumed interpretive program, or a Young Settlers program for kids. Allow at least 2 hours for this special attraction.

From the visitor center, footpaths lead you through the actual site of **"James Cittie,"** where rubbly brick foundations of 17th-century homes, taverns, shops, and statehouses are enhanced by artists' renderings, text, and audio stations. Most complete are the remains of the tower of one of the first brick churches in Virginia (1639). Directly behind the tower is the **Memorial Church,** a 1907 re-creation built by the Colonial Dames of America on the site of the original structure, which, in 1619, housed the first legislative assembly in English-speaking North America. You can rent a recorded tour of the town site to accompany your walk.

At the **Dale House Pottery,** near the church, there are demonstrations (spring through fall) of 17th-century potterymaking by costumed interpreters. A hands-on program for children is offered in summer.

A fascinating **5-mile loop drive** (beginning at the visitor center parking lot) winds through 1,500 wilderness acres of woodland and marsh that have been allowed to return to their natural state in order to approximate the landscape as 17th-century settlers found it. Illustrative markers interpret aspects of daily activities and industries of the colonists—tobacco growing, lumbering, silk and wine production, potterymaking, farming, and so on.

Jamestown Settlement

This indoor-outdoor museum, operated by the Commonwealth of Virginia, is open daily except New Year's Day and Christmas. Basic hours are 9am to 5pm daily. Admission is $9 for adults and $4.25 for children 6 to 12 (under 6 free).

If you're also planning to visit the Yorktown Victory Center (it doesn't have to be the same day), purchase a money-saving **combination ticket** to both museums at $12.50 for adults and $6 for children.

A fast-food restaurant is on the premises and parking is free.

After purchasing tickets, you can enter an orientation **theater** to watch a 20-minute film that provides an introduction to Jamestown. Beyond the theater, three large permanent **museum** galleries feature artifacts, documents, decorative objects, dioramas, and graphics relating to the Jamestown period. The English Gallery focuses on Jamestown's beginnings in the Old World. A Powhatan Indian Gallery explores the origins and culture of the Native Americans who lived near Jamestown. The

Jamestown Gallery deals with the history of the colony during its first century of existence.

Leaving the museum complex, visitors come directly into the **Powhatan Indian Village,** representing the culture and technology of a highly organized chiefdom of 32 tribes that inhabited coastal Virginia in the early 17th century. There are several mat-covered lodges, or "longhouses," which are furnished as dwellings, as well as a garden and a ceremonial dance circle. Historical interpreters tend gardens, tan animal hides, and make bone and stone tools and pottery.

Triangular **James Fort** is a re-creation of the one constructed by the Jamestown colonists on their arrival in the spring of 1607. Inside the wooden stockade are primitive wattle-and-daub structures with thatched roofs representing Jamestown's earliest buildings. Interpreters are engaged in activities typical of early 17th-century life, such as agriculture, animal care, carpentry, blacksmithing, and meal preparation.

A short walk from James Fort are reproductions of the three **ships,** the *Susan Constant, Godspeed,* and *Discovery,* which transported 104 colonists to Virginia in 1607. Visitors can board and explore one or more of the ships.

3 Yorktown

14 miles NE of Williamsburg

Yorktown was the setting for the last major battle of the American Revolution. Here, on October 19, 1781, George Washington wrote to the president of the Continental Congress, "I have the Honor to inform Congress, that a Reduction of the British Army under the Command of Lord Cornwallis, is most happily effected." Though it would be 2 years before a peace treaty was signed and sporadic fighting would continue, the Revolution, for all intents and purposes, had been won.

Today the decisive battlefield is a national park, and the Commonwealth of Virginia has built an interpretive museum explaining the road to revolution, the war itself, and the building of a new nation afterwards. Predating the revolution, the old town of Yorktown itself is worth seeing.

ESSENTIALS

VISITOR INFORMATION   For more information about the Virginia State–run **Yorktown Victory Center,** a stimulating multimedia museum with indoor and outdoor programs located on old route Va. 238, contact P.O. Box JF, Williamsburg, VA 23187 (☎ 804/253-4838). The National Park Service Yorktown and **Yorktown Battlefield Visitor Center** are at the terminus of the Colonial Parkway, P.O. Box 210, Yorktown, VA 23690 (☎ 804/898-3400).

GETTING THERE   By Car   From Williamsburg, drive to the eastern end of the Colonial Parkway.

AREA CODE   The telephone area code is 804.

HISTORY

Though tourist attention focuses to a large degree on the town's role as the final Revolutionary battlefield, Yorktown is also of interest as one of America's earliest Colonial towns.

Before the Revolution   Though a number of settlers lived and farmed in the area by the 1630s, Yorktown's history really dates to 1691, when the General Assembly at Jamestown (then Virginia's capital) passed the Port Act creating a new town on the site. To encourage the development of the town, 50 acres were purchased from

Benjamin Read for 10,000 pounds of "merchantable sweet-scented tobacco and cask," then broken into 85 half-acre lots and sold for 180 pounds of tobacco each. By the end of the century, Yorktown was on the way to becoming a principal mid-Atlantic port and a center of tobacco trade.

In the 18th century, Yorktown was a thriving metropolis with a population of several thousand planters, innkeepers, seamen, merchants, craftsmen, indentured servants, and slaves. After the waterfront officially became part of the town in 1738, Water Street, paralleling the river, was lined with shops, inns, and loading docks.

The Victory at Yorktown   The siege began on September 28, 1781, when American and French troops under Washington occupied a line encircling the town within a mile of the army led by Cornwallis. The allied army of 17,000 men, spread out in camps extending 6 miles, dug siege lines and bombarded the redcoats with cannonfire. When a French fleet sailed up from the Caribbean and defeated the British navy off the Virginia Capes, thereby blocking any hope he had of escaping, Cornwallis's fate was sealed.

Cornwallis compounded his tactical errors by evacuating almost all his positions except for Redoubts (forts) 9 and 10 in order to concentrate his troops closer to town and better defend it. Washington was thus able to move his men to within 1,000 yards of British lines. By October 9, the allies were ready to respond to British artillery. But they didn't wait to respond. The French were the first to fire. Two hours later, George Washington personally fired the first American round. By October 10, the British were nearly silenced. On October 11, the allies moved up about another 500 yards.

On October 14, the French stormed Redoubt 9 while the Continentals made short work of Redoubt 10. Both columns began their assaults at 8pm. The Americans were through by 8:10pm; the French, whose target was stronger, by 8:30pm.

On October 16, following a last-ditch and fruitless attempt to launch an attack on the allies, a desperate Cornwallis tried to escape with his troops across the York River to Gloucester Point, but a violent storm scattered his boats. On October 17 at 10am, a British drummer appeared on the rampart. He beat out a signal indicating a desire to discuss terms with the enemy. A cease-fire was called, and a British officer was led to American lines where he requested an armistice. On October 18, commissioners met at the house of Augustine Moore (see "What to See & Do," below) and worked out the terms of surrender.

At 2pm on October 19, 1781, the French and Continental armies lined Surrender Road, each stretching for over a mile on either side. The French were resplendent in immaculate white uniforms, their officers plumed and decorated; the Americans were in rags and tatters. The British army (about 5,000 British soldiers and seamen), clad in new uniforms, marched between them out of Yorktown to a band playing a tune called "The World Turned Upside Down." Gen. Charles O'Hara of the British Guards represented Cornwallis who, pleading illness, did not surrender in person.

The battle marked the end of British rule in America and made a permanent place for Yorktown in the annals of American history.

After the Revolution   Though it is doubtful that Yorktown would have recovered from the destruction and waste that accompanied the Siege of 1781, it received the coup de grace in the "Great Fire" of 1814 and declined steadily over the years, becoming a quiet rural village. In fact, like Williamsburg, it changed so little that many of the picturesque old streets, buildings, and battle sites have survived intact to this day. Today most of Yorktown—including the surrounding battlefield areas—is part of the 9,300-acre Colonial National Historical Park.

WHAT TO SEE & DO

❂ Yorktown Victory Center

First stop is the Yorktown Victory Center (☎ 804/887-1776), open daily except New Year's Day and Christmas from 9am to 5pm. Set on 21 acres overlooking part of the battlefield of 1781, it offers an excellent orientation to Yorktown attractions, including a film, a living-history program, and museum exhibits. Admission is $6.75 for adults, $3.25 for children 6 to 12 (under 6, free); or you can purchase a **combination ticket** for this and Jamestown Settlement at $12.50 for adults and $6 for children 6 to 12 (under 6 free).

The Road to Yorktown, an evocative 28-minute documentary film produced by David Wolper follows the movements of Generals Washington and Rochambeau and documents the final grueling days of the Revolution.

Visitors follow an open-air timeline walkway, **"Road to Revolution,"** which illustrates the relationship between the colonies and Britain beginning in 1750.

Aspects of the American Revolution are explored in three **gallery exhibits.** "Witnesses to Revolution" focuses on ordinary individuals who recorded their observances of the war and its impact on their lives. "At Water's Edge: The Towns of York and Gloucester" shows those towns' roles as port and urban centers in the 18th century. "Yorktown's Sunken Fleet" uses artifacts recovered from British ships sunk during the siege of Yorktown to describe shipboard life.

In the outdoor **Continental army encampment,** costumed interpreters re-create the lives of men and women who took part in the American Revolution. There are presentations on weaponry, military drills and tactics, medicine, and cookery. Nearby, an 18th-century **farmsite** demonstrates how "middling" farmers—no wealthy plantation owners here—lived and worked.

❂ Yorktown Battlefield Visitor Center

After you've seen the Yorktown Victory Center, head over to **National Park Service Visitor Center** (☎ 804/898-3400), starting point for self-guided auto tours of the battlefield and a full-service information center. Here, too, there's an orientation film. Shown on the hour and half-hour, this 16-minute documentary called *Siege at Yorktown* is about the formal surrender of the British and their German mercenary allies.

Museum displays include Washington's actual military headquarters tent, a replica (which you can board and explore) of the quarterdeck of H.M.S. *Charon,* additional objects recovered from the York River in the excavations, exhibits about Cornwallis's surrender and the events leading up to it, and dioramas detailing the siege. Upstairs, an "on-the-scene" account of the Battle of Yorktown is given by a 13-year-old soldier in the Revolutionary army, his taped narrative accompanied by a sound-and-light show.

National Park Service Rangers are on hand to answer questions. Spring and fall weekends, and daily in summer, they give free **tours** of the British inner defense line. The center is open daily except Christmas from 9am to 5pm, with extended hours spring through fall.

TOURING THE BATTLEFIELD

The National Park Service Visitor Center is the starting point for the 7-mile Battlefield route and the 10.2-mile Encampment route auto tours of the battlefield. You'll be given a map indicating both routes and detailing major sites. At each stop there are explanatory historical markers (sometimes taped narratives as well), but for the most interesting experience, rent a cassette player and tape at the visitor center ($2). Narrated by "British and American colonels," whose polite hostilities to each other are most amusing, the taped commentary further elucidates the battlefield sites. You won't stay in your car the whole time; it's frequently necessary to park, get out, and walk to redoubts and earthworks. A lot of the drive is very scenic, winding through woods and fields abundant with birdlife; the Encampment route is especially beautiful. If you rent the cassette, listen to the introduction in the parking lot; it will tell you when to depart. Auto tour highlights include:

The Grand French Battery   This was a large artillery area in the French section of the first siege line. Here, French soldiers manning cannons, mortars, and howitzers fired on British and German mercenary troops.

The Moore House   When Lord Cornwallis realized the inevitability of his defeat, he sent a message to General Washington: "Sir, I propose a cessation of hostilities for twenty-four hours, and that two officers may be appointed by each side, to meet at Mr. Moore's house, to settle terms for the surrender of the posts of York and Gloucester." General Washington granted Cornwallis just 2 hours to submit general terms. On the afternoon of October 18, 1781, two British commissioners, Col. Thomas Dundas and Maj. Alexander Ross, met in "Mr. Moore's house" with American Col. John Laurens and French representative the vicomte de Noailles. Negotiations went on late into the evening, the British protesting terms of Article III, which required them to march out of Yorktown "with shouldered arms, colors cased that means flags furled, and drums beating a British or German march." They finally agreed to the humiliating exit, and negotiations wound up just before midnight. Washington made a few adjustments, the Articles of Capitulation were signed by Cornwallis and his senior naval officer, and the document was delivered back to Washington.

The Moore House has a long history. In the early 1700s, Lawrence Smith constructed the two-story white-frame building that would become Moore House when the property went to his daughter, Lucy, and her husband, Augustine Moore. Though surviving the battle of Yorktown unscathed, Moore House suffered considerable damage during military action in the Civil War. Shellfire destruction was aggravated by soldiers stripping away siding and other usable wood for fuel. The house was pretty much abandoned (sometimes even used as a cow barn) until John D. Rockefeller Jr. purchased it in 1931 and the National Park Service restored it to its Colonial appearance. It is today furnished with appropriate period pieces, some of which are believed to have been in the house during the surrender negotiations. It's open during summer daily from noon to 4:30pm.

Surrender Field   Here your imagination, stoked by visions from orientation films, can evoke the British march out of Yorktown. William Conrad narrates the story of the surrender scene from a pavilion overlooking the field. Cannons surrendered by the British encircle the pavilion below.

Along the Encampment route, you'll come to the sites of Washington's and Rochambeau's headquarters, a French cemetery and Artillery Park, and allied encampment sites.

TOURING THE TOWN

Self-guided or ranger-led walking tours of Old Yorktown—including some places of interest not related to the famed battle—are available at the Battlefield Visitor Center. Begin your ramble close to the center at:

The Victory Monument   News of the allied victory at Yorktown reached Philadelphia on October 24, 1781. On October 29, Congress resolved "that the United States . . . will cause to be erected at York, in Virginia, a marble column, adorned with emblems of the alliance between the United States and his Most Christian Majesty; and inscribed with a succinct narrative of the surrender of Earl Cornwallis to his excellency General Washington, Commander in Chief of the combined forces of America and France."

All very well in theory, but due to financial difficulties no action was taken for a century. Finally, on October 18, 1881, the cornerstone for the monument was laid by Masons as an appropriate opening to the Yorktown Centennial Celebration. The highly symbolic 98-foot marble shaft overlooking the York River was completed in 1884. The podium is adorned with 13 female figures hand in hand in a solemn dance to denote the unity of the 13 colonies; beneath their feet is the inscription ONE COUNTRY, ONE CONSTITUTION, ONE DESTINY, a moving post–Civil War sentiment. The column itself symbolizes the greatness and prosperity of the nation, and its stars represent the "constellation" of states in the Union in 1881. Atop the shaft is the figure of Liberty.

Cornwallis Cave   According to legend, Cornwallis lived here in two tiny "rooms" during the final days of the siege when he hoped to withdraw to the river and escape overland to New York. The two rooms were carved out by various occupants of the cave—which may at one time have included the pirate Blackbeard—and Confederate soldiers later enlarged the shelter and added a roof. A taped narrative at the entrance tells the story. The cave is at the foot of Great Valley, right on the river.

The Dudley Digges House   You can view the restored 18th-century white weatherboard house on Main Street and Smith Street only from the outside—it's a private residence, not open to the public. Its dormer windows set in the roofline, and surrounding outbuildings, are typical of Virginia architecture in the mid-1700s. Owner Dudley Digges was a Revolutionary patriot who served with Patrick Henry, Benjamin Harrison, and Thomas Jefferson on the Committee of Correspondence. After the war he was rector of the College of William and Mary.

The Nelson House   Scottish merchant Thomas Nelson made three voyages between Great Britain and Virginia before deciding to settle in Yorktown in 1705. He proceeded to sire a dynasty, and by 1707 he had acquired two lots, along with a number of slaves, and built himself a house at Main and Nelson streets. Between 1711 and 1723, he obtained title to several other lots and became co-operator of a ferry, charter member of a trading company, builder of the Swan Tavern, trustee of York's port land, and a large-scale planter. By 1728, he had added 600 acres, a private warehouse and wharf, and a mill to his holdings. He died in 1745 leaving a vast estate, which his descendants—who included several prominent Revolutionary leaders, one of them a signer of the Declaration of Independence—further enlarged.

Though damaged (cannonballs remain embedded in the brickwork), the house survived the Battle of Yorktown (Cornwallis seized it for a command post during part of his occupation), and Nelson's descendants continued to occupy the house through 1907. The National Park Service acquired the house in 1968 and restored it to its original appearance.

It is open daily from 10am to 4:30pm in summer (check at the visitor center for December hours). Ranger-guided tours take 30 to 45 minutes.

The Sessions House   Just across from the Nelson House, this is the oldest house in Yorktown, built in 1692 by Thomas Sessions. At least five U.S. presidents have visited the house, today a private residence off-limits to the public. You may, however, stare at it.

The Customhouse   Dating to 1721, this sturdy brick building at the corner of Main and Read was originally the private storehouse of Richard Ambler, collector of ports. It became Gen. J. B. Magruder's headquarters during the Civil War. Today it is maintained by the Daughters of the American Revolution as a museum.

Grace Episcopal Church   Located on Church Street near the river, Grace Church dates to 1697 and has been an active house of worship since then. Its first rector, the Rev. Anthony Panton, was dismissed for calling the secretary of the colony a jackanapes. Gunpowder and ammunition were stored here during the siege of Yorktown. And during the Civil War the church served as a hospital. It's open to visitors daily from 9am to 5pm. The original communion silver, made in England in 1649, is still in use. Thomas Nelson II is buried in the adjacent graveyard.

The Swan Tavern   For over a century the Swan Tavern, at the corner of Main and Ballard streets (☎ 804/898-3033), was Yorktown's leading hostelry. Originally owned by Thomas Nelson, it was in operation 20 years before Williamsburg's famous Raleigh. The Swan was demolished in 1863 by an ammunition explosion at the courthouse across the street, rebuilt, and destroyed again by fire in 1915. Today it is reconstructed as per historical research, and the premises house a fine antiques shop. Call for hours.

WHERE TO DINE

Consider a **picnic** lunch in a large tree-shaded area at the Victory Center or at a riverside picnic area with tables and grills on Water Street at the foot of Comte de Grasse Street. There's another gorgeous picnic area called **Ringfield,** 7 miles from Williamsburg on the Colonial Parkway.

Nick's Seafood Pavilion

Water Street. ☎ **804/887-5269.** Reservations not accepted. Main courses $8–$35. AE, DC, MC, V. Daily 11am–10pm. AMERICAN/SEAFOOD.

Nick's interior is an exuberant surprise. Several spacious dining rooms are bedecked with reproductions of classic stone statuary, mosaic tiles, plants, fountains, and oil paintings. Soft-shell crabs sautéed in butter, broiled tuna or mahi mahi, and broiled lobster tail are menu standbys, along with nonseafood entrees ranging from pork tenderloin Grecian-style to prime beef shish-kabobs. There's baked Alaska for dessert.

4 James River Plantations

While Williamsburg was the political capital of Virginia during the 18th century, its economic livelihood depended on the great tobacco plantations like Carter's Grove. Several more of the mansions built during that period of wealthy landowners still stand today along the banks of the James River between Williamsburg and Richmond, some occupied to this day by the same families that have produced generals, governors, and two presidents. They provide an authentic feel for 18th-century plantation life.

ESSENTIALS

VISITOR INFORMATION   For information in advance, contact the individual plantations or the **Williamsburg Area Convention & Visitor Bureau,** 201 Penniman Rd., Williamsburg, VA 23187 (☎ 804/253-0192 or 800/368-6511).

GETTING THERE   The plantations are on John Tyler Memorial Highway (Va. 5) between Williamsburg and Richmond. From Williamsburg, take Jamestown Road and bear right on Va. 5. From Richmond, take Main Street east, which becomes Va. 5.

SEEING THE PLANTATIONS

The so-called Plantation Route covers a distance of 55 miles between Williamsburg and Richmond and makes an excellent scenic driving tour between the two cities. Allow a full day to visit all the plantations and to take a break for lunch. We list them here east-to-west as you come to them from Williamsburg. If you're driving from Richmond, start at Shirley and work backwards.

The owners of Sherwood Forest, Evelynton, Berkeley, and Shirley offer a **block ticket** for admission to all of their homes. The cost is $25 for adults (it's less expensive to buy children's tickets to each home). Block tickets can be purchased at any of the four plantations.

Sherwood Forest

Va. 5, 20 miles west of Williamsburg. ☎ **804/829-5377.** Admission $7.50 adults, $7 seniors, $4.50 students, $3 grounds only. Daily 9am–5pm. Closed Christmas.

Owned by President William Henry Harrison in the 1790s, this long, white clapboard house was the home of President John Tyler after he retired from the White House in 1845. It has been continuously occupied by Tyler family members ever since. Then in his sixties, Tyler brought with him a young second wife and commenced to start a new family. The son of that marriage was in his seventies before be began a family, and his son—grandson of President Tyler—still lives upstairs. Built in 1730, the original house is now part of the Main Hall. Tyler extended the one-room-deep home to its present length of 301 feet, making it the longest wood frame house in America. All furnishings are family heirlooms or similar period pieces. A walking tour of the grounds features numerous ancient trees and a number of original plantation outbuildings.

☕ **TAKE A BREAK**   You can break your driving tour of the plantations at **Indian Fields Tavern,** on Va. 5 between Sherwood Forest and Evelynton (☎ 804/829-5004). This fine restaurant in a restored Victorian farmhouse, with screened porches open during warm weather, offers salads of tarragon chicken or fresh yellowfin tuna, burgers, and entrees including quiche, crab cakes, and an unusual mixed grill of local sausages and marinated quail. The signature dish at dinner has crabcakes served over Virginia ham. Reservations are required at dinner. Open daily from 11am to 4pm and 5pm to 9pm. American Express, Discover, MasterCard, and Visa are accepted.

Evelynton

Va. 5, 25 miles west of Williamsburg. ☎ **804/829-5075** or 800/473-5075. Admission $7 for adults, $6 seniors, $3.50 children 6 to 12, under 6 free. Daily 9am to 5pm. Closed Christmas.

Adjacent to and part of the original 1619 Westover Plantation land grant (see "Berkeley," below), this tract was named for William Byrd's daughter Evelyn (pronounced "EVE-lyn"). She is said to have died of a broken heart because her father refused to let her marry her chosen suitor. According to legend, her ghost still roams both houses. Since 1847, Evelynton has been home to the Ruffin family, whose patriarch, noted agriculturist Edmund Ruffin, fired the first shot of the Civil War at Fort Sumter, S.C. The original house was destroyed in 1862, when Gen. George McClellan's Union troops skirmished with Confederates led by J. E. B. Stuart and

John Pelham in the fierce but short-lived Battle of Evelynton Heights. The present structure, a magnificent example of Colonial Revival style, was designed by renowned Virginia architect Duncan Lee and built in 1935.

Berkeley

Va. 5, 30 miles west of Williamsburg. ☎ **804/829-6018.** Admission $8.50 adults, $4 children 6–12, children under 6 free. Daily 8am–5pm. Closed Christmas.

On December 4, 1619, 38 English settlers sent by the Berkeley Company put ashore after a 3-month voyage. They fell on their knees in a prayer of thanksgiving. If you're here on the first Sunday of November, you can participate in the annual celebration commemorating that first official Thanksgiving in the New World.

The aristocratic Harrison family bought Berkeley in 1691. Benjamin Harrison III made it a prosperous operation, and in 1726 his son, Benjamin Harrison IV, built the three-story Georgian mansion. Benjamin Harrison V was a signer of the Declaration of Independence and thrice governor of Virginia. The next generation produced William Henry Harrison, the frontier fighter whose nickname "Old Tippecanoe" helped him get elected as our 9th president. His grandson, another Benjamin Harrison, took the presidential oath 47 years later. George Washington was a frequent guest, and every president through Buchanan enjoyed Berkeley's gracious hospitality.

Berkeley was twice occupied by invading troops. A British army under Benedict Arnold burned the family portraits, practiced target shooting on the cows, and went off with 40 slaves. General George McClellan's Union army trampled the gardens and chopped up the elegant furnishings for firewood. It was during the Yankee occupancy that Gen. Dan Butterfield composed "Taps." After the war, the Harrisons never returned to live at Berkeley.

John Jamieson, a Scottish-born New Yorker who had served as a drummer boy in McClellan's army, purchased the disfigured manor house and 1,400 acres in 1907. His son, Malcolm, has completely restored the house and grounds to their glorious appearances of the early days of the Harrisons' tenure. Following a 10-minute slide presentation, 20-minute guided **tours** of the house are given throughout the day by guides in Colonial dress. Allow at least another half hour to explore the magnificent grounds and gardens.

Sharing Berkeley's lane off Va. 5, **Westover** (☎ 804/829-2882) is the beautiful 1730s Georgian manor house built by Richmond's founder, William Byrd II, directly on the banks of the James. The interior is open to the public only for 5 days during Garden Week (last week in April), although visitors are invited to walk around the grounds and gardens year-round, daily from 9am to 6pm. Admission is $2.

TAKE A BREAK   Berkeley is a good place to stop for lunch, for moderately priced sandwiches, soups, and salads are served in the old carriage house, now appropriately named the **Coach House Tavern** (☎ 804/829-6003). It's open Monday to Saturday from 11am to 3pm, Sunday from 11am to 4pm and 6 to 9pm. American Express, Discover, MasterCard, and Visa are accepted. There also are picnic grounds on Berkeley's premises.

Shirley

Va. 5, Charles City, 35 miles west of Williamsburg. ☎ **804/829-5121.** Admission $7.50 adults, $5 students 13–21, $3.75 children 6–12, children under 6 free. Daily 9am–5pm (last tour at 4:30pm). Closed Christmas.

Another historic James River plantation, Shirley was founded in 1613 and has been in the same family since 1660. The present mansion, built by Edward Hill III or his son-in-law, John Carter (historians are not sure), dates to 1723. Since that time two very distinguished Virginia families—the Hills and the Carters—have occupied Shirley. Because of this continuous ownership, many original furnishings, portraits, and memorabilia remain, making this one of the most interesting plantations open to public view. The carved-walnut staircase, rising three stories with no visible means of support, is the only one of its kind in America. The house survived the Revolution, the Civil War, and Reconstruction, as did the dependencies—a group of superb brick outbuildings, forming a unique Queen Anne forecourt, which include a large two-story kitchen, a laundry house, and two barns. Other original structures are the stable, smokehouse, and dovecote. You can visit the house on 35-minute **tours** given throughout the day; allow at least another 30 minutes to explore the grounds and dependencies.

12 Hampton Roads & the Eastern Shore

Before they moved on to Jamestown in 1607, the 105 colonists in the *Susan Constant, Godspeed,* and *Discovery* first set foot in the New World on the sandy shores of Cape Charles. Although they didn't stay here at Hampton Roads, one of the world's largest natural harbors, later generations did. Today the cities of Norfolk, Virginia Beach, Chesapeake, Portsmouth, Newport News, and Hampton ring the harbor's southern and western shores. Their combined population of some 1.4 million makes sprawling Hampton Roads the most populous metropolitan area in Virginia.

The population swells significantly during the summer months, when the sand and surf of Virginia Beach draw vacationers from around the globe. It also goes up and down depending on deployments by the U.S. Navy, for Hampton Roads has America's largest concentration of naval bases.

Once a bawdy seaport, a rebuilt Norfolk now features an exciting "museum of the future" and a bustling collection of waterfront shops, restaurants, and night clubs. Across the harbor, historic Hampton hosts a very modern air and space museum, and the shipbuilding city of Newport News fittingly is home to a terrific maritime museum.

From Hampton Roads, the 17-mile-long Chesapeake Bay Bridge-Tunnel whisks visitors north to a very different world: Virginia's rural Eastern Shore. There on the Delmarva Peninsula beckon ancient fishing villages like Chincoteague, wildlife refuges teeming with birdlife and wild horses, and the gorgeous Assateague Island National Seashore with 37 miles of pristine, totally undeveloped beach.

1 Norfolk

190 miles SE of Washington, D.C.; 93 miles E of Richmond

Still a major seaport, Norfolk has replaced its notorious waterfront sailor bars and burlesque houses with high-rise offices, condominiums, marinas, museums, shops, nightspots, and a 12,000-seat minorleague baseball park. Interspersed in this revitalized downtown are reminders of Norfolk's past such as historic houses and the old City Hall, now converted into a museum and memorial to World War II hero Gen. Douglas MacArthur.

ESSENTIALS

VISITOR INFORMATION   For information in advance, contact the **Norfolk Convention & Visitors Bureau**, 236 E. Plume St., Norfolk, VA 23510 (☎ 804/441-1852, or 800/368-3097). For motorists arriving from the west via I-64, there is an **information center** on Fourth View Street at Exit 273 in the Ocean View section. It's open during the summer daily from 9am to 7pm, the rest of the year daily from 9am to 5pm. Other information booths are in the Waterside and Nauticus (see "Attractions in Norfolk," below).

AREA CODE   The telephone area code is 804.

GETTING THERE   By Plane   The **Norfolk International Airport,** bordering the Botanical Garden at Norview Avenue, 1¹/₂ miles east of I-64 (☎ 804/857-3351), serves the Norfolk–Virginia Beach metropolitan area. There is no bus service into Norfolk, but taxis, rental cars, and limousines are at the airport.

By Car   From the west, I-64 runs directly from Richmond to Norfolk, then swings around the eastern and southern suburbs, where it meets I-664 to form a beltway around the area. U.S. 460 also runs the length of Virginia to Norfolk, and U.S. 13 and 17 lead here from north or south. If you're coming from Virginia Beach, the Norfolk–Virginia Beach Expressway (Va. 44) becomes I-264, which goes through downtown and Portsmouth. Norfolk is linked to Portsmouth by ferry, bridge, and tunnel, and to Hampton and Newport News by the Hampton Roads Bridge-Tunnel (I-64).

By Train   The nearest **Amtrak** station is 21 miles away in Newport News, at 9304 Warwick Blvd., near Mercury Boulevard (☎ 804/245-3589, or 800/872-7245). An Amtrak Thruway bus connection carries passengers to Norfolk.

By Bus   The **Greyhound/Trailways** terminal is at the corner of Brambleton and Monticello Avenues (☎ 804/627-5641, or 800/231-2222).

GETTING AROUND   The **Tidewater Regional Transit System (TRT)** (☎ 804/640-6300) bus system serves Norfolk, Virginia Beach, Portsmouth, and Chesapeake. Fare is $1.50 anywhere. Exact change is required. TRT has an information and ticket kiosk in the Waterside (see "Attractions in Norfolk," below).

TRT also runs a Norfolk **trolley tour,** with stops at attractions downtown and in the trendy Ghent neighborhood. Visitors can get off at any stop and reboard a later trolley. It operates daily Memorial Day to Labor Day weekends, hourly from 11am to 4pm; throughout September, from noon to 4:30pm. Fare is $3.50 for adults and $1.75 for seniors and children under 12. Tickets may be purchased at the TRT kiosk at the Waterside.

WHAT TO SEE & DO
ATTRACTIONS IN NORFOLK

✪ Chrysler Museum of Art

Olney Road and Mowbray Arch. ☎ **804/622-1211** or 804/622-ARTS for a weekly events update. Admission $3 donation. Tues–Sat 10am–4pm, Sun 1–5pm. Closed New Year's Day, Independence Day, Thanksgiving, and Christmas.

Originally built in 1932 as the Norfolk Museum of Art, this imposing Italian Renaissance building on the Hague Inlet of the Elizabeth River was renamed in 1971 when Walter P. Chrysler Jr. gave a large portion of his collection to the city. It spans artistic periods from ancient Egypt to the 1980s and includes one of the finest and most comprehensive glass collections in the world. Adjoining is an outstanding collection of art nouveau furniture. Other first-floor galleries exhibit ancient Indian, Islamic, Oriental, African, and pre-Columbian art. Most second-floor galleries are devoted to painting and sculpture, particularly Italian baroque and French, including works by Gauguin, Picasso, Renoir, Matisse, Braque, Bernini, and Rouault. American art holdings include 18th- and 19th-century paintings by Charles Willson Peale, Benjamin West, John Singleton Copley, and Thomas Cole, and 20th-century works by Thomas Hart Benton, Calder, Kline, Warhol, Rauschenberg, and Rosenquist. A permanent gallery is devoted solely to photography, showcasing everyone from Walker Evans to Diane Arbus.

✪ Douglas MacArthur Memorial

MacArthur Square, between City Hall Avenue and Plume Street, at Bank Street. ☎ **804/441-2965.** Free admission. Mon–Sat 10am–5pm, Sun 11am–5pm. Closed New Year's Day, Thanksgiving, and Christmas.

When he arrived in Australia after suffering a crushing defeat at the hands of Japanese invaders in the Philippines, General MacArthur uttered the immortal words "I shall return." Here those words, which became a rallying cry for Americans fighting in the Pacific Theater of World War II, are engraved on a bronze plaque, along with excerpts from his other speeches, at the general's final resting place, in Norfolk's old city hall, an imposing domed structure with a columned front portico. Visitors view a film that uses news footage to document the major events of MacArthur's life. Nine galleries are filled with memorabilia ranging from historic World War II surrender documents to the general's famous corncob pipe.

Moses Myers House

323 E. Freemason St. ☎ **804/664-6283.** Admission $3 adults, $1.50 students and seniors, children under 5 free. Apr–Dec, Tues–Sat 10am–5pm, Sun noon–5pm; Jan–Mar, Tues–Sat noon–5pm.

This handsome early-Federal brick town house in Norfolk's oldest residential neighborhood was home to five generations of Myerses from 1792 to 1930. Moses Myers and his wife, Eliza, came to Norfolk in 1787. They were one of the first Jewish families to settle here, and special programs in observance of Jewish holidays are among the museum's annual events. Some 70% of the furniture and decorative arts collections displayed throughout the house is original to the first generation of the family. Two Gilbert Stuart portraits of Mr. and Mrs. Myers hang in the drawing room, which has some distinctive Empire pieces. The fireplace surround has unusual carvings depicting a sun god—with the features of George Washington.

The **Willoughby-Baylor House,** a block away from the Moses Myers House at 601 E. Freemason St., was built in 1794 and is furnished with Georgian and Federal pieces. Admission, hours, and phone are the same for both museums.

Combination tickets for both houses and the Adam Thoroughgood House (see "Historic Attractions" in the Virginia Beach section, below) cost $6 for adults, $4.50 for students and seniors, free for children 5 and under. All three houses are administered by the Chrysler Museum.

✪ NAUTICUS, The National Maritime Center

1 Waterside Drive, at Boush St. ☎ **804/664-1000** or 800/664-1080. General admission $7.50 adults, $6.50 seniors and students 13–17, $5 children 6–12, under 6 free. Single admission to theaters or Virtual Adventures $2.50 adults and students, $1.50 children 6–12, under 6 free. May–Sept, daily 10am–7pm; Oct–Apr, Tues–Sun 10am–5pm. Closed Thanksgiving, Christmas, New Year's Day.

It's appropriate that visitors enter this large battleship-gray building by a gangplank, since it looks like an artist's rendering of a future warship. Inside, kids and adults of

Downtown Norfolk

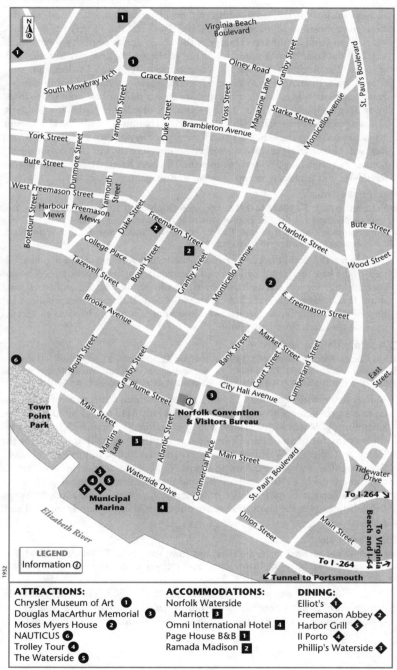

ATTRACTIONS:
Chrysler Museum of Art ❶
Douglas MacArthur Memorial ❸
Moses Myers House ❷
NAUTICUS ❻
Trolley Tour ❹
The Waterside ❺

ACCOMMODATIONS:
Norfolk Waterside
  Marriott ❸
Omni International Hotel ❹
Page House B&B ❶
Ramada Madison ❷

DINING:
Elliot's ❶
Freemason Abbey ❷
Harbor Grill ❺
Il Porto ❹
Phillip's Waterside ❸

all ages can entertain themselves with a plethora of hands-on interactive exhibits, theaters, and a museum, all dedicated to the U.S. Navy and the sea over which it rules. Visitors can stand on the actual bridge of the U.S.S. *Preble*, or pilot a submarine in search of the Loch Ness Monster during one of the world's first "virtual reality" adventures. The Aegis Theater lets them participate in running a battle aboard a destroyer, while in another area they can learn navigation by piloting a ship into San Francisco Harbor. Meanwhile, the Living Sea theater shows films about sealife in the briny depths, simulating a swim among thousands of jellyfish. NAUTICUS also includes a real maritime research laboratory and the **Hampton Roads Naval Museum,** actually operated by the U.S. Navy to tell the story of its presence in Hampton Roads. Real warships often tie up here on weekend visits, since the building sits on the old Banana Pier stretching 700 feet out into the Elizabeth River. After a day here, your school-age kids may want an appointment to Annapolis.

Naval Base Tour

9809 Hampton Blvd. ☎ **804/444-7955.** Admission $5 adults, $2.50 seniors and children. Tickets may be purchased at the TRT kiosk at Waterside from May to September, or at the Naval Base on Hampton Boulevard all year. Call for hours, which vary. Board bus at Waterside or follow Hampton Boulevard north from downtown.

Norfolk has the world's largest naval installation, and visitors can take a guided bus tour of the base, enhanced by informed commentary by naval personnel. The bus goes dockside for looks at aircraft carriers, destroyers, submarines, and other naval ships. It also passes Admiral's Row, a strip of Colonial Revival houses built at the turn of the century for the Jamestown Exposition. There may be visits to selected ships on weekends from 1 to 4:30pm.

✪ Norfolk Botanical Garden

Azalea Garden Road. ☎ **804/441-5385.** Admission $2.50 adults, $1.50 seniors and children 6–12. Daily 8:30am–sunset. Take I-64 to the Norview/Airport exit, pass two lights, and turn left onto Azalea Garden Road at the third light. It's about 4 miles from downtown Norfolk.

A quiet haven with more than 12 miles of floral pathways, the garden can be seen on foot, by trackless train, or by canal boat. From early April to mid-June the grounds are brilliantly abloom with a massive display of azaleas. The Statuary Vista is a beautiful setting for Moses Ezekiel's heroic-size statues (originally intended for the Corcoran Gallery in Washington) of great painters and sculptors—Rembrandt, Rubens, Dürer, and da Vinci, among others. Notable, too, are the rose garden, with a terrace overlook; a classic Japanese hill-and-pond garden; a fragrance garden; and an Italian Renaissance garden with terraces, statuary, a fountain, and a reflecting pool. Behind the pool is the coronation court where the Azalea Queen is crowned each April.

The Waterside

Waterside Drive, between the Omni Hotel and Town Point Park. ☎ **804/627-3300.** Free admission. Summer, Mon–Sat 10am–10pm, Sun noon–8pm; winter, Mon–Sat 10am–9pm, Sun noon–6pm.

A $23-million steel-and-glass pavilion that opened in 1983, The Waterside is the centerpiece of Norfolk's revitalized downtown waterfront. Built by the Rouse Organization—also noted for Baltimore's Inner Harbor, Boston's Faneuil Hall, and New

Norfolk Area

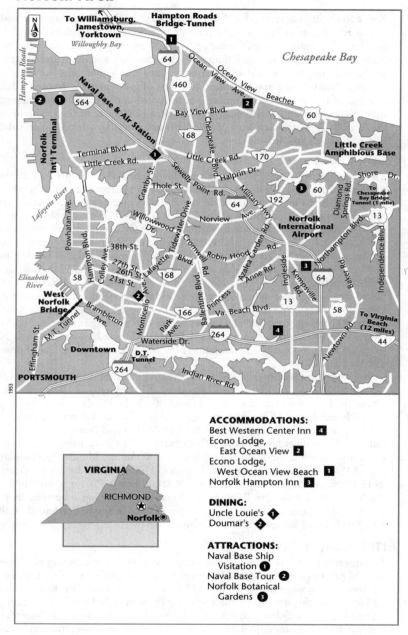

To Williamsburg, Jamestown, Yorktown

Hampton Roads Bridge-Tunnel

Willoughby Bay

Hampton Roads

Chesapeake Bay

Ocean View Ave.

Ocean View Beaches

Naval Base & Air Station

Bay View Blvd.

Little Creek Amphibious Base

Shore Dr.

To Chesapeake Bay Bridge Tunnel (1 mile)

Norfolk Int'l Terminal

Terminal Blvd.

Little Creek Rd.

Little Creek Rd.

Lafayette River

Thole St.

Sewells Point Rd.

Halprin Dr.

Diamond Springs Blvd.

Northampton Blvd.

Independence Blvd.

Granby St.

Willowwood Dr.

Tidewater Drive

Norview

Military Hwy.

Norfolk International Airport

Baker Rd.

Elizabeth River

38th St.

Cromwell Rd.

Robin Hood Rd.

Azalea Garden Rd.

Anne Rd.

Ingleside

Kempsville Rd.

Powhatan Ave.

Hampton Blvd.

Colley Ave.

27th St
26th St
21st St.

Lafayette Blvd.

Ballentine Blvd.

Princess Anne Rd.

Newtown Rd.

To Virginia Beach (12 miles)

West Norfolk Bridge

Brambleton Ave.

Monticello Ave.

Park Ave.

Va. Beach Blvd.

Effingham St.

M.T. Tunnel

Downtown

D.T. Tunnel

Waterside Dr.

PORTSMOUTH

Indian River Rd.

1953

ACCOMMODATIONS:
Best Western Center Inn **4**
Econo Lodge,
   East Ocean View **2**
Econo Lodge,
   West Ocean View Beach **1**
Norfolk Hampton Inn **3**

VIRGINIA

RICHMOND

Norfolk

DINING:
Uncle Louie's **1**
Doumar's **2**

ATTRACTIONS:
Naval Base Ship
   Visitation **1**
Naval Base Tour **2**
Norfolk Botanical
   Gardens **3**

York's South Street Seaport—the Waterside houses more than 30 international food outlets as well as several full-service restaurants and two lively nightclubs. Shops offer a mix of souvenirs, jewelry, fashions, gift items, Virginia products, and crafts that make for pleasurable browsing. A short stroll along the busy waterfront and adjacent marina will bring you to the dock where cruise ships offer harbor tours (see below).

Town Point Park's amphitheater, just west of the Waterside, features a full schedule of free special events throughout the year—concerts, children's theater, magic shows, puppetry, and more. **Harbor Park,** a 12,000-seat stadium, is home to the Norfolk Tides, the New York Mets AAA International League team. For Tides information, call 804/461-5600.

Harbor Cruises

The *Carrie B* (☎ 804/393-4735), a reproduction of a 19th-century Mississippi riverboat, offers daytime and sunset cruises of Norfolk's harbor from the Waterside. Depending on the tour, you can see the shipyard with nuclear subs and aircraft carriers, the naval base, and the site of the Civil War battle between the *Monitor* and the *Merrimac*. It has daily cruises from April through October. A noon sailing takes 1¹/₂ hours and costs $12 for adults, $6 for children. A 2pm tour goes out for 2¹/₂ hours and costs $14 for adults, $7 for children. From June to Labor Day there's also a 2¹/₂-hour sunset cruise leaving at 6pm. It costs $14 for adults, $7 for children.

Also departing from the Waterside, the *Spirit of Norfolk* (☎ 804/627-7771) is like an oceangoing cruise ship, complete with dancing, good food, and entertainment. Offerings include a Fun & Sun Lunch Cruise from noon to 2pm ($20 Tuesday to Friday, $23 Saturday and Sunday), sunset cruises with a show, dancing, and buffet dinner ($32.50 Tuesday to Thursday, $34 Friday, $37 Saturday), and a moonlight party cruise with dancing and cocktails ($15.50) from midnight to 2am Friday and Saturday.

From April to October there are 2- and 3-hour cruises on the *American Rover* (☎ 804/627-7245), a graceful schooner modeled after 19th-century Chesapeake Bay schooners. Prices for these sail-powered cruises along the Elizabeth River begin at $12.50 for adults and $6 for children. Departure point is the Waterside marina.

Ferries once plied the Elizabeth River between Norfolk and Portsmouth every few minutes. The paddlewheel **Elizabeth River Ferry** still makes that short but picturesque trip, departing the Waterside marina every 30 minutes Monday to Thursday from 7:15am to 11:45pm, Friday from 7:15am to 11:45pm, Saturday from 10:15am to 11:45pm, and Sunday from 10:15am to 9:45pm. Fare is 75¢ for adults, 50¢ for children, 35¢ for seniors. In Portsmouth, visitors can browse in the open-air shops in the Olde Harbour Market or take a trolley tour of Olde Towne Portsmouth. Call 804/393-5111, or 804/640-6300 for schedules.

ATTRACTIONS IN HAMPTON

Jamestown was barely two years old when Capt. John Smith sent a contingent of men to build America's first fort on the Hampton River, strategically located on the western shore of Hampton Roads. Thus did Hampton become one of the nation's oldest English-speaking settlements. Blackbeard the Pirate was killed here in 1718 during a fierce battle with Colonial forces (captured members of his crew were later tried and hanged at Williamsburg). Unfortunately there are no remaining structures from those early days, for a Confederate general ordered Hampton burned to the ground rather than permit Union forces holding Fort Monroe to quarter troops and former slaves in the town. Hampton now looks resolutely to the 21st century, since it is home to a major research center of the National Aeronautics and Space Administration.

For **visitor information**, contact the Hampton Visitor Center, 710 Settlers Landing Road, Hampton, VA 23669 (☎ 804/727-1222, or 800/800-2202). The center is on the waterfront a block from the Virginia Air and Space Center (see below).

Casemate Museum

Fort Monroe, Hampton. ☎ **804/727-3391.** Free admission. Daily 10:30am–4:30pm. Closed New Year's Day, Thanksgiving, and Christmas. From Norfolk, take I-64 across the Hampton Roads Bridge-Tunnel to the first exit (268) and follow the Fort Monroe signs.

A must for Civil War buffs is the Casemate Museum at Fort Monroe, where Jefferson Davis was imprisoned in 1865 after the war. Located at the tip of a peninsula and surrounded by a moat, the stone fort was built between 1819 and 1834. Robert E. Lee, a second lieutenant in the Army Corps of Engineers in 1831, was second in command of the detachment that constructed the fort. The fort was so strong that it never fell during the Civil War. The "casemates," or rooms, were originally designed as storage for seacoast artillery. After 1861, they were modified to serve as living quarters for the soldiers stationed at the fort and their families. Visitors can view displays of military memorabilia and enter the sparsely furnished room where Davis was held prisoner. The accusation against Davis—that he had participated in the plot to assassinate Lincoln—was eventually found to be false and Davis was released in 1867.

Hampton University Museum

Hampton University, Hampton. ☎ **804/727-5308.** Free admission. Sept–May, Mon–Fri 8am–5pm, Sat–Sun noon–4pm; June–Aug, Mon–Fri 8am–5pm. From Norfolk, take I-64 across the Hampton Roads Bridge-Tunnel to County Street; then follow signs to the university.

Hampton University, founded in 1868 to provide an education for newly freed African-Americans, boasts among its graduates Booker T. Washington, who himself founded Tuskegee Institute in Alabama. This museum is housed in Academy Building, an 1881 redbrick landmark on the waterfront in the historic section of the campus. Four other landmarks are nearby, including the imposing Memorial Chapel (1886). The museum is noted for its African collection, comprising more than 2,700 art objects and artifacts representing 887 ethnic groups and cultures. Rivaling the African collection in quality and importance, the Native American collection includes works from 93 tribes; it was established in 1878, when the federal government began sending young Native Americans from western reservations to be educated at Hampton. The museum also has notable holdings in works by Harlem Renaissance artists, and extensive Oceanic and Asian objects.

○ Virginia Air and Space Center/Hampton Roads History Center

600 Settlers Landing Rd., Hampton. ☎ **804/727-0900.** Admission $6 adults, $4 seniors and children 3–11, free under 3; combination tickets including the IMAX film $3 more. Memorial Day to Labor Day, Mon–Wed 9am–5pm, Thurs–Sun 9am–7pm; off-season, daily 10am–5pm. From I-64, take Exit 267. Follow Settlers Landing Road to downtown Hampton; the Center will be on the left.

A stunning glass-fronted futuristic structure perched on the edge of Hampton's riverfront, this museum chronicles the history of aviation and space travel and also serves as the official visitor center for NASA's Langley Research Center. The vast interior is separated into various bays that hold individual exhibits on rockets, satellites, and space exploration. The center space has about 10 air vehicles, as well as the world's largest paper airplane, suspended from its 94-foot vaulted ceiling. In the main gallery, the *Apollo 12* command module, complete with reentry burn marks, is an awe-inspiring sight. Visitors to the Space Gallery can don an astronaut's helmet and see themselves on a TV monitor. An IMAX film theater has new films about three times a year.

ATTRACTIONS IN NEWPORT NEWS

Named for Christopher Newport, skipper of the *Discovery* which brought some of the Jamestown settlers to Virginia, Newport News dates back to the early 1600s and has a long maritime tradition. Many of America's most formidable warships have rolled down the ways of Newport News Shipbuilding & Dry Dock Company, the region's largest private employer.

For **visitor information** contact the Newport News Tourism Development Office, 2400 Washington Ave., Newport News, VA 23607 (☎ 804/928-6843, or 800/333-7787).

Mariners' Museum

100 Museum Dr., Newport News. ☎ **804/596-2222.** Admission $6.50 adults, $5.50 seniors, $3.25 students. Daily 10am–5pm. From I-64, take Exit 258A and follow J. Clyde Morris Boulevard (U.S. 17) south to its intersection with Warwick Boulevard, go straight there on Museum Drive.

In a pleasant 550-acre park setting, with a lake, picnic areas, and walking trails, the Mariners' Museum is dedicated to preserving the culture of the sea and its tributaries. Handcrafted ship models, scrimshaw, maritime paintings, decorative arts, working steam engines, and more are displayed in the spacious galleries. Particularly interesting are galleries highlighting the history and culture of the Chesapeake Bay and the Age of Exploration. An 18-minute film narrated by actor James Earl Jones tells about maritime activity the world over. From time to time, costumed historical interpreters, including an 18th-century sea captain and a model ship builder, give demonstrations.

Virginia Living Museum

524 J. Clyde Morris Blvd., Newport News. ☎ **804/595-1900.** Museum $5 adults, $3.25 children 3–12, free under 3. Planetarium admission $2.50 adults, $2 children 3–12, free under 3. Mid-June to Labor Day, Mon–Tues and Fri–Sat 9am–6pm, Thurs 9am–9pm, Sun 10am–6pm; rest of year, Mon–Tues and Fri–Sat 9am–5pm, Thurs 9am–5pm and 7–9pm, Sun noon–6pm. Nature trail closes daily at dusk. From I-64, take Exit 258A and follow J. Clyde Morris Boulevard (U.S. 17) south.

This charming zoolike museum explains the environment of the James River area, beginning with a 60-foot cross-section simulating the river habitat from the Appalachian Mountains to the Atlantic Ocean (the latter represented by a 3,000-gallon tank of sea water filled with fish). A nearby touch-tank lets youngsters handle turtles and other small river animals. Outdoors, a boardwalk nature trail winds along the banks of a picturesque lake. Enclosures contain local wildlife such as otters, beavers, turtles, and birds (including a bald eagle grounded by a gunshot wound). A state-of-the-art planetarium presents various shows explaining the southern skies.

ACCOMMODATIONS

The downtown Norfolk hotels recommended below are within walking distance of the Waterside, and the others are no more than 15 minutes away.

DOWNTOWN HOTELS

✪ Norfolk Waterside Marriott

235 E. Main St., between Atlantic Street and Martin's Lane, Norfolk, VA 23510. ☎ **804/627-4200** or 800/228-9290. Fax 804/628-6452. 404 rms, including 8 suites. A/C TV TEL. $84–$119 single or double. Weekend packages available. AE, CB, DC, DISC, MC, V. Self-parking $8; valet parking $10.

This luxury hotel is an elegantly appointed 24-story high-rise conveniently connected to the Waterside Festival Marketplace via a covered skywalk. Its mahogany-paneled lobby is a masterpiece of 18th-century European style, with fine paintings, a crystal chandelier, potted palm trees, comfortable seating areas with gleaming lamps, and one-of-a-kind antiques. A magnificent staircase leads to the restaurants and lounges. Guest rooms are sumptuously appointed with traditional darkwood furnishings and pretty floral-print draperies and spreads. Sweeping river views are among the extras here. Rooms on the concierge levels enjoy a private lounge where complimentary continental breakfast and afternoon snacks are served.

Dining/Entertainment: The second-level Dining Room is open for breakfast, lunch, and dinner. Stormy's Sports Bar has light fare and evening entertainment, including dancing. The Piano Lounge adjoining the Dining Room has a cozy fireplace and serves cocktails from 4pm.

Services: Valet parking, same-day laundry/valet, room service, babysitting.

Facilities: Atrium-enclosed pool, saunas, whirlpools and sundeck overlooking waterfront, gift shop, business services, health club with Universal equipment.

Omni Waterside Hotel

777 Waterside Dr., Norfolk, VA 23510. ☎ **804/622-6664** or 800/THE-OMNI. Fax 804/ 625-8271. 446 rms, 20 suites. A/C TV TEL. $89–$139 single or double. Children under 16 stay free in parents' room. Weekend and other packages available. AE, CB, DC, DISC, MC, V. Self-parking $3 in adjacent Dominion Tower garage; valet parking $8.50.

Overlooking busy Norfolk Harbor, the Omni is next door to the Waterside Festival Marketplace. Its three-story atrium lobby is enhanced by stunning floral arrangements, and in the sunken Lobby Bar, 30-foot windows overlook the river. The Omni Club Level on the 10th floor offers such special amenities as complimentary continental breakfast, afternoon hors d'oeuvres, free daily newspaper, and nightly turndown with chocolates.

Dining/Entertainment: The Riverwalk offers American fare at all three meals. The Lobby Bar has dancing on Friday and Saturday nights.

Services: Concierge, multilingual staff.

Facilities: Business center, gift and sundries shop, outdoor pool; health club nearby.

Ramada Madison Hotel

345 Granby St., Norfolk, VA 23510. ☎ **804/622-6682** or 800/2-RAMADA. 124 rms. A/C TV TEL. $50–$100 double. Children 12 and under stay free in parents' room. Weekend and other packages available. AE, CB, DC, DISC, MC, V. Free sheltered parking on property.

Built in 1906 at the corner of Granby and Freemason streets as the Southland Hotel and later known as the Madison, the Ramada was the first hostelry in Norfolk to provide indoor plumbing for its guests. Although the Marriott and Omni have eclipsed it, the lobby reflects the hotel's status as Norfolk's grande dame landmark, with crystal chandeliers, polished walnut columns, wing chairs, and a medallion-printed carpet. The original 180 rooms have been renovated and decorated in Colonial style with pale floral-print fabrics and mahogany furnishings. All rooms have remote-control TVs. Dolley's Restaurant serves breakfast and lunch daily. The main restaurant and lounge, Bentley's, is open for drinks and dinner nightly. There is a nominal charge for use of a nearby health and racquetball club.

SUBURBAN ACCOMMODATIONS

Best Western Center Inn

One Best Sq., Norfolk, VA 23502. ☎ **804/461-6600** or 800/237-5517. Fax 804/466-9093. 152 rms. A/C TV TEL. $58–$71 double; $110–$140 suite. Rates include continental breakfast. Weekend and other packages available. AE, CB, DC, DISC, MC, V. Free parking. From I-64, take

I-264 west and exit north onto North Military Highway/U.S. 13; at the red light turn left into Best Square and follow the service road to the inn entrance.

You'll realize this Best Western is something special from the moment you see the tasteful two-story light-gray-stucco complex, set around a nicely landscaped courtyard and garden with park benches and old-fashioned street lamps. All rooms face the courtyard and Olympic-size pool. Accommodations have a summery look, with bamboo furnishings and lavender, pink, and blue spreads and matching draperies. Complimentary continental breakfast is available in the lobby. Next door to the inn are Best Center shops and restaurants, including a branch of the inexpensive Morrison Cafeterias. Military Circle shopping mall is virtually across the street nearby. The Grate Steak restaurant is on site and has a good reputation. Complimentary airport shuttle is offered, and there are a health club, sauna, Jacuzzi, indoor and outdoor pools, coin-op laundry, and conference center.

Econo Lodge

9601 Fourth View St., Norfolk, VA 23503. ☎ **804/480-9611** or 800/768-5425. Fax 804/480-1307. 70 rms, including 22 efficiencies. A/C TV TEL. $48–$60 double. Rates include continental breakfast. Extra person $5. Children under 18 stay free in parents' room. AE, CB, DC, DISC, MC, V. Free parking. From I-64, take Exit 273 to the corner of U.S. 60 (Ocean View Avenue) and Fourth View.

This Econo Lodge, one of the nicest representatives of this chain we've encountered, is across the road from the Chesapeake Bay beach and Harrison fishing pier. The rooms are large, many decorated in tones of green and gold, and all have refrigerators. Efficiencies have full kitchen facilities; microwave ovens are available for a small extra charge. A coin-op laundry, sauna, and Jacuzzi on the premises.

If this Econo Lodge is full, there are four others in the area, including one at 1111 E. Ocean View Beach Ave., Norfolk, VA 23503 (☎ 804/480-1111).

Norfolk Hampton Inn-Airport

1450 Military Hwy., Norfolk, VA 23502. ☎ **804/466-7474** or 800/HAMPTON. 130 rms. A/C TV TEL. $53–$61 double. Rates include continental breakfast. Children 18 and under stay free in parents' room. AE, DC, DISC, MC, V. Free parking. From I-64, take Exit 281 and follow Military Highway south to its intersection with Northampton Boulevard.

Cost-conscious travelers will find that the Hampton gives good value. In addition to comfortable rooms decorated with light-oak furniture, the motel offers many complimentary amenities, among them an airport shuttle, continental breakfast in the lobby, local phone calls, in-room movies, and newspapers. There's an outdoor pool.

BED & BREAKFAST

✪ Page House Inn

323 Fairfax Ave., Norfolk, VA 23507. ☎ **804/625-5033.** Fax 804/623-9451. 4 rms, 2 suites. A/C TEL. $85–$120 double; $130–$145 suite. Rates include breakfast. MC, V. Free parking.

Centrally located in the historic Ghent district and across the street from the Chrysler Museum, this splendid inn is perfectly situated for tourists. Built in 1899 by Herman L. Page, a Welsh immigrant who made good in Norfolk, it is a grand three-story brick Colonial Revival mansion with a dormered roof and double columns punctuating the expansive verandah. It's hard to believe that this exquisite property, owned and enthusiastically operated by Stephanie and Ezio DiBelardino, had stood vacant and desolate for years until the DiBelardinos bought it in 1990. The evidence of Ezio's labors as a master craftsman are evident throughout. The golden-oak paneling, sliding doors, and moldings on the first floor; the hand-carved fireplace in the living room; and the soaring staircase that ascends to the rooftop skylight have been brilliantly restored.

Guest rooms are beautifully furnished with four-poster beds, hand-crocheted spreads, pretty wallpapers, and one-of-a-kind antiques. There is a large dining room, set with Lenox china, where Stephanie serves a gourmet continental breakfast. Afternoon cappuccino, served in the parlor (in front of the fireplace in winter), is another Page House ritual, giving guests a chance to meet one another and enjoy their hosts' graciousness.

DINING
DOWNTOWN

⑤ Elliot's

1421 Colley Ave. ☎ **804/625-0259.** Reservations not necessary. Main courses $8.95–$13.95. AE, CB, DC, DISC, MC, V. Sun–Thurs 11am–10pm, Fri–Sat 11am–midnight. AMERICAN.

Many are the fans of Elliot's, which encompasses five former stores and an airy glass-enclosed patio in Norfolk's trendy Ghent district. An eclectic art deco decor features old photos and advertising signs on the walls, ceiling fans, hanging plants, and etched-glass partitions. Specialties include mile-high nachos with chicken chili and delicious hot crab dip. Fresh-catch selections come broiled, blackened, or with a choice of special sauces. There are also burgers, salads, and vegetarian dishes. And a children's menu is a plus for families. For dessert, you can't beat a homemade fudge brownie topped with ice cream, whipped cream, and chocolate sauce. A selection of domestic and imported beers is available—or have a bottle of house wine. Elliot's offers free dinner delivery to downtown hotels.

Freemason Abbey Restaurant & Tavern

209 W. Freemason St., corner of Boush Street. ☎ **804/622-3966.** Reservations suggested at dinner. Main courses $10–$18. AE, DISC, MC, V. Sun–Thurs 11:30am–10pm, Fri–Sat 11:30am–midnight. AMERICAN.

Did you ever eat in a church? Well, you can here, in an 1873 brick-and-fieldstone building originally occupied by Norfolk's Second Presbyterian Church. The structure has been completely refurbished, exposing the massive cathedral roof trusses and adding a mezzanine that seats about 100 in a casual atmosphere. Etched-glass trim, wood-framed gothic windows, a brass chandelier, and polished wood tables and high-backed booths create a cozy tavern ambiance. The specialty is lobster, and locals flock here on Wednesday nights when a $1\frac{1}{3}$-pound lobster dinner costs only $12. A big draw for meat lovers is the Thursday-night 10-ounce prime rib dinner ($10). Try the she-crab soup for your appetizer; it's a luscious blend of crabmeat and cream with a dash of sherry. Entrees—all served with a salad, potato, oven-fresh rolls, and a steamed vegetable—include grilled salmon, New York strip steak, and seafood pasta. Finish off with Irish Cream coffee or a Freemason cappuccino, made with Frangelico and brandy. Lighter fare for lunch or late-night dinner includes quiches and croissant sandwiches.

Il Porto

The Waterside. ☎ **804/627-4400.** Reservations suggested, especially on weekends. Main courses $10–$15. AE, DC, DISC, MC, V. Daily 11am–4pm; Sun–Thurs 4–11pm, Fri–Sat 4pm–midnight. ITALIAN.

Il Porto has been at the Waterside since the marketplace opened and has expanded several times. Its continuing popularity is due to its great waterfront views and delicious Italian specialties. The candlelit interior evokes the Mediterranean with terra-cotta-tile floors and stucco walls. In good weather you can dine outdoors overlooking the harbor. For a light lunch, have an antipasto (entree-size portion is $6.50) of assorted Italian cold meats, cheeses, and marinated vegetables on salad greens. At dinner, start with mussels in white wine and parsley. Homemade pastas run the gamut from lasagne, manicotti, or linguine with clam sauce to the house special lobster, scallops, fish, and shrimp sautéed in herb butter and tossed with broccoli and pasta. Children's plates of spaghetti and meatballs, lasagne, or veal parmigiana are $6. At night a pianist plays ragtime.

Phillips Waterside

333 Waterside Dr. ☎ **804/627-6600.** Reservations suggested. Main courses $9–$19. AE, CB, DC, DISC, MC, V. Summer, daily 11am–11pm; winter, daily 11:30am–10:30pm (bar open until midnight). SEAFOOD.

Member of a popular regional chain of seafood restaurants, this extravaganza at the Waterside is itself a festival. It seats some 400 diners in a series of dining rooms with blue wrought-iron chairs and tables amid old brick archways, aquariums, stained-glass lamps, a gazebo, nautical items, and hanging plants. Blue tents cover the Deckside Lounge, where there's live entertainment and light fare at night. In the Main Lounge there may be piano bar sing-alongs. But the center of attention is good seafood. At lunch, a fish, a shrimp salad, or a crab cake sandwich is under $7. At dinner, she-crab soup, fresh local oysters, and spiced shrimp are favorite starters. Proceed to Phillips's ultimate seafood adventure: steamed "captain's catch," a bountiful serving that consists of a lobster, snow crab clusters, spiced shrimp, clams, mussels, and oysters. Another fine selection is salmon baked on oak planks from wine barrels.

Schooner's Harbor Grill

The Waterside. ☎ **804/627-8800.** Reservations recommended. Main courses $9–$16. AE, CB, DC, DISC, MC, V. Daily 11am–midnight. AMERICAN.

Dining at Schooner's affords you a lookout over the Waterside marina whether you choose to sit outside on the 200-seat patio overlooking the Elizabeth River or inside, where you can also watch the chefs prepare your meal at the gleaming brass-and-copper grill that's open to view. Spacious and airy, this fun restaurant has red-ceramic-tile floors, checked tablecloths, and ceiling fans with Victorian glass-shaded lamps. For lunch you may want to indulge in spiced jumbo shrimp: A half pound is $6. At night the emphasis is on chargrilled burgers, steaks, fish, and a raw bar with oysters, clams, and shrimp. Barbecued ribs and chicken are also on the menu. The lively bar here provides baskets of Virginia peanuts roasted in the shell.

SUBURBAN RESTAURANTS

Doumar's

19th to 20th streets and Monticello Avenue. ☎ **804/627-4163.** Sandwiches 90¢–$2.45. No credit cards. Mon–Thurs 8am–11pm, Fri–Sat 8am–12:30am. AMERICAN.

This is no modern re-creation of a 1950s drive-in with carhops, curb service, and a 1950s menu, for Doumar's has been just that since the 1930s—which makes it a hip historical attraction. The specialties here are sweet, wafflelike ice-cream cones, some of them from the original cone-making machine invented by Abe Doumar at the St. Louis Exposition in 1904. Abe's great-nephew, present owner Al Doumar, keeps his uncle's invention oiled and working. Barbecue sandwiches, burgers and hot dogs, sundaes, and milkshakes round out the menu.

✪ Uncle Louie's

132 E. Little Creek Rd., Ward's Corner. ☎ **804/480-1225.** Reservations recommended for dinner. Main courses $6–$17. AE, DC, MC, V. Mon–Sat 11am–2am, Sun 10am–10pm (brunch 10am–2pm). Deli, daily 8am–8pm. AMERICAN.

A Very Dismal Swamp

When the early English settlers fanned out from Jamestown, they found their way south blocked by a "vast body of dirt and nastiness." So wrote Colonel William Byrd II, who in 1728 surveyed the Virginia–North Carolina border through this impenetrable region appropriately dubbed the Great Dismal Swamp.

George Washington came to the swamp in 1763 and organized a company to drain and log some 40,000 acres. A 5-mile ditch still bears his name, but Washington's investment went for naught. At the urging of then-governor Patrick Henry, slaves dug the Dismal Swamp Canal from Hampton Roads to North Carolina. Still operating, it is America's oldest manmade waterway. A road constructed on the spoil in 1804 is now U.S. 17 between Portsmouth and Elizabeth City, N.C.

Although much of the swamp was drained over the years, the Great Dismal Swamp National Wildlife Refuge still contains black bear, bobcats, white-tailed deer, otters, and a plethora of birdlife. The last of the swamp's great cypress forest stands along the haunting shores of Lake Drummond, centerpiece of the refuge. The refuge headquarters, off Va. 32 south of Suffolk, provides a boardwalk nature walk and hiking and biking trails to Lake Drummond. Canoes can be launched in the Dismal Swamp Canal on U.S. 17 south of Portsmouth and taken to Lake Drummond via the Federal Feeder Ditch.

For information, contact the refuge at P.O. Box 349, Suffolk, VA 23434 (☎ 804/986-3705). South of the North Carolina line on U.S. 17, the Dismal Swamp Canal Visitor Center (☎ 919/771-8333) is open from Memorial Day through October daily from 9am to 5pm; the rest of the year Tuesday to Saturday from 9am to 5pm. In Virginia, Chesapeake Campground on U.S. 17 (☎ 804/485-0149) rents canoes and has camping facilities.

A sophisticated art deco setting and a multipage menu that includes everything from bagels and lox to shrimp provençal puts Uncle Louie's in a class by itself. Portions are hefty. All-day breakfast fare includes three-egg omelets served with two potato pancakes and a bagel or three cheese blintzes with sour cream. Sunday brunch features challah French toast, eggs Benedict, and eggs Créole. For lunch, huge deli sandwiches come with a choice of coleslaw or potato salad. Dr. Brown's sodas are a perfect accompaniment. Soups, pastas, fresh seafood, choice steaks, and smoked-fish platters are among the offerings. Uncle Louie offers a huge selection of dessert from New York's famous Carnegie Deli. Open until 2am, Louie's bar also serves tropical bar drinks; there is live music Wednesday, Friday, and Saturday nights.

NORFOLK AFTER DARK

For a rundown on evening events, pick up a free copy of *Port Folio,* an entertainment weekly available at the visitors information offices, most hotel lobbies, and the Waterside. In addition to entertainment at hotel lounges, you may be in town during performances of several outstanding companies. The **Virginia Stage Company** puts on five productions annually, October through April, at the restored Wells Theatre, Monticello Avenue and Tazewell Street (☎ 804/627-1234). The Harrison Opera House, Virginia Beach Boulevard and Llewellyn Avenue (☎ 804/627-9545), is home to the **Virginia Opera.**

SCOPE, Brambleton Avenue and St. Paul's Boulevard (☎ 804/441-2161), seats 12,000 for major events—including the circus, ice shows, and concerts. Part of the SCOPE complex, **Chrysler Hall,** Charlotte Street and St. Paul's Boulevard (☎ 804/441-2161), is home to the **Virginia Symphony** and the annual Pops series.

Two clubs—the **Bait Shack** and **Legends of Norfolk**—rock the Waterside after 9pm on Thursday, Friday, and Saturday nights. With live reggae, progressive rock, and beach bands, the Bait Shack draws a younger crowd than the upstairs Legends of Norfolk, whose DJ spins a variety of styles. Call 804/625-LIVE for times and bands.

2 Virginia Beach

18 miles E of Norfolk; 110 miles E of Richmond; 207 miles S of Washington, D.C.

Given its more than 20 miles of unbroken sand and surf, it's not surprising that Virginia Beach comes alive during the summer months with flocks of vacationers. Although big hotels line the beachfront and block off ocean views from everywhere except their rooms, the boardwalk boasts immaculate landscaping, wood benches, small parks, public rest rooms, and attractive white Colonial-style street lamps.

Adding to Virginia Beach's allure as a family vacation destination is the Virginia Marine Science Museum, the most popular museum in the state. History lovers will find several sites, including the First Landing Cross at the spot where the Jamestown settlers first came ashore. And nature lovers can drive a few miles south to the Back Bay National Wildlife Refuge, which attracts migrating birds and protects several miles of beach and marshlands from encroaching development.

ESSENTIALS

ARRIVING   By Plane   Virginia Beach is serviced by **Norfolk International Airport** (☎ 804/857-3351), about 30 minutes (15 miles) from the oceanfront resort area. For airport limousine service, call 804/857-1231.

By Car   From the west, follow I-64 to Va. 44 east (the "44 Expressway" in local parlance), which runs straight to the heart of the oceanfront resort area. U.S. 60 becomes Shore Drive, which deadends at Atlantic Avenue on the northern end of the ocean beach; a right turn takes you to the resort area. From the north or south, U.S. 13 and 17 will take you to I-64.

By Train   The nearest **Amtrak** station is in Newport News, at 9304 Warwick Blvd. (☎ 804/245-3589, or 800/872-7245). An Amtrak Thruway bus connection carries passengers to Virginia Beach.

By Bus   The **Greyhound/Trailways Bus Terminal** is at 1017 Laskin Rd. (☎ 804/422-2998, or 800/231-2222).

VISITOR INFORMATION   For information in planning your trip, or assistance while you're in Virginia Beach, contact the **Visitor Information Center,** 2100 Parks Ave., Virginia Beach, VA 23451 (☎ 804/437-4888, or 800/822-3224). A large board has reservation phones connected to the major hotels and resorts. Particularly helpful is a free **map** showing public restrooms and municipal parking lots in the resort area. The center is at the eastern end of the Va. 44 expressway and is open daily from 9am to 5pm, to 8pm from mid-June to Labor Day. There are **information kiosks** on Atlantic Avenue at 17th, 24th, and 27th streets.

Virginia Beach

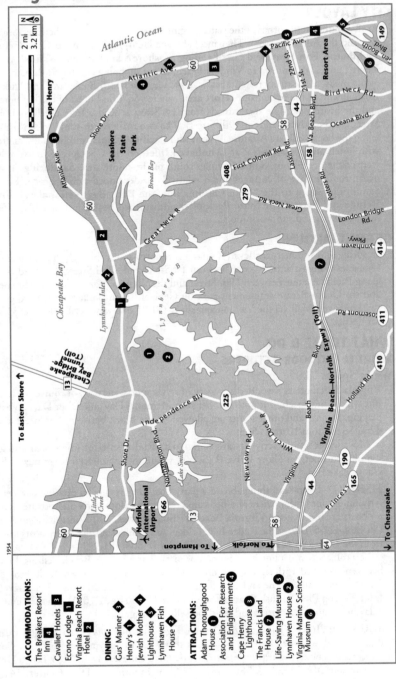

ACCOMMODATIONS:

The Breakers Resort Inn **4**
Cavalier Hotels **3**
Econo Lodge **1**
Virginia Beach Resort Hotel **2**

DINING:

Gus' Mariner **3**
Henry's **1**
Jewish Mother **4**
Lighthouse **5**
Lynnhaven Fish House **2**

ATTRACTIONS:

Adam Thoroughgood House **1**
Association For Research and Enlightenment **4**
Cape Henry Lighthouse **3**
The Francis Land House **7**
Life-Saving Museum **5**
Lynnhaven House **2**
Virginia Marine Science Museum **6**

1954

CITY LAYOUT

At the southeastern corner of the state, Virginia Beach is bordered by the Chesapeake Bay and the Atlantic Ocean. They meet at Cape Henry, now home to **Cape Henry Lighthouse, Fort Story,** and **First Landing/Seashore State Park and Natural Area.** There's no real downtown in Virginia Beach; major shopping and movie theaters are at the malls, as are many restaurants. Va. 44, Virginia Beach Boulevard, and Laskin Road all end at the oceanfront **resort area,** where you'll find most of the big hotels and the boardwalk. The area extends from 1st Street at Rudee Inlet north to 42nd Street (the boardwalk ends at 39th Street). The two main north-south streets paralleling the boardwalk are **Atlantic Avenue** and **Pacific Avenue.** Another popular area with hotels and restaurants is at **Lynnhaven Inlet,** on the Chesapeake Bay 6 miles west of the oceanfront. Some 12 miles south of the resort area, **Sandbridge** is an oceanfront enclave of cottages and a relatively undeveloped public beach. From Sandbridge south to the North Carolina line, the **Back Bay National Wildlife Refuge** and **False Cape State Park** offer undisturbed beach and marshland for hikers, bikers, and sun worshippers.

GETTING AROUND

In spring and summer, **trolleys** (50¢ fare) run north-south through the beach area. One goes along Atlantic Avenue between 1st Street and 42nd Street. A second runs along Pacific Avenue between 19th Street and the Virginia Marine Science Museum and the Ocean Breeze amusement park on General Booth Boulevard. A third goes to Lynnhaven Mall via the Va. 44 expressway ($1.75 one way). Call 804/428-3388 for details.

WHAT TO SEE & DO
SPORT & OUTDOOR ACTIVITIES
Water Sports

Virginia Beach offers a wonderful variety of water sports, starting, of course, with its fine white-sand beach. But note that between Memorial Day and Labor Day, no ball playing, fishing, and other sports are allowed on the beach between 2nd Street and 42nd Street from 10am to 5pm.

Most water sports activities are centered at Rudee Inlet on the ocean and at Lynnhaven Inlet, on Shore Drive (U.S. 60), where the Lynnhaven River meets the Chesapeake Bay.

FISHING Deep-sea fishing aboard a party boat can provide an exciting day's entertainment for both novices and dedicated fishermen. Both party and private charter boats are based at the **Virginia Beach Fishing Center,** 200 Winston Salem Ave. (☎ 804/422-5700), at the Rudee Inlet bridge. At Lynnhaven Inlet, party boats leave from the **D and M Marina,** 3311 Shore Drive (☎ 804/481-7211).

You can also drop a line from numerous piers. The **Virginia Beach Fishing Pier,** between 14th and 15th streets, oceanfront (☎ 804/428-2333), open April through October, has bait for sale and rods for rent. On the Chesapeake Bay, **Lynnhaven Inlet Fishing Pier,** Starfish Road off Shore Drive (☎ 804/481-7071), open 24 hours a day in summer, rents rods and reels and sells crab cages.

SCUBA DIVING The Atlantic Ocean off Virginia Beach is colder and less clear than it is below Cape Hatteras, N.C., but that's not to say you can dive here. For information about dive trips, contact **Atlantic Dive Charters Ltd.,** 1324 Teresa Dr., Chesapeake, VA 23322 (☎ 804/482-9777), or **Lynnhaven Dive Center,** 1413 Great Neck Rd., Virginia Beach, VA 23454 (☎ 804/481-7949).

SWIMMING   During the summer season there are lifeguards on duty along the resort strip from 2nd to 42nd streets; they also handle raft, umbrella, and beach-chair rentals.

You can get away from the summer crowds by driving 12 miles south of Rudee Inlet to the residential beach area of **Sandbridge** and the adjacent **Back Bay National Wildlife Refuge,** and **False Cape State Park** (see "Parks and Wildlife Refuges," below). Take General Booth Boulevard south and follow the signs to Sandbridge and the refuge.

WAVE RUNNING & PARASAILING   You can rent exciting wave runners from **Rudee Inlet Jet Ski Rentals,** which has locations at the Virginia Beach Fishing Center at Rudee Inlet (☎ 804/428-4614), 31st Street at the oceanfront (☎ 804/491-1117), and 1284 Laskin Rd. (☎ 804/428-6156). At Lynnhaven Inlet, **Wave Runners Water Sports Center** (☎ 804/481-4747) rents jet skis and jet boats and also has parasailing over the Chesapeake. At Sandbridge, jet skis, sailboats, fishing boats, and canoes are available from **Sandbridge Boat Rentals,** 3713 Sandpiper Rd. (☎ 804/721-6210). You must be at least 16 years old to operate a jet ski in Virginia.

Land Sports

BIKING, JOGGING & SKATING   You can walk, jog, or run on the boardwalk, or bicycle and skate on the boardwalk bike path. There are biking and hiking trails in **First Landing/Seashore State Park** and in **Back Bay National Wildlife Refuge** (see "Parks and Wildlife Refuges," below). Bikes and in-line skates are available from **Cherie's Bicycle Rentals** (☎ 804/437-8888), which has stands on the oceanfront at 8th, 22nd, 24th, and 37th streets. Cherie's also has clinics for those who want to learn how to skate in-line. **Tom's Bike Rentals** (☎ 804/425-8454) specializes in the northern area, including First Landing/Seashore State Park. His bikes are less expensive than Cherie's, and he delivers to your hotel.

GOLF   The visitor center provides a detailed list of Virginia Beach's nine public golf courses. Among them are the **Hell's Point Golf Course,** 2700 Atwoodtown Rd. (☎ 804/721-3400), designed by Rees Jones, and the **Red Wing Lake Municipal Golf Course,** 1080 Prosperity Road (☎ 804/437-4845).

TENNIS   The city has some 200 public tennis courts, most of which are lighted and free. If you call the city's **Parks Department** (☎ 804/437-4804), they'll be glad to steer you to the one closest to you. The **Owl Creek Municipal Center,** 928 South Birdneck Rd. (☎ 804/422-4716), which has a pro shop, children's play area, and 12 hard-surface and 2 tournament courts, is the major facility.

PARKS & WILDLIFE REFUGES

You don't have to go far from the busy resort area to find open spaces ideal for hiking, biking, camping, and bird-watching.

Between the two resort areas is **First Landing/Seashore State Park,** with 2,270 preserved acres running from the Chesapeake Bay to within two blocks of the ocean. Rabbits, squirrels, and raccoon are among the many species inhabiting this urban park, which has 28 miles of hiking trails. Bikes are prohibited except on the 6-mile Cape Henry Trail, which runs from 64th Street on the beach to the visitor center, entered off Shore Drive (U.S. 60). Admission to the park is $2.50 per vehicle, free for hikers and bikers. The trails are open daily from sunrise to sunset. The visitor center is open from April to November daily from 9am to 6pm. Twenty 2-bedroom cabins can be rented for $510 a week, and a bayside campground has 200 sites for tents and RVs (no hookups) for $19.25 a night. For cabin or camp reservations, call 804/482-2131.

Especially inviting for the bird-watchers is ✪ **Back Bay National Wildlife Refuge,** in the southeastern corner of Virginia at the North Carolina line. Its 7,732 acres of beaches, marshes, and backwaters are on the main Atlantic flyway for migratory birds. No swimming or sunbathing is allowed on the pristine beach here, but you can collect shells, surf cast for fish, and bird-watch. There also are nature trails and a canoe launching spot with marked trails through the marshes. Admission is $4 per vehicle, $2 per pedestrian or biker. The visitor contact station (☎ 804/721-2412) is open Monday to Friday from 8am to 4pm, Sunday from 9am to 4pm. It has nature programs by reservation. From Rudee Inlet, go south on General Booth Boulevard and follow the signs 12 miles to Sandbridge and the refuge.

Canoe, rubber rafts, and aluminum fishing skiffs are available north of the refuge at **Sandbridge Boat Rentals,** 3713 Sandpiper Rd. (☎ 804/721-6210).

There is no vehicular access, but you can hike or bike 4 miles south from the Back Bay visitor station to **False Cape State Park** (☎ 804/426-7128). Swimming and sunbathing are permitted on the beach here, but you must bring your own drinking water. There's an interpretive trail and more than 3 miles of hiking trails. The park is open daily from 9am to 5pm. Primitive camping is by permit only, obtainable at the First Landing/Seashore State Park visitor center (see above).

AMUSEMENT PARKS

The ocean resort area between 15th and 30th streets has the usual collection of electronic games establishments and a haunted house, and at Rudee Inlet there's **Skycoaster,** where you can fly bungee-jumping style from a contraption that looks like the Gateway Arch in St. Louis.

The major fun park here, however, is **Ocean Breeze,** 849 General Booth Boulevard south of Rudee Inlet (☎ 804/442-0718 or 800/678-WILD). Next door to the Virginia Marine Science Museum (see below), this establishment actually includes four amusements: Motor World go-kart track, Shipwreck miniature golf course with waterfalls and a sunken ship, Strike Zone baseball batting cage, and the Wild Water Rapids wave pool. There's also a bungee jumping tower on the premises. Admission to Wild Water Rapids ranges from $8 to $16 for adults, $8 to $11 for children, depending on the day and time. Tickets to everything else are extra. Wild Water Rapids are open from Memorial Day to Labor Day daily from 3pm to 11pm, the other facilities from 10am to 8pm. The park is open weekends during May and September.

HISTORIC ATTRACTIONS

Now part of the U.S. Army's Fort Story, at the north end of Atlantic Avenue, the Jamestown colonists' **First Landing Site** is marked by a cross and plaque where they "set up a Crosse at Chesupioc Bay and named that place Cape Henry" for Henry, Prince of Wales. Also at this site is a monumental relief map showing the French and British naval engagement off Cape Henry during the Revolutionary War and a statue of the French commander. Now known as the **Battle of the Capes,** this decisive battle effectively trapped Cornwallis at Yorktown and helped end British dominion in America. When Cornwallis surrendered, George Washington expressed his gratitude to the French Admiral de Grasse: "I wish it was in my power to express to Congress how much I feel myself indebted to the Count de Grasse and his fleet."

Near the plaque commemorating the battle, visitors can enter the **Old Cape Henry Lighthouse,** the first lighthouse built by authorization of Congress, in 1791. It lit the entrance to Chesapeake Bay until 1881. There is no charge for visitors to enter the grounds of Fort Story. The lighthouse (☎ 804/422-9421) is open mid-March through October 31, daily from 10am to 5pm; admission is $2 for adults, $1 for students and seniors.

Note: To enter Fort Story, you will need a picture identification (driver's license or passport will do).

The oldest brick home in Virginia Beach is the beautiful **Adam Thoroughgood House,** 1636 Parish Rd. (☎ 804/460-0007), near the intersection of Pleasure House Road and Northampton Boulevard (U.S. 13). Probably constructed about 1680 by one of Adam Thoroughgood's grandsons (architectural historians believe its namesake never occupied the house), this picturesque medieval-English-style cottage sits on 4¹/₂ acres of lawn and garden overlooking the Lynnhaven River. The interior has exposed wood beams and whitewashed walls, and although the furnishings did not belong to the Thoroughgood family, they are original to the period and reflect the family's English ancestry. Tours take about 1 hour. The house is open April through December, Tuesday through Saturday from 10am to 5pm and Sunday from noon to 5pm; January through March, Tuesday through Saturday from noon to 5pm. Admission is $3 for adults and $1.50 for seniors and students, free under 5. The house is included in block tickets for the Moses Myers House and Willougby-Baylor House in Norfolk, all administered by the Chrysler Museum (see "What to See & Do" in the Norfolk section, above).

Two other historic houses are open to the public in the Virginia Beach area. Costumed docents provide tours of the **Lynnhaven House,** 4405 Wishart Rd. (☎ 804/460-1688), from the fourth week of April through the end of October, Tuesday through Sunday from noon to 4pm; admission is $2.50 for adults, $1 for seniors and students, and free for children under 6. The **Francis Land House,** 3131 Virginia Beach Blvd. (☎ 804/340-1732), just west of Kings Grant Road, was built as a plantation manor in the mid-18th century but now sits beside one of the area's busiest highways. It is open year-round, Tuesday through Saturday from 9am to 5pm and Sunday from noon to 5pm, with the last tour at 4:30pm. Admission is $2.50 for adults and $1.50 for seniors and students 6 to 18, free for children under 6.

In the heart of the oceanfront resort area, Virginia Beach's **Life-Saving Museum,** 24th Street and Atlantic Avenue (☎ 804/422-1587), is housed in a small white 1903 clapboard building built as a lifesaving station. It recalls rescue missions and shipwrecks along the coast. Open Monday to Saturday from 10am to 5pm, Sunday from noon to 5pm. Admission is $2.50 for adults, $2 for seniors, and $1 for children. The museum has an excellent gift shop with clocks, drawings, books, and other things nautical.

MORE ATTRACTIONS

Association for Research and Enlightenment
67th Street and Atlantic Avenue. ☎ **804/428-3588.** Free admission. Mon–Sat 9am–8pm, Sun 11am–8pm.

The international headquarters carrying on the work of the late psychic Edgar Cayce has a host of free activities daily. You can see a movie that tells about Cayce's psychic talent, which first manifested when, as a young man, he found he was able to enter into an altered state of consciousness and answer questions on any topic. His answers, or "discourses," now called readings, number some 14,305 and have stood the test of extensive research. The movie is shown daily at 3pm; in summer there are guided tours of the building daily at 11:15am and 2:15pm, and a daily lecture at 3pm (see the receptionist for the day's topic). The A.R.E. Bookstore on the first floor has an excellent selection of books and videos about holistic health, parapsychology, life after death, dreams, and even cooking. The Meditation Room on the third floor has a spectacular view of the ocean and is painted with special colors chosen because Cayce readings suggest that they can assist higher consciousness. Outside the center is a Meditation Garden.

○ Virginia Marine Science Museum

717 General Booth Blvd. ☎ **804/425-FISH.** Admission $5.25 adults, $4.75 seniors, $4.50 children 4–12, children under 4 free. Admissions will change as additions come on line. Daily 9am–5pm (with extended summer hours). Closed Thanksgiving and Christmas. From the resort area, go south on Pacific Avenue, which becomes General Booth Boulevard across Rudee Inlet; the museum is less than a mile south of the inlet bridge.

As Virginia's largest aquarium, this entertaining and educational facility focusing on Virginia's marine environment is fittingly located on Owls Creek salt marsh. It even has an outdoor boardwalk that makes the marsh, its waterfowl, and other animals part of the experience. Visitors can see and touch live sea animals, plus try hands-on interactive exhibits such as oyster tonging and forecasting the weather. Under construction during our recent visit, a $35-million expansion was adding sharks, harbor seals, river otters, herons, and egrets to the museum's residents, building an outdoor aviary, expanding the aquarium to 500,000 gallons, and installing an IMAX theater.

The museum also offers boat trips for dolphin watching in summer and whale watching during winter.

WHERE TO STAY

Rates at Virginia Beach hotels rise steeply during summer, so a hotel that's expensive in summer can be surprisingly affordable in spring and fall and downright inexpensive in winter. Therefore, we've listed both summer and winter rates for the hotels below, but categorized the hotels according to their summer rate.

Of course, this is just the tip of the iceberg in Virginia Beach, which had more than 11,000 hotel rooms at last count. All but a few of the major chains are represented here. For example, there are three high-rise Holiday Inns on the oceanfront, including the **Holiday Inn Sunspree,** which is away from the maddening crowds at the 39th Street end of the boardwalk. The **Ramada Plaza Resort,** on the beach at Atlantic and 57th Street, is even more removed from the resort scene. On the south end of the beach, the **Hilton** stands near Rudee Inlet and all of its water sports activities. In between there are a **Sheraton, Days Inn,** and **Comfort Inn,** all on the oceanfront.

You can save by staying a block off the beach. One example here is the **Comfort Inn** at 2800 Pacific Ave., a modern, well-managed hotel with indoor and outdoor pools and an exercise room.

Virginia Beach's only gay-oriented resort is the **Coral Sand Motel,** 23rd and Pacific Ave., Virginia Beach, VA 23451 (☎ 804/425-0872, or 800/828-0872).

HOTELS AT THE OCEAN

○ Cavalier Hotel

42nd Street at the Oceanfront, Virginia Beach, VA 23451. ☎ **804/425-8555** or 800/446-8199. Fax 804/428-7957. 400 rms, 25 suites. A/C TV TEL. Summer, $90–$185 double; winter, $55–$95 double. Extra person $20. Children under 18 stay free in parents' room. Weekend and other packages available. AE, CB, DC, DISC, MC, V. Valet parking $10.

This venerable resort consists of two hotels—the original Cavalier on the hill, built in 1927, and the Cavalier on the ocean, which opened in 1973. Both have been refurbished recently, but the original property still has all the gracious features you'd expect in a fine old resort, including an enclosed verandah with white-wicker furnishings, potted plants, and great ocean views; it evokes memories of the days when F. Scott and Zelda Fitzgerald danced here and lunches were black tie. The lobby is gracious, complete with Colonial-style furnishings and crystal chandeliers. Some of the guest rooms feature European-style baths in black-and-white tile, with pediment sinks, whirlpools, lighted makeup mirrors, bidets, and hairdryers. Furnishings in these individually decorated rooms employ Williamsburg-quality Chippendale reproductions, Colonial-print fabrics, gilt-framed artworks, and museum-quality decorative objects. The heated indoor Olympic-size pool is magnificently tiled and illuminated by a grand skylight.

The oceanfront hotel has contemporary-style rooms, very nicely decorated in pastels, with a shell motif appearing on wall sconces and fabrics. All rooms have oceanfront balconies.

Dining/Entertainment: The elegant Orion rooftop restaurant in the oceanfront hotel is open for cocktails and dinner; the dining room on the lobby floor serves all three meals. The dining room in the hotel on the hill is open seasonally.

Services: Valet parking, room service, concierge, shuttle service between hotels, babysitting.

Facilities: Indoor, outdoor, and kiddie pools; 20-station aerobic fitness course; health club; putting green; four tennis courts; croquet, volleyball, shuffleboard, basketball, bike rentals, and two playgrounds; gift shop; children's activities program in season.

☉ The Breakers Resort Inn

16th Street at the Oceanfront, Virginia Beach, VA 23451. ☎ **804/428-1821** or 800/237-7532. 57 rms and efficiencies. A/C TV TEL. Summer, $116–$195 double; winter, $40–$110 double. Weekend and other packages available. AE, MC, V. Free parking.

One of the more reasonably priced oceanfront hostelries, the Breakers is a small family-operated hotel. A white boxlike nine-story building, its rooms are comfortably furnished with contemporary pieces. All have oceanfront balconies and refrigerators; some rooms with king-size beds contain Jacuzzis. Efficiency apartments have a bedroom with two double beds, a living room with a Murphy bed, and a sitting area. Kitchens are fully equipped. Additional amenities: an outdoor heated pool, coffee shop for poolside dining, and free bicycles.

HOTELS AT LYNNHAVEN INLET

Virginia Beach Resort Hotel

2800 Shore Dr. (U.S. 60), Virginia Beach, VA 23451. ☎ **804/481-9000** or 800/468-2722, 800/422-4747 in Virginia. 295 suites. A/C TV TEL. Summer, $150–$300 double; winter, $90–$230 double. Extra person $10. Weekday and other packages available. AE, DC, MC, V. Free parking.

Situated $3^{1}/_{2}$ miles east of Chesapeake Bay Bridge-Tunnel on 4 acres of Chesapeake Bay beachfront property, this self-contained luxury resort is about 3 miles from the oceanfront resort area. All suites have balconies with bay views, and separate sleeping and living areas, all furnished with sophisticated, contemporary furniture and decorated in pleasing pastel hues. Kitchen areas are equipped with refrigerator and microwave. Utensils are available for a $5 charge, or you may bring your own.

Dining/Entertainment: The Tradewinds Restaurant next to the pool offers wonderful water views and good American fare; the Café by the Bay is for more casual dining.

Services: Room service (6:10am–11pm), nightly turndown on request.

Facilities: Beach, indoor/outdoor pools, health club, sauna, jet-ski rental, volley-ball, children's activities, gift shop, beauty salon, meeting facilities, coin-op laundry, business center.

Econo Lodge

2968 Shore Dr. (U.S. 60), Virginia Beach, VA 23451. ☎ **804/481-0666** or 800/553-2666. Fax 804/481-4756. 41 rms. A/C TV TEL. Summer, $55–$85 single or double; winter, $35–$55 single or double. Extra person $5. AE, CB, DC, DISC, MC, V. Free parking.

This Econo Lodge is attractive with gray-clapboard siding and blue doors. About 2 miles east of the Chesapeake Bay Bridge-Tunnel, it's just a short walk from the Chesapeake Bay beach, or you can take a dip in the motel's heated outdoor pool. Standard motel accommodations all have microwaves and refrigerators. VCRs and tapes are available for rental. Complimentary coffee and doughnuts are served in the reception area every morning.

WHERE TO DINE

Just as Virginia Beach has thousands of hotel rooms, so it also has hundreds of restaurants, especially establishments serving up a bountiful harvest of seafood. We've picked a few of the best to get you started.

Of the many breakfast emporia along Atlantic Avenue, **Pocahontas Pancake & Waffle Shop,** at 35th Street (☎ 804/428-6352), is particularly appealing to kids. There are plenty of reminders of the Native American princess here, including a tee-pee in one corner of the dining room. The menu offers a wide range of inexpensive pancakes and waffles. It's open daily from 7am to 1pm.

RESTAURANTS AT THE OCEAN

✪ Gus' Mariner Restaurant

Atlantic Ave. at 57th St., in Ramada Plaza Resort. ☎ **804/425-5699.** Reservations recommended. Main courses $12–$20, early-bird specials $10. AE, DC, DISC, MC, V. Summer, daily 7am–10pm; off-season, daily 7am–9pm. Early-bird specials daily 3–6pm. SEAFOOD.

One of the few hotel restaurants popular with local residents, Gus's award-winning establishment sits right beside the beach, with gorgeous sea views from its window walls. There's a touch of elegance here, with padded chairs, crisp table linen, and candlelight. Seafood reigns, with old standbys like crab cakes and crab Norfolk augmented by flounder Florentine, paella, and the chef's special blue-corn tortilla wrapped around fresh tuna, salsa, and sour cream. The daily catch is offered with a variety of sauces, from spicy Cajun to cucumber dill. Early-bird specials include varying choices of seafood or meat entrees.

The Jewish Mother

3108 Pacific Ave. ☎ **804/422-5430.** Reservations accepted only for groups of 6 or more. Sandwiches $3.95–$5.85; other items $2.75–$13.95. AE, DISC, MC, V. Daily 8:30am–3am. DELI/AMERICAN.

A fixture on the Virginia Beach dining and nightlife scene since 1975, the Jewish Mother is well loved locally for its outstanding deli sandwiches, oversize egg and omelet platters, and fresh salads. The decor isn't fancy—in fact, the entrance looks more like a neighborhood grocery store, with take-out food items and a bakery case displaying an eclectic variety of desserts, ranging from Key lime pie to baklava and Black Forest cake. The food is top drawer, and after about 9:30pm there's solid entertainment. Live music performances run the gamut from country, blue grass, and blues to zydeco, rock, and acoustic. Depending on the performers, there may be a cover, especially on weekends, ranging from $2 to $15. There is a full bar, an international selection of beers, and arguably the largest array of bottled waters in town.

The Lighthouse

Atlantic Ave. at 1st St., Rudee Inlet. ☎ **804/498-1234.** Reservations accepted. Main courses $15–$25. AE, DC, DISC, MC, V. May–Oct, Mon–Fri noon–10pm, Sat–Sun 10am–11pm; Nov–Apr, Mon–Fri 5–10pm, Sat 5–11pm, Sun 10am–3pm and 5–11pm. SEAFOOD.

The heavy wood beams in this rustic wooden building create a warehouse effect, and great views of the ocean and Rudee Inlet set the stage for a variety of seafood ranging from freshly caught flounder to live Maine lobster. In addition to traditional southern preparations like crab Norfolk, a chargrill perfectly singes the likes of swordfish and salmon steaks. The big draw here, however, is an all-you-can-eat buffet of crab legs, shrimp, and barbecued pork ribs for $25 adults, $11 for children 7 to 12, and $5 for kids under 6. There's also a big Sunday brunch buffet all year.

RESTAURANTS AT LYNNHAVEN INLET

Henry's

3319 Shore Dr. (U.S. 60). ☎ **804/481-7300.** Reservations not accepted Fri–Sat in summer. Main courses $10–$23. AE, DISC, MC, V. May–Sept, Mon–Sat 11am–11pm, Sun 10am–11pm, brunch Sun 10am–2pm. Off-season, Mon–Sat 5–10:30pm, Sun 10am–10pm, brunch Sun 10am–2pm. From the resort area, take Shore Drive (U.S. 60) west for about 6 miles to east side of Lynnhaven Inlet bridge. SEAFOOD.

You'll feel as though you're aboard ship in any one of the casual dining rooms or outdoor decks of this bilevel waterfront dining complex. At the front door, an 8,000-gallon cylindrical aquarium rises two stories and holds marine life native to this area. Gray-tile floors, blond-wood tables, white easy chairs, and lots of mirrors create an appealing contemporary setting. Fresh fish is prepared six different ways—grilled, broiled, fried, blackened, Cajun, or poached—and there are usually over a dozen varieties of fresh fish on the menu. Seafood platters, sautéed combinations, and Henry's famous lump crab cakes are all eminently recommendable. Dessert treats include home-baked cheesecake.

Lynnhaven Fish House

2350 Starfish Rd. ☎ **804/481-0003.** Reservations not accepted. Main courses $17–$23. AE, CB, DC, DISC, MC, V. Daily 11:30am–10:30pm. From the resort area, take U.S. 60 (Shore Drive) to the Lynnhaven Fishing Pier, near the bridge-tunnel. SEAFOOD.

The Lynnhaven Fish House is a Virginia Beach institution, specializing in fresh Chesapeake Bay fish. Its spacious, airy dining room has wraparound windows overlooking the bay. At lunch, a good bet is half a dozen fresh-shucked clams on the half shell with cocktail sauce. Other choices include a crab cake sandwich, shrimp salad on a croissant, seafood pasta salad, or seafood stir-fry. The dinner menu starts off with oysters Rockefeller and selections from the chowder pots. Fresh fish of the day (flounder, sea trout, salmon, mako shark, red snapper, tuna, swordfish, or rainbow trout) are offered broiled, grilled, steamed, or poached, and you have a choice of nine sauces to enhance the flavor. All dinners come with a choice of baked potato, sweet potato, french fries, or black beans and rice; coleslaw, house salad, or Caesar salad; and corn muffins and hush puppies. For dessert, there's moist carrot cake, lavishly frosted, or a refreshing peach Melba.

3 Chincoteague & the Eastern Shore

Chincoteague, 83 miles N of Virginia Beach and Norfolk; 185 miles SE of Washington, D.C.

Miles of uncrowded beaches, countless waterways, abundant wildlife, and down-home cooking and hospitality welcome visitors to the tranquil Eastern Shore. Whether you'd like to take a day cruise to a quaint island out in the Chesapeake Bay, bike along traffic-free back roads, go bird-watching in a wildlife refuge, sun and swim on one of America's great undeveloped beaches, or browse little villages with Native American names like Chincoteague, Wachapreaque, or Onancock, you'll enjoy the gentle pace of this serene area.

Virginia's 70-mile-long end of the Delmarva Peninsula is bordered on one side by the Atlantic Ocean; on the other by the Chesapeake Bay. The ocean side is shielded by a string of barrier islands, many of them now happily preserved in their natural state by the Nature Conservancy (hence, making them impossible to visit without a boat). Fishing towns like Chincoteague and Wachapreague sit inside the barrier islands. On the bay side, creeks cut into the land, creating natural harbors for towns like Onancock, jumping-off point for cruises to the most quaint destination of all, Tangier Island.

ESSENTIALS

VISITOR INFORMATION For information about the area, contact **Virginia's Eastern Shore Tourism Commission,** U.S. 13 South (P.O. Box R), Melfa, VA 23410 (☎ 804/787-2460).

GETTING THERE **By Car** From Norfolk take I-64E, or from Virginia Beach take U.S. 60W, and follow the gull signs to U.S. 13 north and the Chesapeake Bay Bridge-Tunnel, a beautiful 17.6-mile drive across and under the bay ($10 per car). From the Cape Charles end of the bridge, go north on U.S. 13, a 4-lane highway running down the center of the Eastern Shore. To reach Chincoteague, turn east on Va. 175, about 65 miles north of the bridge-tunnel and 5 miles south of the Maryland line.

AREA CODE The telephone area code for the Eastern Shore is 804.

GETTING AROUND There is no public transportation on the Eastern Shore, so you will need either a car or a bike. This flat land is great biking terrain; bikes can be rented at **The Bike Depot,** at the Refuge Motor Inn, 7058 Maddox Boulevard, Chincoteague (☎ 804/336-5511), and at **Piney Island Country Store,** 7085 Maddox Blvd. Chincoteague (☎ 804/336-5188).

CHINCOTEAGUE

With its many motels, inns, restaurants, and proximity to Assateague Island, the village of Chincoteague is the most popular base for exploring the Eastern Shore. Settled by the English in the late 1600s, it sits just south of the Maryland line on Chincoteague Island, 7 miles long by 1 1/2 miles wide and famous for its surrounding bays full of flounder, oyster beds, and clam shoals. Marguerite Henry's children's book, and later film, *Misty of Chincoteague,* aroused wide interest in the annual pony penning and swim, when pony-size wild horses are rounded up on Assateague Island, forced to swim across to Chincoteague, and sold to benefit the local fire department.

For us humans, wonderful Assateague Island is just a short bridge away from Chincoteague. This barrier island is the site of both the Chincoteague National Wildlife Refuge and Assateague Island National Seashore, which together protect the wild ponies' habitat and 37 miles of pristine beach. Assateague is on the main Atlantic flyway, and its population of both migratory and resident birds is simply astounding.

While the town of Chincoteague has its share of tourist facilities, it still retains much of its old fishing-village charm. Rickety old piers still jut out into the water next to modern motels, and watermen in work boats still outnumber tourists on jet skis.

The Eastern Shore

MD.
VA.
Silva
Chincoteague
Nat'l Wildlife
Refuge
Assateague
Island
Chincoteague
New Church
Crisfield
Saxis
Oak Hall
Temperanceville
Sanford
Hallwood
Assateague Island
National Seashore
Great Fox Island
Mappsville
Bloxom
Nelsonia
Guilford
Modest Town
Tangier Island
Tangier
Parksley
Watts Island
Tasley
ACCOMAC
Gargathy Inlet
Onancock
Accomac
Metompkin Island
Onley
Harborton
Melfa
Locustville
Metompkin Inlet
Keller
Pungateague
Wachapreague
Cedar Island
Painter
Wachapreague Inlet
Craddockville
Quimby
Belle Haven
Exmore
Parramore Island
Jamesville
Nassawadox
Franktown
Weirwood
Quinby Inlet
Johnsontown
Birdsnest
NORTHAMPTON
Hog Island
Hog
Island
Bay
Machipongo
Great Machipongo Inlet
Eastville
Cobb
Island
Bay
Cobb Island
Cheriton
Bayview
Sand Shoal Inlet
Oyster
Wreck Island
Cape Charles
New Inlet
Ship Shoal Island
Kiptopeke Beach
Capeville
Townsend
Little Inlet
Kiptopeke
Cape Charles
Smith Island
Fishermans Island
Nat'l Wildlife Refuge
Chesapeake Bay Bridge-Tunnel
Cape Henry
Chesapeake
Beach

Chesapeake Bay

Atlantic Ocean

Scenic Highway

1955

VIRGINIA

Eastern Shore

Accomac ④
Chincoteague National Wildlife Refuge ②
Onancock ⑤
Oyster Maritime Museum ①
Refuge Waterfowl Museum ①
Tangier Island ③
Wachapreague ⑥

Of the nationally recognized chain names, only McDonald's will be seen on this quaint island—and that occurred only after a long and sometimes bitter fight.

ESSENTIALS   Area Layout   Va. 175 crosses the Chincoteague Channel and deadends in the old village at Main Street, which runs north-south along the island's western shore. Turn right at the stoplight to reach the motels, marinas, and bait shops which line Main Street south of the bridge. Turn left at the light for Maddox Boulevard, which heads east from Main Street 9 blocks north of the bridge and goes to Assateague Island. Maddox Boulevard is Chincoteague's prime commercial strip, with a plethora of shops, restaurants, and motels. Church Street goes east 2 blocks north of the bridge and turns into East Side Drive, which goes along the island's eastern shore. Ridge Road and Chicken City Road together run north-south down the middle of the island. On Assateague, there's only one road other than a wildlife drive, and it goes directly to the beach.

Visitor Information   The **Chincoteague Chamber of Commerce,** P.O. Box 258, Chincoteague, VA 23336 (☎ 804/336-6161), operates a visitor center in the traffic circle on Maddox Boulevard, about a mile before the Assateague bridge. It's open from June to October, Monday to Saturday from 9am to 4:30pm, Sunday from noon to 4:30pm. Off-season, it's open Monday to Friday from 9am to 4:30pm.

WHAT TO SEE & DO

Assateague Island

A barrier island protecting Chincoteague Island from the Atlantic Ocean, Assateague Island boasts over 37 miles of pristine **beaches** on its east coast, the northern 25 miles of which are in Maryland. The island is administered by two federal agencies, with the highest degree of protection afforded to wildlife on the Virginia side.

You first enter the **Chincoteague National Wildlife Refuge,** which is open May 1 to September 30, daily from 5am to 10pm; April and October, daily from 6am to 8pm; November 1 to March 31, daily from 6am to 6pm. Owned and managed by the U.S. Fish and Wildlife Service, the refuge accepts the annual entrance passes issued at national parks; otherwise, admission is $4 per car for one week, free for pedestrians and bikers.

Bird-watchers know Assateague Island as a prime Atlantic Flyway habitat where sightings of peregrine falcons, snow geese, great blue heron, and snowy egrets have been made. The annual Waterfowl Week, generally held around Thanksgiving, takes place when a large number of migratory birds use the refuge.

The famous wild horses—called ponies—have lived on Assateague since the 17th century. Local legend says their ancestors swam ashore from a shipwrecked Spanish galleon, but most likely English settlers put the first horses on Assateague, which formed a natural corral. Separated by a fence from their cousins in Maryland, the Virginia horses are now owned by the Chincoteague Volunteer Fire Department, which rounds them up and sells the folds at auction during the famous Pony Pinning during the last week of July (see "Special Events," below).

There is a paved **Wildlife Drive** through the marshes. It begins at the visitor center and is the best place to see the horses. **Assateague Island Tours** (☎ 804/336-6155) conducts 1¹/₂-hour wildlife tours of the refuge from April to mid-November between 10:30am and 5pm. These tours cover 14 miles and usually are the only way to visit most areas of the refuge other than on foot (the sole exception is the refuge's open house at Thanksgiving, when 7 miles of service roads are open to vehicles). The tours cost $7 for adults, $3.50 for children. Book at the refuge visitor center.

The beach itself is in the **Assateague Island National Seashore,** operated by the National Park Service (☎ 804/336-6577). There is a visitor center, two bathhouses, and summertime lifeguards at Tom's Cove, at the end of the road on the island's southern hook. In addition to swimming and sunning, activities at the beach include shell collecting (most productive at the tip of the Tom's Cove spit of land), and hiking. Biking is allowed on the paved roads and along a bike path beside the road from Chincoteague to the Refuge visitors center, then along Wildlife Drive to the Tom's Cove visitors center.

A number of **regulations** apply. Pets and alcoholic beverages are prohibited, even in your vehicle. Off-the-road vehicles are permitted only at Tom's Cove. Surf fishing with a Virginia state license is allowed except on the lifeguard beach at Tom's Cove. Climbing and digging in the sand dunes is illegal. No overnight sleeping is allowed anywhere (backcountry camping is permitted on the Maryland end, a 12-mile hike from the Virginia-end visitor centers). And lastly, thou shalt not feed the horses.

For **information** about the refuge and visitor center seasons and programs, write or call: Refuge Manager, Chincoteague National Wildlife Refuge, P.O. Box 62, Chincoteague, VA 23336 (☎ 804/336-6122).

Museums

You will pass a large airstrip as you drive to Chincoteague on Va. 175. This is NASA's Wallops Flight Facility, a research and testing center for rockets, balloons, and aircraft. The facility also tracks NASA's spacecraft and satellites, including the space shuttles. Across the highway is the **NASA Visitor Center** (☎ 804/824-1344), which explains the facility's history and role in the space program. Kids will get a kick out of seeing a practice space suit from the Apollo 9 moon mission. Admission is free. The visitor center is open from Memorial Day to Labor Day, daily from 10am to 4pm; rest of the year, Thursday to Monday from 10am to 4pm. The center is 5 miles west of Chincoteague.

On Maddox Boulevard, between the traffic circle and the bridge to Assateague, are two small marine-themed museums. The **Oyster and Maritime Museum** (☎ 804/336-6117) tells all about this vital industry. It's open Memorial Day to Labor Day, Monday to Saturday from 10am to 5pm, Sunday from noon to 4pm. Off-season hours are irregular. Admission is $2 for adults, $1 for children 12 and under.

Virtually next door, the **Refuge Waterfowl Museum** (☎ 804/336-5800) has an interesting variety of antique decoys, boats, traps, art, and carvings by outstanding craftspeople. It's open Memorial Day to Labor Day, daily from 10am to 5pm. Admission is $2.50 for adults, $1 for children 12 and under.

SPORTS & OUTDOOR ACTIVITIES

Cruises

While most visitors head for the beach on Assateague, don't overlook the broad bays and creeks which surround Chincoteague. A good way to get out on them is with **Captain Barry's Back Bay Cruises** (☎ 804/336-6508, or 804/824-8471), which depart Landmark Plaza on Main Street. Barry Frishman moved from upstate New York to Chincoteague and set about learning everything he could about the water and what's in it. Now he shares his knowledge by taking guests out on his pontoon boat for 1½-hour early-morning bird-watching expeditions ($15 per person); 4-hour morning or afternoon "adventure quests" in search of crabs, fish, shells, and clams ($30 per person); champagne sunset cruises ($15); and moonlight excursions ($15).

Another way to see the birds at nesting time is on 2-hour nature cruises on the *Osprey* (☎ 804/336-5511), which departs the Town Dock opposite the Fire House on Main Street most evenings from Memorial Day to Labor Day. Prices are $10 for adults, $5 for children. Reservations are required. Purchase tickets at the Refuge Motor Inn on Maddox Boulevard.

East Side Rentals & Marina on East Side Drive (☎ 804/336-3409) also has 1-, 2-, and 3-hour nature cruises priced at $15, $20, and $30 per person, respectively.

Fishing

Chincoteague was a fishing village for centuries before it became a tourist mecca, and it still is. Work and pleasure boats prowl both the back bays and ocean for flounder, croaker, spot, kingfish, drum, striped bass, bluefish, and sharks, to name a few species. Among the pontoon party boats fishing the back bays are *Daisey's Dockside II,* at Daisey's Dockside Pier, South Main Street (☎ 804/336-3345), and the *Chincoteague View,* operating out of East Side Rentals & Marina on East Side Drive (☎ 804/336-3409). They charge about $30 per person. More expensive are the charter boats that go oceanside, including the *Bucktail* (☎ 804/336-5188), the *Patty Wagon II* (☎ 804/336-1459), and the *Mar-shell* (☎ 804/336-1939). Reservations are essential, so call ahead.

Of course, you can do it yourself, either from a rented boat or by throwing your line from a dock. For equipment, supplies, free tide tables, and advice, check in at **Barnacle Bill's Bait & Tackle,** on South Main Street (☎ 804/336-5188). Marinas on East Side Drive that sell bait and rent boats and equipment include **East Side Rentals & Marina** (☎ 804/336-3409), **Snug Harbor Marina** (☎ 804/336-6176), and **Sea Tag Boat Rentals** (☎ 804/336-5555).

Jet Skiing

You can rent these noisy but exciting contraptions at **Snug Harbor Marina** on East Side Drive (☎ 804/336-6176).

Hunting

The marshes in these parts are perfect for hunting ducks, geese, and brants during the fall (dates of annual seasons are announced during the preceding summer). **Randy Birch** (☎ 804/336-6176) and **Fish Tales Hunting Supplies** (☎ 804/336-3474) both offer guide services. Reservations are required.

Kayaking

The waters around Chincoteague are ideal for sea kayaking, and **Tidewater Expeditions** has early-morning and evening trips and an all-day sea clinic, all departing from its shop on East Side Drive (☎ 804/336-3159). Costs for the excursions range from $21 for one-person kayaks to $37 for two persons. The clinic costs $65 per person. The company also rents kayaks and canoes, starting at $10 a hour.

SPECIAL EVENTS

In the last two weeks of July the **Chincoteague Fireman's Carnival,** a fun fest with rides, live entertainment, and food, is climaxed by the famous **pony swim** across the Assateague Channel to Chincoteague Memorial Park. There is no charge for parking or seeing the ponies swim. The ponies are herded to Memorial Park on East Side Drive, where the first colt to come ashore is given away, and many are then sold at auction. The swim takes place on the last Wednesday in July; the remaining ponies swim back to Assateague the following Friday. It's all in a good cause—proceeds go to the fire company's ambulance fund. Another top event is the **Chincoteague Oyster Festival,** when you can get your libido going by gorging on fresh oysters during the first week of October. This event is always sold out in advance, so telephone 804/336-6161 for ticket information.

WHERE TO STAY

If you're looking for a longer-term rental on Chincoteague Island, contact **Chincoteague Island Vacation Cottages,** 6282 Maddox Blvd., Chincoteague, VA

23336 (☎ 804/336-3720, or 800/457-6643); **Island Property Rentals,** 7065 Main St., Chincoteague, VA 23336 (☎ 804/336-3456, or 800/346-2559); and **Bay Company, Inc.,** 6207 Maddox Blvd., Chincoteague, VA 23336 (☎ 804/336-5490). They all have fully furnished cottages in various locations, including some on the waterfront.

Motels

Beach Road Motel

6151 Maddox Blvd. (P.O. Box 557), Chincoteague, VA 23336. ☎ **804/336-6562.** 20 rms, 3 efficiencies. A/C TV TEL. $35–$79 double. Extra adult $5. AE, DC, DISC, MC, V. Free parking. Turn left at the bridge, and drive 8 blocks to Maddox Boulevard.

This owner-operated motel offers very nice rooms in two one-story white-masonry buildings with blue doors. The rooms are immaculate, with all the basics, including refrigerators and beverage hot pots in every room. The efficiencies include a studio, a one-bedroom cottage, and a two-bedroom mobile home with full kitchen facilities. There is an outdoor pool on the property.

Refuge Motor Inn

7058 Maddox Blvd., Chincoteague, VA 23336. ☎ **804/336-5511** or 800/544-8469, ext. 2. Fax 804/336-6134. 70 rms, 2 suites. A/C TV TEL. Summer, $80–$190 double; off-season, $50–$105 double. AE, DC, DISC, MC, V. Free parking.

Located between the traffic circle and the bridge to Assateague, this very attractive motor inn with weathered gray siding nestles on beautifully landscaped grounds shaded by tall pines. The care and attention lavished on decor and facilities at this family-owned spot are evident everywhere. Furnishings are charming. Some rooms have Colonial-style pieces, bleached-pine headboards, decoys, handmade wall hangings, and all the elements of country style. All rooms have refrigerators. First-floor rooms facing the back have sliding doors to private patios where guests can use outdoor grills. There are an observation sundeck on the roof, an exercise room with sauna, glass-enclosed pool and Jacuzzi, children's playground and a pony enclosure, rental bikes, coin-op laundry facilities, and a lobby gift/craft shop.

Waterside Motor Inn

3761 Main St. (P.O. Box 347), Chincoteague, VA 23336. ☎ **804/336-3434.** Fax 804/336-1878. 45 rms. A/C TV TEL. Summer, $90–$145 double; off-season $46–$88 double. Extra person $5. Children under 12 (limit of two children) stay free in parents' room. AE, DC, DISC, MC, V. Free on-site parking. At the bridge entering Chincoteague, turn right; the motel is on the right, about half a mile from the bridge.

All the accommodations at this three-story property have private wooden balconies overlooking Chincoteague Channel, guaranteeing some breathtaking sunset views. Cream-clapboard siding with slate blue trim has a properly nautical look. Rooms are decorated in tones of blue, beige, and green in comfortable contemporary style. All have coffeemakers and refrigerators. The Waterside also offers a Jacuzzi, an exercise room, a tennis court, and a swimming pool, and it's located right on a fishing and crabbing pier.

Bed & Breakfasts

Island Manor House

4160 Main St., Chincoteague, VA 23336. ☎ **804/336-5436.** 8 rms (6 with bath). A/C. $66–$120 double. Rates include full breakfast and afternoon tea. MC, V. Free parking. From the bridge into Chincoteague, turn left onto Main Street and continue about 1¹/₂ blocks; the inn is on the right.

This B&B consists of two white-clapboard houses joined by a one-story garden room with a lovely brick patio and fountain in the back. Originally there was one house, built before the Civil War by two young men. They eventually married sisters, who did not enjoy living under the same roof, so they split the house and moved the front half next door. Today both houses have been handsomely restored and are furnished mainly in Federal style, but also with 17th-, 18th-, and 19th-century pieces collected by hospitable owners Charles Kalmykow and Carol Rogers. In the two first-floor sitting rooms are telephone for guest use and a fireplace. Off one sitting room is a brick courtyard with a fountain.

Miss Molly's Inn Bed & Breakfast

4141 Main St., Chincoteague, VA 23336. ☎ **804/336-6686** or 800/221-5620. 7 rms (5 with bath). A/C. $69–$145 double. Rates include full breakfast and afternoon tea. No credit cards. Closed early Jan–Feb. Free parking. From the bridge into Chincoteague, turn left onto Main Street and continue about 1¹/₂ blocks to the inn, on the left.

This charming 1886 Victorian, with a wide wraparound porch, is named for the daughter of the builder J. T. Rowley, known as "the clam king of the world." Miss Molly, who lived in this house until the age of 84, was a resident when Marguerite Henry stayed here while she was writing *Misty of Chincoteague*. Present innkeepers David and Barbara Wiedenheft have decorated all rooms with an agreeable mix of Victorian and earlier antiques, with lace curtains, pretty coverlets, Tiffany-style lamps, and bibelots adorning mantels and dresser tops. The parlor and dining room have exceptionally fine Victorian pieces—marble-top tables, a curved sofa, original newel-post lamps, and Oriental carpets.

Campgrounds

Chincoteague has several family-oriented campgrounds. At the traffic circle, the **Maddox Family Campground,** 6742 Maddox Blvd., Chincoteague, VA 23336 (☎ 804/336-3111) has 550 campsites. Some sites have views of the Assateague Lighthouse. On the campground are a pool, playground, pavilion, grocery store with RV supplies, rec hall, laundry room, bath houses, dump station, and propane filling station. Shuffleboard, a duck pond, horse shoes, crabbing, and bird-watching are on site. Rates range from $19 for a tent site to $26.50 for full hookup. MasterCard and Visa accepted.

As its name implies, **Pine Grove Campground & Waterfowl Park,** 5283 Deep Hole Rd. (P.O. Box 8), Chincoteague, VA 23336 (☎ 804/336-5200), sits in a very shady pine grove, and it has a parklike area where domestic and exotic waterfowl are bred and raised. There are 100 RV sites and 50 tent sites in separate areas, a pool, laundry room, play area, campstore, dump station, and bath houses. Rates range from $17 to $21. MasterCard and Visa are accepted.

WHERE TO DINE

Etta's Family Restaurant

7452 East Side Dr., at Assateague Channel. ☎ **804/336-5644.** Reservations accepted. Main courses $9–$16. DISC, MC, V (for charges over $15). Summer, daily 11am–9pm; winter, Wed–Mon 8am–9pm. AMERICAN.

Etta's is an unpretentious eatery where service is friendly and food is hearty. It's right next to Memorial Park, and its windows give diners the best view in town of the pony swim. Everything is cooked to order here, so you may have a bit of a wait. Lunch sandwiches include hot beef with gravy, clam strips, and fried oyster. Dinnertime appetizers of creamy crab soup or oyster stew precede entrees like fresh fried or broiled flounder, homemade crabcakes, and fried combination seafood platters. As is true at all restaurants in this family-oriented resort, there's a children's menu.

Landmark Crab House

Landmark Plaza, 6162 Main St., on the bay. ☎ **804/336-5552.** Reservations recommended on weekends. Main courses $11–$17. AE, DC, DISC, MC, V. Mon–Sat 5–10pm, Sun 1–10pm. Closed Dec–Feb. SEAFOOD.

Attracting families to fresh local seafood since 1974, this crab house sits at the end of a pier and is surrounded by decking; wraparound windows provide panoramic views of small fishing vessels tied up for the evening in the channel. The gorgeous Victorian bar, dating to 1897, was brought here from Chicago. The wood-paneled dining room has a nautical motif with ship figureheads, ship models, lanterns, and mounted fish. For an appetizer, you can't beat Chincoteague oysters on the half shell or a bucket of steamed clams. Trips to the salad bar come with all entrees. Landmark specials include half a pound of steamed shrimp with fresh broccoli and hollandaise sauce, soft-shell crabs, and crab imperial. Landlubbers can choose from fresh fried or teriyaki chicken, filet mignon, or New York strip steak. On Friday, Saturday, and holiday evenings there's piano music in the lounge, and the deck bar has entertainment on summer weekends.

Shucking House Café

Landmark Plaza, 6162 Main St., on the bay. ☎ **804/336-5145.** Main courses $8–$12; sandwiches $3.50–$5. AE, DC, DISC, MC, V. Daily 8am–3pm. Closed Dec–Feb. AMERICAN.

Adjoining the Landmark Crab House and under the same owners, the Shucking House Café has a cathedral ceiling, windows overlooking the channel, and seating in red-leather-upholstered booths and small tables. Breakfast options include country ham and biscuits or blueberry pancakes. The lunch menu features soups, chowders, sandwiches, and such seafood entrees as crab cake platter, fried scallops, and seafood au gratin. On Sunday, there's a dinner buffet from 11:30am to 3pm for $10.

Village Restaurant

6576 Maddox Blvd. ☎ **804/336-5120.** Reservations suggested Sat–Sun. Main courses $10–$18.50. AE, DISC, MC, V. Daily 5–10pm. Closed one day off-season. AMERICAN.

The Village Restaurant is gardenlike, with pink-and-green-floral wallpaper, ceiling fans, white trellises, and a gazebolike dining area in the back of the restaurant overlooking a creek and marsh. Shaded lamps provide soft lighting. Appetizers include calamari, stuffed mushroom caps, oyster stew, and oysters or clams on the half shell. Seafood entree choices are uniformly excellent, whether you choose fried oysters, stuffed flounder, or crab imperial. The house seafood platter is piled with fish filet, soft-shell crab stuffed with crab imperial, shrimp, scallops, oysters, clams, and lobster tail. There are nonseafood main dishes like veal parmesan, chicken stir-fry, and filet mignon. All entrees are served with salad, home-baked bread, and a choice of potato, rice, or vegetable of the day.

ONANCOCK

In contrast to Chincoteague's somewhat scruffy fishing-town image, the picturesque town of Onancock, 1 mile west of U.S. 13 and Olney, has a more genteel charm dating back to 1690. Situated on Onancock Creek some 2^1/$_2$ miles from the Chesapeake Bay, it has always made its money from agriculture and trading as well as from the bay. The great ferries and ships that once plied between Norfolk and Baltimore put in here, helping to make Onancock a wealthy town. As a consequence, it has stately churches (many with fish-scale shingle exteriors) and fine historic homes built by wealthy traders and bankers.

ATTRACTIONS

It's worth a stop here to visit **Kerr Place**, a stately Federal mansion built in 1799 by Scottish merchant John Shepherd Kerr on Market Street (Va. 179). This two-story brick manor house is now headquarters for the Eastern Shore of Virginia Historical Society (☎ 804/787-8012) and is beautifully furnished with 18th- and 19th-century antiques. Admission is $3. It's open March through December, Tuesday through Saturday from 9am to 4pm (closed holidays).

While here, linger for a bit at the Town Dock, at the foot of Market Street, in **Hopkins & Bro. store,** built in 1842 and one of the oldest general stores on the East Coast. Part of the store has been turned into a cozy seafood restaurant with great views of the creek.

✪ A Cruise to Tangier Island Hopkins & Bro. store also is departure point for cruises to tiny Tangier Island and its picturesque village of 750 souls out in the Chesapeake Bay. There are no cars on the narrow streets, which seems appropriate to this unspoiled island, discovered by Capt. John Smith in 1608. In fact, the local accent actually harks back to Elizabethan English. This is no glitzy resort. Entertainment consists of walking around the island, perhaps chatting with local watermen, and just enjoying the serenity and fresh sea air. In any case, you'll want to eat at **Hilda Crockett's Chesapeake House,** where home-cooked lunches are served boardinghouse-style from 11:30am to 5pm daily for $11.75. You can also stay overnight at Mrs. Crockett's for a reasonable $40, which includes dinner and breakfast. For details and reservations, the address is simply Tangier Island, Tangier, VA 23440 (☎ 804/891-2331).

The Onancock–Tangier Island ferry operates June through September, daily at 10am, returning at 3pm. Adult fare is $18 round-trip; children 6 to 11, $9; no charge for 5 and under. For reservations call ☎ 804/787-8220.

ACCOMMODATIONS

The town of Olney, 1 mile east of Onancock on U.S. 13, has a modern **Comfort Inn,** the only chain motel between Charles City, Va., and Pocomoke City, Md.

Spinning Wheel Bed & Breakfast

13 North St., Onancock, VA 23417. ☎ **804/787-7311.** 5 rms. A/C. $75–85. Rates include continental breakfast. MC, V. Free parking. From Market Street, turn north on North Street.

Every room in this three-story wood-frame Victorian, built around 1890, has an antique spinning wheel, part of an extraordinary collection belonging to innkeeper Karen Tweedie. She and husband David have added other Eastern Shore antiques throughout, including iron and brass beds. Dormer windows have added unique shapes to the top-level rooms. Both school teachers in Northern Virginia, the Tweedies close this establishment from December through March. When here, they provide free bikes for their guests' use.

DINING

✪ Armando's

10 North St., Onancock. ☎ **804/787-8044.** Reservations accepted 5–6pm only. Main courses $8–$16. AE, MC, V. Tues–Thurs 5–9pm, Fri–Sat 5–10pm. INTERNATIONAL.

Argentine-born Armando Suarez settled in Onancock in 1988 and opened a pizza and sandwich shop. So popular did it quickly become that he opened this fun storefront restaurant adorned with an eclectic mix of pottery, plants, and photos of jazz musicians. Armando's menu is equally eclectic, with some inventive twists such as crab crepes, shrimp margarita (a slightly piquant tequila sauce), and lobster ravioli "drizzled" with sage, butter, and tomato cream sauce. Armando constantly spins jazz CDs and occasionally has live jazz on weekends.

WACHAPREAGUE

Appearing much like Chincoteague must have looked before its days of tourism, the tiny village of Wachapreague (290 permanent residents) sits on the Atlantic coast mainland just 10 miles from Onancock. It overlooks the marshes and waterways that lie between town and an inlet between **Cedar Island** and **Parramore Island,** which protect the bays and marshes here like Assateague does for Chincoteague. At the turn of the 20th century, Wachapreaque was a major resort for the likes of Walter Chrysler, actor Ronald Coleman, and former president Herbert Hoover. They were drawn here by the area's excellent hunting and fishing, and they stayed at the grand Hotel Wachapreague, a four-story Victorian palace surrounded by verandahs and topped by gable windows. Unfortunately the hotel burned down in 1978, but the fishing and hunting here are good as ever.

When you drive into town from U.S. 13 via Va. 180, go straight to the end of the street to the Wachapreaque Hotel, now a fishermen's motel but once a wing of the old hotel. The motel is home to **Skimmer I Cruises** (☎ 804/787-2105), which goes out to Parramore Island, now owned and preserved by the Nature Conservancy, and to Cedar Island, home of beach cottages but inaccessible except by boat. They run from May to October, but the schedule varies depending on the tide and the number of passengers. Accordingly, reservations are essential.

Wachapreague Marina (☎ 804/787-4110) will drop you off at Cedar or Parramore for $60 round-trip, or rent you a boat for do-it-yourself trips for $60 a day, including fuel and a chart. The marina's bait shop will advise on where the fish are biting. If you decide to go out on your own, do it at high tide, since many channels here are very shallow.

ACCOMMODATIONS

✪ Hart's Harbor House and Burton House Bed & Breakfast

9 Brooklyn Ave., Wachapreague, VA 23480. ☎ **804/787-4848** or **804/787-4560.** 10 rms (4 with bath), 2 cottages, 1 cabin. A/C. $65–$85. Rates include full breakfast. MC. From Va. 180, turn left on Brooklyn Avenue 1 block before waterfront.

Born-and-bred Wachapreagers Tom and Pat Hart have turned these two adjacent Victorian houses into a first-rate bed-and-breakfast operation with direct access to the waterfront. Tom salvaged some railing from the Hotel Wachapreague's verandahs and used them to build a charming, gazebolike screened porch on the rear of Burton House (Hart's Harbor House also has a screened porch overlooking the water). Hart's Harbor House's rooms are larger than its neighbor's, and all have baths. All are attractively furnished with Eastern Shore antiques. The cottages and cabin are in the Harts' lot, between the houses and the waterfront. Guests in the main houses are treated to Tom's country breakfast. The Harts also provide free bikes for their guests' use and will arrange cruises, island trips, and hunting and fishing guides.

Appendix

MAJOR AIRLINES

American	800/433-7300
Continental	800/525-0280
Delta	800/221-1212
Northwest	800/225-2525
Southwest	800/435-9792
United	800/241-6522
USAir	800/428-4322

MAJOR CAR RENTAL COMPANIES

Avis	800/831-2847
Alamo	800/327-9633
Budget	800/527-0700
Dollar	800/800-4000
Enterprise	800/325-8007
Hertz	800/654-3131
National	800/227-7368
Thrifty	800/367-2277

MAJOR CHAIN MOTELS & HOTELS

Best Western	800/528-1234
Comfort Inns	800/228-5150
Courtyard by Marriott	800/321-2211
Days Inn	800/325-2525
Doubletree Hotels	800/222-TREE
Econo Lodges	800/446-6900
Fairfield Inn by Marriott	800/228-2800
Hampton Inn	800/HAMPTON
Hilton Hotels	800/HILTONS
Holiday Inn	800/HOLIDAY
Sheraton	800/325-3535
Marriott Hotels	800/228-9290
Motel 6	800/466-8356
Omni Hotels	800/843-6664
Quality Inns	800/228-5151

MAJOR CHAIN MOTELS & HOTELS (CONT.)

Radisson Hotels	800/333-3333
Ramada	800/2-RAMADA
Ritz-Carlton	800/241-3333
Super 8	800/800-8000
Travelodge	800/255-3050

Index

6-21-96 #12⁶⁰

FROMMER'S COMPLETE TRAVEL GUIDES

(Comprehensive guides to sightseeing, dining, and accommodations, with selections in all price ranges from deluxe to budget)

Acapulco/Ixtapa/Taxco, 2nd Ed.
Alaska, 4th Ed.
Arizona '96
Australia, 4th Ed.
Austria, 6th Ed.
Bahamas '96
Belgium/Holland/Luxembourg, 4th Ed.
Bermuda '96
Budapest & the Best of Hungary, 1st Ed.
California '96
Canada, 9th Ed.
Caribbean '96
Carolinas/Georgia, 3rd Ed.
Colorado, 3rd Ed.
Costa Rica, 1st Ed.
Cruises '95-'96
Delaware/Maryland, 2nd Ed.
England '96
Florida '96
France '96
Germany '96
Greece, 1st Ed.
Honolulu/Waikiki/Oahu, 4th Ed.
Ireland, 1st Ed.
Italy '96
Jamaica/Barbados, 2nd Ed.
Japan, 3rd Ed.

Maui, 1st Ed.
Mexico '96
Montana/Wyoming, 1st Ed.
Nepal, 3rd Ed.
New England '96
New Mexico, 3rd Ed.
New York State '94-'95
Nova Scotia/New Brunswick/Prince
    Edward Island, 1st Ed.
Portugal, 14th Ed.
Prague & the Best of the Czech Republic,
    1st Ed.
Puerto Rico '95-'96
Puerto Vallarta/Manzanillo/Guadalajara,
    3rd Ed.
Scandinavia, 16th Ed.
Scotland, 3rd Ed.
South Pacific, 5th Ed.
Spain, 16th Ed.
Switzerland, 7th Ed.
Thailand, 2nd Ed.
U.S.A., 4th Ed.
Utah, 1st Ed.
Virgin Islands, 3rd Ed.
Virginia, 3rd Ed.
Washington/Oregon, 6th Ed.
Yucatan '95-'96

FROMMER'S FRUGAL TRAVELER'S GUIDES

(Dream vacations at down-to-earth prices)

Australia on $45 '95-'96
Berlin from $50, 3rd Ed.
Caribbean from $60, 1st Ed.
Costa Rica/Guatemala/Belize on $35, 3rd Ed.
Eastern Europe on $30, 5th Ed.
England from $50, 21st Ed.
Europe from $50 '96
Greece from $45, 6th Ed.
Hawaii from $60, 30th Ed.

Ireland from $45, 16th Ed.
Israel from $45, 16th Ed.
London from $60 '96
Mexico from $35 '96
New York on $70 '94-'95
New Zealand from $45, 6th Ed.
Paris from $65 '96
South America on $40, 16th Ed.
Washington, D.C. from $50 '96

FROMMER'S COMPLETE CITY GUIDES

(Comprehensive guides to sightseeing, dining, and accommodations in all price ranges)

Amsterdam, 8th Ed.
Athens, 10th Ed.
Atlanta & the Summer Olympic Games '96

Bangkok, 2nd Ed.
Berlin, 3rd Ed.
Boston '96